The Pennsylvania State Grange Cookbook

Credits

This cookbook is a collection of our favorite recipes, which are not necessarily original recipes.

Published by: Favorite Recipes® Press
P. O. Box 305142
Nashville, Tennessee 37230

Library of Congress Number: 92-30345
ISBN: 0-87197-350-2

Printed in the United States of America
First Printing: 1992 25,000 copies

Table of Contents

Pennsylvania State Grange

1604 N. Second Street, Harrisburg, PA 17102

The Grange, officially called THE PATRONS OF HUSBANDRY, was founded in 1867 by Oliver Hudson Kelley. Shortly after the Civil War, Oliver Hudson toured the Southern States for the Bureau of Agriculture. He found the farmers poor, discouraged and without much hope for the future. He believed that a Fraternal organization would attract members and give the farmers a chance to learn modern farming methods and add social activities for the whole family. Thus the Grange was organized, based on the lessons of life and agriculture.

The Grange grew on the basis of its social, legislative and educational programs. TODAY it supplies the needs of ALL PEOPLE, rural and urban alike. It continues to live and grow by providing educational classes, legislative policies, community awareness projects and social activities for the whole family.

The Pennsylvania State Grange is the state's largest rural-farm organization with over 35,000 members and serves over 500 rural communities. It is chartered in 66 of the 67 counties in Pennsylvania.

Proceeds from the Pennsylvania State Grange cookbook enable the subordinate granges to organize community service projects to improve the communities in which they live. It also gives them the opportunity to support causes such as Deaf Awareness, CARE, VOSH, ABC QUILTS, Shelters for Abused Women and Children as well as many other worthwhile causes.

The mission of the Grange is to improve the quality of life in America's communities. The Grange believes that people can achieve happiness, satisfaction and prosperity through unity of action, service to others and fellowship.

THE GRANGE: PEOPLE * PRIDE * PROGRESS

Dedication

To All Pennsylvania Grangers

From the very beginning of the Grange, food and the preparation of food have been an important part of our fraternity. Lifetime friends have been made over an apple butter kettle, an ice cream freezer or while chopping cabbage for coleslaw.

Pennsylvanians, especially Grangers, take great pride in preparing, serving and sharing their favorite recipes. The recipes in this book have been tried and proven in some of the finest kitchens in Pennsylvania...those of Pennsylvania Grangers.

We were really overwhelmed by the response to our plea for recipes, and we truly thank each and every one of you who were willing to share your recipes. They came from all over the state...many more than we will have room to print. Where similar recipes were received, only one name will be printed below as acknowledgment, since one recipe had twelve contributors. The other names will be listed on a contributors page. This will allow more room for recipes.

This book is dedicated to all those members who have contributed recipes for the book and to all those women who cannot resist "collecting" one more cookbook to browse through. This is your book. We hope you will enjoy this one as much as the other four that have been published.

Rebecca Michalka

The Women's Activities Committee
Rebecca Michalka, DWA

Women's Activities Committee

Pennsylvania State Grange

Rebecca Michalka
State Director

Region A	Agnes Wilson
Region B	Anna Gould
Region C	Freda Shreck
Region D	Evelyn Cottrell
Region E	Ruth Posten
Region F	Anna Mary Brenneman
Region G	Martha Snyder
Region H	Eleanor Hill

We gratefully acknowledge and express our thanks to:

MASTER, PENNSYLVANIA STATE GRANGE, William Ringler, who suggested that this book be compiled. His advice, support and encouragement helped to make this project a success.

P. R. DIRECTOR, Steve Robinson, for contacting printers and publishers to acquire bids for printing of the book.

ARTIST, Ruth Livengood, for drawings on Credits page and page 14.

Contributors

Acker, Bertha
Ackerman, Margaret
Adam, Arlene
Adam, Lester A.
Adams, Mrs. Clyde
Adams, Diane
Adams, Esther E.
Adams, Lenora
Alkons, Fred
Alkons, Mary E.
Almgren, Elizabeth
Almgren, Paul G.
Altman, Margaret M.
Alvino, Shirley
Anderson, Helen
Anderson, Martha H.
Angstadt, Anna
Ankney, Betty
Anspach, Hazel L.
Anstadt, Elizabeth
Arnold, Dorothy
Askey, Grace
Askey, Mary E.
Aughenbaugh, Dorothy
Aughey, Dorothy
Aughey, Lura
Aumiller, Connie
Aumiller, Margaret
Aumiller, Patty
Aumiller, Rachel
Aurand, Barbara H.
Ayers, Brian & Dwayne
Ayers, Mona L.
Bachman, Ella
Bacon, Doris J.
Baer, Irene
Bagnick, Jean
Bailey, Lillian
Baker, Leona
Baldwin, Martha B.
Ball, Jean
Balthaser, Catharine
Balthaser, Gladys
Barackman, Margret
Barker, Joan
Barkley, Mrs. Howard
Barlett, Mary K.
Barrett, Viola
Bartges, Belva S.
Bartlett, Edna
Bauer, Margaret S.
Baumgardner, Pauline
Beach, Jolean J.
Bean, Irene
Beatty, Alice
Beatty, Maude
Beaufort, Grace
Beck, Beth
Beck, Betty
Beck, Helen
Beck, Lucille
Beishline, Christine
Benner, Viola C.
Benton, Elaine
Berry, Irene
Best, Bernie
Bestwich, Bessie
Bevington, Buddy
Bevington, Marilyn
Beward, Iva K.
Bibel, Deanna
Bibel, Mary
Billig, Karen
Bish, Minerva
Bishop, Helen
Bitterman, Betty
Blatt, Esther
Blatt, Irene
Blayney, Ivie W.
Blood, Agnes
Bloom, Violet
Blose, Elcy
Blose, Melzena B.
Boak, Helen
Boarts, Olga
Bock, Alice E.
Bocz, Sophie Sally
Bodman, Vivian
Bohn, Anna M.
Book, Marian E.
Borger, Edna
Boroi, Diane
Bortz, Helen E.
Bortz, Virginia E.
Boucher, Nancy
Bowmaster, Mona
Bowser, Janice
Bowser, Karen
Bowser, Susan
Boyce, Ruth
Boyer, Sharon
Boytim, Dorothy E.
Bradnick, Mary L.
Breininger, Mamie A.
Breneman, Judy
Brennan, Marian
Brennaman, Elaine
Brenneman, Anna Mary
Brenneman, Betty
Brest, Esther
Brion, Edith
Bristor, Josephine C.
Broadbent, Helen
Broadbent, Phyllis
Brock, Jewell
Bromley, Ethel
Brooks, Delores
Brooks, Nancy
Brosius, Shelby
Brown, Helen J.
Brown, Lisa
Buchanan, Eunice
Buchko, Peggy
Buckner, Chloe
Buffington, Betty
Buffington, Mary R.
Bullman, Margaret
Bunnell, Eloise
Bupp, Naomi
Burkett, Datha
Burkett, Dolores
Burkett, Elsie

Burkett, L. K.
Burkhart, LaVerne
Burlingame, Doris
Burman, Marion I.
Burns, Alberta G.
Burns, Beatrice
Bush, Marie
Buss, Rose
Byers, Peg
Calhoun, Mary
Caltagarone, Dorothy J.
Calvert, Renee
Campbell, Annie E.
Campbell, Mary
Campbell, Virginia
Campman, Alice
Cape, Almeda
Carle, Hannelore
Carlson, Betty
Carlson, Ruth S.
Carpenter, Mae
Carpenter, Phillip
Case, Phillis M.
Cathcart, Jane
Cauffman, Ardella
Cavalcante, Barbara Ann
Chamberlain, Jeannie
Chapin, Gertrude
Chesnut, Ruth
Chestnut, Nellie
Chiea, Joan
Christian, Margaret
Christman, Anita
Christy, Jean
Chronister, Bonnie
Cioffi, Mary
Clark, Avonell
Clark, Theresa
Clawson, Nina
Cline, Jami
Coleman, Kathleen
Colwell, Gertrude
Conrad, Rose
Cook, A. Elaine
Cook, Mrs. Robert C.
Cool, Lena
Cooper, Sara
Copenhaver, Susan
Costa, Kay
Cottrell, Christine
Cottrell, Evelyn
Coughanour, Helen
Coulter, Margaret
Courter, Elizabeth
Coveleski, Mildred C.
Covert, Alma
Cowan, Madaline
Cowan, Myra
Craig, Anna L.
Cramer, Betty
Cramer, Esther
Cramer, Kathryn
Crater, Carol A.
Crater, Margaret E.
Cree, Kathy
Creitz, Dorothea
Crise, Helen
Christy, Jean
Critzer, Barb
Crosby, Levia
Crowl, Margaret
Crumrine, Vivian
Cummings, Violet
Cunningham, Lonnie
Cupper, Dot
Currie, Frances
Cyphers, Marie
Daneyhower, Elenore P.
Darmofal, Jane
Daub, Fay
Daughenbaugh, Ann
Davidson, Marilyn
Davis, Ethel
Davis, Viola
Davis, Virginia
Dawson, Phyllis
Day, Gladys A.
Day, Oda
Deal, Thelma I.
Dean, Ann
Dean, Eleanora
Deaner, Emma G.
Decker, Wilma
Deibler, Elizabeth
Deibler, Rachel
Delaney, Delphine
Delaney, Dorothy
Delaney, Susan
Deneen, Aura
Dengate, Dorothy
Dentil, Lillian
Dickey, Joan
Diehl, Fern
Dietrich, Dawn
Dietrich, Emily B.
Dietterick, Esther
Dietz, Betty Gail
Dietz, Lucille
Dillan, Agnes
Dixon, Barbara
Dodd, Catherine
Donnell, Charlotte
Donmoyer, Milhe
Dougherty, Tara
Douglass, Marian
Douthit, Charlotte
Drumheller, Carol
Duke, Pansy
Dumbauld, Mildred
Dumbroski, Anna
Dunn, Sandra
Duran, Mildred
Durco, Goldie I.
Durco, Susan
Durlin, Gladys M.
Dusch, Lillian
Eaker, Clara
Ebbert, Ann
Ebersole, Martha
Ebersole, Mary
Ebner, Ellen
Eckhart, Agnes M.
Elensky, Janice
Elliott, Deb
Elliott, Marie
Emert, Melba
Engel, Emma Jean
Epting, Helen S.
Estabrook, Margaret E.
Etchberger, Carol L.
Ewig, Elizabeth
Ewig, Ruth
Ewing, Mary
Ewing, Nancy

Farmery, Ruth
Faul, Margery
Faust, Janice
Faust, Keturah
Faust, Mary C.
Faust, Winnie S.
Feister, Mitzi
Feister, Sharon
Fenstermaker, Martha
Ferrell, Robert U.
Ferris, Sharon
Fetterman, Grace
Fike, Theresa A.
Finkenbinder, Lee Faylor
Fiske, Lorraine
Flannery, Donna T.
Fleeger, Kathryn
Flewellyn, Elaine
Forney, Miriam M.
Fox, Alice B.
Fox, Janice L.
Fox, Maurice J.
Fox, Mrs. Merle U.
Frank, Mary L.
Freer, Marlyn
Frederick, Carrie C.
Frey, Belinda
Frick, Elva M.
Friede, Ethel
Friede, Patty
Fry, Barbara J.
Fuhr, Debbie
Fuller, Ruth Ann
Fulmer, Elizabeth
Fye, Mary
Fye, Mrs. R. L.
Gabel, Betty
Gabel, Linda
Gabel, Viola
Gadsby, Mildred
Gager, Gertrude
Gager, Joseph
Gager, J. William
Gager, Mrs. J. William
Gager, Mavis
Gager, Melissa
Gaiser, Henry
Gannon, Alta
Gardiner, Betty-Jane
Gardner, Elizabeth
Gardner, Ruth
Garman, Ethel
Garman, Mary
Gates, Willowa
Gault, Sarah
Gensamer, Jean
Getgen, Eleanor
Gibson, Evelyn
Gibson, Leone D.
Gilbert, Jane
Gilliland, Agnes
Gilmore, Alice E.
Glass, Lola
Gordon, Peggy
Gould, Anna
Gould, Kathy
Grabe, Elizabeth
Graber, Erma
Grande, Dorothy E.
Graves, Dorothy
Greenwood, Marion
Greis, Dorothy M.
Grindel, Gertrude
Grim, Barbara A.
Grimm, Lois
Grindel, Gertrude
Grove, Betty
Gruber, Ruth E.
Gudehunst, Viola
Guss, Helen
Guthrie, Virginia V.
Gutshall, Patricia A.
Haas, Erla Florelle
Haberman, Bertha
Hackenberry, Carolyn
Haladay, Mary
Haldeman, Pauline
Hall, Betty W.
Halstead, Catherine
Hamer, Rob A.
Hammond, Dorothy
Hammond, Emma L.
Hammond, Hazel
Hamor, Marian G.
Handwork, Barbara
Harding, Dorothy J.
Hare, Mary
Harer, Mildred
Harkelroad, Clem
Harkelroad, Mary
Harkins, Eleanor
Harkness, Hazel
Harman, Madaline
Harmon, Mona
Harnish, Blanch P.
Harper, Vera L.
Harriger, June
Harris, Dot
Harris, Grace
Harting, Mildred E.
Hartle, Dorothy
Hartley, Florence E.
Harvey, Karen
Hartzell, Ruth
Hawk, Mildred
Hay, Stella F.
Hay, Virginia
Hayes, Nada
Haynes, Elouise
Haynes, Luella
Heath, Joyce A.
Hebe, Erma
Hebets, Carol
Hebets, Harold
Heicher, Elmyra
Heinly, Anna
Hendricks, Edith
Henrie, Mrs. R. Neal
Henry, Barbara
Hennessey, Frances
Hepfer, Mary
Hershberger, Grace
Hertzog, Jean H.
Hesselgesser, Frances
Hetherington, Robin A.
Hetrick, Arlene
Hetzell, Judy
Hickernell, Catherine
Hicks, Kim
Hicks, Violet L.
Hill, Eleanor
Hill, Fay
Hill, Mrs. Joseph O.
Hiller, Mary

Himes, Geraldine
Hirschfeld, Rita
Hockenberry, Carolyn
Hoffman, Frances A.
Hoffman, James
Holden, Kenneth
Hollabaugh, Marian
Hollobaugh, Louise
Holloway, Marian
Holman, Kay
Holt, Lorraine
Hopkins, Babe
Horman, Edna K.
Hornick, Eda
Horting, Mildred E.
Horvath, Irene
Hough, Doris L.
Houseknecht, Florence D.
Howell, Adaline
Howell, Nancy
Hoye, Blanche G.
Huber, Betsy
Hubbard, Ida Rachel
Huffman, Cathy
Huling, Bryson Blair
Huling, Hazel G.
Huling, Sherry L.
Hunter, Betty
Hunter, Eleanor N.
Hutchison, Ardelle
Iman, Tami
Irvin, Mrs. Leslie
Irvin, Damaris
Irwin, Lois
Jacobs, Wanda R.
Jacobson, Helen J.
Jameson, Ruth
Jamison, Peggy
Jarrard, Elsie
Jefferis, Vivian C.
Johnn, Jean V.
Johnson, Harry K.
Johnston, Dorothy
Johnston, Ruth Caven
Jones, Della
Jones, Edna S.
Jones, Opal
Juliana, Lisa Huling
Justh, Bertha
Kanouff, Frances
Kauffman, Arlene
Kauffman, Betty Lou
Kauffman, Nettie A.
Kearns, Bernice
Keenan, Lorraine
Keir, Irma
Keck, Mary
Kelly, Mabel L.
Kelso, Janet
Kenny, Alma
Kenny, Lisa
Kennedy, Marjorie
Kent, Mary Jane
Kent, Patricia Lynette
Kephart, Althea
Kessler, Frances
Kessler, Mrs. Glen
Kiefer, Jane
Kiefer, Joan
Kinder, Helen
Kinney, Sandra
Kipps, Dr. Margaret
Knapp, Faye
Knapp, Virginia
Knarr, Roxy
Knight, Esther
Knorr, Velma
Knox, Winnie
Koenig, Amy
Koenig, Doris
Koenig, Lisa
Kolick, Pearl
Kollar, Stella
Kopp, Carol
Korman, Edna K.
Kortz, Dalene
Kozar, Zelda
Kramer, Helen
Kramer, Wayne
Krause, Susan R.
Kreger, Elizabeth
Kretzing, Arlene
Kreider, Mabel
Krider, Helen
Krider, Leona
Kurten, Juanita
Kurtz, Darlene
Kurtz, Ruth E.
LaFaver, May
Lamoreaux, Myrtle
Lanterman, Anna
Lapp, Marjorie
LaRue, Mildred E.
Latimer, Beatrice
Latshaw, Helena B.
Lauer, Evelyn
Laughlin, Eleanor
Laughlin, Kimberley A.
Lawrence, Cleo
Lawson, Helen M.
Leese, Treva
Lehman, Esther
Lehman, Mary
Lehman, Nancy
Lehner, Kit
Lehner, Wandamae
Lengel, Brenda E.
Leonard, Dorrine
Lerch, Mrs. Sherwood
Lerch, Shirley Ann
Letterman, Virginia K.
Levan, Letha
Lichtenwalner, Betty Jane
Lichtenwalner, Thelma
Light, Betty J.
Linder, Evadna
Lindh, Mary
Linn, Kim Huling
Lindner, Charlene F.
Lindner, Mary Ann
Lindner, Travis
Litner, Mary Ann
Litvin, Ruthanne
Lloyd, Gertrude
Lockhart, Tenie
Lohr, Arlene B.
London, Delores
Long, Dorothy M.
Long, Ethel
Long, Pamela
Long, Tracy
Long, Walter R.
Long, Walter W.
Longenberger, Betty

Longenberger, Grace
Longenberger, Nan
Longenecker, Dorothy W.
Lorah, Anna Grace
Love, Bonnie
Lukehart, Edna
Lukens, Anna
Lupp, Eleanora P.
Lutz, Emma
Marion, Lynor
Lyon, Dorothy
Lyon, Twila
Mack, Sarah Ellen
Mackavage, Mary
Madsen, Jane M.
Mains, Pauline
Malm, Doris
Malone, Pearle
Mangel, Virginia
Manley, Emmalena
Marshall, Janice
Martin, Ailene
Martin, Dorothy
Martin, Juanita
Martin, Judy
Martsolf, Nettie
Marzani, June K.
Master, Betty
Matheson, Ethel
Matter, Nancy B.
Matthews, Loretta
Mauser, Joan
McAdams, Ruth
McAlevy, Lois
McAninch, Donna
McAnlis, Lois
McCall, Emily
McCauley, Brenda
McChesney, Mrs. James
McClellan, Janet
McClure, Bertha
McCollough, Vanessa
McCoy, Margaret
McCracken, Mary
McCrory, Pearle K.
McCullough, Helen
McCullough, June
McCullough, Mary Lou
McCurdy, Betty
McElwain, Florence
McFadden, Malissa
McFalls, Bertha
McGary, Donna
McGaughey, Isabelle
McIlwain, Helen
McKelvey, Marcia
McMath, Bernice
McMeans, Esther
McMeans, Vera
McMichael, Esther
McMillin, Howard
McMillin, Ila May
McMillin, June
McMillin, Laura
McMillin, Mary
McMillin, Nancy
McMillin, Roy
McWhirter, Zelma
McWilliams, Jolene
Meier, Renate
Mengel, Helen
Mengel, Katie M.
Mengel, Lillian
Merkel, Shirley
Metrick, Catherine J.
Metzger, Ruth
Michalka, Rebecca
Mihalo, Nancy J.
Miles, A.
Milks, Martha A.
Milliken, Joan
Miller, Audrey
Miller, Beverly J.
Miller, Dorothy M.
Miller, Eleanor
Miller, Hilda
Miller, Nellie
Mills, Helen G.
Minor, Barbara L.
Mitchell, Linda
Mohn, Karen R.
Moll, Katie A.
Montgomery, Carolyn
Mood, Mary
Moore, Gertrude
Moore, Irene
Moore, Jean
Moore, Lois
Morgan, Sally
Morris, Betty L.
Morris, Miriam R.
Mosier, Ruth
Motzer, Mrs. William
Mowrer, Bernice
Mowry, Pat
Mowry, Shirley
Moyer, Anna P.
Moyer, Phyllis
Mullin, Vivian N.
Munsch, Doris
Munson, Mary Jane
Myers, Edith C.
Myers, Lois A.
Nagel, Donna
Nauss, Barbara Harrison
Neal, Mildred R.
Neeley, Mary Jane
Nelson, Hope
Neyhard, Mildred
Nicklin, Jenny
Nicklin, M. J.
Nolf, Amanda
Norburger, Mary
North, Virginia
Null, Melissa
Null, Sandra
Null, Suzanne
Null, Weldell W., Jr.
Nyce, Maria
Oakes, Mary Etta
O'Brien, Susie K.
O'Bryan, Mrs. Ralph
Oesterling, Betty
Ohlin, Irene
Ohlinger, Claude
Ohlinger, Marie E.
Olcus, Rebecca
Orient, Pearl
Osborn, Bettie
Osborne, Mildred
Osborne, Richard L.
Osborne, Ruth E.
Otterman, Ruth
Overly, Mary

Paden, Helen
Paden, Tiffany
Pander, Alice
Pardoe, Mrs. Robert F.
Parrish, Eileen
Patterson, Lucille
Patterson, Lucy
Patton, Edith
Paul, Dorothy Jane
Paul, Paricia L.
Peace, Gladys R.
Peake, Laura Y.
Pecht, Mary Margaret
Pees, Mary E.
Peffer, Abby
Peffer, Anita
Peffer, Jay
Pepper, Naomi
Petergall, Laura M.
Peters, Ada M.
Peters, Esther
Peterson, Beth Ann
Peterson, Jessie
Peterson, Helen M.
Pfautz, Elizabeth
Pflugh, Mrs. Warren
Pier, Thelma
Pifer, Eloise J.
Pifer, Lois M.
Pike, Catherine
Pinnock, Alice
Plank, Lois
Pontius, Betty J.
Porter, Dorothy A.
Post, Catharine
Posten, Ruth
Poust, Ruth
Pressler, Marjorie R.
Preston, Sarah
Preston, Scott
Preto, Ida B.
Price, Louise B.
Proper, Edith
Prosser, Doris
Prosser, Nettie H.
Pursel, James F.
Pyle, Zelma K.
Rabert, Dorothy A.
Rabold, Agnes L.
Rager, Mildred
Raley, Katherine
Ralph, Martha G.
Randolph, Doris E.
Randolph, Edna
Raney, Carolyn
Raney, Joan
Rarig, Florence
Ratchford, Vega G.
Ravenscroft, Ruth
Reaser, Mary
Reddon, Icie
Redic, Helen
Reed, Ann
Reed, Sarah
Reeher, Laura
Reese, Frances
Reese, Glenda
Reffner, Dorothy B.
Reichert, Bertha M.
Reid, Ann
Reilly, Caroline M.
Reilly, Lorene A.
Reinert, Mildred
Reisinger, Faye R.
Remsburg, M. Leone
Remsburg, Shirley E.
Rennard, Jean
Reppert, Jane
Reppert, Jerri
Reyes, Dorothy
Rhoades, Carol A.
Rhoades, Emma W.
Rich, Thelma
Richard, Clare
Richard, Fran
Richards, Lillie
Richards, Sandra
Riedy, Hilda
Riegel, Elvena K.
Riel, Ada
Riggleman, Rose
Riker, Edith
Ringler, Mrs. Mildred
Rishel, Delores
Roberts, Dora
Roberts, Peggy
Robertson, Ellen
Robinson, Mrs. Albert
Robinson, Phyllis
Rodgers, Betty
Rodgers, Lisa
Rodgers, Nancy J.
Roenigk, Mildred
Rogers, Cecil
Rogers, Dorothy
Rogers, Glenora
Rogers, Mary Lou
Roland, Cora
Ross, Edith M.
Ross, Joyce
Ross, Ruth Ann
Rosser, Charlotte
Roth, Grace
Rothrock, Jean F.
Rudy, Patricia
Ruffner, Irene
Ruhf, Luella
Ruhlman, Jean
Rumbaugh, Lois A.
Rumbaugh, Maxine
Rumbaugh, Virginia
Rumberger, Sandra
Rummel, Violet
Rupert, Jerry
Rupert, Stella
Rush, Iva
Sadler, Alta
Sandrock, Velma
Santschi, Viva
Sattazahn, Marlene
Sawhill, Evelyn
Sawhill, Sis
Sayward, Lorraine
Scarpelli, Patricia
Schaeffer, Faye M.
Schaeffer, Marie
Schlegel, Ethel
Schlegel, Lillian
Schlemmer, Edna
Schlemmer, Willie, Jr.
Schlieder, Karmel
Schlosser, Luella
Schnure, Charlotte
Schreckengast, Goldie

Schreiber, Lesta
Schroer, Shirley
Schwartz, Myrtle
Schwarzbach, Catherine
Schwoegl, Margaret
Scott, Dorothy
Sechler, Loretta
Sechrist, Pearl E.
Secules, Madeline
Seiler, Tamra C.
Seiple, Mrs. Jacob S.
Selfridge, Virginia
Shaffer, Arlene
Shaffer, Betty L.
Shaffer, Florence
Shaffer, George
Shaffer, Mae
Shaffer, Veryle
Shannon, Martha
Shaw, Mildred S.
Shawver, Dorothy
Sheesley, Miriam
Sheffer, Gladys
Sheffler, Marie
Sherred, Helen
Shields. Colleen R.
Shirey, Anna Rhine
Showalter, Mary M.
Showalter, Mrs. Melvin
Shreck, Connie
Shreck, Freda
Shull, Charlotte
Shultz, Sandra
Shutt, Mary Kaye
Shutts, Josephine
Sidle, Miriam
Silvis, Lauretta
Simmons, Cora June
Sinclair, Irene
Sinclair, Marie
Sindlinger, Lori
Sipe, Hazel
Sipe, Helen
Sitler, Pauline
Skillington, Jeanne
Slick, Beatrice N.
Slick, Marjorie
Slovinsky, Hilda
Smeltzer, Olive
Smiley, Eleanor
Smith, Blanche
Smith, Clarabelle
Smith, Evelyn
Smith, Josephine
Smith, Shirley J.
Smith, Sue
Smith, Sylvia
Smith, Velma
Snider, Jane
Snyder, Betty
Snyder, Doris
Snyder, Judy
Snyder, Helen F.
Snyder, Louise
Snyder, Martha W.
Snyder, Miriam M.
Snyder, Susan
Snyder, Thelma V.
Snyder, Velma
Soisson, Jean
Sollers, Anna Mae
Sonon, Fern
Sonon, Lester, Jr.
Sonow, Benjamin
Southard, Eva
Spafford, Joanne
Spease, Jean
Speer, Ruth W.
Spengler, Miriam
Springman, Jean
Sprowls, Dolores
Squiers, Kathryn
Steckler, Lucille
Steele, Elizabeth
Steeley, Ruth
Steninger, Geraldine
Stephens, Rose
Sterner, William A.
Stevens, Helen
Stewart, Beverly
Stewart, Ellen
Stewart, Joyce
Stewart, Margaret
Stewart, Mary
Stimmel, Mary
Stiner, Jean
Stitzel, Esther K.
Stokely, Margaret
Stoner, Edith L.
Storm, Margaret M.
Straub, Helen
Stringert, Evelyn K.
Sturgin, Paula
Sullivan, Frances
Supansic, Mildred
Sutliff, Louise
Swanson, Dorothy
Swanson, Virginia
Swartz, Marie
Sylvis, Alice Bish
Syphrit, Mary
Szatkowski, Gerri
Taggert, Helen
Tannehill, Helen B.
Tatters, Helen F.
Tau, Margaret
Tau, Susan
Taydus, Elsie R.
Taylor, Hazel
Templin, Mary Lou
Tenderhope, Marilyn
Tercha, Melinda
Terrell, Robert W.
Terwilliger, Margery
Teudhope, Marilyn
Thoman, Madaline
Thomas, Mildred
Thompson, Aliene
Thompson, Jean
Tomb, Jeanne
Townsend, Margaret
Traub, Marie
Traver, Dorothy
Traver, Ruth B.
Treichler, Brandon
Treichler, Eva
Treichler, Jane
Treichler, Suzanne
Trimble, Ruth
Tromby, Alda L.
Trone, Iva
Trotman, Carol
Trumbull, Matilda
Truscott, Beverly J.

Turner, Beverly
Tush, Eldora
Tush, Jim
Twentier, Mildred
Van Dyke, Cora
Verbeke, Margaret
Verbeke, Martha
Vonada, Ruth E.
Von Wolffradt, Marilyn
Voorhies, Alice
Wade, Virginia
Wadsworth, Ellen Marie
Wagner, Linda
Wagoner, Mrs. Clyde
Wagoner, Jean
Wagoner, Joan
Waidelich, Shirley
Wainwright, Dorothy
Wakefield, Annabel
Walker, Alma
Walker, Mary
Walker, Ruth
Walker, Ruth V.
Wallis, Ruth A.
Walters, Helen Louise
Walton, Ellen
Waltz, Arlene
Waltz, Ruth
Warmkessel, Ruth W.
Warner, Blanch

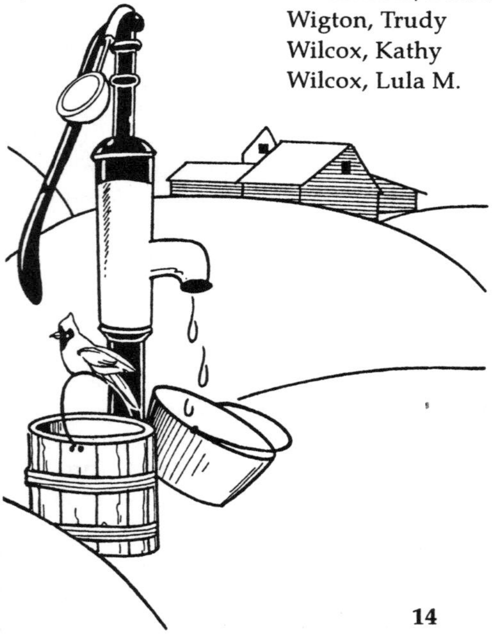

Warren, Miriam
Warrick, Joan
Waskie, Thelma
Watterson, Pam
Weaver, Laura
Weaver, Norma Lee
Weber, Ann
Weeks, Ruth Fitzgerald
Weibley, Shirley
Weigle, Helen
Weir, Pat
Weiss, Barbara
Weitzel, Cleva
Wellhausen, Anna
Wells, Clarabelle
Wensel, Eileen
Werley, Faye M.
Werner, Emily
Wertman, Althea M.
Wescott, Helen
Wessner, Mildred
West, Helen P.
Wetzel, Hope S.
Wetzel, Janice
Whipkey, Mary
Whitacre, Mildred
White, Lynnette
Whited, Janet D.
Whitmoyer, Bessie P.
Whritenour, Barbara
Wigton, Trudy
Wilcox, Kathy
Wilcox, Lula M.
Wilcox, Ruby
Wilhelm, Carol
Williams, Betty Lou
Williams, Judy
Williams, Mark
Williamson, Florence
Wilson, Agnes M.
Wilson, Betty
Wilson, Eleanor
Wilson, Hazel
Wilson, Margaret E.
Wilson, Mary Lou
Wilson, Mrs. Thomas
Windhorst, Elizabeth
Windhorst, Roberta
Winegar, Hazel
Wise, Carol
Wise, Frances
Wise, Inez
Witmer, Carol A.
Wohlbach, Gladys
Wojton, Mary Jo
Wolfe, Cleita
Wolfe, Joyce L.
Wolfe, Lillian
Woods, Catherine
Woods, Katie W.
Woolerton, Althea
Wright, Betty Jo Gifford
Wright, Melva
Yarger, Marlene
Yearich, Ann
Yetter, Karen
Yochum, Effie
Yocum, LeWanda
Yoder, Bess
Yoder, Carolyn
Yoder, Maisie
Yoder, Mary C.
Young, Esther
Young, Helen
Zeafle, Bina
Zeh, Helen
Zerbe, Edna M.
Zimmerman, Carole
Zitney, Jessie D.
Zorich, Rose

VIP Recipes

Yummy Green Beans

1 pound small green beans
2 tablespoons salt or other seasoning
4 quarts boiling water
2 tablespoons butter or margarine
1 large clove of garlic, crushed
Salt and pepper to taste

Cook green beans in salted boiling water in saucepan until tender crisp; drain. Rinse under cold water; pat dry. Melt butter with garlic in small saucepan. Pour over green beans in saucepan. Add salt and pepper; toss. Cook over low heat until heated through. May be heated in microwave on High for 2 minutes. **Yield: 4 servings.**

First Lady Barbara Bush

Bran Muffins

3/4 cup raisins
2 1/2 cups All-Bran cereal
2 cups skim milk
1/2 cup oil
5 eggs, beaten
1 cup honey
2 teaspoons vanilla extract
2 1/2 cups whole wheat flour
1 1/4 teaspoons salt
2 tablespoons sugar
1 tablespoon baking powder
1 cup chopped pecans
2 cups shredded carrots
1 cup drained crushed pineapple
2 apples, coarsely chopped
3/4 cup chopped dates
12 prunes, chopped

Soak raisins and cereal in milk in large bowl for 15 minutes. Stir in mixture of oil, eggs, honey and vanilla. Mix flour, salt, sugar, baking powder, pecans, carrots, pineapple, apples, dates and prunes in bowl. Add to bran mixture; stir just until moistened. Fill greased muffin cups. Bake at 350 degrees for 30 to 40 minutes. May use equivalent amount of egg substitute in place of eggs to reduce cholesterol. **Yield: 24 servings.**

First Lady Barbara Bush

Old-Fashioned Bread Pudding

8 slices raisin bread, lightly buttered
1/2 to 3/4 cup sugar
1/2 teaspoon cinnamon
Additional raisins or fruit to taste
4 cups milk
4 eggs, beaten
1/2 teaspoon salt
2 teaspoons vanilla extract

Cut bread into quarters. Mix sugar, cinnamon and raisins in small bowl. Layer bread and sugar mixture in buttered 9x13-inch baking dish until all ingredients are used. Mix milk, eggs, salt and vanilla in bowl. Pour over bread layers. Bake at 350 degrees for 30 minutes or until puffed and lightly browned. **Yield: 12 servings.**

First Lady Barbara Bush

Mushroom Quiche

$1^1/_4$ pounds mushrooms, sliced
3 green onions, finely chopped
1 clove of garlic, finely chopped
3 shallots, finely chopped
3 tablespoons margarine or butter
$1^3/_4$ teaspoons oregano
$1^3/_4$ teaspoons basil
$1^1/_4$ teaspoons salt
$^3/_4$ teaspoon marjoram
$^1/_4$ teaspoon pepper
$^1/_4$ teaspoon thyme
$^1/_2$ teaspoon dry mustard
4 eggs or egg substitute
$^3/_4$ cup milk or half and half
1 unbaked 9-inch pie shell

Sauté mushrooms, green onions, garlic and shallots in margarine in skillet. Stir in seasonings and dry mustard. Cook for 2 minutes or until liquid is evaporated. Let stand for 5 minutes. Combine eggs and milk in medium bowl; mix well. Stir in mushroom mixture. Spoon into pie shell. Bake in lower third of oven at 375 degrees for 35 to 45 minutes or until set. **Yield: 6 servings.**

First Lady Barbara Bush

Cranberry Squares

$1^1/_2$ cups flour
$1^1/_2$ cups sugar
1 cup melted butter or margarine
2 eggs, well beaten
1 cup chopped nuts
2 cups fresh whole cranberries

Combine flour, sugar, butter and eggs in bowl; mix well. Add nuts and cranberries; mix well. Pour into greased and floured 9x13-inch baking pan. Bake at 325 degrees for 45 to 50 minutes or until golden brown. Cool on wire rack. Cut into squares. **Yield: 2 dozen.**

Dolores A. Barrow, First Lady, The National Grange

Governor Casey's Chocolate Cake

$^3/_4$ cup baking cocoa
2 cups sugar
2 cups flour
$1^1/_2$ teaspoons baking soda
$1^1/_2$ teaspoons baking powder
$1^1/_2$ cups hot water
1 cup safflower oil
2 eggs or egg substitute
2 teaspoons vanilla extract
6 tablespoons margarine, softened
$^1/_2$ cup baking cocoa
$2^2/_3$ cups confectioners' sugar
1 teaspoon vanilla extract

Combine $^3/_4$ cup baking cocoa, sugar, flour, baking soda, baking powder, hot water, oil, eggs and 2 teaspoons vanilla in bowl; mix well. Spoon into 9x13-inch cake pan coated with nonstick cooking spray. Bake at 350 degrees for 40 to 45 minutes. Cool completely. Cream margarine in mixer bowl until light and fluffy. Add $^1/_2$ cup baking cocoa, confectioners' sugar and 1 teaspoon vanilla; beat until of spread consistency. Spread on cooled cake. **Yield: 15 servings.**

Governor Robert P. Casey

Mrs. R's Mincemeat for Pie

$1\frac{1}{2}$ pounds ground beef
$1\frac{1}{2}$ pounds ground pork
2 pounds raisins
2 pounds currants
2 pounds sugar
1 1-pound package brown sugar
2 oranges, ground
2 lemons, ground
4 cups crushed pineapple
3 quarts chopped apples
1 cup molasses
4 cups applesauce
2 teaspoons ground cloves
1 tablespoon cinnamon
1 teaspoon nutmeg

Brown ground beef and ground pork in skillet, stirring until crumbly; drain. Grind in food grinder. Cook raisins and currants in water to cover in large saucepan over low heat until soft; drain. Add ground meat, sugar, brown sugar, ground oranges, ground lemons, pineapple, apples, molasses, applesauce, and seasonings. Cook for 12 minutes. Ladle into hot sterilized quart jars, leaving $\frac{1}{2}$-inch headspace; seal with 2-piece lids. Process in boiling water bath for 10 minutes. May freeze pie filling if desired. **Yield: 8 quarts.**

Mrs. Mildred Ringler, First Lady, Pennsylvania State Grange

Corn Chowder

$\frac{1}{4}$ cup chopped onion
$\frac{1}{4}$ cup butter
$\frac{1}{4}$ cup flour
2 cups milk
2 16-ounce cans whole kernel corn
1 17-ounce can cream-style corn
Salt and pepper to taste

Cook onion in butter in saucepan over low heat just until tender. Stir in flour. Stir in milk gradually. Cook until thickened, stirring constantly. Stir in whole kernel and cream-style corn. Cook until heated through. Add salt and pepper.
Yield: 4 to 5 servings.

Mary R. Buffington, National Grange Lecturer, Kennett #19

The casting of the first cookstove in America took place in Pennsylvania and a long-handled waffle iron was used for the first time over the open hearth in a Pennsylvania farm home.

All-in-One-Dish Supper

4 cups thinly sliced potatoes
1 9-ounce package frozen green beans, thawed
3/4 cup shredded cheese
1/3 cup flour
1 teaspoon salt
1/8 teaspoon pepper
1 15-ounce can tomato sauce
1 pound ground beef
3/4 cup shredded cheese
1/2 cup dry bread crumbs
1/3 cup milk
1 egg
1/4 cup chopped onion

Combine potatoes, green beans, 3/4 cup cheese, flour, salt and pepper in bowl; mix well. Spoon into 7x12-inch baking dish. Pour half the tomato sauce over top. Bake at 350 degrees for 20 minutes. Mix ground beef, 3/4 cup cheese, bread crumbs, milk, egg and onion in bowl. Shape into 24 meatballs. Arrange over tomato sauce layer. Top with remaining tomato sauce. Bake at 350 degrees for 45 to 55 minutes or until potatoes are tender. **Yield: 6 servings.**

Betty-Jane Gardiner, National Director, Women's Activities Committee

Caramel Rolls

2 loaves frozen bread dough, thawed
1 cup packed brown sugar
1 3-ounce package vanilla pudding and pie mix
1/2 cup margarine
2 tablespoons milk
1 teaspoon cinnamon

Pinch dough into small pieces. Arrange in greased 9x13-inch baking pan. Combine brown sugar, pudding mix, margarine, milk and cinnamon in saucepan. Cook over low heat until margarine melts, stirring frequently. Pour over dough. Let rise for 2 1/2 to 3 hours. Bake at 325 degrees for 30 minutes. Cool in pan for 5 to 10 minutes. Remove to serving plate. **Yield: 15 servings.**

Martha Ebersole, Lady Assistant Steward, Pennsylvania State Grange

Chef Salad

5 large heads lettuce
1 bag fresh spinach
1 medium head cabbage
1 small head red cabbage
Flowerets of 1 head cauliflower
1 package carrots, sliced
1 package radishes, sliced
2 pounds thickly sliced boiled ham
2 pounds sliced American cheese
12 tomatoes, cut into wedges
4 green bell peppers, sliced
12 boiled eggs, sliced

Cut lettuce, spinach and cabbages into bite-sized pieces. Combine with cauliflower, carrots and radishes in very large salad bowl; toss. Cut sliced ham and cheese into strips. Arrange tomatoes, green peppers, egg slices, ham and cheese over top. Serve with several types of salad dressing. **Yield: 25 servings.**

Patricia Rudy, Chaplain, Pennsylvania State Grange

Vegetable Turnovers

1 large onion, finely chopped
1 tablespoon oil
1 clove of garlic, finely chopped
2 cups cauliflower flowerets, chopped
2 medium carrots, chopped
1 cup frozen peas, thawed
2 ounces shredded mozzarella cheese
1 cup ricotta cheese
1/4 cup grated Parmesan cheese
2 egg whites
1/8 teaspoon ground nutmeg
1/4 teaspoon salt
1/4 teaspoon pepper
1 recipe 2-crust pie pastry

Sauté onion in oil in skillet for 3 minutes. Add garlic. Sauté for 1 minute. Add cauliflower and carrots. Sauté for 5 minutes. Stir in peas. Sauté for 1 minute longer. Let stand until cooled slightly. Combine cheeses, egg whites, nutmeg, salt and pepper in large bowl. Stir in sautéed mixture. Roll pastry dough into two 11-inch rounds. Spread half the mixture over half the round; fold other side over, sealing edge. Prick top with fork. Repeat with remaining pastry. Place turnovers on greased baking sheet. Bake at 400 degrees for 30 minutes or until golden brown. Serve warm. **Yield: 4 servings.**

Betsy Huber, Pomona, Pennsylvania State Grange

E-Z Chicken Casserole

1 package stuffing mix
8 1/8-inch thick slices chicken or turkey roll
1 10-ounce can cream of chicken soup
1/8 teaspoon paprika
1/8 teaspoon parsley flakes

Prepare stuffing mix using package directions. Spoon stuffing onto chicken slices. Roll up. Place seam side down in greased 8x8-inch baking dish. Spoon undiluted soup over top. Sprinkle with paprika and parsley. Bake at 350 degrees for 25 to 30 minutes or until bubbly. **Yield: 4 servings.**

Ruth E. Osborne, Flora, Pennsylvania State Grange

Rhubarb Crunch

2 cups flour
1 1/2 cups oats
2 cups packed brown sugar
1 cup melted butter
2 teaspoons cinnamon
8 cups chopped rhubarb
2 cups sugar
2 tablespoons cornstarch
2 cups water
2 teaspoons vanilla extract

Combine flour, oats, brown sugar, butter and cinnamon in bowl; stir until crumbly. Press half the mixture into 9x13-inch baking pan. Spread rhubarb over crumb layer. Combine sugar, cornstarch, water and vanilla in saucepan. Cook over medium heat until thickened and clear, stirring constantly. Pour over rhubarb. Sprinkle with remaining crumb mixture. Bake at 350 degrees for 1 hour. **Yield: 12 servings.**

Rebecca Michalka, W. A. Director, Pennsylvania State Grange

Chewy Oatmeal Cookies

3/4 cup butter, softened
1/2 cup sugar
1 1/2 cups packed brown sugar
2 eggs
1 teaspoon vanilla extract
1 1/4 cups flour
1 teaspoon baking powder
1/2 teaspoon baking soda
1 teaspoon salt
2 1/2 cups oats
2/3 cup nuts
1/2 cup Angel Flake coconut

Cream butter, sugar and brown sugar in mixer bowl until light and fluffy. Beat in eggs and vanilla. Sift in flour, baking powder, baking soda and salt; mix well. Add oats, nuts and coconut; mix well. Chill for 2 hours. Roll dough into small balls. Place on cookie sheet. Bake at 350 degrees for 8 to 10 minutes or until golden brown. Remove to wire rack to cool. **Yield: 4 dozen.**

Agnes M. Wilson, Region A, W. A. Director, Wilmington #1477

Apple Crisp

4 cups peeled, sliced apples
2/3 cup packed brown sugar
1/2 cup flour
1/2 cup oats
3/4 teaspoon cinnamon
1/2 cup butter, softened

Place apples in 1 1/2-quart glass baking dish. Mix brown sugar, flour, oats, cinnamon and butter in bowl. Spoon over apples. Microwave on High for 5 minutes or until apples are tender, turning 1/4 turn after 2 1/2 minutes. **Yield: 6 servings.**

Anna Gould, Region B, W. A. Director, Bell Township #2047

Cherry Cheesecake

1 1/4 cups flour
1/2 cup packed brown sugar
1/2 cup butter-flavored shortening
1 cup chopped walnuts, divided
1/2 cup flaked coconut
16 ounces cream cheese, softened
2/3 cup sugar
2 eggs
2 teaspoons vanilla extract
2 21-ounce cans cherry pie filling

Combine flour and brown sugar in bowl. Cut in shortening until crumbly. Stir in half the nuts and coconut. Reserve 1/2 cup mixture for topping. Press remaining mixture into greased 9x13-inch baking pan. Bake at 350 degrees for 15 minutes. Beat cream cheese, sugar, eggs and vanilla in mixer bowl until smooth. Spread over hot baked layer. Bake for 15 minutes. Top with pie filling, spreading to edge. Combine remaining nuts and reserved crumb mixture in small bowl. Sprinkle over pie filling. Bake for 15 minutes. Let stand until cool. Chill in refrigerator. **Yield: 9 servings.**

Freda Shreck, Region C, W. A. Director, White Deer #122

Lemon-Mustard Turkey Cutlets

1 pound turkey breast cutlets
$1/4$ cup flour
$1/4$ teaspoon each salt and pepper
$1\frac{1}{2}$ tablespoons butter
$1/2$ cup whipping cream
2 tablespoons finely chopped onion
2 teaspoons mustard
2 teaspoons lemon juice

Coat cutlets with mixture of flour, salt and pepper; shake off excess. Melt butter in nonstick skillet over medium heat. Add turkey. Cook for 2 minutes on each side or until turkey tests done. Remove to warm serving plate. Pour whipping cream into skillet. Bring to a boil over medium high heat, stirring to deglaze skillet. Add onion, mustard and lemon juice. Cook for 2 minutes or until slightly thickened. Spoon over turkey. Serve immediately. **Yield: 4 servings.**

Evelyn Cottrell, Region D, W. A. Director, Gibson #798

Apricot Dream Dessert

$2\frac{1}{4}$ cups vanilla wafer crumbs
$3/4$ cup margarine
$3/4$ cup confectioners' sugar
2 eggs, beaten
1 teaspoon vanilla extract
1 cup crushed nuts
8 ounces cream cheese, softened
2 packages whipped topping mix, prepared
1 17-ounce can apricots, drained, chopped
1 cup vanilla wafer crumbs

Spread $2\frac{1}{4}$ cups cookie crumbs in 9x13-inch baking pan. Combine margarine, confectioners' sugar, beaten eggs and vanilla in saucepan. Cook over medium heat until thickened, stirring constantly. Let stand until cool. Pour over crumb layer. Combine nuts and cream cheese in bowl; mix well. Spread over custard layer. Fold whipped topping into apricots gently. Spread over cream cheese layer; sprinkle with 1 cup cookie crumbs. **Yield: 12 servings.**

Ruth Posten, Region E, W. A. Director, Deemston #1372

Baked Chicken Salad

2 cups chopped cooked chicken
$1/2$ cup chopped onion
$1/2$ cup chopped green bell pepper
$1/2$ cup chopped celery
$1/2$ cup (about) mayonnaise
2 slices bread, cut into cubes
1 10-ounce can cream of mushroom soup
2 eggs
$1/2$ cup milk
Shredded Cheddar cheese to taste

Combine chicken, onion, green pepper and celery in bowl. Add enough mayonnaise to hold mixture together. Spread half the bread in 2-quart baking dish. Layer chicken salad, remaining bread and soup over top. Mix eggs and milk in bowl. Pour over top. Sprinkle with cheese. Bake at 325 degrees for 1 hour. **Yield: 6 servings.**

Anna Mary Brenneman, Region F, W. A. Director, Scotch Valley #510

Summer Vegetable Bake

2 cups water
3 cups green beans, cut into 1-inch pieces
1½ cups chopped onion
2 10-ounce packages frozen spinach
2 tablespoons butter or margarine
⅓ teaspoon finely chopped garlic
2 tablespoons flour
⅛ teaspoon nutmeg
½ teaspoon salt
⅛ teaspoon pepper
1¾ cups milk
3 ounces cream cheese, cubed
1 cup soft bread crumbs
¼ cup grated Parmesan cheese
2 tablespoons butter, softened

Bring water to a boil in saucepan. Add green beans and onion. Simmer, covered, for 10 minutes. Add spinach. Cook until thawed. Simmer for 5 minutes longer; drain. Spoon vegetables into 2-quart baking dish. Combine 2 tablespoons butter and garlic in saucepan. Cook over medium heat until butter melts. Stir in flour, nutmeg, salt and pepper. Add milk. Cook until thickened, stirring constantly. Stir in cream cheese until melted. Pour sauce over vegetables, stirring to coat. Mix bread crumbs, Parmesan cheese and 2 tablespoons butter in small bowl. Sprinkle over top. Bake at 350 degrees for 20 to 30 minutes. **Yield: 10 servings.**

Martha W. Snyder, Region G, W. A. Director, Plainfield #1727

Banana Pudding Cake

3 egg yolks
2 very ripe bananas
1 teaspoon vanilla extract
½ cup milk
⅓ cup flour, sifted
1 teaspoon artificial sweetener
3 egg whites, stiffly beaten

Beat egg yolks and bananas in bowl until smooth. Add vanilla, milk, flour and sweetener; mix well. Fold in beaten egg whites gently. Spoon mixture into greased 1-quart baking dish. Place in larger pan filled with ½ inch water. Bake at 325 degrees for 30 minutes or until puffed and golden brown. May microwave on Defrost for 15 to 17 minutes, turning dish every 5 minutes. **Yield: 6 servings.**

Eleanor Hill, Region H, W. A. Director, Virginville #1832

Early Pennsylvania cooks developed the tradition of serving meals with "seven sweets and seven sours." Special delicacies included apple butter, spiced peaches, pickled watermelon, pickled beets and red cabbage.

Mandarin Orange Salad

60 Ritz crackers, crushed
1/2 cup melted margarine
1/4 cup sugar
2 11-ounce cans mandarin oranges, drained
12 ounces whipped topping
6 ounces orange juice concentrate
1 14-ounce can sweetened condensed milk

Mix cracker crumbs, margarine and sugar in bowl. Pat into 9x13-inch dish. Beat oranges, whipped topping, orange juice concentrate and condensed milk in mixer bowl. Pour into prepared dish, spreading to edge. Chill until serving time. **Yield: 12 servings.**

Eleanor Wilson, Junior Director, Pennsylvania State Grange

Snowball Cookies

1/2 cup butter, softened
1/4 cup evaporated milk
1/2 teaspoon vanilla extract
1 3/4 cups flour
6 tablespoons confectioners' sugar
1/2 teaspoon salt
1 cup chopped nuts
Additional confectioners' sugar

Cream butter in mixer bowl until light and fluffy. Beat in evaporated milk gradually. Add vanilla; mix well. Sift flour, 6 tablespoons confectioners' sugar and salt together. Add to creamed mixture gradually, mixing well after each addition. Stir in nuts. Shape by teaspoonfuls into balls. Place on floured cookie sheet. Bake at 375 degrees for 10 to 12 minutes. Roll warm cookies in additional confectioners' sugar. **Yield: 3 to 4 dozen.**

Nettie A. Kauffman, Youth and Young Adults Director, Ontelaunee #1617

Golden Apples

3 medium apples, cut into 1/4-inch slices
1/2 cup orange juice
1/4 cup honey
2 tablespoons apricot preserves

Combine apples and orange juice in skillet. Bring to a boil over high heat. Stir in honey and apricot preserves. Simmer, covered, for 5 minutes or until apples are tender. Serve warm with pork or ham. **Yield: 4 to 6 servings.**

Miriam M. Forney, Chairman, 1984 Cookbook Committee, Star #993

Appetizers Beverages and Snacks

Beef and Horseradish Cheese Ball

8 ounces cream cheese, softened
1/4 cup grated Parmesan cheese
1 tablespoon horseradish
1/3 cup chopped, stuffed olives
2 1/2 ounces chipped beef

Combine cream cheese, Parmesan cheese, horseradish, olives and 2 ounces chipped beef in bowl; mix well. Shape into ball. Roll in remaining 1/2 ounce chipped beef to coat. Chill until firm. Serve with crackers. **Yield: 10 servings.**

Carol Wilhelm, Warfordsburg #1889

Holiday Cheese Ball

10 ounces Cheddar cheese, softened
12 ounces cream cheese, softened
6 ounces bleu cheese
2 tablespoons grated onion
1 teaspoon Worcestershire sauce
1 cup finely chopped pecans
1/2 cup chopped fresh parsley

Process Cheddar cheese in food processor until crumbled. Add cream cheese, bleu cheese, onion and Worcestershire sauce. Process until smooth. Add half the pecans and half the parsley; mix well. Spoon into bowl lined with plastic wrap. Chill, covered, for 4 hours. Shape into ball. Roll in remaining pecans and parsley.
Yield: 15 to 20 servings.

Betty W. Hall, Halfmoon #290

Cheese Pineapple

1 1/2 pounds sharp cheese, shredded
8 ounces Swiss cheese, shredded
8 ounces cream cheese, softened
4 ounces bleu cheese, crumbled
4 ounces butter, softened
2 tablespoons lemon juice
1 tablespoon Worcestershire sauce
1/2 cup apple juice
Whole cloves
Paprika to taste
1 pineapple stalk

Combine cheeses and butter in bowl; mix well. Add lemon juice, Worcestershire sauce and apple juice, stirring well. Shape into form of pineapple, smoothing with knife. Make rows of indentations with spoon; arrange cloves in patterns between rows. Sprinkle with paprika; top with pineapple stalk. Chill for several hours. Transfer to serving dish using wide spatula. **Yield: 20 to 25 servings.**

Mary Garman, Mifflin #1725

Pineapple Cheese Ball

16 ounces cream cheese, softened
2 cups chopped walnuts or pecans
1/4 cup chopped green bell pepper
2 tablespoons minced onion
1 8-ounce can crushed pineapple, drained
1 tablespoon Crazy salt

Combine cream cheese, half the walnuts, green pepper, onion, pineapple and salt in bowl; mix well. Shape into ball; roll in remaining walnuts. Chill until firm.
Yield: 20 servings.

Kim Huling Linn, Shavers Creek #353

So Easy Cheese Ball

16 ounces Velveeta cheese, softened
8 ounces cream cheese, softened
Chopped walnuts

Combine Velveeta cheese and cream cheese in mixer bowl. Beat at low speed until smooth. Shape into ball; roll in chopped walnuts. Chill in refrigerator until firm. May shape like yule log for holiday season. Serve with crackers.
Yield: 10 to 15 servings.

Maisie Yoder, Bell Township #2047

Cheese Ring

16 ounces sharp Cheddar cheese, shredded
1 cup chopped pecans
3/4 cup mayonnaise
1 onion, grated
1 clove of garlic, pressed
1/2 teaspoon Tabasco sauce
1 cup strawberry preserves

Combine cheese, pecans, mayonnaise, onion, garlic and Tabasco in bowl; mix well. Spoon into ring mold; chill. Unmold onto serving plate. Spoon preserves into center. Serve with crackers. **Yield: 20 to 24 servings.**

Kay Costa, Gillett #884

Olive Cheese Balls

2 cups finely shredded Cheddar cheese
1/2 cup butter, softened
1 cup flour
1 teaspoon paprika
48 large pimento-stuffed olives

Combine cheese, butter, flour and paprika in bowl; mix well. Shape 1 tablespoon mixture around each olive. Store in freezer. Arrange on baking sheet. Bake at 400 degrees for 20 minutes or until golden. **Yield: 48 servings.**

Marie E. Ohlinger, Ontelaunee #1617

Spinach Squares

1 10-ounce package frozen chopped spinach
2 eggs, beaten
1 cup sour cream
1 tablespoon grated onion
1/2 cup grated Parmesan cheese
1 tablespoon flour
1 tablespoon butter
1 teaspoon salt
1/8 teaspoon pepper

Cook spinach using package directions; drain well. Combine with eggs, sour cream, onion, Parmesan cheese, flour, butter, salt and pepper in bowl; mix well. Pour into greased 9x9-inch baking pan. Bake at 350 degrees for 25 to 30 minutes or until firm. Cut into small squares to serve. **Yield: 25 servings.**

Susan Copenhaver, Milford #773

Stuffing Balls

1 loaf Italian bread
1 small onion, chopped
2 stalks celery, chopped
1 cup margarine
1 10-ounce can cream of chicken soup
2 eggs, beaten
Salt and pepper to taste
1 soup can water

Tear bread into small pieces; place in bowl. Sauté onion and celery in margarine in skillet for 5 minutes. Pour over bread. Combine half the soup with eggs, salt and pepper in small bowl. Mix with bread mixture. Shape into small balls. Place in 9x13-inch baking pan. Mix remaining soup with water until smooth. Pour over balls. Bake, covered with foil, at 300 degrees for 1 hour. Remove foil. Bake for 15 minutes longer. **Yield: 8 to 10 servings.**

Clara Eaker, Murphy #735

Tuna Miniatures

2 cups crushed cornflakes
1/3 cup milk
1/4 cup mayonnaise
1 7-ounce can tuna, drained, flaked
1 tablespoon chopped parsley
1/4 cup minced onion
1/2 teaspoon Worcestershire sauce
1 teaspoon lemon juice
1/4 teaspoon salt
1/8 teaspoon pepper

Combine half the cornflakes with milk in bowl. Add mayonnaise, tuna, parsley, onion, Worcestershire sauce, lemon juice, salt and pepper; mix well. Shape into 1-inch balls. Roll in remaining cornflakes. Place on greased baking sheet. Bake at 425 degrees for 15 minutes or until heated through. Serve immediately.
Yield: 16 to 20 servings.

Frances Wise, Amity #1540

Bleu Cheese Dip

4 ounces bleu cheese, crumbled
2 cups mayonnaise
1/2 cup catsup
Garlic powder to taste

Combine bleu cheese, mayonnaise, catsup and garlic powder in bowl; mix well. Serve with fresh vegetables. **Yield: 20 servings.**

Theresa Clark, Valley #1420

Cheeseburger Dip

16 ounces Velveeta cheese
1 10-ounce can cream of mushroom soup
1 10-ounce can chili-tomatoes
1 pound ground beef, cooked

Melt cheese in saucepan over low heat. Add soup, tomatoes and cooked ground beef; mix well. Pour into warming dish. Serve with tostito chips. **Yield: 20 servings.**

Joyce Stewart, Cherry Hill #1214

Dried Beef Dip

1 5-ounce jar dried beef
8 ounces cream cheese, softened
1/2 cup sour cream
2 tablespoons milk or cream
1 teaspoon prepared horseradish
Chopped pecans to taste
1 tablespoon butter

Combine dried beef, cream cheese, sour cream, milk and horseradish in bowl; mix well with fork. Spoon into 1 1/2-quart casserole; sprinkle with pecans. Dot with butter. Bake at 350 degrees for 20 to 30 minutes or until heated through. **Yield: 16 servings.**

Kathryn Fleeger, Mountain #1307

Fruit Dip

1/2 cup sugar
Juice and grated rind of 1 orange
Juice and grated rind of 1 lemon
1 cup pineapple juice
2 eggs, beaten
4 teaspoons cornstarch
8 ounces cream cheese

Combine sugar, orange juice and rind, lemon juice and rind, pineapple juice, eggs and cornstarch in top of double boiler; mix well. Simmer over low heat until thickened, stirring constantly. Beat cream cheese in mixer bowl until light and fluffy. Add cooked mixture, stirring well. Chill until serving time. Serve with variety of fresh fruits. **Yield: 20 to 24 servings.**

Miriam Spengler, Harmony #1692

Pepperoni Dip

2 10-ounce cans cream of celery soup
8 ounces cream cheese, softened
8 ounces pepperoni, thinly sliced and quartered

Combine soup and cream cheese in saucepan. Cook over low heat until smooth, stirring frequently. Stir in pepperoni. Serve warm in slow-cooker or chafing dish with rye or pumpernickle bread. **Yield: 30 servings.**

Catherine Hickernell, Vernon #936

Pizza Dip

8 ounces cream cheese, softened
1/2 cup sour cream
1 teaspoon oregano
1/8 teaspoon garlic salt
1/8 teaspoon crushed red pepper
1/4 cup chopped green onions
1/2 cup chopped pepperoni
1/4 cup chopped green bell pepper
1/2 cup pizza sauce
1/2 cup shredded mozzarella cheese

Combine cream cheese, sour cream, oregano, garlic salt, red pepper, green onions, pepperoni and green pepper in bowl; mix well. Spread in round shallow baking dish. Cover with pizza sauce. Bake at 350 degrees for 5 minutes. Sprinkle with mozzarella cheese. Bake for 5 minutes longer or until cheese is melted. Serve hot or cold with crackers or chips. **Yield: 8 to 10 servings.**

Betty Snyder, New Vernon #608

Shrimp Dip

1 4-ounce can tiny shrimp, rinsed, drained
1/4 cup chili sauce
2 teaspoons lemon juice
1 teaspoon prepared horseradish
1/2 teaspoon salt
1/8 teaspoon pepper
Dash of Tabasco sauce
1 cup sour cream

Chop shrimp into tiny pieces; set aside. Combine chili sauce, lemon juice, horseradish, salt, pepper, Tabasco sauce and sour cream in bowl; mix well. Fold in shrimp. Chill for 1 to 2 hours before serving. Serve with fresh vegetables or crackers.
Yield: 6 to 8 servings.

Lilliam Wolfe, Bloomingdale #536

For low-fat dips, try unsweetened applesauce or a mixture of equal parts yogurt and cottage cheese processed in the blender and seasoned with herbs or spices.

Easy Crescent Snacks

1 8-count package crescent rolls
8 ounces cream cheese, softened
Onion flakes and oregano to taste

Unroll crescent roll dough, separating into 4 squares. Spread with cream cheese; sprinkle with onion flakes and oregano. Roll up; cut into 1/2-inch slices. Place on baking sheet. Bake at 350 degrees for 5 to 10 minutes or until light brown.
Yield: 32 to 36 servings.

Jane Reppert, Virginville #1832

Ham Roll-Ups

8 slices ham
8 ounces cream cheese, softened
8 green onions, trimmed

Spread ham slices with cream cheese. Place green onion in middle; roll to enclose green onion. Cut each slice into 1-inch pieces. Arrange on serving plate with wooden picks. May substitute pickles or asparagus for green onions. **Yield: 16 servings.**

Eleanor Harkins, Jackson #1506 and Helen Kramer, Burgettstown #1502

Meatball Appetizers

1 1/2 pounds ground beef
2 eggs, beaten
1/4 cup milk
1 cup plain bread crumbs
1/4 cup chopped onion
1 1/2 teaspoons chopped parsley
1 1/2 teaspoons salt
1/8 teaspoon pepper
3 tablespoons oil
1 10-ounce bottle of chili sauce
1/2 cup grape jelly
1 tablespoon instant coffee powder

Combine ground beef, eggs, milk, bread crumbs, onion, parsley, salt and pepper in bowl; mix well. Shape into tiny meatballs. Brown in large skillet; remove and drain well. Stir in chili sauce, jelly and coffee powder, mixing with pan drippings. Simmer for 4 minutes, stirring occasionally. Add meatballs. Simmer for 10 minutes longer. Serve with wooden picks. **Yield: 15 servings.**

Sandra Null, Eldred #1604

Arrange spices and herbs in alphabetical order in your spice shelf to eliminate searching for the correct one.

Tangy Sweet Meatballs

2 pounds ground beef
1 cup ginger ale
1 cup catsup
1/4 cup honey
1/4 cup Worcestershire sauce
1/4 cup vinegar

Shape ground beef into bite-sized balls. Place on baking sheet. Bake at 350 degrees for 20 to 30 minutes, turning occasionally; drain well. Combine ginger ale, catsup, honey, Worcestershire sauce and vinegar in saucepan; mix well. Stir in meatballs. Simmer for 1 hour, stirring occasionally. Serve with wooden picks. May substitute bite-sized hot dogs for meatballs. **Yield: 15 servings.**

Patty Friede, Stony Point #1694

Crabby Mushrooms

1 6-ounce can crab meat, rinsed, drained, flaked
2 teaspoons fresh lemon juice
1/3 cup finely chopped black olives
1/4 cup mayonnaise
2 tablespoons chopped fresh parsley
1/4 teaspoon garlic powder
1/4 teaspoon onion powder
24 fresh mushrooms, stems removed
Freshly grated Parmesan cheese

Toss crab meat with lemon juice in medium bowl. Add olives, mayonnaise, parsley, garlic powder and onion powder; mix well. Spoon mixture into mushroom caps. Sprinkle with Parmesan cheese. Arrange mushrooms on baking sheet sprinkled with water; cover with foil. Bake at 400 degrees for 12 to 15 minutes; remove foil. Bake for 5 minutes longer or until golden. **Yield: 24 servings.**

Helen B. Tannehill, Miller's Run #2020

Stuffed Mushrooms

12 large mushrooms
2 tablespoons butter
1 onion, finely chopped
1/4 cup finely chopped green bell pepper
1/2 cup chopped pepperoni
1/2 cup finely crushed butter crackers
1 clove of garlic, minced
3 tablespoons grated Parmesan cheese
1 tablespoon parsley flakes
1/2 teaspoon salt
1/4 teaspoon oregano
1/3 cup chicken broth

Rinse mushrooms and remove stems. Set caps aside; chop stems finely. Melt butter in skillet. Sauté onion, green pepper, pepperoni and mushroom stems until tender; remove from heat. Stir in cracker crumbs, garlic, cheese, parsley, salt and oregano. Add chicken broth, mixing well. Spoon stuffing into mushroom caps. Place in shallow baking pan with small amount of water. Bake at 325 degrees for 25 minutes. **Yield: 12 servings.**

Jolene McWilliams, Red Brush Community #2085

Hot Mushroom Turnovers

8 ounces cream cheese, softened
1/2 cup butter or margarine, softened
1 1/2 cups flour
8 ounces mushrooms, minced
1 large onion, minced
3 tablespoons butter or margarine
1/4 cup sour cream
1 teaspoon salt
1/4 teaspoon thyme
2 tablespoons flour
1 egg, beaten

Beat cream cheese, 1/2 cup butter and 1 1/2 cups flour in mixer bowl until creamy. Shape into ball; wrap in plastic wrap. Chill for 1 hour. Sauté mushrooms and onion in 3 tablespoons butter in skillet until tender. Add sour cream, salt, thyme and 2 tablespoons flour; mix well and set aside. Remove dough from refrigerator; roll out to 1/8-inch thickness. Cut into circles with 2 3/4-inch cutter. Place 1 teaspoon mushroom mixture on circles; brush edge with egg. Fold over to enclose filling. Seal edges; prick top with fork. Place on baking sheet. Brush with remaining egg. Bake at 425 degrees for 12 to 14 minutes or until golden brown. **Yield: 42 servings.**

Karen Harvey, East New Castle #1536

Noel Nibblers

1 pound ground beef
1/4 cup chopped onion
1/2 teaspoon salt
1 pound hot dogs, cut into 1-inch pieces
1 10-ounce jar peach or apricot preserves
1 cup barbecue sauce
1 20-ounce can pineapple chunks, drained

Combine ground beef, onion and salt in bowl; mix well. Shape into 1-inch meatballs. Brown in skillet, turning occasionally; drain. Add hot dogs. Combine preserves with barbecue sauce in bowl; mix well. Pour over meatballs and hot dogs. Simmer for 20 minutes, stirring occasionally. Add pineapple. Cook until heated through.
Yield: 40 servings.

Barbara L. Minor, Buckhorn #1119

Party Rye Pizazz

2 cups shredded sharp cheese
1 cup mayonnaise
1 2-ounce can chopped black olives, drained
2 tablespoons chopped onion
1 loaf party rye bread
8 ounces bacon, crisp-fried, chopped

Combine cheese, mayonnaise, olives and onion in bowl; mix well. Spread over party rye slices; top with bacon. Arrange on baking sheet. Bake at 350 degrees for 15 minutes. May freeze before baking. **Yield: 40 servings.**

Ethel Matheson, Montmorenci #1704

Saucy Sausage and Frank Snacks

1 16-ounce can cranberry sauce
2 tablespoons spicy brown mustard
1 teaspoon lemon juice
1 pound fully-cooked smoked sausage
8 ounces frankfurters, cut into 1/2-inch slices

Combine cranberry sauce, mustard and lemon juice in saucepan. Cook over medium low heat until smooth and heated through, stirring constantly. Remove casing from sausage; cut into 1/2-inch slices. Add sausage and frankfurters to sauce. Bring to a boil; reduce heat. Simmer for 20 minutes. Serve warm with wooden picks. **Yield: 30 servings.**

Maisie Yoder, Bell Township #2047

Barbecued Water Chestnuts

1 8-ounce can water chestnuts, drained
8 ounces bacon, cut into small pieces
1/2 cup mayonnaise
1 cup packed brown sugar
1 cup chili sauce

Wrap chestnuts in bacon, securing with wooden picks. Place in shallow baking dish. Combine mayonnaise, brown sugar and chili sauce in bowl; mix well. Pour over chestnuts. Bake at 350 degrees for 1 hour. **Yield: 6 to 8 servings.**

Suzanne Null, Eldred #1604

Zucchini Appetizers

4 eggs, slightly beaten
1/2 cup grated Parmesan cheese
1/2 teaspoon oregano
1/2 teaspoon salt
Dash of pepper
2 tablespoons finely chopped parsley
1/2 teaspoon seasoned salt
1/2 cup oil
1 clove of garlic, minced
1 cup biscuit mix
1/2 cup finely chopped onion
3 cups thinly sliced zucchini

Combine eggs, cheese, oregano, salt, pepper, parsley, seasoned salt, oil, garlic and biscuit mix in bowl; mix well. Fold in onion and zucchini. Pour into greased 9x13-inch baking pan. Bake at 350 degrees for 30 minutes or until golden brown. Cut into 1 1/2-inch squares. Serve warm or cold. **Yield: 24 servings.**

Helen Guss, Milford #773

Vegetable Pizza

2 8-count cans crescent rolls
16 ounces cream cheese, softened
1 cup mayonnaise
1 envelope ranch salad dressing mix
3/4 cup chopped green bell pepper
3/4 cup chopped onions
3/4 cup chopped broccoli
3/4 cup chopped cauliflower
1/2 cup chopped tomato
1 2-ounce can sliced black olives, drained
1 carrot, shredded
1 cup shredded Cheddar cheese

Spread crescent roll dough over ungreased 7x11-inch baking sheet. Bake at 375 degrees for 10 to 12 minutes or until golden brown. Beat cream cheese, mayonnaise and salad dressing mix in mixer bowl until light and fluffy. Spread over cooled crust. Top with green pepper, onions, broccoli, cauliflower, tomato, olives, carrot and cheese. Cover with waxed paper, pressing down slightly. Chill; cut into squares to serve. **Yield: 20 servings.**

Virginia Mangel, Eureka #244

Pickled Eggs and Red Beets

1 16-ounce can beets
3/4 cup beet juice
3/4 cup vinegar
1 teaspoon salt
1/2 cup packed light brown sugar
12 hard-boiled eggs

Drain beets, reserving 3/4 cup juice. Combine juice, vinegar, salt and brown sugar in saucepan. Bring to a boil, stirring frequently; remove from heat. Place beets and eggs in container; pour warm mixture over top. Chill, covered, overnight.
Yield: 12 servings.

Margaret M. Storm, Pleasant Hill #1861

Pink Apple-Lime Punch

6 cups cranberry juice cocktail
4 cups apple juice
1/4 cup fresh lime juice
2 6-ounce cans frozen lemonade concentrate
4 1/2 cups water

Combine juices, concentrate and water in large bowl; mix well. Chill until serving time. Serve over ice. Garnish with mint sprigs. **Yield: 25 servings.**

Frances A. Hoffman, Northumberland #218

Frosty Apple Delight

1 gallon cold milk
1 12-ounce can apple juice concentrate
$1^1/_2$ quarts vanilla ice cream, softened
Cinnamon and nutmeg to taste

Combine milk, concentrate and ice cream in large bowl. Beat until frothy. Pour into chilled punch bowl. Add cinnamon and nutmeg. **Yield: 25 servings.**

Betty Buffington, Community #2048

Banana Cooler

2 bananas, sliced
2 tablespoons honey or maple syrup
2 cups cold milk
2 cups vanilla ice cream, softened

Combine bananas, honey and a small amount of milk in blender container. Process until almost smooth. Add remaining milk and ice cream. Process for 1 minute or until smooth and frothy. Serve in chilled glasses garnished with banana slices. **Yield: 4 servings.**

Madeline Secules, Troy #182

Banana Punch

4 cups sugar
8 cups water
5 bananas, mashed
$^1/_2$ cup lemon juice
1 12-ounce can frozen orange juice concentrate
1 46-ounce can pineapple juice
$^1/_2$ gallon pineapple sherbet, softened

Combine sugar and water in saucepan. Bring to a boil. Simmer for 5 minutes. Let stand to cool. Mix bananas and lemon juice in bowl. Combine syrup and banana mixture in punch bowl. Add concentrate and pineapple juice; mix well. Add sherbet at serving time. **Yield: 30 servings.**

Claude H. Ohlinger, Ontelaunee #1617

Fruit Punch

1 46-ounce can orange juice
1 46-ounce can pineapple juice
4 16-ounce bottles of ginger ale or 7-Up
1 12-ounce can apricot nectar
1 12-ounce can frozen lemonade concentrate

Combine orange juice, pineapple juice, ginger ale, apricot nectar and lemonade concentrate in large container; mix well. Pour into punch bowl. Add ice. **Yield: 30 servings.**

Hilda Miller, Seipstown #1657

Fruit Slush Mix

4 cups sugar
4 cups water
1 6-ounce can frozen orange juice concentrate
1/2 cup lemon juice
1 46-ounce can pineapple juice
Ginger ale

Combine sugar and water in saucepan. Cook until sugar is dissolved. Add concentrate, lemon juice and pineapple juice; mix well. Pour into ice cube trays. Freeze until firm. Remove from trays; store in plastic bags. Combine several cubes with ginger ale to cover in glass for 1 serving. Let stand for 15 minutes; stir. Use cubes within 6 months. **Yield: 20 to 25 servings.**

Elizabeth Kreger, Kingwood #1765

Non-Alcoholic Piña Colada Mix

2 6-ounce cans frozen lemonade concentrate
1 46-ounce can pineapple juice
1 can coconut milk
7-Up

Combine concentrate, pineapple juice and coconut milk in blender container. Process until blended. Pour into freezer-proof container. Freeze until firm. Combine 2 tablespoons mix with 7-Up in glass for 1 serving. **Yield: 10 servings.**

Joanne Spafford, DuBois #808

Orange Punch

6 6-ounce cans orange juice
1 1/2 cups corn syrup
5 quarts ginger ale
1/4 cup lime juice

Combine orange juice, corn syrup, ginger ale and lime juice in bowl; mix well. Pour into punch bowl. Garnish with pineapple slices. **Yield: 25 servings.**

Jerri Reppert, Deemston #1372

Raspberry Punch

1 46-ounce can Hawaiian punch
1 6-ounce can frozen lemonade concentrate
3 16-ounce bottles of 7-Up
1 quart raspberry sherbet

Combine punch, concentrate and 7-Up in bowl; mix well. Pour into punch bowl. Add sherbet at serving time. **Yield: 30 servings.**

Edith Riker, Mt. Nebo #1872

Quick Root Beer

2 cups sugar
4 teaspoons root beer concentrate
1 teaspoon yeast

Combine sugar, concentrate and yeast in large container; mix well. Add enough water to measure 1 gallon. Pour into 1-gallon glass jar. Let stand, covered, in sunshine for 4 hours. **Yield: 30 servings.**

Carol Kopp, Gideon #2010

Ruby Party Punch

2 envelopes strawberry drink mix
6 to 8 cups ice water
1 6-ounce can frozen pineapple juice concentrate
1 6-ounce can frozen orange juice concentrate
1 cup sugar
1 12-ounce bottle of strawberry soda
1 2-liter bottle of carbonated water, chilled

Combine drink mix, water, concentrates and sugar in large container; mix well. Pour into punch bowl. Add soda and carbonated water; mix well. **Yield: 45 servings.**

Agnes M. Wilson, Wilmington #1477

Hot Wassail

2 cups apple cider
6 whole cloves
2 teaspoons ground nutmeg
14 cups apple cider
1 6-ounce can frozen lemonade concentrate
1 6-ounce can frozen orange juice concentrate
1 cup packed brown sugar
Cinnamon sticks

Combine 2 cups cider, cloves and nutmeg in 6-quart saucepan. Simmer over low heat for 10 minutes. Add 14 cups cider, concentrates and brown sugar. Cook until heated through, stirring occasionally; do not boil. Add cinnamon sticks. May keep warm in slow cooker. **Yield: 36 servings.**

Tami Iman, Jackson #1506

Freeze lemonade and orange juice in ice trays to serve in iced tea.

Oyster Crackers

1 cup popcorn oil
1 envelope ranch salad dressing mix
1 16-ounce package oyster crackers

Mix oil and salad dressing mix in small bowl. Pour over crackers in large bowl, stirring frequently. Drain on paper towels. **Yield: 6 servings.**

Madaline Harman, Shavers Creek #353

Garlic Oyster Crackers

1 16-ounce package oyster crackers
1 envelope ranch salad dressing mix
2 teaspoons dillweed
1/2 teaspoon garlic salt
1/2 teaspoon lemon pepper
1 cup oil

Place crackers in large bowl. Stir in dressing mix, dillweed, garlic salt and lemon pepper. Pour oil over all; stir. Let stand for 1 hour. Stir frequently until all oil is absorbed. **Yield: 6 servings.**

Loretta Sechler, Kingwood #1765

Caramel Corn

2 8-ounce packages popcorn, popped
1 cup margarine
2 cups packed brown sugar
1/2 cup corn syrup
1/2 teaspoon vanilla extract
1 tablespoon peanut butter
1/2 teaspoon baking soda

Place popcorn in large roasting pan. Melt margarine in saucepan. Add brown sugar and corn syrup. Bring to a boil. Boil for 5 minutes. Remove from heat. Add vanilla, peanut butter and baking soda; stir until mixture is no longer foamy. Pour over popcorn, stirring until coated. Bake at 250 degrees for 1 hour, stirring at 15 minute intervals. Store in airtight containers. **Yield: 40 servings.**

Dorothy W. Longenecker, Shavers Creek #353

Cracker Jack

1 cup molasses
1 cup sugar
1 tablespoon vinegar
2 tablespoons water
1 tablespoon butter
1 teaspoon baking soda
5 quarts popped popcorn

Combine molasses, sugar, vinegar and water in saucepan. Bring to a boil. Stir in butter. Cook to hard-crack stage, stirring frequently. Stir in baking soda. Pour over popcorn in large bowl. Stir well. May add peanuts if desired. **Yield: 40 servings.**

Carol Wise, Harmony #1112

Holiday Snack Mix

3 cups cinnamon toast cereal
2 cups chocolate bear-shaped graham snacks
2 cups peanuts
1½ cups red and green candy-coated chocolate pieces

Mix cereal, snacks, peanuts and candy in large bowl. Store in airtight container. **Yield: 18 servings.**

Carol A. Crater, Logan #109

Peanut Butter Popcorn Drops

¼ cup popcorn
1½ tablespoons oil
¼ cup honey
½ cup chunky peanut butter
¼ cup honey
½ cup grated coconut

Pop popcorn in oil using package directions. Spread in 8x8-inch pan. Cook ¼ cup honey in saucepan over medium heat for 1 minute. Add peanut butter. Cook for 5 minutes, stirring occasionally. Remove from heat. Stir in ¼ cup honey. Dot over popcorn. Shape into 1½-inch balls. Roll in coconut. **Yield: 10 servings.**

Elizabeth Ewig, Harmony #1112

Piña Colada-Rice Krispie Treats

6 cups Rice Krispies
1 cup packed coconut
5 tablespoons butter
1 10-ounce package miniature marshmallows
¾ teaspoon coconut extract
¾ teaspoon pineapple extract
¾ teaspoon rum extract
⅓ cup finely chopped candied pineapple

Combine cereal and coconut in large bowl sprayed with nonstick cooking spray; toss well. Melt butter in saucepan. Add marshmallows and flavorings. Cook over medium heat until marshmallows are melted, stirring occasionally. Add candied pineapple; stir until coated. Add to cereal mixture, stirring until coated. Pat into 9x13-inch pan sprayed with nonstick cooking spray. Cool in pan. Cut into squares. **Yield: 15 servings.**

Betty J. Light, North Jackson #1740

Substitute tortillas, split pita rounds, English muffins or split French loaves for the traditional crust for quick and easy pizza snacks.

Easy Popcorn Balls

1/2 cup popcorn
1/2 cup margarine
1 10-ounce package marshmallows
1/4 teaspoon salt

Pop popcorn using package directions. Place in large bowl. Combine margarine, marshmallows and salt in saucepan. Cook until of syrup consistency. Pour over popcorn. Shape into balls using greased hands. **Yield: 20 servings.**

Marie Sinclair, Sanborn #2016

Popcorn Tree

5 quarts popped popcorn
1/2 cup margarine
1 16-ounce package marshmallows
2 pounds assorted gumdrops and jellied candies

Place popcorn in large bowl. Melt margarine in saucepan. Add marshmallows. Cook until marshmallows are melted, stirring frequently. Drizzle over popcorn, stirring to coat. Shape into large ball using lightly greased palms. Place on large baking sheet. Shape into 11-inch tall firm cone. Spear candies 2 at a time on toothpicks. Insert into cone in desired pattern. **Yield: 40 servings.**

Bernie Best, Mt. Joy #537

Pretzel Snacks

1 cup melted margarine
1 envelope onion soup mix
1 pound large hard pretzels, broken

Mix melted margarine and soup mix in small bowl. Add to pretzels in large bowl; mix well. Spoon into 9x13-inch baking pan. Bake at 200 degrees for 2 hours, stirring at 20 minute intervals. **Yield: 8 servings.**

Florence D. Houseknecht, Canusarago #27

Italian Pretzels

1 pound pretzels, broken into small pieces
1 cup vegetable or olive oil
1 envelope ranch salad dressing mix
1/2 teaspoon dillweed
1/2 teaspoon lemon pepper
1/2 teaspoon garlic powder

Spread pretzels on jelly roll pan. Combine oil, dressing mix, dillweed, lemon pepper and garlic powder in bowl; mix well. Pour over pretzels. Bake at 325 degrees for 15 minutes. Store in airtight tin container for 24 to 48 hours before serving.
Yield: 8 servings.

Brenda McCauley, Virginville #1832

Spiced Pretzels

1 pound pretzels, broken into pieces
2/3 cup oil
1 envelope ranch salad dressing mix
1/4 teaspoon dillweed
1/2 teaspoon garlic salt

Place pretzels in microwave-safe dish. Combine oil, dressing mix, dillweed and garlic salt in small bowl; mix well. Pour over pretzels, tossing to coat. Microwave on High for 6 minutes, stirring every 2 minutes. Cool and store in airtight container. **Yield: 8 servings.**

Donna McGary, Penn #534

People's Puppy Chow

1 cup milk chocolate chips
1 cup semisweet chocolate chips
1 cup peanut butter
1/2 cup margarine
1 16-ounce package Crispix cereal
2 cups confectioners' sugar

Combine chocolate chips, peanut butter and margarine in saucepan. Cook over low heat until melted, stirring occasionally. Pour over cereal in large bowl; toss until coated. Stir in confectioners' sugar; toss or shake until coated. **Yield: 10 servings.**

Helen J. Jacobson, Mahoning Valley #1649

Texas Trash Snack

2 6-ounce packages corn chips
1 quart popped popcorn
1 8-ounce package pretzels
1 8-ounce package corn balls
1 cup chopped pecans
1/2 teaspoon garlic salt
1 clove of garlic, crushed
1 teaspoon salt
1 teaspoon curry powder
1/2 cup melted margarine

Place corn chips, popcorn, pretzels, corn balls and pecans in large roasting pan. Mix garlic salt, garlic, salt, curry powder and melted margarine in bowl. Pour over popcorn mixture; toss well. Bake at 250 degrees for 1 hour, stirring occasionally. **Yield: 16 servings.**

Mary Lou Wilson, Bradford #1219

Keep a blackboard in your kitchen for grocery lists, household chores and family reminders.

Party Snack

1/2 package Cheerios
1/2 package Rice Chex
1/2 package Wheat Chex
6 ounces thin pretzels
6 ounces salted peanuts
6 ounces cashews
1 teaspoon onion salt
1 teaspoon celery salt
1 teaspoon garlic salt
1 teaspoon MSG
3/4 cup melted butter

Combine cereals, pretzels, peanuts, cashews, onion salt, celery salt, garlic salt and MSG in bowl; mix well. Stir in melted butter. Spoon into baking pan. Bake at 200 degrees for 2 hours, stirring occasionally. **Yield: 30 servings.**

Betty Jane Lichtenwalner, Macungie #1569

Pecan Snack

1 egg white
1 tablespoon water
1 pound pecans or walnuts
3/4 cup sugar
1 teaspoon cinnamon
1 teaspoon salt

Beat egg white with water in large bowl until frothy. Add pecans; mix well. Mix sugar, cinnamon and salt in small bowl. Stir into pecan mixture. Spread on baking sheet. Bake at 250 degrees for 1 hour, stirring every 15 minutes. **Yield: 10 servings.**

Mary Ebersole, Charlesville #698

Microwave Sugar-Glazed Walnuts

1/2 cup butter or margarine
1 cup packed brown sugar
1 teaspoon cinnamon
4 cups walnut halves

Microwave butter in microwave-safe bowl on High for 1 minute. Stir in brown sugar and cinnamon. Microwave on High for 2 minutes. Stir in walnuts. Microwave for 3 to 5 minutes longer or until walnuts are evenly glazed. Cool before serving. **Yield: 10 servings.**

Thelma Rich, Keystone #2

To enhance the flavor of shelled walnuts, microwave them on High for 4 minutes. Add 1 teaspoon margarine for each 1/2 cup walnuts if desired.

Healthy Cereal

3/4 cup honey
1/4 cup water
1/4 cup oil
1 tablespoon vanilla extract
6 cups rolled oats
1 1/2 cups chopped pecans
1 1/2 cups shredded coconut
1/2 teaspoon salt
1 tablespoon cinnamon
1 tablespoon nutmeg
1 cup wheat germ

Combine honey, water and oil in large saucepan. Cook until heated through. Stir in vanilla. Add oats, pecans, coconut, salt, cinnamon and nutmeg; mix well. Spread on baking sheet. Bake at 250 degrees for 1 hour, stirring every 20 minutes. Add wheat germ; mix well. Store in airtight container. **Yield: 20 servings.**

Rebecca Michalka, Burgettstown #1502

Granola

6 cups oats
1/2 cup packed brown sugar
3/4 cup wheat germ
1/2 cup flaked coconut
1/4 cup sesame seed
1 cup chopped walnuts
1/2 cup dry milk powder
2/3 cup honey
2/3 cup oil
2 tablespoons water
1 1/2 teaspoons vanilla extract
1 cup raisins

Combine oats, brown sugar, wheat germ, coconut, sesame seed, walnuts and dry milk powder in large bowl; mix well. Mix honey, oil, water and vanilla in small bowl. Stir into oat mixture. Spread on 2 large baking sheets. Bake at 300 degrees for 25 to 35 minutes or until lightly toasted, stirring twice. Let stand to cool, stirring 3 times. Crumble into pieces. Add raisins. Store in airtight container. **Yield: 28 servings.**

Joan Mauser, North Jackson #1740

Homemade Cereal

5 cups oats
1 cup chopped almonds
1 cup unrefined sesame seed
1 cup sunflower seed
1 cup shredded coconut
1 cup soy flour
1 cup dry milk powder
1 cup wheat germ
1 cup honey
1 cup oil

Combine oats, almonds, sesame seed, sunflower seed, coconut, flour, dry milk powder and wheat germ in bowl; mix well. Stir in mixture of honey and oil. Spread on 2 large baking sheets. Bake at 300 degrees for 1 hour or until browned. May add desired amount of dried fruit after baking. **Yield: 30 servings.**

Zelda Kozar, Dunkard Township #2045

Salads

Cinnamon-Apple Salad

1 6-ounce package cherry or strawberry gelatin
2 cups boiling water
$1/2$ cup red hot cinnamon candies
$1\frac{1}{2}$ cups (about) boiling water
2 cups chopped apples
2 cups chopped celery
$1/2$ cup nuts (optional)

Dissolve gelatin in 2 cups boiling water in bowl. Place candies in measuring cup. Add enough boiling water to measure 2 cups; stir until candies dissolve. Add to gelatin; mix well. Chill until partially set. Stir in apples, celery and nuts. Spoon into serving bowl. Chill until firm. **Yield: 8 to 10 servings.**

Alta Gannon, Slippery Rock #1441

Stuffed Apple Rings Salad

2 or 3 red Delicious apples
Pineapple or lemon juice
8 ounces cream cheese, softened
2 to 3 tablespoons honey
$1/3$ cup finely chopped dates
$1/4$ cup chopped pecans

Core apples; cut into $3/4$-inch thick rings. Dip in juice; drain. Beat cream cheese in mixer bowl at medium speed until smooth. Add honey. Beat until light and fluffy. Stir in dates and pecans. Arrange apple rings on serving plate. Spoon cream cheese mixture into centers of apple rings. **Yield: 4 to 6 servings.**

Mary Ebersole, Charlesville #698

Caramel-Apple Salad

3 cups chopped unpeeled apples
1 8-ounce can crushed pineapple, drained
1 cup dry-roasted peanuts
1 cup miniature marshmallows
1 cup raisins (optional)
1 3-ounce package butterscotch instant pudding mix
8 ounces whipped topping

Combine apples, pineapple, peanuts, marshmallows, raisins, pudding mix and whipped topping in bowl; mix well. Spoon into serving bowl. Chill until serving time. **Yield: 8 to 10 servings.**

Ellen Robertson, Charleston Valley #54

Dreamy Apricot Salad

2 3-ounce packages apricot gelatin
2/3 cup sugar
2/3 cup water
2 jars baby food apricots
1 20-ounce can crushed pineapple
1 14-ounce can sweetened condensed milk
8 ounces cream cheese, softened
1 1/2 cups chopped nuts

Combine gelatin, sugar and water in saucepan. Bring to a boil, stirring until gelatin and sugar dissolve. Remove from heat. Stir in apricots and undrained pineapple. Let stand until cool. Beat condensed milk and cream cheese in mixer bowl until smooth. Stir in gelatin mixture and nuts. Spoon into 9x13-inch glass dish. Chill overnight. Serve with additional whipped topping and nuts. **Yield: 20 to 24 servings.**

Chloe Buckner, Mahoning Valley #1649

Banana Salad

1 cup sugar
1 tablespoon flour
1 tablespoon vinegar
1 egg, beaten
1/2 cup water
1 tablespoon butter
2 or 3 bananas, sliced
Roasted peanuts or walnuts

Combine sugar, flour, vinegar, egg, water and butter in saucepan; mix well. Cook over medium heat until thickened, stirring constantly. Let stand until cool. Combine banana slices and nuts in bowl. Pour cooled sauce over top; toss gently. Serve immediately. **Yield: 4 to 6 servings.**

Mary Lou McCullough, Big Beaver #1578

Champagne Salad

8 ounces cream cheese, softened
1/2 cup sugar
1 6-ounce package frozen strawberries, thawed
1 cup drained crushed pineapple
2 bananas, chopped
12 ounces whipped topping

Beat cream cheese and sugar in mixer bowl until smooth. Add strawberries, pineapple, bananas and whipped topping; mix well. Spoon into 9x13-inch dish. Freeze until firm. **Yield: 15 servings.**

Barbara Henry, Vernon #936

Cherry Waldorf Gelatin Salad

1 3-ounce package cherry gelatin
1 cup boiling water
3/4 cup cold water
1/2 cup chopped apple
1/2 cup chopped banana
1/4 cup chopped celery

Dissolve gelatin in boiling water in bowl. Add cold water. Chill until partially set. Stir in apple, banana and celery. Spoon into 4-cup mold. Chill until set. Unmold onto serving plate. **Yield: 6 servings.**

Lena Cool, Frankfort Springs #1989

Cranberry Gelatin Salad

2 cups cranberries, coarsely chopped
1 cup chopped carrot
1 cup chopped celery
1 package lemon gelatin
1 package cherry gelatin
1 cup sugar
3 cups boiling water
1 cup chopped apple
1 cup chopped seedless grapes
1 cup chopped orange
1 cup nuts

Combine cranberries, carrot and celery in large bowl. Dissolve gelatins and sugar in boiling water in bowl. Pour over cranberry mixture. Let stand, covered, for 15 minutes. Combine apple, grapes, orange and nuts in medium bowl; mix well. Stir into gelatin mixture. Chill in refrigerator, stirring occasionally until partially set. Spoon into 4-quart dish. Chill overnight or until set. Serve on lettuce leaves with crackers. **Yield: 8 to 12 servings.**

Mamie A. Breininger, Shartlesville #1512

Cranberry Salad

2 cups cranberries, finely ground
3/4 cup sugar
3 cups miniature marshmallows
2 cups chopped apples
1 cup green grapes, cut into halves
1/2 cup walnuts, chopped
1/4 teaspoon salt
1 cup whipping cream, whipped

Combine cranberries, sugar and marshmallows in bowl; mix well. Chill overnight. Add apples, grapes, walnuts, salt and whipped cream; mix well. Spoon into serving dish. Chill until serving time. **Yield: 8 to 10 servings.**

Helen McCullough, Jackson #1506

Fruit Salad

2 20-ounce cans pineapple chunks
2 16-ounce cans mixed fruit
2 17-ounce cans apricots, chopped
3 11-ounce cans mandarin oranges
1 3-ounce package tapioca pudding mix
Sliced bananas
1 3-ounce package vanilla instant pudding mix

Drain canned fruits, reserving liquids. Prepare tapioca pudding mix with 2 cups reserved liquid using package directions. Let stand until cool. Pour over banana slices in bowl; toss until coated. Prepare vanilla pudding mix with 1 1/2 cups reserved liquid using package directions. Combine vanilla pudding, banana mixture and drained fruits in bowl; mix well. Chill until serving time. **Yield: 16 to 20 servings.**

Helen Taggart, Slippery Rock #1441

Hawaiian Shells

1 cup uncooked shell macaroni
3 peeled oranges, sectioned
2 bananas, sliced
3/4 cup flaked coconut
1 cup pineapple yogurt

Prepare macaroni using package directions. Rinse with cold water; drain. Combine with oranges, banana slices, coconut and yogurt in bowl; mix well. Spoon into serving dish. Chill completely. **Yield: 4 servings.**

Lillian Wolfe, Bloomingdale #536

Hollywood Salad

3 peeled oranges, chopped
2 peeled grapefruit, chopped
2 peeled apples, chopped
3 bananas, chopped
1 cup broken nuts
3 tablespoons lemon juice
6 tablespoons oil
1/4 teaspoon salt
1/4 teaspoon paprika
Lettuce leaves

Combine oranges, grapefruit, apples, bananas and nuts in bowl; mix well. Combine lemon juice, oil, salt and paprika in jar; shake well. Spoon fruit mixture onto lettuce-lined serving plate. Add salad dressing just before serving.
Yield: 10 to 12 servings.

Myrtle M. Schwartz, Harmony #1692

Hostess Salad

1 16-ounce can crushed pineapple
1/2 cup sugar
2 3-ounce packages lemon gelatin
6 ounces cream cheese, softened
2 cups cold water
1 12-ounce can evaporated milk, partially frozen
Salt to taste
1 cup finely chopped celery
1 cup chopped nuts

Combine undrained pineapple and sugar in saucepan. Bring to a boil over medium heat, stirring until sugar dissolves. Boil for 5 minutes. Remove from heat. Stir in gelatin until dissolved. Beat cream cheese in mixer bowl until smooth. Add hot gelatin mixture gradually, mixing well after each addition. Stir in cold water. Chill until partially set. Beat ice-cold evaporated milk in cold mixer bowl until stiff peaks form. Add salt to celery. Fold celery, nuts and whipped evaporated milk into chilled gelatin mixture gently. Spoon into 10x16-inch pan. Chill overnight. **Yield: 15 servings.**

Opal Jones, Gretna #1543

Christmas Gelatin Salad

1 3-ounce package lime gelatin
1 cup boiling water
3/4 cup cold water
1 3-ounce package lemon gelatin
1 cup boiling water
1 cup miniature marshmallows
6 ounces cream cheese, softened
1/2 cup mayonnaise
1 cup whipped cream
1 20-ounce can crushed pineapple, drained
1 3-ounce package raspberry gelatin
1 cup boiling water
3/4 cup cold water

Dissolve lime gelatin in 1 cup boiling water in bowl. Add 3/4 cup cold water. Pour into 9x13-inch dish. Chill until firm. Dissolve lemon gelatin in 1 cup boiling water in mixer bowl. Stir in marshmallows until dissolved. Add cream cheese. Beat until light and fluffy. Chill until partially set. Stir in mayonnaise, whipped cream and pineapple. Spoon over congealed layer. Chill until set. Dissolve raspberry gelatin in 1 cup boiling water in bowl. Add 3/4 cup cold water. Spoon over congealed layers. Chill until set. **Yield: 18 to 20 servings.**

Betty Lou Williams, Vernon #936

Gelatin Salad

1 6-ounce package strawberry gelatin
3 cups boiling water
1 16-ounce can whole cranberry sauce, mashed
1 package frozen strawberries, thawed

Dissolve gelatin in boiling water in bowl. Stir in cranberry sauce and strawberries. Spoon into 9x13-inch dish. Chill until set. Serve on lettuce-lined salad plates. **Yield: 8 servings.**

Mrs. Clyde Adams, Greenbrier #1148

Quick and Easy Gelatin Salad

2 11-ounce cans mandarin oranges
1 20-ounce can crushed pineapple
1 3-ounce package orange gelatin
2 3-ounce packages vanilla tapioca pudding mix
2 cups whipped topping

Drain mandarin oranges and pineapple, reserving liquid. Add enough water to reserved liquid to measure 3 cups. Combine with gelatin and pudding mix in saucepan. Cook over medium heat until thickened, stirring constantly. Let stand until cool. Stir in remaining ingredients. Spoon into serving dish. Chill completely. **Yield: 10 servings.**

Catherine Hickernell, Vernon #936

Lemon-Lime Salad

1 3-ounce package lemon instant pudding mix
2 cups hot water
1 3-ounce package lime gelatin
1 cup (scant) cold water
1 8-ounce can crushed pineapple
Whipped topping
Nuts

Prepare pudding mix with 2 cups hot water using package directions. Stir in gelatin until dissolved. Add cold water and crushed pineapple; mix well. Spoon into serving dish. Chill until set. Serve with whipped topping and nuts. **Yield: 6 servings.**

Alberta G. Burns, Plum Creek Valley #1702

Maple Salad

16 ounces cream cheese, softened
1/2 cup maple syrup
1 13-ounce can crushed pineapple
1 cup chopped dates
1/2 cup chopped nuts
12 ounces whipped topping

Beat cream cheese with maple syrup in mixer bowl until smooth. Add pineapple, dates and nuts; mix well. Fold in whipped topping gently. Spoon into 9x9-inch dish. Freeze until firm. Remove from freezer 15 minutes before serving. **Yield: 8 servings.**

Blanche G. Hoye, Plain Grove #1431

Mint Salad

1 3-ounce package lime gelatin
1 13-ounce can crushed pineapple
1 16-ounce package miniature marshmallows
1 8-ounce package butter mints, crushed
8 to 12 ounces whipped topping

Combine gelatin, undrained pineapple and marshmallows in bowl; mix well. Chill for 12 hours, stirring occasionally. Fold in crushed mints and whipped topping gently. Spoon into serving dish. Freeze until firm. **Yield: 6 to 8 servings.**

Ruth Chestnut, West Salem #1607

Peach Double-Decker Salad

1 16-ounce can sliced peaches, drained
2 tablespoons apricot brandy (optional)
2 3-ounce packages orange gelatin
2 cups boiling water
1½ cups cold water
4 ounces whipped topping

Chop peaches. Sprinkle brandy over peaches. Dissolve gelatin in boiling water in bowl. Add cold water. Chill until partially set. Divide gelatin into 2 portions. Stir peaches into 1 portion. Spoon into 6-cup mold. Chill for 10 minutes or until partially set. Fold whipped topping into remaining gelatin gently. Spoon over peach layer. Chill until firm. Unmold onto serving plate. **Yield: 10 servings.**

Marie Sinclair, Sanborn #2016

Pear Salad

1 3-ounce package lime gelatin
1¾ cups boiling water
½ cup pear juice
¼ teaspoon salt
1 teaspoon vinegar
3 ounces cream cheese, softened
⅛ teaspoon ginger
2 cups drained chopped pears

Dissolve gelatin in boiling water in bowl. Stir in pear juice, salt and vinegar. Pour half the mixture into 5x9-inch loaf pan. Let remaining gelatin stand at room temperature until mixture is slightly thickened. Add cream cheese and ginger. Beat until smooth. Stir in pears. Spoon over congealed layer. Chill until firm. Serve on lettuce-lined salad plate. **Yield: 8 servings.**

Leone D. Gibson, Charlesville #698

Perfection Salad

2 envelopes unflavored gelatin
½ cup cold water
2 cups hot water
2 teaspoons salt
½ cup vinegar
2 tablespoons lemon juice
½ cup sugar
1 cup shredded cabbage
2 cups chopped celery
2 pimentos, chopped

Soften gelatin in cold water in bowl. Stir in hot water, salt, vinegar, lemon juice and sugar. Let stand until cool. Stir in cabbage, celery and pimentos. Spoon into 9x13-inch dish. Chill until firm. May substitute ¼ cup chopped red and green bell pepper for pimentos if desired. **Yield: 12 to 15 servings.**

Helen Redic, Mt. Pleasant #1687

Creamy Pineapple-Orange Gelatin Salad

1 8-ounce can crushed pineapple
1 3-ounce package orange gelatin
1 cup buttermilk
1¾ cups whipped topping
½ cup chopped pecans
6 lettuce leaves

Bring undrained pineapple to a boil in saucepan. Remove from heat. Stir in gelatin until dissolved. Let stand until cool. Stir in buttermilk. Fold in whipped topping and pecans. Spoon into 8x8-inch serving dish. Chill for 4 hours or until firm. Serve on lettuce-lined salad plate. Garnish with mandarin orange slices. **Yield: 6 servings.**

Betty Cramer, Cherry Hill #1214

Pineapple-Cream Cheese Salad

1 20-ounce can crushed pineapple
1 cup sugar
1 3-ounce package orange gelatin
8 ounces cream cheese, softened
1 12-ounce can evaporated milk, chilled

Combine undrained pineapple and sugar in saucepan. Bring to a boil. Stir in gelatin until dissolved. Add cream cheese; mix well. Let stand until cool. Beat ice-cold evaporated milk in cold mixer bowl until stiff peaks form. Fold into gelatin mixture. Spoon into serving dish. Chill until firm. May substitute lemon or lime gelatin for orange gelatin. **Yield: 6 servings.**

Susan Tau, Hayfield #800

Imitation Fried Egg Salad

8 pineapple slices
8 lettuce leaves
1 cup whipping cream, whipped
8 peach halves

Place 1 pineapple slice on lettuce-lined salad plate. Cover slice completely with whipped cream. Place 1 peach half cut side down on whipped cream. Repeat with remaining ingredients. **Yield: 8 servings.**

Helen Wescott, New Lebanon #1445

Pink Fluff

2 cups yogurt
1 3-ounce package vanilla instant pudding mix
16 ounces whipped topping
1 21-ounce can cherry pie filling
Nuts

Combine yogurt, pudding mix and whipped topping in bowl; mix well. Fold in pie filling gently. Spoon into serving dish. Top with nuts. Chill until serving time. **Yield: 8 servings.**

Margaret M. Storm, Pleasant Hill #1861

Pistachio Salad

1 3-ounce package pistachio instant pudding mix
12 ounces whipped topping
1 30-ounce can fruit cocktail
1 cup cooked rice
1 cup miniature marshmallows

Combine pudding mix, whipped topping, undrained fruit cocktail, rice and marshmallows in large bowl. Stir with rubber spatula until well mixed. Spoon into serving dish. Chill until serving time. **Yield: 10 servings.**

Marilyn Davidson, Bald Eagle #1390

Rainbow Gelatin

1 3-ounce package cherry gelatin
4 cups boiling water
2 cups cold water
1 3-ounce package lemon gelatin
1 3-ounce package orange gelatin
1 3-ounce package lime gelatin
2 envelopes unflavored gelatin
1/2 cup cold water
2 cups milk
1 cup sugar
2 cups sour cream
2 teaspoons vanilla extract

Dissolve cherry gelatin in 1 cup boiling water in small bowl. Add 1/2 cup cold water. Prepare each remaining flavored gelatin separately using same method. Do not chill. Soften unflavored gelatin in 1/2 cup cold water. Combine milk and sugar in saucepan. Cook until mixture is hot and sugar dissolves. Stir in unflavored gelatin until dissolved. Let stand until cool. Stir in sour cream and vanilla. Pour cherry gelatin into 9x13-inch dish. Chill for 30 minutes or until firm. Add alternating layers of 1 1/2 cups sour cream mixture, lemon, orange and lime gelatins, chilling for 30 minutes after each gelatin layer. Chill until firm. **Yield: 12 servings.**

Virginia Hay, Hillcrest #1674

Raspberry Delight Salad

1 3-ounce package raspberry gelatin
1 cup boiling water
1 cup vanilla ice cream
3 tablespoons orange juice
1 8-ounce can crushed pineapple
1/2 cup chopped pecans
1 medium banana, sliced

Dissolve gelatin in boiling water in bowl. Stir in ice cream until dissolved. Add orange juice; mix well. Let stand until partially set. Add mixture of undrained pineapple, pecans and banana slices to gelatin; mix well. Spoon into 4-cup mold. Chill until firm. **Yield: 6 servings.**

Elizabeth Ewig, Harmony #1112

Raspberry Gelatin

1 6-ounce package raspberry gelatin
2 cups boiling water
1 cup cold water
2 cups applesauce
1 10-ounce package frozen red raspberries, thawed

Dissolve gelatin in boiling water in bowl. Add cold water. Stir in applesauce and raspberries. Spoon into serving dish. Chill until firm. **Yield: 8 servings.**

Hazel Wilson, Big Beaver #1578

Rice Gelatin

1 6-ounce package orange gelatin
2 cups boiling water
1 20-ounce can crushed pineapple
8 ounces whipped topping
1 to 1 1/2 cups cooked rice

Dissolve gelatin in boiling water in bowl. Stir in pineapple. Chill until partially set. Add whipped topping and rice; mix well. Spoon into 9x13-inch dish. Chill until firm. Serve on lettuce-lined salad plate. **Yield: 12 servings.**

Lorraine Keenan, Aleppo #2054

Sea Breeze

1 20-ounce can crushed pineapple
3 3-ounce packages lime or lemon gelatin
2 cups boiling water
1 20-ounce can lemon pie filling
1 package whipped topping mix

Drain pineapple, reserving juice. Add enough cold water to reserved juice to measure 2 cups. Dissolve gelatin in boiling water in bowl. Add reserved pineapple juice. Chill until partially set. Beat in pie filling. Reserve 1 cup mixture for topping. Stir pineapple into remaining mixture. Spoon into 9x13-inch dish. Chill until firm. Prepare whipped topping mix using package directions. Fold into reserved gelatin mixture gently. Spread over congealed layer. Chill until serving time.
Yield: 12 servings.

Alma Covert, Bloomingdale #536

Waldorf Zip Salad

1 3-ounce package lemon gelatin
1 cup boiling water
1 cup cold ginger ale
1 cup chopped apple
1/3 cup thinly sliced celery
1/3 cup chopped nuts

Dissolve gelatin in boiling water in bowl. Stir in cold ginger ale gradually. Chill until partially set. Fold in apple, celery and nuts gently. Spoon into 9x9-inch serving dish. Chill until firm. **Yield: 6 to 9 servings.**

Mary Stimmell, Morning Star #1271

Yum-Yum Salad

3 eggs
1/4 cup lemon juice
1/4 cup sugar
1/3 cup pineapple juice
6 ounces cream cheese, softened
1 20-ounce can pineapple chunks, drained
1 16-ounce package miniature marshmallows
1 cup whipping cream, whipped

Combine eggs, lemon juice, sugar and pineapple juice in top of double boiler. Cook over medium heat until thickened, stirring constantly. Let stand until cool. Stir in cream cheese. Fold in pineapple, marshmallows and whipped cream gently. Spoon into serving dish. Chill until firm. May also add bananas, grapes and walnuts before congealing. **Yield: 10 to 12 servings.**

Margaret Tau, Hayfield #800

Argentine Corned Beef Salad

6 pimento-stuffed olives
1 12-ounce can corned beef
2 hard-boiled eggs, chopped
1/2 cup finely chopped celery
1/2 cup finely chopped pickle
1/4 cup finely chopped onion
Garlic salt to taste
1 cup mayonnaise
1 hard-boiled egg, sliced

Chop olives, reserving 4 pimentos for garnish. Combine olives with corned beef, chopped eggs, celery, pickle, onion, garlic salt and mayonnaise in bowl; mix well. Spoon onto lettuce leaves. Top with reserved pimentos and sliced egg. **Yield: 4 servings.**

Arlene B. Lohr

Chili Supper Salad

2 15-ounce cans chili with beans
10 cups assorted salad greens
4 medium tomatoes, seeded, chopped
2 cups shredded cheese

Heat chili in saucepan over medium heat, stirring occasionally. Toss salad greens, chopped tomatoes and half the cheese in large bowl. Top with chili and remaining cheese. May substitute homemade chili for canned chili. **Yield: 6 servings,**

Elizabeth Pfautz, Shermanata #1796

Leftover chicken or ham mixed with chopped celery, sliced water chestnuts, green grapes and mayonnaise makes a delicious salad for luncheons.

Cauliflower-Ham Salad

Flowerets of 1/2 head cauliflower
1 tablespoon oil
1 tablespoon sugar
2 teaspoons cornstarch
2 teaspoons minced onion
1/2 cup chopped celery
1 teaspoon prepared mustard
1/2 teaspoon garlic salt
1/4 teaspoon salt
Pepper to taste
2/3 cup water
1/3 cup vinegar
2 cups cooked ham, cut into 1 1/2-inch strips
6 cups torn lettuce
1 cup halved cherry tomatoes

Cook cauliflowerets in boiling water in saucepan until tender. Drain and slice lengthwise; set aside. Combine oil, sugar, cornstarch, onion, celery, mustard, garlic salt, salt and pepper in electric skillet. Stir in water and vinegar. Cook at 300 degrees until mixture is thick and bubbly, stirring constantly. Add cauliflower and ham. Cook until heated through. Add lettuce. Cook 30 minutes longer. Serve immediately topped with cherry tomatoes. **Yield: 8 servings.**

Virginia Wade, Vernon #936

Spinach and Lamb Salad with Yogurt Dressing

8 ounces fresh spinach, torn
1 medium green bell pepper, cut into thin strips
1/2 cup sliced mushrooms
1 cup crumbled feta cheese
1 1/2 cups sliced cooked lamb
1 medium tomato, cut into wedges
1 cup low-fat yogurt
1/4 cup sugar
2 tablespoons vinegar

Combine spinach, green pepper, mushrooms and cheese in bowl, tossing gently. Arrange on serving plate. Place lamb in center of plate; top with tomato wedges. Combine yogurt, sugar and vinegar in small bowl; mix well. Serve over salad. **Yield: 6 servings.**

Thelma V. Snyder, Willard #1440

Chicken Curry Salad

4 cups chopped cooked chicken
2 cups chopped celery
2 tablespoons lemon juice
Salt and pepper to taste
1 13-ounce can pineapple chunks, drained
1 16-ounce can seedless grapes
1 cup slivered toasted almonds
1/2 cup sour cream
1/2 cup mayonnaise
1 1/2 teaspoons curry powder

Combine chicken, celery, lemon juice, salt, pepper, pineapple, grapes and almonds in salad bowl, tossing gently to mix. Beat sour cream, mayonnaise and curry powder in small bowl until smooth. Pour over salad, tossing to coat. Garnish with sliced hard-boiled eggs. **Yield: 12 servings.**

Marie Elliott, Hookstown #1980

Chicken-Pineapple Salad

2 cups chopped cooked chicken
1/2 cup pineapple tidbits
1/4 cup chopped celery
1/2 cup mayonnaise-type salad dressing

Combine chicken, pineapple, celery and salad dressing in bowl; mix well. Serve on individual plates lined with lettuce leaves. **Yield: 4 servings.**

Geraldine Himes, Roseville #1290

Chicken-Vegetable-Pasta Toss

1 16-ounce package macaroni
1 envelope vegetable soup mix
2 cups sour cream
1/2 cup mayonnaise
1/2 cup green olives
1 tablespoon lemon juice
3 cups chopped cooked chicken
2 medium tomatoes, cut into wedges
2 hard-boiled eggs, cut into wedges

Cook macaroni using package directions. Drain and rinse with cold water; set aside. Combine soup mix, sour cream and mayonnaise in large bowl; mix well. Toss olives with lemon juice in small bowl. Add to mayonnaise mixture with chicken, macaroni and tomato wedges. Toss gently to coat. Spoon into salad bowl. Top with egg wedges. **Yield: 6 to 8 servings.**

Helen Anderson, West Pike Run #1928

Turkey and Fruit Salad

4 cups chopped cooked turkey
1 cup pineapple tidbits
1 cup chopped nuts
1 cup seedless grapes
1 1/2 cups mayonnaise

Combine turkey, pineapple, nuts, grapes and mayonnaise in salad bowl. Toss gently to mix. Chill before serving. **Yield: 6 to 8 servings.**

Agnes M. Wilson, Wilmington #1477

For quick individual ***Salades Niçoise****, place chunks of solid-pack tuna on lettuce-lined plates. Add drained green beans, sliced cooked potatoes, cherry tomatoes, hard-boiled egg quarters, black olives and a light vinaigrette.*

Indian Melon Salad

2 cups chopped cooked chicken or turkey
1 5-ounce can sliced water chestnuts, drained
8 ounces seedless green grapes
1/2 cup chopped celery
1 cup mayonnaise
1/2 teaspoon curry powder
1 tablespoon lemon juice
1/4 teaspoon salt
1/8 teaspoon freshly ground pepper
1 teaspoon soy sauce
1 cup honeydew melon balls
1 cup cantaloupe melon balls
Lettuce cups

Combine chicken, water chestnuts, grapes and celery in bowl. Mix mayonnaise, curry powder, lemon juice, salt, pepper and soy sauce in small bowl, stirring to blend. Pour over chicken mixture, tossing to coat. Chill for several hours. Add honeydew and cantaloupe melon balls before serving. Spoon into individual lettuce cups. **Yield: 4 to 6 servings.**

Kay Costa, Gillett #884

Seafood Flakes Salad Supreme

1 pound imitation crabmeat
1 6-ounce can tiny shrimp, drained
2 small zucchini, thinly sliced
1/2 cup thinly sliced celery
2 green onions, thinly sliced
1/2 tablespoon lemon juice
1 teaspoon dried tarragon
3/4 cup mayonnaise-type salad dressing
1/2 cup sour cream

Combine crabmeat, shrimp, zucchini, celery, green onions, lemon juice and tarragon in large bowl. Mix salad dressing and sour cream in small bowl. Pour over crabmeat mixture, tossing well to coat. Chill before serving. Serve on bed of lettuce and tomatoes. May also use to stuff pita pocket bread. **Yield: 4 to 6 servings.**

Sharon Ferris, Dawson #419

Creole Salad

1 1/2 cups red kidney beans, drained
1 cup cooked brown rice
1 pound cooked peeled shrimp
1/4 cup chopped onion
1/4 cup chopped celery
1/4 cup chopped red or green bell pepper
1 hard-boiled egg, chopped
1/2 cup Dijon mustard
1 tablespoon oil
1 tablespoon vinegar
1/4 cup mayonnaise
1/2 teaspoon dried thyme

Combine kidney beans, rice, shrimp, onion, celery, bell pepper and egg in large bowl. Mix mustard, oil, vinegar, mayonnaise and thyme in small bowl until smooth. Pour over salad, tossing to coat. Garnish with tomato wedges. May substitute chopped cooked chicken for shrimp or use both. **Yield: 6 to 8 servings.**

Dorothy Reyes, Port Matilda #1284

Holiday Seafood Salad

2 cups flaked tuna
8 ounces lobster, cooked, chopped
$1\frac{1}{2}$ pounds shrimp, cooked, chopped
2 ounces cooked flaked crabmeat
$1\frac{1}{2}$ cups chopped celery
$\frac{1}{2}$ cup chopped green bell pepper
1 teaspoon salt
1 cup mayonnaise
1 tablespoon lemon juice
$\frac{1}{8}$ teaspoon pepper
3 tablespoons unflavored gelatin
$\frac{1}{2}$ cup cold water

Combine tuna, lobster, shrimp, crabmeat, celery, green pepper, salt, mayonnaise,lemon juice and pepper in large bowl. Soften gelatin in cold water. Place in saucepan filled with hot water, stirring until dissolved. Pour over seafood mixture, stirring gently to mix. Spoon into $5\frac{1}{2}$-cup fish mold, packing lightly. Chill overnight. Unmold onto bed of lettuce. Garnish with olive slices for "eyes" and with cherry tomatoes. **Yield: 8 to 10 servings.**

Aliene Thompson, Middletown #684

Low-Calorie Tuna Salad

1 16-ounce can bean sprouts, drained
1 teaspoon minced onion flakes
1 cup chopped celery
2 tablespoons chopped green bell pepper
1 7-ounce can tuna, drained, flaked
$\frac{1}{4}$ cup low-calorie mayonnaise

Combine bean sprouts and onion flakes in saucepan. Add enough water to cover. Cook over medium heat for 20 minutes or until tender. Drain and chill. Combine with celery, green pepper, tuna and mayonnaise; mix well. Spoon into serving bowls. **Yield: 3 servings.**

Elizabeth Gardner, Center Road #502

Tuna Salad

1 6-ounce can water-pack tuna, drained
$\frac{1}{2}$ cup chopped unpeeled cucumber
3 tablespoons mayonnaise
$\frac{1}{8}$ teaspoon onion powder
$\frac{1}{8}$ teaspoon dry mustard

Toss tuna and cucumber in bowl. Combine mayonnaise, onion powder and mustard in small bowl; mix well. Pour over tuna mixture, stirring to mix. Chill in refrigerator. Serve on lettuce leaves for main-dish salad or may use for sandwich filling. **Yield: 3 servings.**

Dot Harris, Iona #272

JB's Marinated Antipasto Salad

Flowerets of 1 head cauliflower
Flowerets of 1 bunch broccoli
1 pound mushrooms, sliced
2 medium purple onions, sliced
1 5-ounce can black olives, drained
1 cup mild pepper rings, drained
3 cups Italian salad dressing
2 cups Italian cheese salad dressing

Combine cauliflower, broccoli, mushrooms, onions, olives and pepper rings in order listed in large bowl with airtight lid. Combine salad dressings in jar; shake to mix well. Add to salad; mix well. Marinate, covered, in refrigerator for 6 hours to overnight, shaking several times to coat well. **Yield: 8 to 10 servings.**

Jeannie Chamberlain, Stony Point #1694

Aspic to Remember

1 package lemon gelatin
1 cup boiling water
3/4 cup tomato juice
1 tablespoon vinegar
1 teaspoon sugar
1/2 cup chopped cabbage
1/2 cup chopped celery
1/4 cup chopped green bell pepper

Dissolve gelatin in boiling water in bowl. Stir in tomato juice, vinegar and sugar. Add cabbage, celery and green pepper. Spoon into mold. Chill until set. Unmold onto serving plate. **Yield: 8 servings.**

Jean F. Rothrock, Sebring #1047

Taco-Bean Salad

1 cup cooked beans, rinsed, drained
1 11-ounce can corn, rinsed, drained
1 onion, chopped
1 green bell pepper, chopped
1 red bell pepper, chopped
1/4 cup catsup
1/4 cup vinegar
1/4 cup oil
3 tablespoons brown sugar
1 tablespoon chili powder
1 1/2 tablespoons mustard
1 teaspoon salt
1/4 teaspoon pepper
1 6-ounce package tortilla chips, crushed

Combine beans, corn, onion and chopped bell peppers in bowl. Combine catsup, vinegar, oil, brown sugar, chili powder, mustard, salt and pepper in saucepan. Bring to a boil; reduce heat. Simmer for 10 minutes. Add to salad with chips; toss to mix well. **Yield: 8 servings.**

Rose Riggleman, Penn Line #1784

Red Beet Salad

1 3-ounce package lemon gelatin
1 cup boiling water
1 cup cold water
1 tablespoon grated onion
1 tablespoon vinegar
1/2 teaspoon salt
1 cup chopped celery
1/4 cup chopped olives
2 cups chopped cooked beets

Dissolve gelatin in boiling water in bowl. Stir in cold water. Add onion, vinegar and salt. Chill until partially set. Fold in celery, olives and beets. Chill until set. **Yield: 6 servings.**

Lauretta Silvis, DuBois #808

Broccoli Salad

1/2 cup flour
1 1/2 cups sugar
1/2 teaspoon salt
1/2 cup vinegar
1 1/2 cups water
1 cup mayonnaise
2 teaspoons dry or prepared mustard
2 bunches broccoli, chopped
2 red onions, thinly sliced
1 3-ounce jar bacon bits

Mix flour, sugar and salt in saucepan. Stir in vinegar and water. Cook until thickened, stirring constantly. Cool to room temperature. Stir in mayonnaise and mustard. Combine with broccoli, onions and bacon bits in salad bowl; mix well. Chill, covered, in refrigerator for up to several days. **Yield: 15 to 20 servings.**

Janet McClellan, Logan #109

Cabbage Salad

2 cups shredded cabbage
1/2 cup grated carrot
1 8-ounce can juice-pack crushed pineapple
1/3 cup raisins
1 1/2 cups chopped apple
2 tablespoons lemon juice
1/2 cup chopped peanuts (optional)

Combine cabbage, carrot, undrained pineapple, raisins, apple and lemon juice in 1 1/2-quart bowl; mix well. Marinate, covered, in refrigerator overnight. Add peanuts at serving time; mix well. **Yield: 6 servings.**

Florence Williamson, Bottle Run #1301

Use sweet pickle juice instead of vinegar in coleslaw for a different and delicious taste.

Sweet and Sour Red Cabbage

2 cups coarsely chopped red cabbage
3 tablespoons sugar
1/4 cup water
2 tablespoons vinegar
1 teaspoon margarine
1/2 teaspoon salt
1 medium unpeeled Granny Smith apple, cut into thin wedges

Combine cabbage, sugar, water, vinegar, margarine and salt in medium saucepan; mix well. Cook over medium-low heat for 8 minutes or until cabbage is tender. Add apple. Simmer, covered, for 5 minutes. Simmer, uncovered, for 10 minutes longer or until most of the liquid has evaporated. Serve hot. **Yield: 4 servings.**

Ann Ebbert, Stony Point #1694

Red Cabbage Salad

1 head red cabbage, shredded
1 head cauliflower, chopped
1 pound bacon, crisp-fried, crumbled
1 onion, finely chopped
2 1/2 cups low-calorie mayonnaise
1/4 cup grated Parmesan cheese
1 teaspoon salt
Pepper to taste

Combine cabbage, cauliflower, bacon and onion in large bowl; mix well. Combine mayonnaise, Parmesan cheese, salt and pepper in small bowl, stirring until smooth. Pour over cabbage mixture, stirring to coat. Chill before serving. May also add chopped fresh mushrooms. **Yield: 6 to 8 servings.**

Jerry Rupert, Shavers Creek #353

Cabbage Patch Salad

2 cups elbow macaroni, cooked
1 cup chopped tomatoes
2 cups chopped cabbage
1/2 cup chopped green bell pepper
Thousand Island salad dressing

Combine cooked macaroni, tomatoes, cabbage, green pepper and enough salad dressing to moisten. Toss lightly; chill. Arrange in cabbage-lined salad bowl. May add additional salad dressing before serving. **Yield: 6 to 8 servings.**

Mildred R. Neal, Slippery Rock #1441

Add toasted sesame seed to salads for a rich nutty flavor. Toasting intensifies the flavor.

Hot Slaw

2 tablespoons butter
4 cups shredded cabbage
1/2 cup water
1 teaspoon salt
2 tablespoons sugar
2 tablespoons vinegar
1/2 teaspoon dry mustard
1/2 cup sour cream

Melt butter in large saucepan. Add cabbage, water and salt. Simmer, covered, for 10 minutes. Add sugar, vinegar and dry mustard; mix well. Simmer for 5 minutes longer. Stir in sour cream before serving. **Yield: 4 servings.**

Belinda Frey, West Branch #136

Carrot and Mushroom Salad

2 cups sliced cooked carrots
1 14-ounce can artichoke hearts, drained, cut into quarters
8 ounces fresh mushrooms, cut into halves
1 cup halved ripe olives
1/4 cup chopped red bell pepper
2/3 cup vinegar
2/3 cup oil
1/4 cup chopped onion
2 cloves of garlic, minced
1 teaspoon salt
1/4 teaspoon pepper
1 teaspoon basil
1 teaspoon oregano

Combine carrots, artichoke hearts, mushrooms, olives and bell pepper in bowl; toss gently. Combine vinegar, oil, onion, garlic, salt, pepper, basil and oregano in saucepan; mix well. Bring mixture to a boil; reduce heat. Simmer for 10 minutes, stirring frequently. Pour over vegetables. Chill, covered, for several hours before serving. **Yield: 4 to 6 servings.**

Vera McMeans, Blanco #2099

Fiesta Corn Salad

2 16-ounce cans corn, drained
2 cups chopped tomatoes
2 cups chopped peeled cucumbers
1 cup chopped celery
1 cup chopped green or red bell pepper
4 green onions, sliced
1 cup prepared Italian salad dressing

Combine corn, tomatoes, cucumbers, celery, bell pepper, green onions and salad dressing in bowl; mix well. Chill several hours before serving. **Yield: 6 servings.**

Helen Crise, Mendon #855

Cottage Cheese-Cucumber Mold

1 3-ounce package lime gelatin
1 cup boiling water
1 cup cottage cheese
1/2 cup mayonnaise-type salad dressing
1 cup chopped cucumber
1/4 cup sliced black olives
1 tablespoon chopped onion

Dissolve gelatin in boiling water in small bowl. Combine cottage cheese and salad dressing in medium bowl. Add gelatin mixture, stirring well. Chill until partially set. Fold in cucumber, olives and onion. Pour into 1-quart mold. Chill until firm. Unmold onto serving plate; top with additional salad dressing if desired.
Yield: 4 to 5 servings.

Pearle Malone, Mendon #855

Cucumber and Sour Cream Salad

3 medium cucumbers, peeled, thinly sliced
1 1/2 cups sour cream
1 tablespoon chopped dill
1 tablespoon sugar
2 to 3 tablespoons vinegar
1/2 teaspoon pepper
1 1/2 teaspoons salt

Place cucumbers in bowl. Pour in enough boiling water to cover. Let stand for 15 to 20 minutes to soften; drain. Pour ice water over cucumbers. Let stand several minutes; drain. Chill in refrigerator for 15 to 20 minutes. Combine sour cream, dill, sugar, vinegar and pepper in small bowl; mix well. Sprinkle cucumbers with salt. Add sour cream mixture, stirring gently to mix. **Yield: 4 servings.**

Virginia Savage Selfredge, Brandywine #60

Eight-Layer Salad

1 head lettuce, chopped
Salt, pepper and sugar to taste
1 pound bacon, crisp-fried, crumbled
6 hard-boiled eggs, sliced
1 10-ounce package frozen peas, thawed
1 medium sweet onion, sliced
1 cup mayonnaise
1 cup mayonnaise-type salad dressing
4 ounces Swiss cheese, grated

Arrange half the lettuce in 3-quart glass bowl; sprinkle with salt, pepper and sugar. Layer with bacon, sliced eggs, remaining lettuce, salt, pepper, sugar, peas, onion slices and mixture of mayonnaise and salad dressing. Top with Swiss cheese. Chill, covered, for 12 hours to overnight. May also add layer of shaved baked or boiled ham. Garnish with olives and pickles. **Yield: 16 to 20 servings.**

Ruth Caven Johnston, Wilmington #1477

Pasta Slaw

8 ounces linguini
3/4 cup coleslaw dressing
1/4 cup chopped onion
3/4 teaspoon prepared mustard
2 cups chopped red or green cabbage
1/2 cup chopped green bell pepper
1/2 cup grated carrot

Cook pasta using package directions; drain and rinse. Combine coleslaw dressing, onion and mustard in large bowl; mix well. Add pasta, stirring to coat. Chill, covered, for 1 hour to overnight. Add cabbage, green pepper and carrot before serving, tossing well. **Yield: 10 servings.**

Ruth Ravenscroft, Ohiopyle #1933

Pea Salad

1 20-ounce package frozen peas
1/2 cup sour cream
1 cup mayonnaise
1 medium onion, chopped
1/4 teaspoon sugar
1 pound bacon, crisp-fried, crumbled

Cook peas using package directions; drain and cool. Combine sour cream, mayonnaise, onion and sugar in bowl; mix well. Fold in peas and bacon. Chill before serving. **Yield: 6 to 8 servings.**

Hope Nelson, Brokenstraw #407

Family-Style Potato Salad

8 medium potatoes, cooked, peeled, cubed
3 hard-boiled eggs, chopped
1/2 cup chopped cucumber
1/2 cup chopped onion
1/4 cup chopped green bell pepper
3 tablespoons chopped pimento
1 cup mayonnaise
3 tablespoons sugar
3 tablespoons vinegar
1 tablespoon prepared mustard
1 1/2 teaspoons salt
1/4 teaspoon pepper

Combine potatoes, eggs, cucumber, onion, green pepper and pimento in 5-quart bowl; mix well. Mix mayonnaise, sugar, vinegar, mustard, salt and pepper in medium bowl, stirring until smooth. Pour over potato mixture, tossing to coat. Chill, covered, before serving. **Yield: 18 servings.**

Carol A. Rhoades, Perry Valley #1804

Country Rice Salad

3 cups chilled cooked rice
1/4 cup sweet pickle relish
1 2-ounce jar chopped pimento, drained
1/3 cup finely chopped green onions
1/4 cup finely chopped green bell pepper
1/4 cup finely chopped celery
3 hard-boiled eggs, chopped
1/2 cup mayonnaise
1/4 cup prepared mustard
2 tablespoons sugar
1 teaspoon vinegar
1/4 teaspoon salt
1/8 teaspoon pepper
1 to 2 tablespoons milk

Combine rice, relish, pimento, green onions, green pepper, celery and eggs in large bowl. Mix mayonnaise, mustard, sugar, vinegar, salt, pepper and milk in small bowl, stirring to blend. Pour over rice mixture, stirring to coat. Chill, covered, for several hours before serving. **Yield: 10 servings.**

Pauline Haldeman, Carter Camp #1563

Vegetable-Rice Salad

1 cup mayonnaise
1 tablespoon vinegar
1 small clove of garlic, minced
1 teaspoon salt
1/4 teaspoon pepper
2 cups cooked rice
1 10-ounce package frozen peas, thawed
1/2 cup shredded carrot
1/4 cup chopped green onions

Combine mayonnaise, vinegar, garlic, salt and pepper in bowl; mix well. Add rice, peas, carrot and green onions, stirring to moisten. Chill, covered, before serving. **Yield: 6 servings.**

Helen M. Peterson, Ackley #870

Rodeo Salad

1 7-ounce package macaroni and cheese dinner
2 cups kidney beans, drained
1/4 cup sliced onion
1/3 cup sliced sweet pickle
1/2 cup mayonnaise-type salad dressing

Prepare macaroni and cheese dinner using package instructions. Add kidney beans, onion, pickle and salad dressing; mix well. Chill before serving.
Yield: 4 to 6 servings.

Keturah Faust, Northumberland #218

Soda Cracker Salad

1 package saltine crackers, crushed
1 cup mayonnaise
1/2 cup chopped green bell pepper
1/2 cup chopped celery
1/2 cup chopped onion
1/2 cup chopped sweet pickles or sweet relish
3 hard-boiled eggs, chopped
Sugar and pepper to taste

Combine crackers, mayonnaise, green pepper, celery, onion, pickles, eggs, sugar and pepper in 1 1/2-quart bowl; mix well. Chill, covered, overnight. **Yield: 4 to 6 servings.**

Effie Yochum, Steuben #858

Spinach Salad

1 pound fresh spinach, torn
1 8-ounce can water chestnuts, drained, sliced
4 hard-boiled eggs, chopped
6 slices crisp-fried bacon, crumbled
1 small onion, thinly sliced
1/2 cup packed brown sugar
1/2 cup oil
1/3 cup vinegar
1/3 cup catsup
1 tablespoon Worcestershire sauce

Combine spinach, water chestnuts, eggs, bacon and onion in large bowl; set aside. Mix brown sugar, oil, vinegar, catsup and Worcestershire sauce in small bowl, stirring to blend. Pour over spinach mixture, tossing to coat. Chill until serving time. **Yield: 4 to 6 servings.**

Ethel Schlegel, Star #993

Spinach and Mushroom Salad

1 pound fresh spinach, torn
8 ounces fresh mushrooms, sliced
1 8-ounce can water chestnuts, drained
1 cup oil
2/3 cup sugar
1/3 cup catsup
1/4 cup wine vinegar
1 tablespoon Worcestershire sauce
1/2 medium onion, grated or minced
8 to 10 slices crisp-fried bacon, crumbled

Combine spinach, mushrooms and water chestnuts in bowl. Mix oil, sugar, catsup, vinegar, Worcestershire sauce and onion in small bowl, stirring well. Pour over spinach mixture, tossing to coat. Sprinkle crumbled bacon over top. Chill. **Yield: 4 to 6 servings.**

Jean H. Hertzog, Pioneer #1777

Sweet Potato Salad

2 cups cooked sweet potatoes, cubed
1 apple, chopped
1 cup chopped celery
1 11-ounce can mandarin oranges, drained
1 8-ounce can pineapple tidbits, drained
1/2 cup chopped walnuts
1/2 teaspoon salt
1/4 cup sour cream
1/4 cup mayonnaise
2 tablespoons milk

Combine sweet potatoes, apple, celery, mandarin oranges, pineapple and walnuts in large bowl. Mix salt, sour cream, mayonnaise and milk in small bowl, stirring to blend. Pour over sweet potato mixture. Chill before serving. Spoon onto lettuce-lined plates. **Yield: 8 servings.**

Virginia B. Guthrie, Aleppo #2054

Marinated Tomatoes

3 large tomatoes, thickly sliced
1/3 cup olive oil
1/4 cup red wine vinegar
1 teaspoon salt
1/4 teaspoon pepper
1/2 clove of garlic, minced
2 tablespoons chopped onion
1 tablespoon chopped fresh parsley
1 tablespoon chopped fresh basil or 1 teaspoon dried basil

Place tomato slices in large shallow dish. Combine oil, vinegar, salt, pepper, garlic, onion, parsley and basil in jar. Cover and shake until well mixed. Pour over tomatoes. Marinate, covered, in refrigerator for several hours. **Yield: 4 to 6 servings.**

Dorothy Aughenbaugh, Bradford #1219

Tossed Salad with Fruit and Nuts

1 cup fresh spinach, torn
6 cups romaine lettuce, torn
1 cup seedless red or green grapes, cut into halves
1/2 cup toasted slivered almonds
1 11-ounce can mandarin oranges, drained
1/2 cup oil
1/4 cup vinegar
1/4 cup sugar
1/2 teaspoon salt
1 avocado, sliced (optional)

Combine spinach, lettuce, grapes, almonds and mandarin oranges in large bowl; mix well. Combine oil, vinegar, sugar and salt in jar; cover. Shake well to mix. Pour over salad, tossing to coat. Top with avocado slices. **Yield: 6 to 8 servings.**

Margret Barackman, Penn Line #1784

Bacon Dressing

1 egg, beaten
1 1/2 cups sugar
1 cup vinegar
8 slices bacon

Beat egg with sugar and vinegar in bowl. Chop bacon into 3/8-inch pieces. Fry in 10-inch skillet until crisp. Add egg mixture. Bring to a boil, stirring constantly. Cook for 1 minute, stirring constantly. Serve over salads or potatoes. **Yield: 8 servings.**

Mary L. Frank, Bottle Run, #1301

Bleu Cheese Dressing

8 ounces bleu cheese, crumbled
3/4 cup tomato purée
2 cups mayonnaise
2 tablespoons sugar
1 teaspoon parsley
1 teaspoon minced garlic
1 tablespoon lemon juice
1/4 teaspoon celery seed
1/2 teaspoon oregano
1 teaspoon MSG
1 teaspoon salt
1/4 teaspoon pepper

Combine bleu cheese, tomato purée, mayonnaise, sugar, parsley, garlic, lemon juice, celery seed, oregano, MSG, salt and pepper in bowl; mix until smooth. Chill, covered, overnight before serving. Store in airtight container in refrigerator. **Yield: 12 servings.**

Joan Kiefer, Rush #1167

Cooked Salad Dressing

1/3 cup flour
1/2 cup sugar
2 teaspoons salt
2 teaspoons dry mustard
1/8 teaspoon paprika
1 cup water
3/4 cup vinegar or lemon juice
2 eggs, beaten
1 tablespoon butter, softened

Combine flour, sugar, salt, mustard and paprika in glass bowl. Add water and vinegar gradually, stirring constantly. Microwave on High for 8 to 10 minutes or until bubbly, stirring twice. Stir small amount of hot mixture into eggs; add eggs to mixture, beating well. Stir in butter. Chill, covered with plastic wrap. **Yield: 2 1/2 cups.**

Lois A. Myers, Fort Granville #1902

French Dressing

3 cups sugar
1 cup vinegar
1 cup oil
1 medium onion, chopped
3 tablespoons catsup
3 tablespoons mustard or horseradish

Mix sugar and vinegar in saucepan. Heat until sugar is dissolved. Cool to room temperature. Combine with oil, onion, catsup and mustard in blender container. Process until smooth. **Yield: 4 cups.**

Joan Milliken, Tuscarora #774

Fruit Salad Dressing

1/2 cup mayonnaise-type salad dressing
1/4 cup confectioners' sugar
1/2 cup whipping cream, whipped
1 tablespoon grated orange rind

Combine salad dressing, confectioners' sugar, whipped cream and orange rind in bowl; mix gently. Chill in refrigerator. **Yield: 8 servings.**

Betty Oesterling, Eureka #244

Honey-Vinaigrette Salad Dressing

1/2 cup olive oil
1/2 cup cider vinegar
1/2 cup water
1/2 cup honey
1/3 cup catsup
1 tablespoon lemon juice
1 to 3 cloves of garlic, minced
1 small onion, minced
1 teaspoon paprika
1 teaspoon celery salt

Combine olive oil, vinegar, water, honey, catsup, lemon juice, garlic, onion, paprika and celery salt in 4-cup glass measure. Microwave on Medium-High for 3 minutes. Whisk until well mixed. Let stand until cool. Store in airtight container in refrigerator. **Yield: 20 servings.**

Mary Ann Lindner, Ringtown Valley #2100

*Make **Thousand Island Salad Dressing** by combining half a small bottle of catsup or chili sauce, 3 cups mayonnaise, 2 tablespoons prepared mustard, 1 cup sweet pickle relish and enough relish juice to make of desired consistency.*

Salt-Free Herbed Salad Dressing

1 tablespoon water
1/2 teaspoon dry mustard
1/4 cup wine vinegar
1/2 teaspoon onion powder
1/2 teaspoon sugar
1/4 teaspoon thyme
1/4 teaspoon marjoram
1/4 teaspoon basil
1/2 cup oil

Combine water and dry mustard in jar with lid. Let stand until dry mustard is dissolved. Add vinegar, onion powder, sugar, thyme, marjoram and basil; mix well. Let stand, covered, for several hours to overnight. Add oil. Store, covered, in refrigerator. Shake well before using. **Yield: 3/4 cup.**

Sophie Sally Bocz, Brush Valley #1785

Italian Dressing

8 cups oil
2 2/3 cups cider vinegar
1 cup lemon juice
8 teaspoons sugar
8 teaspoons garlic powder
4 teaspoons dry mustard
4 teaspoons oregano
2 teaspoons basil
Pepper to taste

Combine oil, vinegar, lemon juice, sugar, garlic powder, dry mustard, oregano, basil and pepper in large jar with lid. Shake, covered, to mix well. Store in refrigerator. **Yield: 3 quarts.**

Ethel Davis, Elder #503

Eggless Mayonnaise

1/4 cup evaporated milk, chilled
1 tablespoon vinegar
1 tablespoon lemon juice
1/2 teaspoon confectioners' sugar
1/4 teaspoon dry mustard
1/4 teaspoon paprika
1/2 teaspoon salt
Cayenne pepper to taste
1 cup oil or olive oil, chilled

Combine evaporated milk, vinegar, lemon juice, confectioner's sugar, dry mustard, paprika, salt and cayenne pepper in bowl. Beat with rotary beater until smooth. Add oil 1/3 at a time, mixing well after each addition. Serve immediately. **Yield: 1 1/2 cups.**

Jean V. Johnn, Hemlock #2051

Cooked Mayonnaise

2 tablespoons flour
2/3 cup sugar
1/2 teaspoon dry mustard
1 teaspoon salt
1/2 cup water
1/2 cup vinegar
2 eggs, beaten

Mix flour, sugar, dry mustard and salt in saucepan. Blend in water and vinegar. Cook until thickened, stirring constantly. Stir a small amount of hot mixture into eggs; add eggs to hot mixture gradually, beating constantly until smooth. **Yield: 1 1/2 cups.**

Grace Fetterman, Harrold #1984

Strawberry Dressing

1 10-ounce package frozen strawberries, thawed, drained
2/3 cup light mayonnaise
1 cup strawberry yogurt

Crush strawberries in bowl. Add mayonnaise, stirring well. Fold in yogurt. Chill, covered, for 1 hour. Serve over honeydew wedges and strawberries. **Yield: 2 1/2 cups.**

Thelma V. Snyder, Willard #1440

Potato Salad Dressing

2 tablespoons flour
3/4 cup sugar
2 eggs
1 cup vinegar
1 cup cream or evaporated milk
1 tablespoon prepared mustard
2 tablespoons butter
1 teaspoon salt

Combine flour, sugar, eggs, vinegar, cream, mustard, butter and salt in saucepan; mix well. Cook until thickened, stirring constantly. **Yield: 3 cups.**

Frances Currie, East New Castle #1536

Sweet and Sour Salad Dressing

1 1/2 cups vinegar
3 cups oil
2 cups sugar
1 onion, finely chopped
2 teaspoons celery seed
1 tablespoon dry mustard
2 teaspoons salt

Combine vinegar, oil, sugar, onion, celery seed, dry mustard and salt in blender container. Process until smooth. **Yield: 6 cups.**

Gertrude Chapin, Wilmington #1477

Tasty Salad Dressing

1 10-ounce can tomato soup
3/4 cup vinegar
1 cup oil
1 cup sugar
1 teaspoon Worcestershire sauce
1 tablespoon mustard
1/2 teaspoon salt
1/2 teaspoon pepper

Combine soup, vinegar, oil, sugar, Worcestershire sauce, mustard, salt and pepper in bowl; mix well. Store in airtight container in refrigerator. Serve over lettuce salads. **Yield: 3 1/2 cups.**

Minerva Bish, Reynoldsville #1825

Dressing for Tossed Salad

1/2 cup chili sauce
1/2 cup catsup
1/2 cup vinegar
1 cup oil
1 cup sugar
1 teaspoon salt
1/2 teaspoon pepper

Combine chili sauce, catsup, vinegar, oil, sugar, salt and pepper in jar with lid; shake to mix well. Store in refrigerator. **Yield: 3 1/2 cups.**

Sarah Ellen Mack, Turbot #249

Ranch Dressing Mix

2 tablespoons salt
2 teaspoons MSG
2 teaspoons parsley flakes
1 teaspoon garlic powder
1/2 teaspoon onion powder
1 teaspoon pepper

Combine salt, MSG, parsley flakes, garlic powder, onion powder and pepper in airtight container. Mix well before using. To make dressing, combine 1 tablespoon dressing mix with 1 cup mayonnaise and 1 cup plain yogurt and chill for 24 hours. **Yield: 5 tablespoons mix.**

Susan Bowser, Winfield #1105

Make a dressing for vegetable salads of 2 cups mayonnaise, 1 envelope ranch salad dressing mix and 1 cup sour cream.

Soups and Sandwiches

Cream of Asparagus Soup

4 cups 1/2-inch asparagus pieces
1 cup water
1/4 cup finely chopped green onions
5 tablespoons butter
5 tablespoons flour
1/2 teaspoon salt
1/4 teaspoon white pepper
4 cups milk
1 cup water
1 tablespoon instant chicken bouillon

Cook asparagus in 1 cup water in saucepan until tender; drain, reserving cooking liquid. Sauté green onions in butter in saucepan until tender. Stir in flour, salt and pepper. Cook over medium heat for 1 minute, stirring constantly. Stir in milk, 1 cup water, reserved cooking liquid and bouillon gradually. Cook until thickened, stirring constantly. Stir in asparagus. Cook until heated through. **Yield: 6 servings.**

Doris Malm, Diamond #2027

Quick and Easy Barley Soup

1 onion, chopped
3 carrots, chopped
3 potatoes, chopped
3 stalks celery, chopped
2 tablespoons parsley flakes
1/4 teaspoon pepper
2 quarts water
3 tablespoons beef soup base
1/2 cup quick-cooking barley

Combine onion, carrots, potatoes, celery, parsley flakes, pepper, water and soup base in 4-quart saucepan. Bring to a boil. Stir in barley. Cook for 30 minutes or until vegetables and barley are tender, stirring occasionally. **Yield: 6 servings.**

Elizabeth Windhorst, Pleasant Hill #1505

Oven-Baked Bean Soup

1 pound mixed dried beans
1 pound chopped lean ham
1 ham bone
3 quarts water
2 stalks celery, chopped
1 onion, chopped
2 carrots, chopped
1 8-ounce can tomato sauce
Salt and pepper to taste

Combine dried beans, ham, ham bone, water, celery, onion, carrots, tomato sauce, salt and pepper in Dutch oven; mix well. Bake at 325 degrees for 4 to 4 1/2 hours or until of desired consistency. **Yield: 10 servings.**

Karen Harvey, East New Castle #1536

Serbian Bean Soup

3 16-ounce cans green beans
3 large potatoes, chopped
2 carrots, chopped
1/2 cup chopped celery
1/4 cup chopped tomatoes
4 cups water
1 onion, chopped
3 1/2 tablespoons oil
3 tablespoons flour
Salt and pepper to taste

Combine green beans, potatoes, carrots, celery, tomatoes and water in saucepan. Cook until vegetables are tender. Sauté onion in oil in skillet. Stir in flour. Cook until brown. Add to soup. Simmer for 5 minutes longer. Season with salt and pepper. **Yield: 8 servings.**

Rose Zorich, Carmichaels #1389

White Bean Soup

1/3 cup chopped celery
1/3 cup chopped carrot
1/3 cup chopped onion
1 teaspoon minced garlic
2 tablespoons butter or margarine
1 16-ounce can white beans
2 cups water
1 envelope chicken gravy mix
8 ounces chopped ham or smoked sausage
1/2 teaspoon thyme
1/8 teaspoon pepper

Cook celery, carrot, onion and garlic in butter in covered medium saucepan over medium-low heat for 5 minutes or until tender. Add beans, water, gravy mix, ham, thyme and pepper; mix well. Bring to a boil over medium-high heat; reduce heat. Simmer, covered, for 15 minutes. Simmer, uncovered, for 5 minutes longer. **Yield: 4 servings.**

Janice Wetzel, Macungie #1569

Beefy Soup

1 pound ground beef
1 48-ounce can V-8 juice
2 onions, chopped
2 cups grated carrots
2 10-ounce cans cream of celery or cream of mushroom soup
Grated cabbage (optional)

Brown ground beef in saucepan, stirring until crumbly; drain. Add V-8 juice, onions, carrots, soup and cabbage; mix well. Simmer for several hours. May cook in slow cooker for 8 hours if preferred. **Yield: 8 servings.**

Arlene Waltz, Lycova #2006

Cream of Broccoli Soup

1 large bunch fresh broccoli, chopped
1/4 cup melted margarine
1/4 cup flour
1 10-ounce can cream of chicken soup
2 cups half and half
3 cups shredded Cheddar cheese
Paprika, salt and pepper to taste

Cook broccoli in water in saucepan until tender; drain. Blend melted margarine and flour in large saucepan. Combine soup with enough water to measure 2 cups. Add to saucepan. Cook over medium heat until thickened and smooth, stirring constantly. Add half and half; reduce heat. Stir in cheese until melted. Add broccoli. Cook just until heated through. Season with paprika, salt and pepper to taste.
Yield: 6 servings.

Barbara L. Minor, Buckhorn #1119

Cheesy Broccoli Soup

3/4 cup chopped onion
1/2 cup chopped carrot
2 tablespoons oil
6 cups water
5 chicken bouillon cubes
1 teaspoon salt
1 10-ounce package frozen chopped broccoli, cooked
4 cups thin noodles, cooked
6 cups milk
1 pound process cheese, chopped

Sauté onion and carrot in oil in saucepan until brown. Add water, bouillon cubes and salt. Bring to a boil. Stir in broccoli and noodles. Cook for 3 minutes. Add milk and cheese. Cook until cheese melts. **Yield: 12 servings.**

Pearle K. McCrory, Long Branch Community #2072

Cauliflower and Ham Chowder

1 cup thinly sliced celery
2 cups sliced fresh or frozen cauliflower
1 14-ounce can chicken broth
1 1/4 cups water
1 10-ounce can cream of potato soup
1 cup evaporated milk
2 tablespoons cornstarch
1/8 teaspoon pepper
1/4 cup water
2 cups chopped cooked ham
1/2 cup shredded Cheddar cheese

Combine celery, cauliflower, chicken broth and 1 1/4 cups water in saucepan. Cook until vegetables are tender; do not drain. Combine potato soup and evaporated milk in bowl; mix well. Stir in mixture of cornstarch, pepper and 1/4 cup water. Add to cauliflower mixture with ham. Simmer for 10 minutes or until of desired consistency, stirring frequently. Stir in cheese at serving time. **Yield: 4 to 6 servings.**

Mrs. Clyde Wagoner, Chippewa #1592

Pennsylvania Chicken Soup

1 chicken, cut up
1 large onion, chopped
1 bay leaf
1/2 teaspoon thyme
8 peppercorns
Salt to taste
1/4 teaspoon saffron
Pepper to taste
2 cups corn
6 ounces uncooked egg noodles

Rinse chicken well. Combine with next 4 ingredients in water to cover in heavy saucepan. Bring to a boil over high heat. Stir in salt; reduce heat to medium-low. Simmer, covered, for 30 minutes or until chicken is tender. Remove chicken from broth and strain broth. Cool chicken slightly. Cut into bite-sized pieces, discarding skin and bones. Bring broth to a boil in saucepan. Add saffron, salt and pepper. Simmer for 15 minutes. Add chicken and corn. Bring to a boil. Stir in noodles. Simmer for 5 minutes or until noodles are tender. Serve immediately. **Yield: 10 to 12 servings.**

Viola C. Benner, North Woodbury #1923

Chicken and Dumplings Soup

2 packages cut-up chicken
4 or 5 stalks celery
1 onion
1 tablespoon salt
2 14-ounce cans chicken broth
2 10-ounce cans cream of chicken soup
1/4 package wide noodles
3 cups baking mix
1 cup milk or water

Rinse chicken well. Combine with celery, onion, salt and water to cover in saucepan. Cook until chicken is tender. Remove chicken and strain cooking liquid. Bone chicken and return to cooking liquid in saucepan. Add canned broth and soup. Bring to a boil. Add noodles. Combine baking mix and milk in bowl; mix well. Drop by 1/2 to 1 teaspoonfuls into simmering soup. Cook, uncovered, for 10 minutes. Cook, covered, for 10 minutes longer. **Yield: 8 to 10 servings.**

Mary Bibel, Mendon #855

Homemade Cream of Chicken Soup

3/4 cup minced celery
1 large onion, minced
3 tablespoons butter
2 14-ounce cans chicken broth
3 cups chopped potatoes
1 10-ounce package frozen peas and carrots
2 cups chopped cooked chicken
1/8 teaspoon sage
1/2 teaspoon thyme
2 teaspoons seasoned salt
1/2 teaspoon white pepper
1 cup half and half
1 cup milk

Sauté celery and onion in butter in heavy saucepan over medium-high heat until tender. Add chicken broth and potatoes. Cook for 20 minutes. Stir in peas and carrots, chicken, sage, thyme, seasoned salt and pepper. Add half and half and milk. Cook until heated through. **Yield: 8 servings.**

Betty Jane Lichtenwalner, Macungie #1569

Manhattan Clam Chowder

1 16-ounce can stewed tomatoes
4 potatoes, chopped
1 carrot, chopped
2 stalks celery, chopped
1 onion, minced
3 cups water
2 7-ounce cans minced clams
Parsley to taste

Combine tomatoes, potatoes, carrot, celery, onion and water in saucepan. Cook until vegetables are tender. Add undrained clams and parsley. Cook until heated through. **Yield: 4 servings.**

Winnie S. Faust, Bernville #1887

New England Clam Chowder

1 10-ounce can clams
2 medium onions, cut into quarters
3 tablespoons margarine
2 medium potatoes, peeled, chopped
1 cup boiling water
1/2 teaspoon salt
1/8 teaspoon pepper
1 tablespoon flour
2 tablespoons cold water
2 cups milk

Drain clams, reserving liquid. Sauté onions in margarine in large skillet until tender. Add potatoes, boiling water, reserved clam liquid, salt and pepper. Simmer for 30 minutes, adding additional boiling water if needed for desired consistency. Stir in mixture of flour and cold water. Cook until thickened, stirring constantly. Stir in milk and clams. Cook just until heated through. Serve with chowder crackers. **Yield: 4 servings.**

Sandra Null, Eldred #1604

Corn Chowder

5 slices bacon
2 cups chopped potatoes
1 cup sliced onion
1 16-ounce can whole kernel corn
1 10-ounce can cream of mushroom soup
2 cups milk
1 teaspoon salt
Pepper to taste
2 tablespoons flour

Fry bacon in skillet until crisp. Remove and crumble bacon; reserve 2 tablespoons drippings. Cook potatoes and onion in boiling salted water in saucepan until tender; do not drain. Stir in undrained corn, mushroom soup, milk, 1 teaspoon salt and pepper. Blend reserved bacon drippings with flour in small bowl. Add to soup. Cook until thickened, stirring constantly. Simmer for 5 minutes longer, stirring frequently. Top servings with bacon. **Yield: 6 to 8 servings.**

Susan R. Krause, Star #993

Pennsylvania Corn Chowder

6 large crackers
1 cup milk
4 slices bacon, chopped
1 large onion, sliced
4 large potatoes, chopped
2 cups water
2 cups corn
1/4 teaspoon paprika
1 teaspoon salt
1/4 teaspoon pepper

Combine crackers with milk in bowl. Let stand for several minutes. Fry bacon in 4-quart saucepan until brown. Add onion. Sauté for 5 minutes. Add potatoes and water. Cook until potatoes are tender. Stir in cracker mixture, corn, paprika, salt and pepper. Cook until heated through. **Yield: 4 to 6 servings.**

Esther Dietterick, Light Street #31

Hearty Soup

1 pound mild Italian sausage
1 medium green bell pepper, chopped
1 medium onion, chopped
1 28-ounce can tomatoes
2 8-ounce cans tomato sauce
2 8-ounce cans water
1 tablespoon chicken bouillon
3/4 teaspoon garlic powder
3/4 cup uncooked small macaroni
Shredded mozzarella or Cheddar cheese

Brown sausage with green pepper and onion in large saucepan. Add tomatoes, tomato sauce, water, chicken bouillon and garlic powder; mix well. Simmer, covered, for 15 minutes. Stir in macaroni. Simmer for 10 to 12 minutes or until macaroni is tender. Top servings with cheese. **Yield: 4 to 6 servings.**

Jeanne Tomb, Alert #905

Mil's Low-Calorie Soup

2 cups thinly sliced carrots
2 cups thinly sliced celery
2 cups chopped cabbage
1 8-ounce package frozen green beans
1 onion, chopped
1 27-ounce can chopped tomatoes
3 envelopes low-sodium beef-flavored soup mix
3 tablespoons Worcestershire sauce
Salt and pepper to taste

Combine carrots, celery, cabbage, green beans, onion, tomatoes, soup mix, Worcestershire sauce, salt and pepper in slow-cooker. Add enough water to cover. Cook, covered, on High for 5 hours, stirring occasionally. Serve hot or cold.
Yield: 14 to 16 servings.

Mildred K. Duran, Burgettstown #1502

Fresh Mushroom and Barley Soup

1/2 cup pearl barley
1 pound mushrooms, thinly sliced
6 large carrots, sliced 1/8 inch thick
1 medium onion, chopped
1 tablespoon oil
2 tablespoons butter
6 cups chicken broth
Salt to taste
1/2 teaspoon freshly ground pepper
1/4 cup chopped fresh dill or 1 1/2 teaspoons dried dill
2 tablespoons fresh lemon juice

Soak barley in hot water to cover in bowl for 20 minutes. Sauté mushrooms, carrots and onion in oil and butter in large heavy saucepan for 5 minutes. Drain barley. Add barley, chicken broth, salt, pepper and half the dill to sautéed mixture. Simmer for 45 minutes. Add remaining dill and lemon juice. **Yield: 4 to 6 servings.**

Mildred K. Duran, Burgettstown #1502

French Onion Soup

3 large purple or white onions, thinly sliced
1/4 cup butter
2 14-ounce cans beef broth
1/2 cup water
2 teaspoons Worcestershire sauce
4 slices French bread, toasted, buttered
Grated Parmesan cheese
4 slices mozzarella cheese

Sauté onions in butter in saucepan until tender. Add beef broth, water and Worcestershire sauce. Bring to a boil; reduce heat. Simmer, covered, for 25 minutes. Spoon into 4 ovenproof bowls. Place on baking sheet. Place 1 slice of bread on each serving; sprinkle with Parmesan cheese. Top with mozzarella cheese. Broil until cheeses melt. **Yield: 4 servings.**

Joanne Spafford, DuBois #808

Cheesy Onion and Ham Chowder

3 medium potatoes, chopped
1 cup chopped onion
3 tablespoons butter
3 tablespoons flour
Pepper to taste
3 cups milk
1 1/2 cups chopped cooked ham
1 1/2 cups shredded cheese

Cook potatoes in water in saucepan until tender. Drain, reserving cooking liquid. Add enough water to reserved liquid to measure 1 cup. Sauté onion in butter in saucepan. Stir in flour and pepper. Add milk and reserved cooking liquid. Cook until thickened, stirring constantly. Stir in ham and cheese. Cook just until cheese melts. **Yield: 4 servings.**

Cora Van Dyke, Sebring #1047

Rivel Soup

1 cup flour
1/2 teaspoon salt
1 egg, beaten
1 quart chicken or beef broth
1 cup whole kernel corn, crushed

Combine flour, salt and egg in bowl; mix until crumbly. Bring broth to a boil in saucepan. Rub flour mixture through hands into boiling broth. Add corn. Cook for 10 minutes. **Yield: 8 servings.**

Mildred Wessner, Virginville #1832

Hearty Potato and Sauerkraut Soup

5 cups chicken broth
1 10-ounce can cream of mushroom or cream of chicken soup
1 quart sauerkraut, drained
8 ounces fresh mushrooms, sliced (optional)
1 1/2 cups chopped potatoes
1 cup chopped carrots
1 cup chopped onion
1 cup chopped celery
12 to 16 ounces smoked Polish sausage, chopped
1/2 to 1 cup chopped cooked chicken
2 tablespoons vinegar
2 teaspoons dried dillweed or 1 1/2 teaspoons dillseed
1/2 teaspoon pepper
2 slices bacon, crisp-fried, crumbled
2 hard-boiled eggs, chopped (optional)

Combine chicken broth, mushroom soup, sauerkraut, mushrooms, potatoes, carrots, onion, celery, sausage, chicken, vinegar, dillweed and pepper in 4-quart slow cooker; mix well. Cook on Low for 10 to 12 hours or until vegetables are tender and soup is of desired consistency. Skim surface if necessary. Sprinkle servings with bacon and chopped egg. May cook in large saucepan on stove top if preferred.
Yield: 6 to 8 servings.

Shelby Brosius, Shannondale #1865

Potato and Bacon Soup

4 cups chopped peeled potatoes
3/4 cup sliced green onions
3/4 cup chopped celery
1 10-ounce can chicken broth
1 cup low-fat cottage cheese
2 cups skim milk
6 slices bacon, crisp-fried, crumbled
1/4 teaspoon pepper

Combine potatoes, green onions, celery and chicken broth in 3-quart saucepan. Bring to a boil; reduce heat. Simmer, covered, for 15 minutes or until vegetables are tender. Remove and reserve 1 cup vegetables. Purée remaining vegetable mixture and cottage cheese 1/2 at a time in blender. Return to saucepan. Stir in milk, bacon, pepper and reserved vegetables. Heat just to serving temperature; do not boil. This is a low-fat soup. **Yield: 8 servings.**

Patty Friede, Stony Point #1694

Salmon Soup

1 16-ounce can salmon
2 16-ounce cans milk
2 cups chopped cooked broccoli
Minced onion to taste (optional)

Drain and flake salmon, discarding skin and bones. Combine 1 can milk with broccoli in blender container; process until smooth. Combine salmon, broccoli mixture, remaining milk and onion in 3-quart saucepan. Cook until heated through, stirring frequently. Sprinkle servings with cheese. Serve with oysters crackers. **Yield: 4 to 6 servings.**

Mamie A. Breininger, Shartlesville #1512

Shrimp Bisque

1 cup sliced fresh mushrooms
2 tablespoons chopped chives
1 clove of garlic, minced
1/4 cup butter
3 tablespoons flour
1 14-ounce can chicken broth
1 pound medium shrimp, peeled, deveined
1 cup half and half
1 tablespoon chopped parsley

Sauté mushrooms, chives and garlic in butter in deep saucepan until tender, stirring occasionally. Stir in flour. Add chicken broth. Bring to a boil, stirring constantly. Stir in shrimp; reduce heat. Add half and half and parsley. Cook until shrimp are cooked through. **Yield: 6 servings.**

Karen Bowser, DuBois #808

Taco Soup

1 pound ground beef
1/4 cup chopped onion
1 8-ounce can tomato sauce
1 16-ounce can tomatoes
1 16-ounce can whole kernel corn
1 16-ounce can kidney beans
1 2-ounce package taco seasoning mix
Shredded Cheddar cheese
Sour cream

Brown ground beef in large saucepan, stirring until crumbly; drain. Add onion, tomato sauce, undrained tomatoes, undrained corn, undrained beans and taco seasoning mix; mix well. Simmer for 15 minutes. Top servings with cheese and sour cream. Serve with nacho chips for dipping soup. **Yield: 6 servings.**

Nancy J. Rodgers, Plain Grove #1431

Turkey and Bean Soup

1 pound dried beans
2 turkey drumsticks
1 gallon water
1½ teaspoons thyme
Salt and pepper to taste
¾ cup chopped onion
¾ cup chopped carrot
1 sprig of fresh rosemary
¾ cup chopped celery
1 cup chopped peeled potato

Soak beans in water to cover overnight. Rinse turkey well. Combine with water, thyme, salt and pepper in large saucepan. Simmer for several hours or until very tender. Remove turkey, reserving broth. Cut turkey into bite-sized pieces, discarding bones. Drain beans. Add beans to broth with onion, carrot and rosemary. Simmer for 1 to 1½ hours or until beans are tender. Add celery and potato. Cook until vegetables are tender. Stir in turkey. Cook until heated through.
Yield: 6 to 8 servings.

Jean F. Rothrock, Sebring #1047

Busy-Day Vegetable Soup

1 pound ground beef
½ cup chopped onion
Salt and pepper to taste
2 16-ounce cans stewed tomatoes
2 16-ounce cans mixed vegetables
1 14-ounce can beef broth
1 cup uncooked noodles

Brown ground beef in large saucepan, stirring until crumbly. Add onion. Cook until onion is tender; drain. Season with salt and pepper. Stir in tomatoes, mixed vegetables, beef broth and noodles. Simmer, covered, for 15 minutes or until noodles are tender. **Yield: 8 to 10 servings.**

Nina Clawson, Bell Township #1756

Chinese Vegetable Soup

1 pound ground beef
1 16-ounce can bean sprouts, drained, rinsed
1 16-ounce can mixed Chinese vegetables, drained, rinsed
1 28-ounce can stewed tomatoes
Oregano, garlic powder, salt and pepper to taste
Tomato juice (optional)

Brown ground beef in saucepan, stirring until crumbly; drain. Add bean sprouts, mixed vegetables, tomatoes, oregano, garlic powder, salt and pepper; mix well. Simmer until heated through, adding tomato juice if needed for desired consistency.
Yield: 8 servings.

Marilyn Bevington, Sandy Creek #2021

Peppered Vegetable Soup with Meatballs

2 cups chopped carrots
4 cups tomatoes
3 potatoes, chopped
1½ cups chopped celery
¼ cup chopped parsley
2 small onions, chopped
8 cups water
1 tablespoon sugar
2 teaspoons each oregano and basil
3 bay leaves
4 teaspoons salt
2 teaspoons pepper
2 pounds ground beef
½ cup bread crumbs
2 eggs
2 tablespoons milk
2 teaspoons salt
½ teaspoon pepper
2 16-ounce cans green beans
1 12-ounce can corn

Combine first 13 ingredients in large saucepan. Simmer for 30 minutes. Combine ground beef, bread crumbs, eggs, milk, 2 teaspoons salt and ½ teaspoon pepper in bowl; mix well. Shape into 1-inch meatballs. Drop into soup. Simmer for 30 minutes or longer. Add green beans and corn. Simmer for 10 minutes longer. Discard bay leaves. **Yield: 12 servings.**

Della Jones, Jefferson #1373

Wedding Soup with Meatballs

1 chicken, cut up
8 cups water
8 ounces ground turkey or ground beef
1 tablespoon bread crumbs
2 tablespoons grated Parmesan cheese
1 tablespoon parsley flakes
½ teaspoon pepper
1 10-ounce package frozen spinach
3 egg whites
½ cup grated Parmesan cheese

Rinse chicken well. Combine with water in saucepan. Cook until tender. Combine next 5 ingredients in bowl; mix well. Shape into tiny meatballs. Remove chicken from broth. Drop meatballs into simmering broth. Simmer for 20 minutes. Add spinach. Cook for 10 minutes. Chop chicken into bite-sized pieces, discarding skin and bones. Add to soup; reduce heat. Combine egg whites and ½ cup cheese in bowl; mix well. Drop by tablespoonfuls into soup. Cook for 5 minutes longer. **Yield: 10 servings.**

Nettie Martsolf, Jefferson #1373

Wonderful Zucchini Soup

1 large onion, chopped
2 tablespoons margarine
2 cups boiling water
2 chicken bouillon cubes
8 cups chopped zucchini
⅛ teaspoon garlic powder
½ teaspoon salt
¼ cup chopped parsley

Sauté onion in margarine in saucepan. Add water, bouillon, zucchini, garlic powder and salt; mix well. Cook until zucchini is tender. Combine with parsley in blender container; process until smooth. **Yield: 6 to 8 servings.**

Eleanor Harkins, Jackson #1506

Won Ton Soup

1 cup flour
1 teaspoon salt
2 egg yolks or 2 whole eggs
1 tablespoon water
1 pound ground pork
8 ounces ground ham
Onion powder, garlic powder and pepper to taste
1 cup chopped onion
3 tablespoons oil
6 cups beef broth or stock

Mix flour and salt in bowl. Add egg yolks and water; mix to form dough. Let rest for 30 minutes. Brown ground pork and ham with onion powder, garlic powder and pepper in skillet, stirring frequently; drain. Roll dough very thin on floured surface. Cut into small squares. Place a small amount of meat mixture into center of each square. Fold over dough to enclose filling; press edges to seal. Sauté onion in oil in saucepan. Add beef broth. Bring to a simmer. Drop won tons into simmering broth. Simmer until cooked through. **Yield: 8 servings.**

Trudy Wigton, Pleasant Hill #1505

Dried Beef Sandwich Filling

4 ounces dried beef
4 ounces sharp cheese
1 medium onion
1 medium green bell pepper
2 eggs, beaten
1 tablespoon flour
1 6-ounce can tomato purée

Grind dried beef, cheese, onion and green pepper together. Combine with eggs, flour and tomato purée in saucepan. Cook for 10 minutes or until thickened, stirring constantly. Cool to room temperature. Store in refrigerator. **Yield: 20 servings.**

Lauretta Silvis, DuBois #808

Pizza Burgers

1 6-ounce can tomato paste
1/2 cup catsup
3/4 teaspoon each oregano and garlic salt
2 tablespoons flour
1/2 cup dry milk powder
3/4 cup water
1 cup shredded process cheese
1 pound ground beef
8 sandwich buns, split, toasted
1/2 cup grated Parmesan cheese

Combine tomato paste, catsup, oregano and garlic salt in bowl; set aside. Mix flour and dry milk powder in saucepan. Stir in water until smooth. Cook over medium heat until thickened, stirring constantly; do not boil. Stir in process cheese until melted. Brown ground beef in skillet, stirring until crumbly; drain. Arrange buns cut side up on baking sheet. Layer tomato mixture, cheese sauce, ground beef and Parmesan cheese on buns. Bake at 400 degrees for 12 to 15 minutes or broil until bubbly. May be prepared in advance, frozen or refrigerated and baked as needed. **Yield: 8 servings.**

Ruth Waltz, Bottle Run #1301

Pizza Sandwiches

8 ounces chopped ham
8 ounces Swiss cheese
2 tablespoons chopped onion
1/2 cup margarine
2 tablespoons parsley
2 teaspoons mustard
1/8 teaspoon garlic powder
8 sandwich buns

Process ham and cheese in blender until finely ground. Combine with next 5 ingredients in bowl; mix well. Spread on sandwich buns. Wrap individually in foil. Bake at 350 degrees for 25 minutes or until heated through. **Yield: 8 servings.**

Betty Lou Williams, Vernon #936

Silver Bullets

8 ounces ham, chopped
8 ounces Cheddar cheese, shredded
1/4 cup chopped onion
2 hard-boiled eggs, chopped
1/2 cup thinly sliced olives
2 tablespoons sweet pickle relish
3 tablespoons mayonnaise
1/2 cup chili sauce
10 hot dog buns

Mix first 7 ingredients in bowl. Stir in chili sauce. Spread on hot dog buns. Wrap each in foil; place on baking sheet. Bake at 400 degrees for 10 minutes. **Yield: 10 servings.**

Joan Barker, DuBois #808

Brunch Pockets

1/2 cup chopped cooked ham
1/4 cup chopped green bell pepper
2 tablespoons butter
1/8 teaspoon pepper
4 eggs, beaten
1/4 cup shredded Cheddar cheese
2 6-inch pita bread rounds

Combine ham, green pepper, butter and pepper in round glass dish. Microwave on High for 3 minutes, stirring after 1 1/2 minutes. Stir in eggs. Microwave for 2 1/2 minutes or until eggs are set, stirring with fork every 30 seconds. Stir in cheese. Cut pita rounds into halves. Spoon ham and egg mixture into pockets. **Yield: 4 servings.**

Ethel Friede, Stony Point #1694

Bacon Sandwich Filling

12 hard-boiled eggs
1 pound bacon, crisp-fried, crumbled
Chopped olives
Hellman's mayonnaise
1 loaf rye or whole wheat bread

Mash eggs in bowl. Add bacon, olives and enough mayonnaise to make of desired consistency; mix gently. Spread between slices of bread. **Yield: 10 servings.**

Kathryn Fleeger, Mountain #1307

Chicken Salad Sandwiches for-a-Crowd

12 pounds chicken breasts and legs
4 medium onions
1 bunch celery, finely chopped
2 cups mayonnaise-type salad dressing
4 teaspoons prepared mustard
3/4 cup vinegar
2/3 cup sugar
Salt and pepper to taste
50 homemade sandwich rolls

Rinse chicken well. Cook in water to cover in stockpot until very tender; drain. Remove chicken from bones, discarding bones and skin. Grind chicken with onions. Combine with celery, salad dressing, mustard, vinegar, sugar, salt and pepper in bowl; mix well. Spread on rolls. **Yield: 50 or more servings.**

Peg Byers, Wilmington #1477

Hot Cheesy Chicken Heros

2 cups chopped cooked chicken
1 1/2 cups chopped celery
1 tablespoon grated onion
3 tablespoons sweet pickle relish
1/2 cup mayonnaise
Salt to taste
1/8 teaspoon pepper
4 large semihard rolls
4 ounces Cheddar cheese, shredded

Combine chicken, celery, onion, relish, mayonnaise, salt and pepper in bowl; mix well. Cut slice from top of each roll; remove bread centers. Fill with chicken mixture. Place on baking sheet. Bake at 375 degrees for 25 to 30 minutes or until heated through. Top with cheese. Bake just until cheese melts. **Yield: 4 servings.**

Emma L. Hammond, Fairview #1351

Tuna-Cheese Melts

1 7-ounce can tuna, drained, flaked
2 or 3 hard-boiled eggs, chopped
1 tablespoon milk
Mayonnaise-type salad dressing to taste
12 slices bread
Marie's Creamy Italian Garlic Salad Dressing
12 slices cheese
Butter or margarine, softened

Combine tuna and eggs in bowl. Blend milk with enough salad dressing to moisten tuna mixture in bowl. Add to tuna mixture; mix well. Spread 1 side of bread slices with Italian dressing. Fill each sandwich with tuna mixture and 2 slices cheese. Spread outsides of sandwiches with butter. Grill until golden brown. May add tomato slices if desired. **Yield: 6 servings.**

Jane Darmofal, Kutztown #1836

Sloppy Tom Barbecued Sandwiches

1 pound ground turkey
1 small onion, chopped
2 stalks celery, chopped
1 green bell pepper, chopped
1/2 cup chili sauce
1/4 cup each tomato paste and water
2 teaspoons mustard
6 sandwich rolls

Brown ground turkey with vegetables in skillet, stirring frequently; drain. Add next 3 ingredients; mix well. Simmer for 15 minutes. Serve on rolls. **Yield: 6 servings.**

Arlene Hetrick, Twin East Hanover #2089

Cheese Sandwich Spread

6 eggs
1 pound longhorn cheese, at room temperature
1 4-ounce can pimentos
Salt and pepper to taste
1 cup mayonnaise

Cook eggs in water in saucepan until hard-boiled. Cool slightly. Grind with cheese and pimentos. Combine with salt and pepper in mixer bowl. Add mayonnaise; beat for 5 minutes or until smooth. Store in refrigerator. **Yield: 6 cups.**

Mary Stimmell, Morning Star #1271

Pimento Cheese Spread

2 eggs, slightly beaten
2 tablespoons margarine
2 tablespoons sugar
3 tablespoons vinegar
1 2-ounce jar chopped pimentos
1 small onion, chopped
8 ounces cream cheese, softened
20 slices bread

Combine eggs, margarine, sugar and vinegar in saucepan. Cook over medium heat until thickened, stirring constantly. Drain pimentos, reserving liquid. Add pimentos, onion and cream cheese to egg mixture; mix well. Add several drops of pimento juice if desired for color. Spread between slices of bread. **Yield: 10 servings.**

Janet McClellan, Logan #109

Baked Tomato and Cheese Sandwiches

12 slices bread
Butter, softened
6 tomato slices
6 thin onion slices
6 Old English cheese slices

Spread inner sides of bread with butter. Arrange half the bread on baking sheet. Layer tomato, onion and cheese slices on bread; top with remaining bread. Butter tops of sandwiches. Bake in moderate oven until tops are golden brown and cheese is melted. **Yield: 6 servings.**

Elsie Burkett, Elder #503

Meats

Marinated Roast Beef

1 3 to 4-pound rolled rump roast
1 to 2 teaspoons bacon drippings
Salt, pepper, garlic powder and oregano to taste
2 beef bouillon cubes
1 cup water
1 tablespoon butter or margarine
1/4 teaspoon basil
1/4 teaspoon rosemary
1/4 teaspoon parsley flakes

Brown roast in bacon drippings in large roasting pan. Sprinkle with salt, pepper, garlic powder and oregano. Bake, covered, at 325 degrees for 1 to 1 1/2 hours or to desired degree of doneness. Remove roast to warm platter; cool. Add bouillon cubes, water, butter and herbs to pan drippings; mix well. Slice cooled beef very thinly. Place in broth. Heat until warmed through before serving. **Yield: 6 to 8 servings.**

Theresa A. Fike, Logan #109

Beef Marinade

1 small onion, chopped
2 tablespoons vinegar
1/4 cup water
2 tablespoons each catsup and oil
1 tablespoon brown sugar
1 teaspoon salt
1/2 teaspoon Tabasco sauce
1 to 1 3/4 pounds beef steak

Combine first 8 ingredients in shallow dish; mix well. Add steak, turning once to coat. Marinate, covered, in refrigerator for 4 hours, turning steak after 2 hours. Drain, reserving marinade. Cook beef to desired degree of doneness by favorite method, using reserved marinade for basting. May serve remaining marinade as sauce. **Yield: 4 to 6 servings.**

Doris Koenig, Central #1650

Spicy New England Pot Roast

3 tablespoons flour
2 teaspoons salt
1/4 teaspoon freshly ground pepper
1 4-pound beef roast
3 tablespoons bacon drippings
1/2 cup freshly grated horseradish or 1 4-ounce jar prepared horseradish
1 cup whole cranberry sauce
1 stick cinnamon, broken
4 whole cloves
1 cup beef broth
16 small white onions
1 bunch carrots, cut into 3-inch lengths

Combine flour, salt and pepper in small dish. Coat roast with mixture. Brown roast in bacon drippings in heavy casserole. Pour off and reserve pan drippings. Combine horseradish, cranberry sauce, cinnamon, cloves and broth in small bowl; mix well. Pour over roast. Bring to a boil; reduce heat. Simmer, covered, for 2 hours or until roast is tender. Brown onions in reserved pan drippings in skillet. Add carrots. Cook for 2 minutes longer; drain. Add vegetables to broth. Cook for 25 minutes longer or until vegetables and roast are tender. **Yield: 8 servings.**

Irene Horvath, Odin #1254

Quick Sauerbraten

2 pounds stew beef
1 large onion, cut into quarters
Oil for browning
1 teaspoon salt
3 cups vinegar
3 cups water
1 teaspoon pickling spices
12 gingersnaps

Brown beef with onion in a small amount of oil in large heavy saucepan. Add salt, vinegar and water. Tie pickling spices in cheesecloth; add to beef. Cook over low heat for 1 1/2 hours. Drain off 2 cups pan drippings. Add gingersnaps to pan drippings to soften. Return to saucepan. Remove spices. Simmer until sauce is thickened, stirring frequently. Serve with noodles or mashed potatoes. **Yield: 4 to 6 servings.**

Hannelore Carle, Sebring #1047

Breaded Steak

1 package hamburger or hot dog buns, crumbled
1/2 teaspoon salt
1 teaspoon pepper
1/2 cup grated Romano cheese
1 egg
2 tablespoons water
8 portions cubed steak
Oil for frying

Combine bread crumbs, salt, pepper and cheese in bowl. Beat egg with water. Dip steaks in egg mixture; coat with bread crumb mixture. Place on waxed paper-lined baking sheet. Chill for 2 hours. Fry in small amount of oil in skillet until browned on both sides. **Yield: 8 servings.**

Carole Zimmerman, Ackley #870

Round Steak

2 tablespoons flour
3/4 teaspoon salt
1/8 teaspoon pepper
1 1/2 pounds round steak, 1 1/2 inches thick
3 tablespoons shortening
2 onions, sliced
2 tablespoons flour
3/4 teaspoon salt
2 teaspoons brown sugar
1 cup frozen grapefruit juice concentrate, thawed

Combine 2 tablespoons flour, 3/4 teaspoon salt and pepper in bowl; mix well. Sprinkle steak with mixture. Pound mixture in with a meat mallet. Cut steak into serving portions. Brown on both sides in hot shortening in skillet. Remove steak; add onions. Sauté until light brown. Stir in 2 tablespoons flour, 3/4 teaspoon salt and brown sugar. Cook until smooth paste forms, stirring constantly. Stir in grapefruit juice. Add steak. Simmer, covered, over low heat for 1 1/2 hours or until tender. **Yield: 4 to 6 servings.**

Betty McCurdy, Boot Jack #1680

Steak Diane

3 ½-inch thick sirloin strip steaks, trimmed
2 tablespoons butter
2 tablespoons oil
2 tablespoons brandy
2 tablespoons minced green onions
1 tablespoon chopped parsley
1 10-ounce can beef consommé, chilled
Salt and pepper to taste
1 cup Worcestershire sauce

Pound steaks with meat mallet to ¼-inch thickness. Brown in hot butter and oil in skillet for 1 minute on each side. Pour brandy over steaks; ignite. Shake pan over high heat until flame is extinguished. Add green onions and parsley, stirring well. Add consommé one spoonful at a time, stirring well. Bring to a boil. Spoon 2 tablespoons of mixture onto warm platter. Remove steaks to platter and keep warm. Cook remaining broth until reduced by half, stirring occasionally. Stir in Worcestershire sauce. Pour over steaks. Serve with French-fried potatoes. **Yield: 6 to 8 servings.**

Laura Y. Peake, Charleston Valley #54

Oven Swiss Steak

1½ pounds boneless round steak, ¾ inch thick
¼ cup flour
1 teaspoon salt
2 cups stewed tomatoes
½ cup chopped celery
½ cup chopped carrots
2 tablespoons chopped onion
½ teaspoon Worcestershire sauce
4 slices American cheese

Slice steak into 4 serving portions. Pat mixture of flour and salt onto each side of steak. Reserve any remaining flour. Brown steak in hot oil in skillet. Remove steak to shallow baking dish, reserving pan drippings. Stir reserved flour into pan drippings to form paste. Add next 5 ingredients; mix well. Bring to a boil, stirring constantly. Pour over steak. Bake, covered, at 350 degrees for 2 hours or until tender. Place cheese over steaks. Bake until cheese is melted. **Yield: 4 servings.**

Marilyn Davidson, Bald Eagle #1390

Italian Beef Stew

1½ pounds beef stew meat
¼ cup flour
1 teaspoon salt
3 tablespoons oil
8 ounces sweet Italian sausage, sliced
2 cups tomato juice
1 teaspoon sugar
1 teaspoon Italian seasoning
1 1-pound eggplant, peeled, cubed

Coat stew meat with mixture of flour and salt. Brown in hot oil in large heavy skillet. Add sausage to skillet. Brown lightly. Stir in tomato juice, sugar and Italian seasoning. Bring to a boil; reduce heat. Simmer for 1 hour or until meat is tender. Add eggplant cubes. Cook, covered, for 20 minutes longer or until eggplant is tender. Serve over cooked spaghetti or noodles. **Yield: 4 to 6 servings.**

Mary Hare, Gillett #884

Orange Beef and Broccoli Stir-Fry

1 pound top sirloin, trimmed, thinly sliced
4 teaspoons soy sauce
2 teaspoons grated fresh ginger or 1/2 teaspoon ground ginger
1 teaspoon grated orange rind
1 tablespoon oil
2 cups broccoli flowerets
1 red bell pepper, cut into strips
2/3 cup picante sauce
1/2 teaspoon sugar (optional)
1/3 cup orange juice
1 tablespoon cornstarch
3 green onions, cut diagonally into 1-inch pieces
Slivered almonds (optional)

Combine sirloin with soy sauce, ginger and orange rind in bowl; toss well. Let stand for 10 minutes. Heat oil in wok or large skillet. Stir-fry sirloin slices until meat is no longer pink. Remove to warm platter. Add broccoli, red pepper, picante sauce and sugar. Simmer, covered, for 3 minutes or until vegetables are tender-crisp. Mix orange juice with cornstarch in small bowl. Add to wok with sirloin and green onions. Stir-fry for 1 minute or until sauce is thickened. Sprinkle with almonds. Serve over hot steamed rice. **Yield: 4 to 6 servings.**

Willowa Gates, Corry #55

Beef Turnovers

2 cups chopped cooked roast beef
3 ounces cream cheese, softened
2 tablespoons sweet relish
1 small onion, chopped
1 8-count can crescent rolls
2 tablespoons melted butter
Seasoned bread crumbs

Combine roast beef, cream cheese, relish and onion in bowl; mix well. Unroll crescent rolls, forming 4 squares. Spoon equal portion of mixture in center of each square. Fold up corners to enclose filling, sealing edges. Arrange in baking pan. Drizzle with melted butter; sprinkle with bread crumbs. Bake at 350 degrees for 20 minutes or until golden brown. **Yield: 4 servings.**

Emma L. Hammond, Fairview #1351

Dried Beef Casserole

1 10-ounce can cream of mushroom soup
1 cup milk
1 cup shredded Cheddar cheese
3 tablespoons chopped onion
1 cup uncooked macaroni
4 ounces dried beef, cut into bite-sized pieces
2 hard boiled eggs, chopped

Mix soup with milk in bowl, stirring until creamy. Stir in cheese, onion, macaroni and dried beef. Add eggs, stirring gently. Spoon into buttered 1 1/2-quart baking dish. Chill for 3 to 4 hours to overnight. Bake at 350 degrees for 1 hour.
Yield: 4 to 6 servings.

Norma Lee Weaver

Home-Cured Corned Beef

7 quarts water
3 cups pickling salt
1 egg
1 6 to 9-pound beef brisket
3 cloves of garlic
20 whole cloves
20 peppercorns
1 bay leaf
6 sprigs fresh thyme

Pour water into earthenware or stainless steel crock. Add pickling salt, stirring to dissolve. Place unshelled raw egg in brine. Continue adding salt gradually until egg floats; remove egg. Add brisket, garlic, cloves, peppercorns, bay leaf and thyme. Soak in mixture for 3 days. Bake using preferred recipe. Discard bay leaf before serving. **Yield: 1 brisket.**

Eva Southard, Gideon #2010

Corned Beef and Noodle Casserole

1 12-ounce package noodles
1 6-ounce can tomato paste
1 12-ounce can corned beef
2 3/4 cups water
2 green bell peppers, chopped
2 onions, chopped
Salt and pepper to taste

Cook noodles using package directions; drain. Mix tomato paste, corned beef, water, green peppers, onions, salt and pepper in bowl. Stir in noodles. Pour into casserole. Bake at 375 degrees for 20 minutes. **Yield: 12 servings.**

Peg Byers, Wilmington #1477

Reuben Casserole

1 16-ounce can sauerkraut
1 12-ounce can corned beef, crumbled
2 cups shredded Swiss cheese
1/2 cup light mayonnaise
1/4 cup Thousand Island salad dressing
2 tomatoes, sliced
1/4 cup pumpernickel or rye bread crumbs
2 tablespoons melted butter

Spoon undrained sauerkraut into 1 1/2-quart microwave-safe baking dish. Layer with corned beef and cheese. Mix mayonnaise and salad dressing in small bowl until blended. Spread over cheese. Top with tomato slices. Toss bread crumbs with butter in bowl. Sprinkle over tomatoes. Microwave on Medium for 12 to 14 minutes or bake at 350 degrees for 45 minutes. Let stand for 5 minutes before serving.
Yield: 6 to 8 servings.

Naomi Pepper, Iona #272

Fluffy Burgers

6 slices dry Vienna bread
1 large onion, chopped
1 pound ground round or ground chuck
3 eggs
2 tablespoons cracker meal
Salt and pepper to taste

Soak bread in cold water in bowl until soft; squeeze to remove moisture. Fry onion in nonstick skillet. Combine bread, onion, ground round, eggs, cracker meal, salt and pepper in bowl; mix well until bread disappears. Shape into large meatballs. Flatten with fingers dipped into cold water. Cook over medium coals to desired degree of doneness. **Yield: 6 servings.**

Hope Nelson, Brokenstraw #407

Mushroom Burgers

8 ounces mushrooms, finely chopped
8 ounces lean ground beef
Salt and pepper to taste
Pinch of garlic powder

Mix mushrooms, ground beef, salt, pepper and garlic powder in bowl. Shape into 4 patties. Cook in skillet over medium heat to desired degree of doneness. Serve on toasted hamburger rolls with mustard, catsup or both. **Yield: 4 servings.**

Betty J. Light, North Jackson #1740

Amish Casserole

1 pound ground beef
2 cups cooked medium noodles
1 cup shredded sharp Cheddar cheese
1 10-ounce can cream of chicken soup
1/2 cup shredded sharp Cheddar cheese
2 cups canned tomatoes

Brown ground beef in skillet, stirring until crumbly; drain. Layer ground beef, noodles, 1 cup cheese, soup, 1/2 cup cheese and tomatoes in 3-quart casserole. Bake at 350 degrees for 40 minutes. **Yield: 6 servings.**

Lucille Beck, Reynoldsville #1825

Ground Beef and String Beans Casserole

2 1/2 pounds ground beef
1 large onion, chopped
2 16-ounce cans string beans
2 10-ounce cans tomato soup
2 cups mashed potatoes
1 cup shredded cheese

Brown ground beef with onion in skillet, stirring frequently; drain. Layer ground beef mixture, string beans, soup, potatoes and cheese in casserole. Bake at 375 degrees for 30 minutes. **Yield: 12 servings.**

Nancy Lehman, Lycova #2006

Quick and Easy Casserole

1 onion, chopped
2 tablespoons shortening
1 pound ground beef
1 16-ounce can cream-style corn
3 cups seasoned mashed potatoes

Cook onion in shortening in skillet until tender. Add ground beef. Cook until lightly browned, stirring frequently; drain. Place in greased casserole. Spread corn over beef mixture. Top with mashed potatoes. Bake at 350 degrees for 25 minutes. **Yield: 4 servings.**

Bonnie Chronister, Mifflin #1725

Fred's Gringo Chili

2 onions, chopped
2 cloves of garlic, crushed
2 tablespoons olive oil
1½ pounds ground beef
1 15-ounce can peeled tomatoes
¼ cup tomato paste
1 bay leaf
1 green bell pepper, chopped
1 teaspoon ground cumin
1 teaspoon dried oregano
¼ teaspoon cayenne pepper
Salt and black pepper to taste
1 cup beef stock
1 tablespoon mild chili powder
1 15-ounce can pinto or kidney beans

Cook onions and garlic in hot oil in large heavy skillet until tender. Add ground beef. Cook until browned, stirring frequently; drain. Add tomatoes, tomato paste, bay leaf, green pepper, cumin, oregano, cayenne pepper, salt, black pepper, beef stock and chili powder; mix well. Bring to a boil. Simmer, covered, for 1 hour, stirring occasionally. Add beans. Simmer for 20 to 30 minutes or until heated through. Remove bay leaf. **Yield: 10 servings.**

Fred Alkons, Virginville #1832

Chuck Wagon Chowder

2 pounds ground beef
¼ cup chopped onion
¼ cup green bell pepper strips
½ teaspoon salt
¼ teaspoon hot sauce
1 cup uncooked noodles
3 cups chopped tomatoes
1 10-ounce package frozen peas
1 cup shredded American cheese

Brown ground beef in skillet, stirring until crumbly; drain. Add onion, green pepper, salt, hot sauce, noodles, tomatoes and peas; mix well. Simmer, covered, for 30 minutes or until noodles are tender. Sprinkle with cheese. Let stand for 5 minutes. **Yield: 15 servings.**

Betty Gail Dietz, Mt. Nebo #1872

Stuffed Cabbage Casserole

$1\frac{1}{2}$ pounds ground beef
1 onion, chopped
$\frac{1}{2}$ green bell pepper, chopped
2 cloves of garlic, minced
$\frac{3}{4}$ cup uncooked rice
$\frac{1}{2}$ head cabbage, shredded
1 46-ounce can tomato or V-8 juice

Brown ground beef with onion, green pepper and garlic in skillet, stirring frequently; drain. Layer ground beef mixture, rice and cabbage $\frac{1}{2}$ at a time in 9x13-inch baking dish. Pour juice over all. Bake, covered with foil, at 350 degrees for 1 hour and 15 minutes. **Yield: 8 servings.**

Kimberley A. Laughlin, Hookstown #1980

Halupkies

6 cabbage leaves
1 pound ground beef
Salt and pepper to taste
1 egg, beaten
$\frac{1}{4}$ cup rice, cooked
2 tablespoons shortening
1 onion, thinly sliced
$\frac{1}{2}$ cup chopped green bell pepper
1 10-ounce can tomato soup
1 soup can water
1 teaspoon chopped parsley
$\frac{1}{2}$ cup chopped celery
Juice of 1 lemon
1 teaspoon sugar

Rinse cabbage leaves. Cook in water to cover in saucepan until tender. Drain on paper towels. Combine ground beef, salt, pepper, egg and rice in bowl; mix well. Place 2 tablespoons ground beef mixture on each cabbage leaf. Roll tightly; secure with wooden picks. Place in large baking dish. Melt shortening in skillet. Add onion, green pepper, tomato soup, water, parsley, celery, lemon juice and sugar; mix well. Simmer for 10 minutes. Pour over cabbage rolls. Cook for 1 hour and 30 minutes. **Yield: 6 servings.**

Cleita Wolfe, Bloomingdale #536

For a quick stew, shape 1 pound of ground chuck into meatballs and brown them with a sliced onion. Add a can of corn, a can of lima beans and a can of chopped tomatoes and simmer for 45 minutes.

Mexican Lasagna

1 pound lean ground beef
1 10-ounce can refried beans
2 teaspoons dried oregano
1 teaspoon ground cumin
3/4 teaspoon garlic powder
12 lasagna noodles, uncooked
2 1/2 cups water
2 1/2 cups picante sauce or salsa
2 cups sour cream
3/4 cup finely chopped green onions
1 2-ounce can sliced black olives
1 cup shredded Monterey Jack cheese

Brown ground beef in skillet, stirring until crumbly; drain. Add beans, oregano, cumin and garlic powder; mix well. Arrange 4 noodles in 9x13-inch baking pan. Layer ground beef mixture and remaining noodles 1/2 at a time in prepared pan. Pour mixture of water and picante sauce over all. Bake, tightly covered with foil, at 350 degrees for 1 hour and 30 minutes or until noodles are tender. Mix sour cream, green onions and olives in bowl. Spoon over casserole. Sprinkle with cheese. Bake, uncovered, for 5 minutes or until cheese is melted. **Yield: 12 servings.**

Pat Weir, Unionville #1971

Baked Sausage-Beef Meatballs

1 1/2 pounds lean ground beef
1 pound mild bulk sausage
3 cups baking mix
1/2 cup milk

Combine ground beef, sausage, baking mix and milk in bowl; mix well. Shape into 1-inch balls. Place on foil-lined baking sheet. Bake at 350 degrees for 30 minutes. **Yield: 12 servings.**

Diane Boroi, Valley #1420

Swedish Meatballs

1 pound ground beef
8 ounces ground pork
3/4 cup bread crumbs
1 tablespoon minced parsley
1 teaspoon Worcestershire sauce
2 teaspoons salt
1/4 teaspoon pepper
1 egg
1/2 cup milk
1/2 cup chopped onion
1/4 cup oil
1/4 cup flour
1 teaspoon paprika
2 cups boiling water
3/4 cup sour cream

Combine ground beef, ground pork, bread crumbs, parsley, Worcestershire sauce, salt, pepper, egg, milk and onion in bowl; mix well. Shape into small balls. Combine oil, flour, paprika, boiling water and sour cream in skillet; mix well. Cook until thickened. Add meatballs. Cook for 20 minutes or until cooked through. May substitute 1 can mushroom soup for sour cream. **Yield: 10 servings.**

Edna Bartlett, East Sullivan #821

Chinese Meat Loaf

1 pound ground beef
1 cup chopped onion
3 cups chopped celery
2 4-ounce cans mushrooms, drained
1 10-ounce can chicken with rice soup
1 10-ounce can cream of mushroom soup
2 cups chow mein noodles
1/2 cup cashews (optional)
1/4 cup chow mein noodles

Brown ground beef with onion and celery in skillet, stirring frequently; drain. Add mushrooms, soups, 2 cups noodles and cashews; mix well. Spoon into casserole. Top with 1/4 cup noodles. Bake at 350 degrees for 45 minutes. Serve with rice. **Yield: 8 servings.**

Mildred R. Neal, Slippery Rock #1441

Easy Meat Loaf

1 1/2 pounds ground beef
1 10-ounce can chicken gumbo soup

Combine ground beef and soup in bowl; mix well. Spoon into loaf pan. Bake at 350 degrees for 1 hour. **Yield: 10 servings.**

Olga Boarts, Mt. Joy #537

Speckhackbraten (German Meat Loaf)

10 slices stale white bread, crusts trimmed
1 cup finely chopped onion
2 tablespoons finely chopped parsley
Lard for frying
2 pounds ground beef
7 slices bacon, cut into 1-inch pieces
1/2 carrot, minced
2 tablespoons flour
2 eggs
2 teaspoons salt
1/8 teaspoon pepper
3 slices bacon, cut into halves
1 onion, minced
2 tablespoons flour
1 tomato, sliced
4 cups boiling soup stock
Salt and pepper to taste

Soak bread in cold water in bowl for 30 seconds; squeeze out moisture. Sauté chopped onion and parsley in lard in skillet until onion is translucent. Combine bread, sautéed mixture, ground beef, bacon pieces, carrot, 2 tablespoons flour, eggs, 2 teaspoons salt and 1/8 teaspoon pepper in bowl; mix well. Shape into loaf. Place in greased roasting pan. Press bacon halves firmly across top of loaf. Bake at 375 degrees for 1 hour or until cooked through. Remove meat loaf to warm serving platter. Place roasting pan on stove. Add additional lard to pan drippings if necessary to measure 2 to 3 tablespoons liquid. Cook minced onion in drippings until brown. Add 2 tablespoons flour; mix well. Cook until brown. Add tomato; mash with fork. Cook for 2 to 3 minutes longer. Add soup stock slowly; stir well with fork. Simmer for 5 minutes. Strain gravy and serve with meat loaf. **Yield: 12 servings.**

Mary Lehman, Pine Grove Area #2090

Meat Loaf in Crust

2 pounds ground beef
1/4 cup chopped onion
2 eggs, slightly beaten
1/2 cup dry bread crumbs
1/2 cup chili sauce
1/2 teaspoon salt
1/4 teaspoon pepper
1 teaspoon Worcestershire sauce
1 tablespoon water
1 8-count can crescent rolls
1 egg white, slightly beaten

Combine ground beef, onion, eggs, bread crumbs, chili sauce, salt, pepper, Worcestershire sauce and water in bowl; mix well. Shape into loaf. Place in shallow baking pan. Bake at 350 degrees for 50 minutes to 1 hour or until cooked through. Cool for 10 minutes. Remove to baking sheet. Roll dough into 10x15-inch rectangle. Place over loaf; trim excess. Brush with egg white. Bake for 20 to 25 minutes longer or until golden brown. **Yield: 12 servings.**

Jean H. Hertzog, Pioneer #1777

Meat Loaf Dinner

2 pounds ground beef
1 cup cracker meal or dry bread crumbs
1 onion, grated
1 8-ounce can tomato sauce
3 eggs
1 teaspoon salt
1 teaspoon pepper
3 to 4 carrots, peeled, cut into halves
3 to 4 potatoes, peeled, cut into halves
1 onion, chopped
1 green bell pepper, sliced (optional)
4 cups water
1 to 2 tablespoons catsup
2 teaspoons Gravy Master or Kitchen Bouquet
1 to 2 teaspoons sugar
Salt and pepper to taste

Combine ground beef, cracker meal, grated onion, 1/3 can tomato sauce, eggs, 1 teaspoon salt and 1 teaspoon pepper in bowl; mix well. Shape into oval loaf. Place in small roasting pan or Dutch oven. Surround with carrots, potatoes, chopped onion and green pepper. Mix water, catsup, Gravy Master, half the remaining tomato sauce and sugar in bowl. Pour over vegetables, leaving top of loaf dry. Spread loaf with remaining tomato sauce. Sprinkle vegetables with salt and pepper. Bake, covered, at 350 degrees for 1 to 1 1/2 hours or until cooked through. **Yield: 8 servings.**

Margaret Verbeke, Reynoldsville #1825

Add sage sparingly to meat loaves for a different flavor.
Sage is the leaf of a shrub grown in Greece and Yugoslavia.

Sicilian Meat Roll

2 eggs, beaten
1 cup soft bread crumbs
2/3 cup tomato sauce
2 tablespoons chopped parsley
1/2 teaspoon crushed oregano
1/4 teaspoon salt
1/4 teaspoon pepper
1 small clove of garlic, minced
2 pounds lean ground beef
8 thin slices boiled ham
1 1/2 cups shredded mozzarella cheese
3 slices mozzarella cheese, cut into halves diagonally

Combine eggs, bread crumbs, tomato sauce, parsley, oregano, salt, pepper and garlic in bowl; mix well. Add ground beef; mix well. Pat into 10x12-inch rectangle on waxed paper. Top with ham slices, leaving small margin around edges. Sprinkle with shredded cheese. Roll up from short end; seal edges and ends. Place seam side down in 9x13-inch baking pan. Bake at 350 degrees for 55 minutes to 1 hour or until cooked through. Top with cheese slices. Bake for 3 to 5 minutes longer or until cheese is melted. **Yield: 10 servings.**

Helen McIlwain, Spring Church #1803

Stuffed Meat Loaf

1/2 cup chopped onion
1/2 cup chopped celery
2 tablespoons butter
4 cups dry bread cubes
1/2 teaspoon salt
1/4 teaspoon pepper
3 pounds ground beef
1 envelope onion soup mix
1/3 cup catsup
1 egg
2 tablespoons (or more) water

Sauté onion and celery in butter in skillet until tender. Add bread, salt and pepper; mix well. Set aside. Combine ground beef, soup mix, catsup, egg and water in bowl; mix well. Place 3/4 of the ground beef mixture into casserole. Shape to bottom and sides of dish. Spread onion mixture over loaf. Top with remaining ground beef mixture. Bake, covered, at 350 degrees for 1 hour and 15 minutes. Serve with onion soup gravy and mashed potatoes. **Yield: 12 servings.**

Mary Jo Wojton, Mt. Joy #537

Meat loaf will not stick if you place a slice of bacon on the bottom of the baking pan.

Stuffed Beef Logs

$1^1/_2$ pounds lean ground beef
$^3/_4$ cup fine dry bread crumbs
$^1/_2$ cup finely chopped onion
1 egg, lightly beaten
1 teaspoon salt
4 teaspoons Worcestershire sauce
6 sticks Cheddar cheese
6 slices bacon
8 teaspoons Worcestershire sauce

Combine ground beef, bread crumbs, onion, egg, salt and 4 teaspoons Worcestershire sauce in bowl; mix well. Divide into 6 portions. Shape each portion into roll around a cheese stick. Wrap with bacon slices. Place in foil-lined baking pan. Brush with 8 teaspoons Worcestershire sauce. Bake at 475 degrees for 15 to 18 minutes or until cooked through. **Yield: 6 servings.**

Mary Hepfer, Shermanata #1796

Vegetable Soup Meat Loaf

1 pound ground beef
1 10-ounce can vegetable soup
$^1/_2$ cup bread crumbs
2 tablespoons flour
1 tablespoon minced parsley
1 egg, beaten
$^1/_8$ teaspoon Mrs. Dash seasoning or pepper
4 slices bacon (optional)

Combine ground beef, soup, bread crumbs, flour, parsley, egg and seasoning in bowl; mix well. Shape into loaf. Place 2 slices bacon in baking pan. Add meat loaf. Top with 2 slices bacon. Bake at 350 degrees for 45 minutes to 1 hour or until cooked through. May add $^1/_4$ cup each finely chopped onion, celery and green bell pepper. **Yield: 8 servings.**

Mary Lou Templin, Millers Run #2020

Moore than Beans

1 pound ground beef
8 ounces bacon, chopped
1 onion, chopped
$^1/_3$ cup packed brown sugar
$^1/_3$ cup sugar
$^1/_4$ cup catsup
$^1/_4$ cup barbecue sauce
2 tablespoons prepared mustard
2 tablespoons molasses
$^1/_2$ teaspoon salt
$^1/_2$ teaspoon chili powder
$^1/_2$ teaspoon pepper
1 16-ounce can kidney beans, drained
1 16-ounce can pork and beans
1 40-ounce can butter beans

Brown ground beef and bacon in skillet; drain. Add onion. Cook until onion is tender. Add brown sugar, sugar, catsup, barbecue sauce, mustard, molasses, salt, chili powder and pepper; mix well. Stir in beans. Spoon into 3-quart casserole. Bake at 350 degrees for 1 hour. Enjoy this Moore Township recipe. **Yield: 8 servings.**

Ethel Schlegel, Star #993

Pepperoni and Ground Beef Casserole

8 ounces shell macaroni
8 ounces ground beef
1 teaspoon salt
1/8 teaspoon pepper
1 teaspoon minced fresh parsley or 1/4 teaspoon dried parsley
1 24-ounce jar spaghetti sauce
1 4-ounce can tomato sauce
1 4-ounce can mushrooms
4 ounces pepperoni, sliced
1 cup grated Parmesan cheese
8 ounces mozzarella cheese, shredded

Cook macaroni using package directions; drain and rinse. Brown ground beef in skillet, stirring until crumbly; drain. Add salt, pepper and parsley. Stir in spaghetti sauce and tomato sauce. Cook until heated through. Add mushrooms, pepperoni, Parmesan cheese and half the mozzarella; mix well. Stir in macaroni. Spoon into 3-quart casserole. Top with remaining mozzarella cheese. Bake at 350 degrees for 30 minutes. **Yield: 6 servings.**

Mary Bibel, Mendon #855

Summer Stuffed Peppers

8 yellow, green or red bell peppers
1 1/2 pounds lean ground beef
1/2 clove of garlic, minced
1 onion, minced
1/2 cup finely chopped cabbage
1 carrot, shredded
1/2 cup shredded zucchini
1 28-ounce can chopped tomatoes
1/2 cup uncooked long grain rice
1 tablespoon brown sugar
1/4 teaspoon dried basil
Pepper to taste

Cut tops from peppers; remove stems from tops. Chop enough of the tops to measure 1/3 cup. Remove seed and membranes from bell peppers. Cook peppers in saucepan in boiling water to cover until tender-crisp; rinse with cold water. Brown ground beef in skillet over medium heat, stirring until crumbly; drain. Add garlic, onion, cabbage, carrot, zucchini and chopped bell pepper. Sauté until vegetables are tender. Add tomatoes with juice, rice, brown sugar, basil and pepper; mix well. Simmer, covered, over low heat for 20 minutes or until rice is tender. Spoon hot mixture into peppers. Serve on platter garnished with parsley leaves or sprigs of mint.
Yield: 8 servings.

Willowa Gates, Corry #55

To make a quick Meat Loaf Wellington, cover meat loaf with refrigerator crescent dinner rolls for last 15 minutes of baking time.

Super-Quick Stuffed Peppers

12 ounces ground beef
1 small onion, chopped
1 15-ounce can red kidney beans, drained
1 8-ounce can tomato sauce
1/2 teaspoon sugar
1/4 teaspoon thyme
1/8 teaspoon pepper
Salt to taste
3 large green bell peppers
1 teaspoon salt
1/2 cup water
1 tablespoon cornstarch
2 tablespoons shredded Cheddar cheese

Cook ground beef and onion in 3-quart saucepan over medium-high heat for 10 minutes or until brown and tender, stirring occasionally. Add beans, tomato sauce, sugar, thyme, pepper and salt to taste; mix well. Bring to a boil; reduce heat. Simmer for 10 minutes. Cut peppers into halves; discard seeds. Place in 12-inch skillet. Add 1/2 inch water and 1 teaspoon salt. Bring to a boil over high heat; reduce heat. Simmer for 5 minutes or until tender-crisp; drain. Stir mixture of 1/2 cup water and cornstarch into ground beef mixture. Cook until thickened. Place peppers cut side up on warm platter. Spoon meat mixture into peppers. Sprinkle with cheese. **Yield: 6 servings.**

Connie Shreck, White Deer #122

Country Pie

1/2 cup tomato sauce
1/2 cup bread crumbs
1 pound ground beef
1/4 cup chopped onion
1/4 cup chopped green bell pepper
1/2 teaspoon salt
1/8 teaspoon pepper
1/8 teaspoon vinegar
1 1/3 cups minute rice
1 cup water
1 1/2 cups tomato sauce
1 cup shredded Cheddar cheese
1/2 teaspoon salt

Combine 1/2 cup tomato sauce, bread crumbs, ground beef, onion, green pepper, 1/2 teaspoon salt, pepper and vinegar in bowl; mix well. Pat into 9-inch pie plate, fluting edge. Mix rice, water, 1 1/2 cups tomato sauce, cheese and 1/2 teaspoon salt in bowl. Spoon into prepared pie plate. Bake at 350 degrees for 25 minutes. **Yield: 6 servings.**

Helen Redic, Mt. Pleasant #1687

Reduce cholesterol and add variety in your recipes by substituting ground turkey for all or part of ground beef.

Quick Crescent Taco Pie

1 8-count can crescent rolls
1 cup crushed corn chips
1 1/2 pounds ground beef
1 envelope taco seasoning mix
1/2 cup water
1/2 cup mild chunky salsa
1 cup sour cream
6 slices American cheese
1/2 cup crushed corn chips

Press dough into 10-inch pie plate; seal perforations. Sprinkle with 1 cup corn chips. Brown ground beef in skillet, stirring until crumbly; drain. Add seasoning mix, water and salsa. Simmer for 5 minutes. Spoon over corn chips. Spread with sour cream. Cover with cheese slices. Sprinkle with 1/2 cup corn chips. Bake at 375 degrees for 20 minutes or until golden brown. **Yield: 6 servings.**

Alma Kenny, Westfield #1514

Ground Beef Pie

3/4 cup chopped onion
2 tablespoons oil
1 1/2 cups flour
1 1/2 teaspoons baking powder
1/2 teaspoon salt
1 teaspoon celery seed
1/4 cup shortening
1 egg
1/3 cup cold milk
1 onion, chopped
1 pound ground beef
3/4 teaspoon salt
1/8 teaspoon pepper
2 cups green beans, drained
1 16-ounce can corn, drained
1 10-ounce can tomato soup

Cook 3/4 cup onion in oil in skillet until tender. Sift flour, baking powder and salt together. Stir in celery seed. Cut in shortening until crumbly. Stir in cooked onion. Add mixture of egg and milk gradually, stirring until dough is moistened. Turn onto floured board. Knead for 30 seconds. Roll out; cut with biscuit cutter. Cook remaining onion in skillet until tender. Add ground beef, salt and pepper; mix well. Cook until lightly browned. Add green beans, corn and soup. Bring to a boil. Spoon into greased 3-quart casserole. Top with biscuits. Bake at 450 degrees for 10 to 15 minutes or until biscuits are done. **Yield: 8 servings.**

Velma Sandrock, Red Brush Community #2085

Keep dried mushrooms, mushroom flakes or mushroom powder on the shelf to use in main dish recipes when you have no fresh mushrooms.

Meat Crust Pie

1 pound ground beef
1 cup soft bread crumbs
1/2 cup milk
1 tablespoon chopped onion
1 tablespoon Worcestershire sauce
3/4 teaspoon salt
1/8 teaspoon pepper
2 cups cooked mixed vegetables
1 cup cooked tomatoes, drained
Cooked green pepper rings

Mix first 7 ingredients in bowl. Pack into 9-inch pie plate, covering bottom and side. Top with second pie plate. Bake at 350 degrees for 7 minutes. Remove top pie plate. Bake for 3 minutes longer. Spoon mixed vegetables and tomatoes over prepared meat crust. Top with pepper rings. Bake for 20 minutes longer. **Yield: 6 servings.**

Frances A. Hoffman, Northumberland #218

Beef Upside-Down Pie

2 1/2 tablespoons shortening
1/4 cup sliced onion
1 10-ounce can tomato soup
8 ounces lean ground beef
1 1/2 cups flour
1 tablespoon baking powder
1 teaspoon salt
1 teaspoon paprika
1 teaspoon dried celery
1/4 teaspoon pepper
2 1/2 tablespoons shortening
3/4 cup milk or water

Melt 2 1/2 tablespoons shortening in 9-inch skillet. Add onion. Cook until tender. Add soup and ground beef. Bring to a boil. Sift flour, baking powder, salt, paprika, celery and pepper together. Add 2 1/2 tablespoons shortening; mix well. Stir in milk. Spread over ground beef mixture. Bake at 425 degrees for 20 minutes or until heated through. Invert onto serving plate. **Yield: 8 servings.**

Dot Cupper, Sebring #1047

Cheeseburger Pizza

2 10-count cans biscuits
12 ounces ground beef
1/2 onion, chopped
Chopped mushrooms to taste
Chopped green bell pepper to taste
1 10-ounce can Cheddar cheese soup
1 teaspoon prepared mustard
Hot pepper sauce to taste
Salt, pepper, oregano and basil to taste
1 8-ounce can chopped tomatoes, drained
1/2 cup shredded mozzarella cheese
1/2 cup grated Parmesan cheese

Spread dough in 12-inch circle on greased baking sheet or pizza pan. Bake at 400 degrees for 10 minutes. Brown ground beef with onion in skillet, stirring frequently. Add mushrooms and green pepper. Cook for 2 minutes; drain. Stir in soup, mustard, hot pepper sauce and seasonings. Spread over prepared crust, leaving 1/2-inch margin. Top with tomatoes and cheeses. Bake at 400 degrees for 5 minutes or until edge is golden brown. **Yield: 6 servings.**

Inez Wise, Progress #96

Pizza Cups

1 10-count can biscuits
12 ounces ground beef
1 8-ounce can tomato paste
1 tablespoon minced onion
1/2 teaspoon salt
Italian seasoning to taste (optional)
1/2 to 3/4 cup shredded mozzarella cheese

Press dough into and up sides of greased muffin cups. Brown ground beef in skillet; drain. Add tomato paste, onion, salt and seasoning; mix well. Cook over low heat for 5 minutes, stirring frequently. Fill muffin cups with 1/4 cup ground beef mixture. Sprinkle with cheese. Bake at 400 degrees for 12 minutes. **Yield: 12 servings.**

Jean Ruhlman, Hemlock #2051

Pop-Up Pizza

1 1/2 pounds ground beef
1 cup chopped onion
1 cup chopped green bell pepper
1 clove of garlic, minced, or garlic salt to taste
1/2 teaspoon oregano
1/8 teaspoon salt
1/2 cup water
1/8 teaspoon hot sauce
1 2/3 cups tomato sauce
1 envelope spaghetti sauce mix
6 to 8 slices mozzarella cheese
1 cup milk
1 tablespoon oil
2 eggs
1 cup flour
1/2 teaspoon salt
1/2 cup grated Parmesan cheese

Brown ground beef in large skillet; drain. Add onion, green pepper, garlic, oregano, 1/8 teaspoon salt, water, hot sauce, tomato sauce and spaghetti sauce mix; mix well. Simmer for 10 minutes, stirring occasionally. Spoon into ungreased 9x13-inch baking pan. Top with cheese slices. Combine milk, oil and eggs in mixer bowl; beat at medium speed for 1 minute. Add flour and 1/2 teaspoon salt; beat for 2 minutes longer or until smooth. Pour over cheese slices, covering completely. Sprinkle with grated cheese. Bake at 400 degrees for 25 to 30 minutes or until puffed and deep golden brown. Serve immediately. **Yield: 10 servings.**

Betty Ankney, Somerset #1697

One of the best ways to remove fat from ground beef is to microwave it in a colander. Place a bowl under the colander to collect the fat as it cooks out of the beef.

German Pizza

1 pound ground beef
1/2 onion, chopped
1/2 green bell pepper, chopped
1/2 teaspoon salt
1/2 teaspoon pepper
2 tablespoons butter or margarine
6 potatoes, peeled, finely shredded
1 teaspoon salt
3 eggs, beaten
1/3 cup milk
2 cups shredded Cheddar or mozzarella cheese

Brown ground beef with onion, green pepper, 1/2 teaspoon salt and pepper in skillet over medium heat; drain and remove from skillet. Melt butter in skillet over low heat. Spread potatoes over melted butter. Sprinkle with 1 teaspoon salt. Top with ground beef mixture. Pour mixture of eggs and milk over all. Cook, covered, for 30 minutes or until potatoes are tender. Top with cheese. Cook, covered, for 15 minutes or until cheese is melted. Cut into wedges or squares to serve. **Yield: 6 servings.**

Virginia Hay, Hillcrest, #1674

Pizza Casserole

8 ounces noodles
8 ounces sausage
1 1/2 pounds ground beef
1/2 cup chopped onion
1/2 cup chopped green bell pepper
1/2 teaspoon Italian seasoning
1 8-ounce can pizza sauce
1 16-ounce jar spaghetti sauce
1 tablespoon Worcestershire sauce
1 4-ounce can mushrooms
1 teaspoon basil
1 cup shredded Cheddar cheese
8 ounces mozzarella cheese, shredded
1/4 cup grated Parmesan cheese
8 ounces pepperoni, sliced

Cook noodles using package directions; drain. Brown sausage and ground beef in skillet, stirring frequently; drain. Add onion, green pepper and Italian seasoning; mix well. Cook for 15 minutes. Add pizza sauce, spaghetti sauce, Worcestershire sauce, mushrooms and basil; mix well. Simmer for 15 minutes. Layer half the noodles, half the sauce, Cheddar cheese, remaining noodles, remaining sauce, mozzarella cheese, Parmesan cheese and pepperoni in 9x12-inch baking dish. Bake at 350 degrees for 35 minutes. **Yield: 8 servings.**

Ruth E. Gruber, Stony Point, #1694

Bake meat loaf in greased muffin cups for a speedy supper. Cooking time will be reduced and individual servings will be ready.

Baked Spaghetti Supper

7 ounces spaghetti
1 envelope onion soup mix
1 tablespoon flour
1 cup sour cream
1 pound ground beef
2 tablespoons butter
1/4 cup flour
2/3 cup instant nonfat dry milk powder
1/2 teaspoon salt
1/8 teaspoon pepper
2 cups water
Buttered bread crumbs

Cook spaghetti using package directions; drain. Mix half the soup mix, 1 tablespoon flour and sour cream in bowl. Stir into spaghetti. Spoon into 2-quart buttered casserole, making well in center. Brown ground beef in butter in skillet, stirring occasionally; remove from heat. Add 1/4 cup flour, dry milk powder, salt, pepper and remaining soup mix; mix well. Stir in water gradually. Cook until thickened, stirring constantly. Spoon onto center of spaghetti. Top with crumbs. Bake at 350 degrees for 25 minutes or until crumbs are browned. **Yield: 6 servings.**

Mary Mood, Briar Creek #146

Baked Ham Slice Sauterne

1 3-pound ham slice
1/2 cup packed brown sugar
3 tablespoons cornstarch
1 1/2 cups water
1 tablespoon margarine
1/2 cup raisins
1/2 cup Sauterne

Place ham in large skillet; add enough water to cover. Bring to a boil. Remove ham; place in greased baking dish. Combine brown sugar and cornstarch in small saucepan. Add 1 1/2 cups water and margarine. Cook for 5 minutes over medium heat, stirring constantly. Remove from heat. Stir in raisins and Sauterne. Pour sauce over ham. Bake at 350 degrees for 45 minutes or until ham is done.
Yield: 4 to 6 servings.

Jean Thompson, Mt. Pleasant #1687

Breaded Ham Croquettes

2 cups ground cooked ham
1 cup mashed potatoes
1 tablespoon chopped onion
1 tablespoon chopped parsley
Salt and pepper to taste
1 tablespoon water
1 egg, beaten
1/2 to 1 cup fine dry bread crumbs

Combine ham, potatoes, onion, parsley, salt and pepper in bowl; mix well. Chill in refrigerator until firm. Shape into 8 croquettes. Beat water and egg in small bowl. Dip croquettes in egg mixture; coat with bread crumbs. Fry in a small amount of hot oil in skillet until golden brown. **Yield: 4 servings.**

Colleen R. Shields, Avis #1959

Broccoli and Ham Roll-Ups

6 to 8 slices cooked ham
6 to 8 slices Swiss cheese
1 10-ounce package frozen broccoli spears, thawed
1/2 cup chopped onion
2 tablespoons margarine
2 tablespoons flour
1/2 teaspoon salt
1/4 teaspoon basil
1/8 teaspoon pepper
1 cup milk

Layer each ham slice with Swiss cheese. Place broccoli spears in center; roll up to enclose, securing with wooden picks if necessary. Place in shallow baking dish. Sauté onion in margarine until tender. Stir in flour, salt, basil and pepper. Add milk. Cook over low heat until thickened, stirring constantly. Pour sauce over ham rolls. Bake, covered, at 350 degrees for 25 minutes. **Yield: 6 to 8 servings.**

Thelma Waskie, Roaring Creek Valley #2041

Ham Balls in Dill Sauce

1 pound ground ham
1 pound ground pork
1/2 cup cornflake crumbs
1/4 cup finely chopped onion
1/2 cup milk
2 eggs, beaten
1 teaspoon prepared mustard
1/8 teaspoon pepper
2 tablespoons butter
2 tablespoons flour
1/2 teaspoon salt
1 cup milk
1/2 cup sour cream
1 tablespoon prepared mustard
1/2 teaspoon dillweed

Combine ham, pork, cornflake crumbs, onion, 1/2 cup milk, eggs, 1 teaspoon mustard and pepper in bowl; mix well. Shape into 24 balls. Place in greased shallow baking pan. Bake at 350 degrees for 30 to 40 minutes or until cooked through; drain. Melt butter in saucepan. Stir in flour and salt to form paste. Add milk. Cook over low heat until thickened and smooth, stirring constantly. Stir in sour cream, mustard and dillweed. Cook over very low heat until heated through, stirring frequently. Spoon over ham balls. Serve as Easter dinner with fresh asparagus. May prepare as appetizer by making small ham balls using 1 teaspoon mixture for each. Serve with dill sauce as a dip. **Yield: 6 servings.**

Jenny Nicklin, Hemlock #2051

Chop leftover ham and add to macaroni and cheese, scrambled eggs, quiche or dried beans or lentils.

Ham and Cauliflower Casserole

1 10-ounce package frozen cauliflower
1 cup chopped cooked ham
1 tablespoon butter
1 tablespoon flour
1/2 teaspoon salt
1/8 teaspoon pepper
3/4 cup milk
1/4 cup crushed crackers
1 to 2 tablespoons grated Parmesan or American cheese

Cook cauliflower using package directions; drain. Place in buttered 1-quart baking dish. Sprinkle with ham. Melt butter in saucepan. Stir in flour, salt and pepper. Add milk gradually. Cook over low heat until thickened and smooth, stirring constantly. pour over ham and cauliflower. Sprinkle with cracker crumbs and cheese. Bake at 350 degrees for 30 minutes or until golden. **Yield: 3 to 4 servings.**

Jean Wagoner, Chippewa #1592

Ham and Cheese Casserole

16 slices pullman bread
2 tablespoons (about) butter
8 slices sharp cheese
8 slices boiled ham
6 eggs
3 cups milk
1/2 teaspoon dry mustard
1 4-ounce can mushrooms, drained
1 cup crushed cornflakes
1/2 cup melted butter

Butter bread on one side. Place 8 slices in greased 9x13-inch baking dish. Top with cheese, ham and remaining bread, buttered side up. Combine eggs, milk and mustard in bowl; mix well. Pour over top layer. Chill, covered, overnight. Sprinkle top with mushrooms and cornflakes. Drizzle with melted butter. Bake at 350 degrees for 45 minutes. Let stand for 15 minutes before serving. **Yield: 8 servings.**

Doris Munsch, Mt. Nebo #1872

Ham Crêpes Ensenada

12 thin slices ham
12 flour tortillas
1 pound Monterey Jack cheese, cut into 1/2-inch sticks
1 4-ounce can green chilies, cut into 1/4-inch strips
1/2 cup flour
1/2 cup melted butter
1 quart milk
3 cups shredded Cheddar cheese
1 teaspoon prepared mustard
1/2 teaspoon salt
1/8 teaspoon pepper
Paprika to taste

Place 1 slice ham on each tortilla. Top each with 1 stick Monterey Jack cheese and 1 chili strip. Roll up; secure with wooden picks. Place in greased 9x13-inch baking pan. Stir flour into melted butter in saucepan. Add milk, Cheddar cheese, mustard, salt and pepper. Cook until blended and smooth, stirring frequently. Pour over crepes. Sprinkle with paprika. Bake at 350 degrees for 45 minutes. **Yield: 6 servings.**

Susan Tau, Hayfield #800

Ham and Sweet Potato Hash

1 pound cooked ham, cut into ½-inch chunks
1½ cups cubed, cooked sweet potatoes
2 medium onions, minced
½ large green bell pepper, chopped
1 tablespoon chopped fresh basil
Salt and freshly ground pepper to taste
¾ cup heavy cream
3 tablespoons butter
4 to 6 poached eggs
Chopped parsley

Combine ham, sweet potatoes, onions, green pepper, basil, salt, pepper and cream in bowl; mix well. Melt butter in large heavy skillet over medium heat. Spread mixture evenly in skillet. Cook for 10 minutes over low heat until browned and crusty. Transfer to platter, browned side up. Top with poached egg per person and parsley. **Yield: 4 to 6 servings.**

Lois M. Pifer, Henderson #1315

Ham and Tater Logs

1 small onion, chopped
1 cup mashed potatoes
½ cup chopped cooked ham
1 egg, beaten
½ cup flour
½ cup bread crumbs
¼ cup oil

Sauté onion in nonstick skillet until tender. Combine with potatoes, ham, egg and flour in bowl; mix well. Shape mixture into 2- or 3-inch logs. Roll in bread crumbs. Fry in oil in skillet until browned, turning once. May substitute cooked ground beef, crumbled bacon or cooked sausage for ham. **Yield: 4 servings.**

June K. Marzani, Unity #1710

Ham Loaf

1 pound ground ham
1 pound ground pork
½ cup milk
2 cups cornflakes
2 eggs, beaten
1 8-ounce can crushed pineapple

Combine ham, pork, milk, cornflakes and eggs in bowl; mix well. Shape into loaf; place in loaf pan. Bake at 350 degrees for 1 hour. Pour crushed pineapple over top of ham loaf. Bake for 30 minutes longer. **Yield: 6 to 8 servings.**

Anna Mae Sollers, Shavers Creek #353

Very Popular Ham Loaf

$1\frac{1}{4}$ pounds ground ham
12 ounces ground pork
$\frac{1}{2}$ teaspoon pepper
$\frac{1}{2}$ teaspoon onion salt
1 teaspoon dry mustard
1 tablespoon brown sugar
2 eggs, beaten
2 large shredded wheat cereal biscuits
$\frac{3}{4}$ cup milk
1 tablespoon dry mustard
$\frac{1}{4}$ cup water
$\frac{1}{2}$ cup packed brown sugar
$\frac{1}{4}$ cup vinegar

Combine ham, pork, pepper, onion salt, 1 teaspoon dry mustard, 1 tablespoon brown sugar and eggs in bowl; mix well. Soak wheat biscuits in enough milk to make 1 cup. Pour into ham mixture; mix well. Shape into loaf; place in loaf pan. Combine 1 tablespoon mustard, water, $\frac{1}{2}$ cup brown sugar and vinegar in small bowl, stirring until sugar is dissolved. Brush over ham loaf. Bake at 325 degrees for $1\frac{1}{2}$ hours, basting occasionally with brown sugar sauce. **Yield: 6 to 8 servings.**

Helen Broadbent, Shavers Creek #353

Pineapple Upside-Down Ham Loaf

3 tablespoons butter
$\frac{1}{3}$ cup packed light brown sugar
6 to 8 pineapple slices
6 to 8 maraschino cherries
1 pound ground cooked ham
10 ounces ground pork
2 cups bread crumbs
2 eggs, beaten
1 cup milk
1 teaspoon salt
$\frac{1}{8}$ teaspoon pepper
$\frac{1}{2}$ teaspoon dry mustard

Melt butter in saucepan. Stir in brown sugar. Pour into 8x8-inch pan. Place pineapple slices over sugar mixture with cherry in center. Combine ham, pork, bread crumbs, eggs, milk, salt, pepper and mustard in bowl; mix well. Spread evenly over pineapple slices. Bake at 350 degrees for $1\frac{1}{2}$ hours. Invert onto serving platter. Cut into squares to serve. **Yield: 6 servings.**

Jerri Reppert, Deemston #1372

One-Dish Ham Dinner

1 4-ounce package rice
1 16-ounce can yams
3 slices cooked ham
$\frac{1}{4}$ cup raisins
$\frac{1}{3}$ cup pineapple
$\frac{1}{3}$ cup pineapple juice
$\frac{1}{4}$ teaspoon ground cloves
8 marshmallows

Cook rice using package directions. Spread in buttered $2\frac{1}{2}$-quart casserole. Arrange yams around edge of casserole. Place ham slices in middle. Combine raisins, pineapple, pineapple juice, cloves and marshmallows in saucepan. Cook over low heat until warmed through, stirring frequently. Pour over ham and yams. Bake, covered, at 350 degrees for 35 to 40 minutes. **Yield: 4 servings.**

Tami Iman, Jackson #1506

Hawaiian Ham Patties

1½ pounds ground cooked, smoked ham
1 teaspoon grated onion
1 tablespoon chopped parsley
1 tablespoon prepared mustard
1 egg, beaten
2 tablespoons pineapple juice
8 pineapple slices
½ cup crushed cornflakes

Combine ham, onion, parsley, mustard, egg and pineapple juice in large bowl; mix well. Shape into 8 patties. Roll in crushed cornflakes. Place pineapple slices in 8x10-inch shallow baking dish. Place ham patty on each slice. Bake at 375 degrees for 30 minutes. **Yield: 8 servings.**

Dorothy Dengate, Logans Valley #664

Ham Cream Potato Scallops

5 pounds potatoes
3 tablespoons butter
¼ cup flour
¼ cup chopped onions
½ cup chopped celery
1 pound chopped cooked ham
1 10-ounce can chicken broth
¼ cup mayonnaise
1 cup American cheese spread
Salt and pepper to taste

Boil potatoes in water until partially done. Cool, peel and slice ¼ inch thick. Layer in greased 2-quart casserole. Melt butter in saucepan. Stir in flour to blend. Add onions, celery, ham, chicken broth, mayonnaise and cheese spread; mix well. Cook over medium heat until thickened, stirring constantly. Stir in salt and pepper. Spoon over potatoes; toss well. Bake at 275 degrees for 1 hour. **Yield: 6 to 8 servings.**

Mary Lou Wilson, Bradford #1219

Schnitz 'n Gnepp

2 to 3 cups dried apple schnitz
1½ pounds smoked ham
4 cups water
Salt to taste
3 tablespoons brown sugar
2 potatotes, cubed (optional)
1½ cups flour
2 teaspoons baking powder
1 egg, beaten
Milk

Soak apple schnitz for 2 to 3 hours. Cook ham in 4 cups water until done. Add schnitz, salt, brown sugar and potatoes, stirring well. Remove ham and set aside. Combine flour, baking powder and egg in bowl; mix well. Stir in enough milk to moisten. Drop gnepp by tablespoonfuls into ham broth. Simmer for 10 minutes. Simmer, tightly covered, for 10 minutes longer. May add a small amount of milk to broth before adding gnepp. **Yield: 4 to 5 servings.**

Mrs. Sherwood Lerch, Harmony #1692

Lamb à la King

1/2 cup canned mushrooms
3 tablespoons melted butter
3 tablespoons flour
1 1/4 cups scalded milk
Salt and pepper to taste
2 cups chopped cooked lamb
2 tablespoons chopped pimento
1 green bell pepper, chopped
1 egg yolk, well beaten

Brown mushrooms in 1 tablespoon butter in skillet; set aside. Combine remaining melted butter, flour and milk in top of double boiler. Cook until thick and smooth, stirring constantly. Add salt, pepper, mushrooms, lamb, pimento and green pepper; mix well. Cook until mixture begins to boil; remove from heat. Stir a small amount of hot mixture into beaten egg yolk. Beat egg yolk into hot mixture. Bring to a boil, stirring constantly. Serve over buttered toast, patty shells or with border of mashed potatoes or rice. **Yield: 6 servings.**

Helena B. Latshaw, Ontelaunee #1617

Baked Liver

1 1/2 pounds beef liver, trimmed
Flour
Paprika to taste
Bacon drippings
1 large onion, thinly sliced
1 1/2 cups water
2 beef bouillon cubes
2 teaspoons Worcestershire sauce
1/2 cup catsup

Rinse liver and pat dry. Coat with mixture of flour and paprika. Brown quickly in bacon drippings in skillet. Remove liver to greased 2-quart baking dish, reserving pan drippings. Top with onion slices. Add water, bouillon cubes, Worcestershire sauce and catsup to bacon drippings; mix well. Pour over liver and onion slices. Bake, covered, at 350 degrees for 1 hour. **Yield: 4 servings.**

Arlene Kretzing, Mt. Dempsey #2083

Liver and Onions with Beef Bouillon

2 large onions, chopped
1 clove of garlic, minced
1 beef bouillon cube
1/2 cup water
1 tablespoon oil or margarine
4 slices beef liver

Combine onions, garlic, bouillon cube, water and oil in skillet. Cook over medium heat until onions are tender. Add liver and additional water if necessary. Simmer until liver is cooked through. **Yield: 4 servings.**

Rose Zorich, Carmichaels #1389

Pork Chop Casserole

4 thick-cut pork chops
1 teaspoon salt
1/8 teaspoon pepper
1/2 cup flour
2 tablespoons shortening
2/3 cup uncooked rice
3 cups boiling salted water
4 thick slices tomato
4 green bell pepper rings
4 thin slices onion
Salt and pepper to taste

Rinse pork chops. Sprinkle with 1 teaspoon salt and 1/8 teaspoon pepper; coat with flour. Brown on both sides in shortening in skillet. Place in greased 8x12-inch casserole; set aside. Rinse rice. Cook in salted water for 5 minutes. Pour rice and liquid into casserole around pork chops. Place a tomato slice, green pepper ring and onion slice on each pork chop. Season with salt and pepper. Bake at 350 degrees for 1 hour, adding additional water if necessary. **Yield: 4 servings.**

Laura Weaver, Fernwood #1329

Pork Chops à l'Orange

4 1-inch thick center-cut pork chops
Salt, pepper and paprika to taste
1/2 cup orange juice
5 tablespoons sugar
1 1/2 teaspoons cornstarch
1/4 teaspoon salt
1/4 teaspoon cinnamon
10 whole cloves
1/2 cup orange juice
4 to 6 orange slices

Trim fat from pork chops. Render fat over low heat in skillet; discard, reserving drippings. Sprinkle pork chops with salt, pepper and paprika. Cook over medium-high heat in reserved drippings until golden brown on both sides. Reduce heat to low; add 1/2 cup orange juice. Simmer, tightly covered, for 45 minutes to 1 hour or until tender, turning chops occasionally. Combine sugar, cornstarch, 1/4 teaspoon salt, cinnamon, cloves and 1/2 cup orange juice in saucepan. Cook over medium heat until thick and clear, stirring constantly. Arrange pork chops on serving platter; pour orange sauce over top. Garnish with orange slices. **Yield: 4 servings.**

Aliene Thompson, Middletown #684

Pork 'n Corn Roast

4 to 6 pork chops
1 tablespoon prepared mustard
1 cup boiling water
2 cups cream-style corn
2/3 cup soft bread crumbs
2 tablespoons finely chopped onion
1 tablespoon finely chopped green bell pepper
1 teaspoon salt
1/2 teaspoon pepper

Spread pork chops with mustard. Brown on both sides in nonstick skillet; discard pan drippings. Place pork chops in 2-quart shallow baking dish. Pour in boiling water. Mix remaining ingredients in bowl. Spread over pork chops. Bake, covered, at 350 degrees for 15 minutes. Bake, uncovered, for 45 minutes or until tender. **Yield: 4 servings.**

Ruth Waltz, Bottle Run #1301

Pork and Sauerkraut

1 3-pound rib-end pork roast
Salt and pepper to taste
Flour
3 tablespoons oil
1 or 2 packages sauerkraut, drained
2 cups hot water

Sprinkle roast with salt, pepper and flour. Brown on all sides in oil in 6-quart Dutch oven. Add sauerkraut and water; cover. Bring to a boil; reduce heat to medium. Simmer, covered, for 2 1/2 hours or until cooked through. May substitute pork chops or spare ribs for pork roast. **Yield: 6 to 8 servings.**

Lucille Beck, Reynoldsville #1825

Slow-Cooker Barbecued Spareribs

4 pounds country-style spareribs
1 10-ounce can tomato soup
1/2 cup cider vinegar
1/2 cup packed brown sugar
1 tablespoon soy sauce
1 teaspoon celery seed
1 teaspoon salt
1 teaspoon chili powder

Cut spareribs into serving pieces. Layer in slow-cooker. Combine tomato soup, vinegar, brown sugar, soy sauce, celery seed, salt and chili powder in bowl; mix well. Pour mixture over spareribs. Cook, covered, on High for 6 to 8 hours. Skim fat from juices before serving. **Yield: 4 to 5 servings.**

Marcia McKelvey, Harveys #1444

Barbecued Ribs

1 to 2 pounds pork or beef ribs
Sliced onions
2 tablespoons white vinegar
2 tablespoons Worcestershire sauce
1/2 teaspoon salt
1 teaspoon paprika
1/2 teaspoon red pepper
1/2 teaspoon black pepper
2 teaspoons chili powder
2/3 cup catsup
2/3 cup water

Cut ribs into serving portions. Brown on both sides in skillet. Place in large baking pan; cover with sliced onions. Combine vinegar, Worcestershire sauce, salt, paprika, red pepper, black pepper, chili powder, catsup and water in bowl; mix well. Pour over ribs. Bake, covered with foil, at 350 degrees for 1 1/2 to 2 hours or until cooked through. **Yield: 4 servings.**

Patricia Scarpelli, Shaver's Creek #353

Pork Stir-Fry

2 tablespoons cornstarch
1¼ cups water
⅓ cup soy sauce
⅓ cup light or dark corn syrup
2 tablespoons corn oil
1 pound boneless pork, cut into thin strips
Garlic powder to taste
2 tablespoons corn oil
2 cups chopped broccoli flowerets
2 onions, cut into wedges
1 carrot, cut into 2-inch strips
8 ounces mushrooms, sliced

Combine cornstarch, water, soy sauce and corn syrup in bowl, stirring until smooth; set aside. Heat 2 tablespoons oil over medium-high heat in wok or large skillet. Sprinkle pork with garlic powder. Stir-fry for 5 minutes or until tender; remove pork from wok. Heat remaining 2 tablespoons oil. Add broccoli, onions and carrot strips. Stir-fry for 2 minutes. Add mushrooms. Stir-fry for 1 minute or until vegetables are tender-crisp. Add pork; pour prepared sauce over all. Bring to a boil; reduce heat to medium. Cook for 1 minute, stirring constantly. Serve over rice.
Yield: 4 to 6 servings.

Jane Reppert, Virginville #1832

Sweet and Sour Pork

2 to 3 pounds pork, cubed
2 eggs
½ teaspoon salt
½ teaspoon flour
3 tablespoons water
½ cup vinegar
½ cup packed brown sugar
2 tablespoons cornstarch
¾ cup water
1 8-ounce can pineapple chunks, drained
1 to 2 tomatoes, cut into wedges

Brown cubed pork on all sides in skillet; remove and set aside, reserving pan drippings. Beat eggs, salt, flour and 3 tablespoons water in bowl. Dip pork in mixture. Fry in skillet until golden brown; drain. Combine vinegar, brown sugar, cornstarch and ¾ cup water in saucepan; mix well. Simmer until heated through. Add pork cubes. Stir in pineapple just before serving. Garnish with tomato wedges.
Yield: 6 to 8 servings.

Trudy Wigton, Pleasant Hill #1505

Fresh lime served with pork dishes enhances the flavor.
It can also be used in marinades for grilled pork.

Festive Sweet and Sour Pork

1 pound lean pork, cut into strips
1/4 teaspoon salt
1/4 teaspoon pepper
2 tablespoons oil
1 20-ounce can juice-pack pineapple chunks
1/2 cup pineapple juice
2 tablespoons cornstarch
1/4 cup chicken broth
1/4 cup white vinegar
2 tablespoons sugar
2 tablespoons catsup
1 tablespoon soy sauce
1/4 teaspoon ground ginger
2 cups broccoli flowerets
1 red bell pepper, cut into chunks
4 scallions, cut in 1-inch lengths

Sprinkle pork with salt and pepper. Heat oil over medium-high heat in large skillet. Cook pork for 3 to 6 minutes or until cooked through, stirring constantly. Remove to warm platter; cover. Drain pineapple, reserving 1/2 cup juice. Add reserved juice and cornstarch to skillet, stirring well. Add chicken broth, vinegar, sugar, catsup, soy sauce and ginger; mix well. Cook over medium-low heat until mixture comes to a boil, stirring constantly. Add broccoli and red pepper. Simmer, covered, for 2 to 3 minutes. Add pineapple, scallions and pork. Simmer for 1 minute or until heated through. Serve over hot rice. **Yield: 4 servings.**

Helen Coughanour, Rostraver #919

Nana Sieben's Screpples

1 1/2 pounds lean pork
1 1/2 pounds beef
2 quarts water
3 teaspoons salt
2 teaspoons ground cloves
4 cups buckwheat flour
3 cups all-purpose flour
Butter

Force pork and beef together through food grinder. Place in 5-quart saucepan with water, salt and cloves. Cook over medium heat until done. Add buckwheat and all-purpose flours alternately a small amount at a time, stirring constantly until soft dough forms. Add more buckwheat flour if necessary for desired consistency. Remove form heat. Press mixture into loaf pans sprinkled with water. Chill until firm. Slice into 1/8 to 1/4-inch thickness. Fry in butter until browned. Serve with eggs or as main dish with vegetables. **Yield: 5 to 6 loaves.**

Doris L. Hough, Fulton #66

Spices usually associated with desserts, such as cinnamon and cloves, are delicious additions to pork dishes.

Creole Franks

3 slices bacon, chopped
1/3 cup chopped onion
2/3 cup pineapple juice
1/2 cup catsup
Dash of chili powder
1 pound hot dogs
2 tablespoons chopped green bell pepper

Fry bacon in skillet until partially cooked. Add onion. Sauté until tender. Stir in pineapple juice, catsup and chili powder; mix well. Score hot dogs diagonally at 1-inch intervals. Add to sauce. Cook, covered, until mixture comes to a boil; reduce heat. Add green pepper. Simmer for 8 to 10 minutes. **Yield: 6 servings.**

Janet Kelso, Vernon #936

Frankfurter Corn Bake

3 eggs, slightly beaten
1 cup fine dry bread crumbs
1/4 cup finely chopped onion
1 teaspoon salt
2 17-ounce cans cream-style corn
1 teaspoon dry mustard
6 to 8 frankfurters, cut into 1/2-inch pieces
Catsup

Combine eggs, bread crumbs, onion, salt, corn, mustard and 2/3 of the frankfurters in 2-quart casserole; mix well. Place remaining frankfurters on top. Bake at 375 degrees for 30 minutes or until knife inserted in center comes out clean. Garnish with catsup. **Yield: 6 to 8 servings.**

Lillian Schlegel, Virginville #1832

Hot Dogs in Blankets

1 pound hot dogs
Pickle relish to taste
8 slices bread, crusts trimmed
8 slices bacon

Slit hot dogs lengthwise; fill with pickle relish. Wrap bread around each hot dog. Roll bacon over bread. Place on baking sheet. Bake at 400 degrees for 15 minutes. **Yield: 8 servings.**

Betty Gabel, Oliver #1069

A quick surprise for the kids in your family is a big piece of grilled bologna basted with their favorite barbecue sauce.

Broccoli-Sausage Casserole

2 10-ounce packages frozen chopped broccoli
1 pound bulk Italian sausage, cooked, drained
$1/2$ cup melted margarine
1 pound mozzarella cheese, shredded
1 package Brownberry seasoned croutons
1 10-ounce can cream of mushroom soup

Cook broccoli using package directions; drain. Combine with sausage, margarine, cheese, croutons and soup in bowl; mix well. Spoon into 12x15-inch glass baking dish. Bake, covered, at 350 degrees for 25 minutes. **Yield: 10 to 12 servings.**

Chloe Buckner, Mahoning Valley #1649

Crunchy Sausage Casserole

2 6-ounce packages long-grain and wild rice mix
1 pound bulk pork sausage
$1/2$ pound ground beef
1 8-ounce can sliced water chestnuts, drained
1 large onion, chopped
1 8-ounce can sliced mushrooms, drained
3 tablespoons light soy sauce
3 to 4 stalks celery, chopped
1 2-ounce package sliced almonds

Cook rice using package directions; set aside. Brown sausage and ground beef in skillet, stirring until crumbly; drain. Add water chestnuts, onion, mushrooms, soy sauce and celery; mix well. Spoon into ungreased 2 or 3-quart casserole. Sprinkle with almonds. Bake at 325 degrees for 50 minutes. **Yield: 6 to 8 servings.**

LaVerne Burkhart, Gouglersville #1743

Hynka's Kielbasa Casserole

1 quart sliced yellow or green beans
4 potatoes, cut into $1\frac{1}{2}$-inch cubes
1 onion, chopped
2 slices rye-caraway seed bread, cubed
1 pound kielbasa, sliced 1 inch thick
Catsup

Cook beans in water in saucepan until partially done; set aside. Boil potatoes in water in saucepan until partially done; set aside. Sauté onion in large nonstick skillet until tender. Add bread, kielbasa, beans, potatoes and enough catsup to lightly coat vegetables. Cook until vegetables are tender, stirring frequently. **Yield: 4 servings.**

Catherine J. Metrick, Unionville #1971

Link Sausage with Apples

1 pound link sausage
6 sweet potatoes, peeled, sliced
6 medium onions, sliced
Salt, pepper and paprika to taste
6 apples, peeled, cored and cut into halves

Place sausage in saucepan with enough water to cover. Bring to a boil. Remove from heat; drain. Place in large baking dish. Layer with sweet potatoes and onions; sprinkle with salt, pepper and paprika. Bake, covered, at 400 degrees for 1 hour. Add apples. Bake, covered, until apples are tender. **Yield: 6 servings.**

Margaret E. Estabrook, Chippewa #1592

Pennsylvania Dutch Dinner

1 pound bulk sausage
1 tablespoon margarine
1 2-pound can sauerkraut, drained
1 10-ounce package noodles

Brown sausage with margarine in Dutch oven, stirring until crumbly. Stir in sauerkraut. Bake, covered, at 300 degrees for 2 hours. Cook noodles using package directions; drain. Add to sauerkraut mixture, stirring well. Bake, covered, for 20 minutes longer. **Yield: 6 to 8 servings.**

Thelma Pier, Sparta #110

Sausage and Cider

1 pound country sausage
1/4 cup water
2 tablespoons butter
1 onion, chopped
2 tablespoons chopped parsley
1 tablespoon flour
1 cup apple cider
Apple slices

Cut sausage into serving portions; prick casing with fork. Simmer, covered, in water in skillet for 20 minutes; drain off water. Cook until sausage is evenly browned. Remove to warm platter. Melt butter in skillet. Sauté onion until golden. Stir in parsley and flour. Add apple cider. Cook until mixture comes to a boil, stirring constantly. Place sausage in sauce. Cook until heated through, stirring occasionally. Garnish with apple slices. **Yield: 4 to 6 servings.**

Lee Taylor Finkenbinder, Mifflin #1725

*Layer 2 to 3 pounds cooked sausage, 3 cans of sauerkraut, 2 sliced onions, 10 sliced potatoes and 4 sliced apples in electric skillet. Pour 3 cups apple juice over the top and simmer, covered, for 45 minutes. This is an **Easy Skillet Meal** for 12 people.*

Smoked Sausage

1 pound smoked sausage, thinly sliced
1 16-ounce can white corn, drained
1 onion, sliced
1½ cups medium-cut green beans
2 potatoes, cubed
1 green bell pepper, finely chopped
1 10-ounce can cream of tomato soup
Shredded American or processed cheese
Buttered bread crumbs

Place half the sausage in 2-quart casserole. Layer with corn, onion, green beans, potatoes, green pepper and remaining sausage. Pour soup over top. Sprinkle with cheese and bread crumbs. Bake at 350 degrees for 1 hour. **Yield: 10 servings.**

Katie W. Woods, Alleghenyville #2065

Stuffed Sausage Roll

2 pounds bulk sausage
2 cups chopped apples
2 small onions, chopped
2 cups bread crumbs

Pat out sausage on waxed paper into ½ inch thick rectangle. Combine apples, onions and bread crumbs in bowl; mix well. Spread over sausage. Roll up as for jelly roll, tucking in edges. Place in baking dish. Bake at 350 degrees for 45 minutes. **Yield: 6 to 8 servings.**

Luella Haynes, Waterford #423

Spaghetti Pizza

1 pound spaghetti, cooked
1 egg, beaten
⅓ cup milk
¼ cup melted butter
½ cup shredded mozzarella cheese
1 30-ounce jar spaghetti sauce
¼ cup grated Parmesan cheese
2 cups shredded mozzarella cheese
Sliced pepperoni

Combine spaghetti, egg, milk, butter and ½ cup mozzarella cheese in bowl; mix well. Spread over greased 10x15-inch baking pan. Spoon spaghetti sauce over top. Sprinkle with Parmesan cheese, 2 cups mozzarella cheese and pepperoni. Bake at 350 degrees for 35 to 40 minutes or until bubbly. **Yield: 10 servings.**

Patricia L. Paul, Hillcrest #1674

Sausage will shrink less and spatter less if rolled lightly in flour before frying.

Vienna 'n Noodles

1/2 cup chopped onion
1/2 cup chopped celery
1 cup grated carrots
1/4 cup butter
3 tablespoons flour
1 teaspoon salt
1 1/2 cups milk
1/2 cup mayonnaise
1/2 teaspoon Worcestershire sauce
2 cups cooked noodles
2 5-ounce cans Vienna sausages in beef stock, drained, sliced

Sauté onion, celery and carrots in butter in skillet for 5 minutes. Stir in flour, salt and milk. Cook until thickened, stirring constantly. Stir in mayonnaise, Worcestershire sauce, noodles and sausages. Spoon into 1 1/2-quart casserole. Bake, covered, at 350 degrees for 25 minutes. **Yield: 4 servings.**

Mrs. Glen Kessler, Valley #1184

Hasen Kacka (Rabbit Cake)

1 rabbit
1/2 cup rabbit broth
1 1/2 tablespoons flour
1 teaspoon salt
1/4 teaspoon pepper
2 cups hot mashed potatoes
1 tablespoon minced parsley
1 egg, well beaten
4 cups torn day-old bread
2 tablespoons melted butter or margarine
1 onion,, minced
1/2 cup chopped celery

Cook rabbit in water to cover until tender. Drain, reserving 1/2 cup broth. Shred meat, discarding bones. Mix with 5 tablespoons broth, flour, salt and pepper in bowl; set aside. Combine potatoes, parsley and egg in medium bowl; mix well. Soak bread in cold water; squeeze dry. Stir into potato mixture with butter, onion and celery. Alternate layers of potato filling and rabbit mixture in 1 1/2-quart baking dish. Drizzle with remaining 3 tablespoons broth. Bake at 350 degrees for 25 minutes or until browned. May substitute chopped chicken or turkey for rabbit. **Yield: 4 servings.**

Esther Dietterick, Light Street #31

Use wine and tomatoes to tenderize less tender cuts of meat; they act to break down tougher fibers. Salt meat after it cooks to preserve the natural juices.

Cream Cheese and Venison Popover

1 pound ground venison
1/2 cup chopped onion
8 ounces cream cheese, cubed
1/4 cup water
1/2 teaspoon salt
1/2 teaspoon crushed oregano
1/4 teaspoon ground cumin
Pepper to taste
2 teaspoons Worcestershire sauce
2 eggs, beaten
3/4 cup flour
1/2 teaspoon salt
3/4 cup milk
1 tablespoon cornmeal
1 tomato, chopped

Brown venison in skillet, stirring until crumbly; drain. Add onion. Cook until tender. Add cream cheese and water. Cook over low heat until melted, stirring frequently. Stir in 1/2 teaspoon salt, oregano, cumin, pepper and Worcestershire sauce. Combine eggs, flour, 1/2 teaspoon salt and milk in bowl; mix well. Pour into greased 9-inch round baking dish. Sprinkle with cornmeal. Pour cream cheese mixture over cornmeal. Bake at 400 degrees for 35 minutes. Top with tomato. May substitute ground beef for venison. **Yield: 6 to 8 servings.**

Tamra C. Seiler, Fort Granville #1902

Scrumptious Venison

3 pounds ground venison
1 cup fine cracker crumbs
1/2 cup milk
1 teaspoon salt
Dash of pepper
Flour
1 10-ounce can cream of mushroom soup
1 soup can milk

Combine venison, cracker crumbs, 1/2 cup milk, salt and pepper in bowl; mix well. Spread over baking sheet to 1-inch thickness. Chill until firm. Cut into squares. Dust with flour. Brown in shortening in skillet on both sides. Place in baking dish. Beat soup and milk in small bowl until smooth. Pour over squares. Bake at 350 degrees for 30 minutes. **Yield: 12 servings.**

Joan Mauser, North Jackson #1740

Venison Meat Loaf

2 pounds lean ground venison
1/4 pound ground pork shoulder
1/2 cup seasoned bread crumbs
1 egg, beaten
1/2 cup thinly sliced mushrooms
1 onion, chopped
2 shallots, chopped
1/4 cup grated Romano cheese
1/2 cup grated Parmesan cheese
2 slices bacon

Mix venison and pork in large bowl. Add bread crumbs and egg, stirring to mix. Stir in mushrooms, onion, shallots, Romano and Parmesan cheeses. Pat into 5x9-inch loaf pan. Place bacon slices over top. Bake at 350 degrees for 1 hour. **Yield: 6 servings.**

Hazel Taylor, Odin #1254

Spanish Venison Steak

$1^1/_2$ to 2 pounds venison steak
1 green bell pepper, chopped
1 onion, chopped
2 tablespoons oil
Salt and pepper to taste
4 cups spaghetti sauce
Brown sugar to taste

Brown steak, green pepper and onion over medium heat in oil in large skillet; drain. Season with salt and pepper. Add spaghetti sauce and brown sugar. Cook until heated through, stirring occasionally. Pour into baking dish. Bake at 350 degrees for $1^1/_2$ hours or to desired degree of doneness. **Yield: 4 servings.**

Alice Bish Sylvis, Reynoldsville #1825

Venison Jerky

$^1/_2$ cup soy sauce
$^1/_2$ cup Worcestershire sauce
2 teaspoons MSG
2 teaspoons seasoned salt
$^2/_3$ teaspoon garlic salt
2 teaspoons onion powder
1 pound venison cut into $^1/_4$x1-inch slices

Combine soy sauce, Worcestershire sauce, MSG, seasoned salt, garlic salt and onion powder in shallow bowl; mix well. Add venison slices. Marinate, covered, for 12 hours to overnight. Place venison on baking sheet. Dry in 200-degree oven for 5 to 8 hours. Store in airtight container for up to 2 years. **Yield: 16 servings.**

Barb Critzer, Brokenstraw #407

Basic Seasoning Salt

$^1/_2$ cup salt
1 tablespoon celery salt
1 tablespoon onion salt
1 teaspoon paprika
1 tablespoon pepper

Combine salt, celery salt, onion salt, paprika and pepper in shaker jar. **Yield: $^3/_4$ cup.**

Gertrude Chapin, Wilmington #1477

No-Salt Seasoning

$^1/_2$ teaspoon garlic powder
$^1/_2$ teaspoon onion powder
$^1/_4$ teaspoon thyme
$^1/_2$ teaspoon paprika
$^1/_4$ teaspoon ground celery seed
$^1/_2$ teaspoon dry mustard
$^1/_2$ teaspoon pepper

Mix garlic powder, onion powder, thyme, paprika, celery seed, dry mustard and pepper in small bowl. Store in airtight container in dry place. **Yield: 1 tablespoon.**

Jean Christy, Conneaut #955

Special Seasoning

3 ounces dried mixed vegetables
1/2 teaspoon parsley flakes
1/4 teaspoon dried green and red bell peppers
1/4 teaspoon garlic powder
1/8 teaspoon thyme
1/4 teaspoon onion powder
1/4 teaspoon paprika
1/8 teaspoon ground celery seed
1/4 teaspoon dry mustard

Combine mixed vegetables, parsley flakes, dried peppers, garlic powder, thyme, onion powder, paprika, celery seed and dry mustard in blender container; process until well blended. Use as substitute seasoning for salt. **Yield: 1/4 cup.**

Hazel G. Huling, Shavers Creek #353

Salt Substitute

5 teaspoons onion powder
1 tablespoon garlic powder
1 tablespoon paprika
1 tablespoon dry mustard
1 teaspoon thyme
1/2 teaspoon celery seed
1/2 teaspoon white pepper

Combine onion powder, garlic powder, paprika, dry mustard, thyme, celery seed and white pepper in airtight container; mix well. Store in cool dry place. **Yield: 5 tablespoons.**

Ethel Friede, Stony Point #1694

Spicy Salt Substitute

1 teaspoon chili powder
2 teaspoons oregano
2 tablespoons dry mustard
1 tablespoon garlic powder
2 tablespoons paprika
6 tablespoons onion powder
2 tablespoons poultry seasoning
2 teaspoons pepper

Combine chili powder, oregano, dry msutard, garlic powder, paprika, onion powder, poultry seasoning and pepper in shaker; mix well. **Yield: 1 cup.**

Dorothy R. Hammond, Charleston Valley #54

Red spices will retain their flavor and color longer if stored in the refrigerator.

Sweet and Sour Sauce

1/4 cup cornstarch
1/2 cup packed brown sugar
2/3 cup vinegar
2 cups pineapple juice
2 tablespoons soy sauce
1 teaspoon salt

Combine cornstarch, brown sugar, vinegar, pineapple juice, soy sauce and salt in saucepan; mix well. Cook until thickened, stirring constantly. Serve over meatballs. May substitute orange juice for pineapple juice. **Yield: 3 cups.**

Ruby Wilcox, Watson #1068

Tomato Gravy

1/4 cup butter
2 cups canned tomatoes
Pinch of baking soda
2 tablespoons flour
2 cups milk
Salt to taste

Melt butter in large skillet. Cook until brown. Add tomatoes and baking soda. Simmer for several minutes. Blend flour and milk in bowl. Add to skillet gradually, stirring constantly. Cook until thickened, stirring constantly. Season with salt. Serve over bread, crushed crackers or mashed potatoes. **Yield: 6 servings.**

Nettie H. Prosser, Montour Valley #2005

Raisin Sauce for Ham

1 cup raisins
1 3/4 cups water
1/3 cup packed brown sugar
1 1/4 tablespoons cornstarch
1/4 teaspoon cinnamon
1/4 teaspoon dry mustard
1/4 teaspoon ground cloves
1/4 teaspoon salt
1 tablespoon butter
1 tablespoon vinegar

Cook raisins in water in saucepan for several minutes. Mix brown sugar, cornstarch, cinnamon, dry mustard, cloves and salt in small bowl. Stir into raisins. Cook for 15 minutes, stirring frequently. Stir in butter and vinegar. Serve with ham.
Yield: 2 cups.

Marie E. Ohlinger, Ontelaunee #1617

*For an **Easy Tartar Sauce**, combine 1 cup mayonnaise, 1 teaspoon grated onion, 2 tablespoons minced dill pickle, 1 tablespoon minced parsley and 2 teaspoons chopped pimento.*

Homemade Steak Sauce

1 cup catsup
1/4 cup white vinegar
2 tablespoons brown sugar
1 tablespoon prepared mustard
2 tablespoons soy sauce
1/4 cup lemon juice
1/4 cup dry white wine or water
1/2 cup chopped onion
1 large clove of garlic

Combine catsup, vinegar, brown sugar, mustard, soy sauce, lemon juice, wine, onion and garlic in saucepan; mix well. Simmer for 30 minutes or to desired consistency and color, stirring occasionally. Cool to room temperature. Strain. Store in covered container in refrigerator. **Yield: 2 1/2 cups.**

Ruby Wilcox, Watson #1068

Steak Marinade

1/2 cup packed brown sugar
1/2 cup soy sauce
1/2 cup tomato juice
1/2 cup oil
Garlic powder to taste

Combine brown sugar, soy sauce, tomato juice, oil and garlic powder in bowl. Use as overnight marinade for steak. **Yield: 2 cups.**

Lois McAlevy, Logan Valley #664

Soy Marinade

1/2 cup soy sauce
1/2 cup lemon juice
1/2 cup oil
3 tablespoons catsup
3 or 4 cloves of garlic, minced
1/4 teaspoon pepper

Combine soy sauce, lemon juice, oil, catsup, garlic and pepper in bowl; mix well. Use to marinate less tender cuts of meat for 6 hours to overnight. **Yield: 1 1/2 cups.**

Ruby Wilcox, Watson #1068

Creamy Horseradish Sauce

1 tablespoon cornstarch
1 tablespoon cold water
1 cup hot beef broth
1 4-ounce jar prepared horseradish
2 tablespoons sour cream
2 tablespoons low-fat yogurt
1/4 teaspoon sugar

Blend cornstarch and water in saucepan. Add broth gradually. Cook until thickened and smooth, stirring constantly. Add horseradish, sour cream, yogurt and sugar. Cook just until heated through; do not boil. Serve hot or cold. **Yield: 1 1/4 cups.**

Helen J. Brown, Somerset #1697

Horseradish Sauce

1/2 cup drained prepared horseradish
1 tablespoon vinegar
3/4 teaspoon salt
1/4 teaspoon pepper
1/2 cup whipping cream

Combine horseradish, vinegar, salt and pepper in bowl; mix well. Whip cream in mixer bowl until soft peaks form. Fold into horseradish mixture. **Yield: 1 cup.**

Jean V. Johnn, Hemlock #2051

Easy Barbecue Sauce

3/4 cup catsup
1/4 cup water
1/4 cup packed brown sugar
1 tablespoon mustard
1/2 teaspoon lemon juice
2 tablespoons Worcestershire sauce
1 onion, chopped

Combine all ingredients in saucepan. Cook until of desired consistency. **Yield: 2 cups.**

Lillian Dentil, Buffalo #1523

Barbecue Sauce

1 cup tomato soup
3/4 cup water
3 tablespoons vinegar
2 tablespoons Worcestershire sauce
1/4 teaspoon cinnamon
1 teaspoon paprika
1 teaspoon chili powder
1/8 teaspoon ground cloves
1 teaspoon salt
1/4 teaspoon pepper
2 medium onions, sliced

Combine all ingredients in saucepan; mix well. Cook until of desired consistency. Use to baste meat and fish. **Yield: 2 cups.**

Jean V. Johnn, Hemlock #2051

Microwave Barbecue Sauce

1 cup chili sauce
3/4 cup water
1/4 cup lemon juice
1/2 cup packed brown sugar
1 envelope onion soup mix
1 teaspoon dry mustard
1/8 teaspoon garlic powder

Combine chili sauce, water, lemon juice, brown sugar, soup mix, dry mustard and garlic powder in medium glass bowl; mix well. Microwave on High for 5 minutes. Microwave on Medium-High for 8 to 10 minutes or until thickened to desired consistency, stirring occasionally. Use as basting sauce on ribs, chicken or hamburgers. **Yield: 2 cups.**

Cathy Woods, Pleasant Hill #1505

Poultry and Seafood

Barbecued Chicken

10 chicken thighs or legs
1 10-ounce can Diet Pepsi
1 10-ounce bottle of catsup

Rinse chicken and pat dry. Place skin side down in baking pan. Combine Pepsi and catsup in bowl, mixing well. Pour over chicken. Bake at 375 degrees for 40 minutes; turn chicken. Bake for 40 minutes longer or until tender. May serve sauce over potatoes or noodles. **Yield: 5 servings.**

Jean Rennard, Chester Valley #1496

Breaded Chicken

1 chicken, cut into serving pieces
1 8-ounce bottle of Italian salad dressing
Flour
1 egg, beaten
Bread crumbs

Rinse chicken and pat dry. Pour salad dressing over chicken in shallow dish. Marinate in refrigerator overnight; drain marinade. Roll chicken in flour. Dip in egg. Coat with bread crumbs. Place in baking dish. Bake, covered, at 350 degrees for 1 hour. Bake, uncovered, for 30 minutes longer or until chicken is brown and tender. **Yield: 4 to 6 servings.**

Anna Lanterman, Kaylor #1396

Bulgarian Chicken

5 cups coarsely chopped cabbage
1 16-ounce can sauerkraut, drained
1/2 cup uncooked rice
3/4 cup water
1 cup chopped onion
3 tablespoons oil
2 16-ounce cans tomatoes
2 2 1/2-pound chickens, cut into serving pieces
1/2 teaspoon salt
1/8 teaspoon pepper

Layer cabbage, sauerkraut and rice in 9x13-inch baking dish. Pour water over top. Sauté onion in hot oil in skillet until tender. Spoon onion and tomatoes over rice layer. Rinse chicken and pat dry. Season with salt and pepper. Arrange pieces skin side up over top layer. Bake at 375 degrees for 1 1/2 hours or until chicken is tender and golden brown. **Yield: 8 servings.**

Lorraine Keenan, Aleppo #2054

Baked or roasted chicken has fewer calories than stewed chicken. Always remove skin to further reduce calories.

Chicken Cacciatore

1 onion, chopped
1/4 cup water
1 cup canned tomatoes
1/2 teaspoon garlic powder
1 teaspoon oregano
1/8 teaspoon pepper
1/2 cup tomato purée
4 chicken pieces, skinned

Combine onion, water, tomatoes, garlic powder, oregano, pepper and tomato purée in 2-quart saucepan. Simmer for 10 minutes, stirring occasionally. Rinse chicken and pat dry. Place in large skillet. Pour tomato mixture over top. Simmer, covered, over low heat for 45 to 50 minutes or until chicken is tender. Cook uncovered for 15 minutes longer or until sauce is thickened. **Yield: 4 servings.**

Cathy Woods, Pleasant Hill #1505

Chicken Paprikash with Egg Dumplings

1 onion, chopped
2 teaspoons oil
1 1/2 teaspoons paprika
1/2 teaspoon salt
1/2 teaspoon pepper
1 clove of garlic, chopped
1 chicken, cut into serving pieces
2 cups water or chicken broth
1 cup sour cream
2 cups flour
3 eggs, beaten
1 teaspoon salt
1/2 cup water
1 to 2 teaspoons butter

Sauté onion in oil in large skillet until tender. Add paprika, salt, pepper and garlic. Rinse chicken and pat dry. Brown in skillet for 10 minutes. Add water. Simmer for 45 to 60 minutes or until chicken is tender. Stir in sour cream just before serving. May add 1 to 2 tablespoons of mixture of flour and water to thicken sauce if needed. Combine 2 cups flour, eggs, salt and water in bowl, mixing well. Cut in butter. Roll out on board scalded with hot water. Drop small pieces of dough into boiling salted water. Cook for 5 minutes or until dumplings float to surface. Remove with slotted spoon. Butter lightly before serving with chicken. **Yield: 4 servings.**

Olga M. Boarts, Mt. Joy #537

Chicken Parmesan

2 chicken legs, skinned
1 14-ounce can Italian-style stewed tomatoes
1 tablespoon cornstarch
1/4 teaspoon oregano
2 tablespoons grated Parmesan cheese

Rinse chicken and pat dry. Place in baking dish. Combine tomatoes, cornstarch and oregano in small bowl, mixing well. Pour over chicken. Sprinkle with cheese. Bake at 350 degrees for 1 hour. **Yield: 2 servings.**

Winnie S. Faust, Bernville #1887

Slow-Cooker Chicken

1 chicken, cut into serving pieces
6 cups cubed potatoes
4 cups coarsely chopped carrots
1 10-ounce can cream of chicken soup

Rinse chicken and pat dry. Place in slow cooker with potatoes and carrots; cover with soup. Cook, covered, on High for 1 hour. Reduce temperature to Low. Cook for 2 hours longer. A complete meal, just fix and forget. **Yield: 4 to 6 servings.**

Ila May McMillin, Westfield #1514

Easy Baked Chicken

1 cup uncooked brown rice
1 3-pound chicken, cut into serving pieces
1 envelope onion soup mix
1 10-ounce can cream of chicken soup
2 soup cans water
1/4 cup melted butter or margarine

Spread rice in greased 9x13-inch baking dish. Rinse chicken and pat dry. Arrange over rice. Combine onion soup mix, chicken soup, water and butter in bowl; mix well. Pour over chicken. Bake, covered, at 350 degrees for 1 1/2 to 2 hours or until tender. **Yield: 4 to 6 servings.**

Deb Elliott, Hookstown #1980

Filipino Chicken (Manok Adobo)

1 3-pound chicken, cut into serving pieces
1 cup vinegar
2 tablespoons soy sauce
3 to 4 teaspoons salt
1 teaspoon whole black peppercorns
4 bay leaves, crushed
8 to 10 cloves of garlic, mashed or minced
4 celery tops and leaves, chopped

Rinse chicken and pat dry. Place in shallow pan. Combine vinegar, soy sauce, salt, peppercorns, bay leaves, garlic and celery in bowl; mix well. Pour over chicken. Marinate in refrigerator for 2 to 3 hours. Transfer chicken and marinade to skillet. Simmer until marinade is reduced by half and chicken is tender. The chicken will have a slight pickled and peppered flavor. For a milder flavor, marinate for 3 hours instead of 2. **Yield: 4 to 6 servings.**

Alice Campman, Chandlers Valley #846

Fried Chicken

1 egg
1/2 cup milk
2 tablespoons garlic salt
1 tablespoon paprika
1 tablespoon pepper
1/4 tablespoon poultry seasoning
1 cup flour
2 to 3 pounds chicken pieces
Oil for frying

Beat egg with milk in small bowl; set aside. Combine garlic salt, paprika, pepper, poultry seasoning and flour in plastic bag, shaking to mix. Rinse chicken and pat dry. Dip in egg mixture. Shake in flour mixture to coat. Heat 1/2 to 1 inch oil in electric skillet. Fry chicken at 365 degrees until brown. Reduce heat to 275 degrees. Cook for 30 to 40 minutes or until tender, turning chicken frequently. **Yield: 4 to 6 servings.**

Elmyra Heicher, Shermanata #1796

Grilled Chicken

1 cup soy sauce
1 cup packed brown sugar
2 cloves of garlic, minced, pressed
1/2 teaspoon ginger
1 tablespoon oil
2 chickens, cut into serving pieces

Combine soy sauce, brown sugar, garlic, ginger and oil in saucepan. Simmer for several minutes, stirring frequently. Rinse chicken and pat dry. Place in shallow dish. Pour marinade over chicken, turning to coat. Marinate in refrigerator for 3 hours to overnight, turning occasionally; drain. Broil in oven or grill over medium coals until chicken is tender and golden brown. **Yield: 8 servings.**

Carolyn Yoder, White Deer #122

Oven-Baked Chicken

2 1/2 to 3 pounds chicken pieces
1/2 cup melted butter or margarine
2 cups cornflake crumbs
Salt and pepper to taste

Rinse chicken and pat dry. Dip in melted butter; coat with cornflake crumbs. Arrange chicken in baking dish. Season with salt and pepper. Drizzle with remaining melted butter; sprinkle with remaining cornflake crumbs. Bake at 375 degrees for 1 hour or until tender. May substitute potato flakes or cornmeal for cornflake crumbs.
Yield: 4 servings.

Edith C. Myers, Mt. Joy #537

Oven-Fried Chicken

1/4 cup butter or margarine
2 cups herb-seasoned stuffing mix, crushed
1 teaspoon salt
2 to 3 pounds chicken pieces
1 egg
1 tablespoon water

Melt butter in shallow baking pan; set aside. Combine stuffing mix and salt in plastic bag. Rinse chicken and pat dry. Dip in mixture of egg and water; toss in stuffing mix to coat. Place skin side down in melted butter. Bake at 425 degrees for 30 minutes; turn. Bake for 15 minutes longer or until tender. **Yield: 4 servings.**

Ruth Ravenscroft, Ohiopyle #1933

Scalloped Potato and Chicken Casserole

4 cups sliced peeled potatoes
4 onions, sliced
Salt, pepper and thyme to taste
1/2 cup hot water
1 13-ounce can evaporated milk
3 slices bacon
6 pounds chicken pieces
2 tablespoons butter
Paprika to taste

Layer potatoes and onions in large roasting pan. Sprinkle with salt, pepper and thyme. Add hot water. Reserve 1/4 cup evaporated milk. Pour remaining evaporated milk over vegetables. Fry bacon in large skillet until crisp; drain. Rinse chicken and pat dry. Brown on all sides in butter in skillet. Arrange in pan with potatoes. Crumble bacon over top. Bake, covered, at 400 degrees for 1 hour. Pour reserved 1/4 cup evaporated milk over top; sprinkle with paprika. Bake, uncovered, for 30 minutes longer. **Yield: 8 servings.**

Kim Hicks, Pioneer #1777

Chicken and Hashed Browns

1 1-pound package frozen hashed brown potatoes, thawed
1 2 1/2-pound chicken, cut into serving pieces
1 10-ounce can mushroom soup
1 envelope chicken gravy mix
1/2 cup sour cream
1 teaspoon salt
1/4 teaspoon pepper
1 tablespoon chopped onion
1 1/3 cups water

Spread hashed browns in greased 9x13-inch baking pan. Rinse chicken and pat dry. Arrange over hashed browns. Combine soup, gravy mix, sour cream, salt, pepper, onion and water in bowl; mix well. Pour over chicken and hashed browns. Bake at 350 degrees for 40 minutes to 1 hour or until tender. **Yield: 4 servings.**

Jean Stiner, Eldred #1604

Chicken and Vegetable Casserole

4 whole chicken breasts, skinned, boned
2 cups quartered potatoes
3 to 4 carrots, cut into chunks
1 onion, chopped
1 stalk celery, chopped
1 cup frozen lima beans
Salt to taste
1 soup can water
1 10-ounce can cream of chicken soup

Rinse chicken and pat dry. Place in 6-quart casserole. Add potatoes, carrots, onion, celery, lima beans, salt and water. Pour chicken soup over all. Bake at 350 degrees for 1½ hours or until chicken and vegetables are tender. **Yield: 6 to 8 servings.**

Elizabeth Pfautz, Shermanata #1796

Chicken à la Heckman

6 to 8 whole chicken breasts, cut into halves
1 8-ounce bottle of French salad dressing
1 envelope onion soup mix
1 16-ounce can cranberry sauce

Rinse chicken and pat dry. Place in 9x13-inch baking pan. Combine salad dressing, soup mix and cranberry sauce in bowl; mix well. Pour over chicken. Bake, covered, at 325 degrees for 1½ hours. Bake uncovered for 30 minutes longer or until brown. Serve with rice pilaf. **Yield: 6 to 8 servings.**

Hazel Wilson, South Buffalo #1908

Cheese-Stuffed Chicken Breasts

½ cup chopped onion
2 teaspoons parsley flakes
¼ teaspoon salt
Pepper and garlic salt to taste
4 slices cheese, chopped
2 cups dry bread crumbs
1 egg, beaten
4 boneless chicken breasts
4 slices cheese
¼ cup melted butter
½ cup flour
¼ cup grated Parmesan cheese

Combine onion, parsley, salt, pepper, garlic salt, chopped cheese, bread crumbs and egg in bowl; mix well. Rinse chicken and pat dry. Place 1 slice cheese on each chicken breast. Top with bread crumb mixture. Roll up to enclose filling, securing with wooden pick. Dip in melted butter; coat with flour and Parmesan cheese. Place in baking pan. Bake at 375 degrees for 40 minutes or until chicken is tender.
Yield: 4 servings.

Judy Breneman, Mifflin #1725

Dilled Lemon Chicken

1½ pounds boneless chicken breasts
¼ cup margarine or butter
½ cup dry white wine
1 tablespoon lemon juice
¼ teaspoon salt
⅛ teaspoon dried dillweed
½ lemon, thinly sliced
2 green onions, sliced

Sauté chicken breasts in margarine in 10-inch skillet for 5 minutes on each side or until light brown. Combine wine, lemon juice, salt and dillweed in small bowl; pour over chicken. Place lemon slices on chicken. Bring to a boil; reduce heat. Simmer, covered, for 10 to 15 minutes or until chicken is tender. Remove chicken with slotted spoon to warm platter. Boil wine mixture for 3 minutes or until reduced by half, stirring constantly. Pour over chicken. Sprinkle with green onions. **Yield: 6 servings.**

Karen Yetter, Valley #1360

Hawaiian Chicken

4 chicken breasts
1 cup flour
1 teaspoon cinnamon
1 teaspoon ginger
1 teaspoon ground cloves
½ teaspoon onion powder
½ teaspoon garlic powder
½ cup oil
1 13-ounce can pineapple chunks
½ teaspoon sugar
1 cup uncooked rice

Rinse chicken and pat dry. Combine flour, cinnamon, ginger, cloves, onion powder and garlic powder in bowl. Dip chicken in mixture. Brown on both sides in oil in skillet. Add pineapple and sugar. Simmer for 45 minutes or until chicken is tender. Cook rice using package directions. Serve with chicken. **Yield: 4 servings.**

Jean Bagnick, Hope #898

Chicken in-a-Pot

½ cup butter or margarine
1 onion, chopped
6 boneless chicken breasts
1 8-ounce package poultry stuffing mix
Salt and pepper to taste
½ cup butter or margarine

Dot bottom of heavy 6-quart casserole with ½ cup butter; sprinkle with onion. Rinse chicken and pat dry; season with salt and pepper. Alternate layers of chicken and poultry stuffing mix over onion. Dot with remaining ½ cup butter. Bake, tightly covered, at 350 degrees for 1½ to 2 hours or until chicken is tender. Chicken, gravy and stuffing are all ready to eat. **Yield: 6 servings.**

Peggy A. Roberts, White Deer #122

Italian Chicken Cutlets

Chicken cutlets or chicken breast filets
Salt and pepper to taste
Italian seasoned bread crumbs
Flour
Garlic powder to taste
Chopped fresh parsley or parsley flakes
Grated Parmesan cheese to taste
Oregano to taste
Oil for frying

Rinse chicken and pat dry; season with salt and pepper. Combine next 6 ingredients in shallow bowl. Roll chicken pieces in mixture to coat. Fry in hot oil in skillet until tender and golden brown; drain. **Yield: variable.**

Jean Spease, Virginville #1832

Chicken Kiev

6 whole chicken breast filets, split
2 cups sour cream
1/4 cup lemon juice
4 teaspoons Worcestershire sauce
1 1/2 teaspoons garlic salt
1 teaspoon salt
1 teaspoon paprika
1 6-ounce package stuffing mix, finely crushed
1/2 cup melted margarine or butter

Rinse chicken and pat dry. Place in shallow dish. Combine sour cream, lemon juice, Worcestershire sauce, garlic salt, salt and paprika. Pour over chicken, turning to coat well. Chill, covered, overnight. Remove chicken, taking up as much of sour cream mixture as possible. Roll in stuffing mix to coat. Place in 8x11-inch baking dish. Drizzle with half the melted margarine. Bake at 350 degrees for 45 minutes. Drizzle with remaining margarine. Bake for 15 minutes longer. **Yield: 6 servings.**

Beatrice N. Slick, North Woodbury #1923

Lemon-Apricot Chicken

1 tablespoon melted butter
1 egg
2 tablespoons water
1 cup baking mix
1 tablespoon grated lemon rind
1/4 teaspoon garlic powder
6 chicken breast filets
3 tablespoons melted butter
2/3 cup apricot preserves
2 tablespoons lemon juice
1/2 teaspoon soy sauce
1/4 teaspoon ground ginger

Coat 11x15-inch baking sheet with 1 tablespoon melted butter. Beat egg and water in small bowl. Combine baking mix, lemon peel and garlic powder in shallow dish. Rinse chicken and pat dry. Flatten between sheets of waxed paper to 1/2-inch thickness. Dip in egg; coat with baking mix mixture. Arrange on prepared baking sheet. Drizzle 3 tablespoons butter over chicken. Bake at 425 degrees for 20 minutes; turn. Bake for 10 minutes longer. Remove to warm serving platter. Combine remaining ingredients in saucepan; mix well. Simmer until heated through, stirring frequently. Cut chicken crosswise into 1/2-inch slices; drizzle with sauce. Garnish with lemon slices. **Yield: 6 servings.**

Erma Hebe, Sebring #1047

Chicken Breasts Parmesan

1/3 cup fine dry bread crumbs
1 tablespoon minced parsley
3 tablespoons grated Parmesan cheese
2 egg whites
2 teaspoons water
1 pound chicken breast filets
1 tablespoon olive oil
1 lemon, cut into quarters

Combine bread crumbs and parsley on plate. Spread Parmesan cheese on separate plate. Beat egg whites with water in small bowl. Rinse chicken and pat dry. Flatten between sheets of waxed paper to 1/4-inch thickness. Dip into cheese, egg mixture and bread crumb mixture, coating well. Place chicken on rack. Chill in refrigerator for 20 minutes. Cook in hot oil in 10-inch heavy skillet over medium high heat for 3 to 4 minutes on each side or until chicken is cooked through. Drain and transfer to warm platter. Garnish with lemon quarters. **Yield: 6 servings.**

Marion Greenwood, Schnecksville #1684

Ham and Cheese Chicken Rolls

4 chicken breast filets
4 thin slices cooked ham
4 thin slices Swiss cheese
2 tablespoons oil
1 10-ounce can cream of broccoli soup
1/3 cup milk
1/4 cup sliced green onions
1/8 teaspoon crushed thyme

Rinse chicken and pat dry. Flatten between sheets of waxed paper. Layer each chicken breast with slice of ham and cheese. Roll up as for jelly roll, securing with wooden picks. Cook in hot oil in skillet for 10 minutes or until brown; drain. Stir in soup, milk, green onions and thyme. Bring to a boil; reduce heat. Simmer, covered, for 10 minutes or until chicken is cooked through, stirring occasionally. Transfer chicken to serving plate, removing wooden picks. Spoon sauce over top. May prepare chicken rolls omitting oil and soup mixture by dipping in chicken coating mix and baking at 400 degrees for 20 minutes. **Yield: 4 servings.**

Vivian C. Jeffries, Rural Valley #1750

Pizza Chicken

6 chicken breasts
1 15-ounce jar pizza sauce
1 cup shredded mozzarella cheese

Rinse chicken and pat dry. Place in baking dish. Bake at 350 degrees for 30 minutes. Pour pizza sauce over top. Bake for 30 minutes longer. Sprinkle with cheese. Bake for 5 minutes longer or until cheese is melted. **Yield: 8 servings.**

Mary Haladay, Berwick #1917

One-Dish Chicken Stir-Fry

1½ to 2 pounds boneless chicken, cut into strips
3 tablespoons margarine
1 chicken bouillon cube
1 cup chopped carrots
½ cup chopped celery
1 10-ounce can cream of broccoli soup
1 soup can milk
½ soup can water
1 tablespoon soy sauce
Garlic salt and onion powder to taste
2 cups uncooked rice

Sauté chicken strips in margarine in skillet until brown. Add bouillon cube, carrots and celery. Cook until tender-crisp, stirring occasionally. Stir in next 6 ingredients. Simmer, covered, for 10 minutes or until chicken is tender. Cook rice using package directions. Spoon onto serving plate; top with chicken mixture. May substitute noodles for rice. **Yield: 4 to 6 servings.**

Lisa Koenig, Central #1650

Chicken and Pea Pods

1½ pounds boneless chicken, cut into strips
½ cup chicken broth
6 tablespoons low-sodium soy sauce
1 tablespoon cornstarch
3 packets artificial sweetener
1 teaspoon ground ginger
⅓ cup rice vinegar
8 ounces pea pods
1½ cups sliced mushrooms
½ cup each chopped broccoli, zucchini, red bell pepper, green bell pepper and green onions

Rinse chicken and pat dry. Heat chicken broth in wok until hot. Add chicken. Stir-fry for 5 minutes or until cooked through. Combine soy sauce, cornstarch, artificial sweetener, ginger and rice vinegar in small bowl; mix well. Pour over chicken. Add pea pods, mushrooms, broccoli, zucchini, bell peppers and green onions. Stir-fry until sauce thickens. Serve over cooked rice. **Yield: 10 servings.**

Caroline M. Reilly, Scotch Valley #510

Quick Pepper Chicken

2 chicken breast filets, cut into ½ inch thick strips
2 scallions, diagonally sliced
1 tablespoon corn oil
¼ teaspoon crumbled savory
1 small green bell pepper, cut into ½-inch strips
1 small red bell pepper, cut into ½-inch strips
Tarragon to taste
¼ teaspoon coarsely ground pepper
1 to 2 tablespoons lemon juice
¼ cup dry white wine

Rinse chicken and pat dry. Sauté with scallions in oil in skillet for 4 to 5 minutes or until light brown. Add remaining ingredients. Cook, covered, over low heat for 6 to 8 minutes or until peppers are tender. **Yield: 2 servings.**

Sophie Sally Bocz, Brush Valley #1785

Quick Saucy Chicken Stir-Fry

2 tablespoons oil
1 cup broccoli flowerets
1 cup caulifloweretts
3/4 cup 2-inch julienned carrots
1/4 cup sliced green onions
1 clove of garlic, minced
3 chicken breast filets, cut into 1-inch pieces
1/2 cup mayonnaise-type salad dressing
1/2 teaspoon ground ginger
1 tablespoon soy sauce

Heat 1 tablespoon oil over medium-high heat in skillet or wok. Add broccoli, cauliflower, carrots, green onions and garlic. Stir-fry for 4 to 5 minutes or until tender-crisp; remove to warm platter. Add remaining 1 tablespoon oil. Stir-fry chicken for 4 minutes or until tender; remove from heat. Add cooked vegetables, salad dressing, ginger and soy sauce, stirring well to mix. Serve over hot cooked rice. **Yield: 4 servings.**

Evelyn Smith, Plain Grove #1431

Chicken in-a-Biscuit

3 ounces cream cheese, softened
2 tablespoons milk
2 cups chopped cooked chicken
2 tablespoons chopped pimento
2 tablespoons minced onion
1/2 teaspoon salt
Pepper to taste
1 8-count package crescent rolls
1/4 cup melted butter
1/4 cup Italian-seasoned bread crumbs

Mix cream cheese with milk in bowl until smooth. Stir in next 5 ingredients. Separate crescent rolls into 2 large rectangles; cut into 4x5-inch rectangles. Place 1 heaping tablespoon chicken mixture on each rectangle. Fold up to enclose filling, sealing edges. Place seam side down on baking sheet. Brush with butter; sprinkle with bread crumbs. Bake at 350 degrees for 25 minutes. **Yield: 6 servings.**

Gertrude J. Colwell, East Great Bend #940

Cheesy Chicken Casserole

1 16-ounce package frozen broccoli, carrots and water chestnuts, thawed
4 chicken breasts, cooked, cut into bite-sized pieces
2 4-ounce cans mushrooms, drained
1/2 cup margarine
2 tablespoons flour
1 cup milk
8 ounces Velveeta cheese, cubed
1 6-ounce package stuffing mix

Place vegetables in 9x13-inch baking dish. Layer with chicken and mushrooms. Melt margarine in small saucepan. Blend in flour. Stir in milk gradually. Add cheese. Cook until sauce thickens and cheese is melted, stirring constantly. Pour over mushroom layer. Top with stuffing mix. Bake, covered with foil, at 375 degrees for 35 minutes. **Yield: 6 to 8 servings.**

Sally Morgan, Fairview #1351

Chicken Noodle Casserole

5 to 6 whole chicken breasts, cooked, chopped
1 pound fresh mushrooms, sliced
3 10-ounce cans cream of mushroom soup
3 cups sour cream
1 cup mayonnaise
1 16-ounce package noodles, cooked
Salt and pepper to taste
1 cup sherry or brandy
1 8-ounce package stuffing mix

Combine chicken, mushrooms, soup, sour cream, mayonnaise, noodles, salt and pepper in large bowl; mix well. Spoon into greased baking dish. Top with stuffing mix. Bake at 350 degrees for 30 minutes. **Yield: 6 to 8 servings.**

Kay Holman, Mt. Nebo #1872

Chicken Chow Mein Casserole

2 1½-ounce cans chow mein noodles
4 cups chopped cooked chicken
2 cups thinly sliced celery
1 10-ounce can cream of chicken soup
1 10-ounce can cream of celery soup
1 10-ounce can cream of mushroom soup
1 cup mayonnaise
½ cup chicken broth

Combine noodles, chicken, celery, soups, mayonnaise and chicken broth in large bowl; mix well. Spoon into greased 9x13-inch baking pan. Bake at 350 degrees for 1 hour. Garnish with shredded cheese. May substitute turkey for chicken.
Yield: 8 to 10 servings.

Mildred K. Duran, Burgettstown #1502

Classic Chicken à la King

6 tablespoons butter
9 tablespoons flour
¾ teaspoon salt
Dash of pepper
3 cups chicken broth
1 cup cream
1 cup sliced mushrooms
Chopped green bell pepper to taste
2 cups chopped cooked chicken
½ cup sliced pimentos
2 egg yolks, beaten
¼ cup sherry
Tart shells or toast

Melt butter in saucepan. Blend in flour, salt and pepper. Add chicken broth gradually. Bring to a boil. Cook for 2 minutes or until thickened, stirring constantly; remove from heat. Stir in cream. Pour sauce into top of double boiler. Sauté mushrooms and green pepper in skillet until tender. Add sautéed vegetables, chicken and pimentos to sauce. Heat over hot water, stirring constantly. Just before serving, stir a small amount of hot mixture into egg yolks; stir egg yolks and sherry into hot mixture. Spoon mixture into prepared tart shells or over toast. **Yield: 4 to 6 servings.**

Pat Rudy, Mt. Nebo #1872

Chicken à la King with Vegetables

1/4 cup butter or margarine
1/4 cup flour
1 cup milk
1 10-ounce can cream of chicken soup
1/2 cup milk or chicken broth
1/2 cup chopped celery
1/2 cup peas
1/3 cup chopped carrots
1/4 cup chopped parsley
2 to 3 cups chopped cooked chicken
3 hard-boiled eggs, sliced
1 teaspoon salt
Pastry shells or toast

Melt butter in large heavy saucepan. Blend in flour. Stir in 1 cup milk gradually. Cook over low heat until thickened, stirring constantly. Add cream of chicken soup and 1/2 cup milk. Bring mixture to a slow boil, stirring frequently. Sauté celery, peas and carrots in skillet until tender-crisp. Add to sauce with parsley, chicken, eggs and salt, stirring to mix. Bring to a boil; reduce heat. Simmer until heated through, stirring frequently. Spoon into prepared pastry shells or over toast.
Yield: 6 to 8 servings.

Katie M. Mengel, Centerport #1600

Chicken Loaf

3 cups finely chopped cooked chicken
1 cup cooked rice
1/2 cup chopped celery
2 tablespoons chopped parsley
1 tablespoon grated onion
1 teaspoon salt
3/4 teaspoon poultry seasoning
1/4 teaspoon pepper
3 eggs
1 cup milk

Combine chicken, rice, celery, parsley, onion, salt, poultry seasoning and pepper in large bowl; mix well. Beat eggs and milk in small bowl; stir into chicken mixture. Pour into buttered 4x8-inch loaf pan. Place loaf pan in larger pan half-filled with boiling water. Bake for 1 hour or until knife inserted near center comes out clean.
Yield: 6 to 8 servings.

Gertrude Chapin, Wilmington #1477

Double-stuff a chicken by spooning stuffing under the skin of the breast. Loosen skin carefully with fingers, working from the neck cavity.

Chicken Sandwich Squares

3 ounces cream cheese, softened
3 tablespoons mayonnaise
1 1/4 cups chopped cooked chicken
1 cup shredded Cheddar cheese
1/4 cup thinly sliced celery
1/4 cup sliced onion
1 tablespoon chopped pimento
1/2 teaspoon garlic salt
Dash of pepper
2 cups baking mix
1/2 cup cold water
2 tablespoons melted margarine
1/2 cup crushed corn chips

Combine cream cheese, mayonnaise, chicken, cheese, celery, onion, pimento, garlic salt and pepper in large bowl; mix well. Combine baking mix and cold water in medium bowl, stirring until soft dough forms. Beat vigorously for 20 strokes. Turn onto floured surface; knead 5 times. Roll into 12x18-inch rectangle. Cut into 6 squares. Spoon 1/3 cup chicken mixture onto each square. Fold up corners to enclose filling, sealing edges. Brush with margarine; dip in corn chip crumbs. Arrange squares on ungreased baking sheet. Bake at 350 degrees for 20 minutes or until golden brown. **Yield: 6 servings.**

Virginia Mangel, Eureka #244

Chicken Soufflé

1 large loaf white bread, crust trimmed, cut in half
1 cup chopped green bell pepper
1 cup chopped onion
1 cup chopped celery
2 teaspoons butter
4 cups chopped cooked chicken
1 cup mayonnaise
Salt and pepper to taste
3 cups milk
3 eggs
2 10-ounce cans cream of mushroom soup
1 cup shredded sharp cheese
Paprika

Line nonstick 10x15-inch baking pan with half the bread. Sauté green pepper, onion and celery in butter in skillet until tender. Mix with chicken, mayonnaise, salt and pepper in bowl. Spoon over bread. Layer with remaining bread. Beat milk with eggs in small bowl. Pour over bread. Spoon soup over top; sprinkle with cheese and paprika. Bake at 325 degrees for 1 1/4 hours. **Yield: 6 to 8 servings.**

Agnes M. Eckhart, Friendship #1799

Marinate chicken in Italian or Russian salad dressing in refrigerator and then grill for an easy and flavorful dish.

Chinese Chicken Casserole

1 10-ounce can cream of mushroom soup
1 10-ounce can Cheddar cheese soup
1 15-ounce can evaporated milk
3 cups chopped cooked chicken
1 teaspoon salt
3 cups cooked green beans
1 cup chopped celery
1/2 to 3/4 cup chow mein noodles
1/2 cup slivered almonds
1 3-ounce can French-fried onions

Combine soups and evaporated milk in large bowl; mix well. Stir in chicken, salt, green beans, celery, chow mein noodles and almonds. Pour into baking dish. Sprinkle French-fried onions over top. Bake, covered with foil, at 350 degrees for 35 minutes. Bake, uncovered, for 10 minutes longer. **Yield: 6 to 8 servings.**

Bernice Mowrer, Shavers Creek #353

Company Chicken Casserole

2 cups broken spaghetti, cooked
4 cups chopped cooked chicken
1 1/2 cups chopped ham
1/2 cup chopped green bell pepper
1/4 cup chopped pimento
2 10-ounce cans mushroom soup
1 cup chicken broth
1 onion, grated
1/2 teaspoon celery seed
1 4-ounce can mushrooms, drained
Shredded cheese

Combine spaghetti, chicken, ham, green pepper, pimento, mushroom soup, chicken broth, onion, celery seed and mushrooms in large bowl; mix well. Pour into baking dish; cover with foil. Bake at 325 degrees for 1 hour. Remove foil; sprinkle with shredded cheese. Bake until cheese is melted. **Yield: 6 to 8 servings.**

Helen Kramer, Burgettstown #1502

Stuffed Chicken Shells

1 16-ounce package jumbo pasta shells
1 6-ounce package chicken-flavored stuffing mix
4 cups chopped cooked chicken
1/2 cup chopped celery
1/2 cup chopped onion
1 cup mayonnaise-type salad dressing
2 10-ounce cans cream of chicken soup
1 soup can water

Cook shells using package directions; drain and cool. Prepare stuffing mix using package directions. Combine with chicken, celery, onion and salad dressing; mix well. Spoon stuffing mixture into cooked shells; place in baking pan. Chill in refrigerator overnight. Pour mixture of chicken soup and water over shells. Bake at 350 degrees for 1 hour. **Yield: 6 to 8 servings.**

Ruth Hartzell, Red Brush Community #2085

Barbecued Pheasant

2 pheasant
Salt and pepper to taste
Flour
1 tablespoon shortening
1 medium onion, chopped
1 tablespoon brown sugar
1 tablespoon cornstarch
1/4 cup catsup
2 tablespoons vinegar
3 tablespoons Worcestershire sauce
1/2 teaspoon salt
1/4 teaspoon pepper
2 cups cooked tomatoes

Rinse pheasant and pat dry; cut into serving portions. Sprinkle with salt, pepper and flour. Brown in 2 teaspoons hot shortening in skillet. Arrange in shallow baking dish. Sauté onion in remaining shortening in saucepan until tender. Stir in brown sugar and cornstarch. Add catsup, vinegar, Worcestershire sauce, 1/2 teaspoon salt, 1/4 teaspoon pepper and tomatoes, stirring well after each addition. Cook for 20 minutes or until thickened, stirring frequently. Pour over pheasant. Cook, covered, at 300 degrees for 1 hour. **Yield: 2 to 3 servings.**

Fern Sonon, Virginville #1832

Ground Turkey Chili

1/4 cup chopped onion
1 clove of garlic, minced
5 tablespoons oil
1 pound ground turkey
1 6-ounce can tomato paste
3 tablespoons chili powder
1/4 teaspoon oregano
1/4 teaspoon paprika
2 15-ounce cans tomato sauce
2 15-ounce cans kidney beans, drained

Sauté onion and garlic in 1 tablespoon oil in skillet until tender. Add remaining oil. Warm over medium heat but do not overheat. Add turkey. Cook slowly, stirring until crumbly; drain. Combine remaining ingredients in large saucepan; mix well. Stir in turkey mixture. Cook for 1 1/2 to 2 hours or until of desired consistency, stirring occasionally. **Yield: 8 to 10 servings.**

Nettie Martsolf, Jefferson #1373

Turkey and Bean Chili

1 pound ground turkey
1 large onion, chopped
1 small green pepper, chopped
1 teaspoon garlic powder
2 14-ounce cans pinto beans
2 15-ounce cans red kidney beans
1 14-ounce can tomatoes
1 tablespoon brown sugar
1 teaspoon chili powder
1/2 teaspoon salt
1/8 teaspoon pepper

Cook turkey, onion and green pepper with garlic powder in large saucepan until light brown. Stir in undrained beans, tomatoes, brown sugar, chili powder, salt and pepper; mix well. Bring to a boil; reduce heat to low. Simmer, covered, for 30 minutes. Garnish with shredded cheese. **Yield: 8 servings.**

Joyce A. Heath, Fort Granville #1902

Quick and Easy Dinner

1 package macaroni and cheese dinner
1/2 cup milk
1/4 cup chopped onion
1 tablespoon margarine
1 10-ounce can cream of mushroom or celery soup
1 cup chopped cooked turkey
Buttered bread crumbs

Prepare macaroni and cheese dinner using package directions, but use only 1/2 cup milk. Sauté onion in margarine until tender. Stir into macaroni and cheese. Add soup and turkey, stirring well. May add additional milk for desired consistency. Pour into 8x8-inch casserole. Sprinkle with buttered bread crumbs. Bake at 350 degrees for 30 minutes or until light brown. **Yield: 4 servings.**

Agnes Blood, Cherry Hill #1214

Creamy Turkey Lasagna

8 ounces lasagna noodles
1 10-ounce can cream of chicken soup
1 10-ounce can cream of mushroom soup
1 cup grated Parmesan cheese
1 cup sour cream
1 cup chopped onion
1 cup chopped ripe olives
1/4 cup chopped pimento (optional)
1/2 teaspoon garlic salt
3 cups chopped, cooked turkey
16 ounces sliced American cheese

Cook lasagna noodles using package directions; drain. Combine soups, Parmesan cheese, sour cream, onion, olives, pimento and garlic salt in bowl; mix well. Fold in turkey. Spread small amount of mixture in 9x13-inch pan. Alternate layers of noodles, turkey mixture and cheese slices 1/3 at a time, ending with cheese. Bake at 350 degrees for 40 to 45 minutes or until brown. **Yield: 6 to 8 servings.**

Ada Riel, Chandlers Valley #846

Turkey Cheese Puffs

3 ounces cream cheese, softened
2 tablespoons margarine, softened
2 tablespoons milk
2 cup chopped cooked turkey
1/8 teaspoon pepper
1 8-count can crescent rolls

Beat cream cheese and margarine at medium speed in mixer bowl until smooth. Add milk. Beat until light and fluffy. Stir in turkey and pepper. Separate crescent roll dough into 4 rectangles, sealing perforations. Spoon 1/2 cup turkey mixture in center of each rectangle. Fold up to enclose filling, pinching edges to seal. Place on ungreased baking sheet. Bake at 350 degrees for 20 to 25 minutes or until golden brown. May substitute chicken for turkey. Garnish with cream sauce. **Yield: 4 servings.**

Ruth Caven Johnston, Wilmington #1477

Turkey Loaf

1/4 cup margarine
3 tablespoons flour
2 cups milk
2 eggs, beaten
1 teaspoon salt
1/4 teaspoon pepper
3 cups chopped cooked turkey
1/4 cup minced onion
3 tablespoons margarine
2 cups herb-flavored stuffing mix
1 1/2 cups chopped celery
3/4 cup wheat germ
2 tablespoons lemon juice
Mustard sauce

Melt 1/4 cup margarine in saucepan. Blend in flour. Add milk gradually. Cook over medium heat until thickened, stirring constantly. Remove from heat; cool. Beat in eggs, salt and pepper. Fold in turkey. Sauté onion in 3 tablespoons margarine in skillet until tender. Mix with stuffing mix, celery, wheat germ and lemon juice. Add to turkey mixture. Spoon into foil-lined 5x9-inch loaf pan. Bake at 375 degrees for 1 hour or until firm. Remove to serving platter. Serve with mustard sauce made from sour cream and 2 tablespoons prepared mustard. May substitute left-over stuffing for stuffing mix made with onion and celery. **Yield: 6 servings.**

Dorothy J. Caltagarone, Reynoldsville #1825

Low-Calorie Turkey Loaves

2 egg whites or 1 egg
1/4 cup skim milk
2 pounds ground turkey breast
1 pound ground chuck
1 cup oat bran
2 slices oat bran or whole wheat bread, crumbled
1/2 cup chopped onion
1/4 cup chopped green bell pepper (optional)
2 tablespoons chopped parsley
1 1/2 teaspoons salt
1/4 teaspoon pepper
Herbs and seasonings to taste
1 8-ounce can tomato sauce
1 tablespoon brown sugar
1 tablespoons Worcestershire sauce
1 teaspoon prepared mustard

Beat egg whites with skim milk in bowl. Add turkey, ground chuck, oat bran, bread crumbs, onion, green pepper, parsley, salt, pepper and herbs; mix well. Combine tomato sauce, brown sugar, Worcestershire sauce and mustard in small bowl; mix well. Add 2/3 of the sauce to the turkey mixture, stirring well. Spoon into two 5x7-inch loaf pans. Bake at 350 degrees for 1 1/2 hours, basting with remaining sauce. May substitute 3 tablespoons catsup mixed with 1 tablespoon water for canned tomato sauce, reducing brown sugar to 2 teaspoons. **Yield: 12 servings.**

Katie M. Mengel, Centerport #1600

Sweet and Sour Turkey Patties

2 cups soft fine bread crumbs
1/4 cup chopped onion
1 teaspoon salt
1/2 cup water
1 pound ground turkey
1 cup sliced onion
1/3 cup packed brown sugar
1 tablespoon flour
1/4 cup vinegar
2 tablespoons water
2 teaspoons prepared mustard

Combine bread crumbs, chopped onion, salt and 1/2 cup water in bowl; mix well. Let stand for 5 minutes. Stir in turkey. Shape into 6 patties. Brown patties in skillet on both sides. Top with sliced onion. Combine brown sugar, flour, vinegar, 2 tablespoons water and mustard in small bowl; mix well. Spoon over patties. Simmer, covered, for 35 minutes. **Yield: 6 servings.**

Sara Cooper, Briar Creek #146

Turkey Noodle Dandy

1 12-ounce package noodles
1 pound ground turkey
1/3 cup chopped onion
8 ounces cream cheese, softened
1 cup cottage cheese
1 cup sour cream
2 8-ounce cans tomato sauce
Sugar to taste

Cook noodles using package directions; drain. Sauté turkey and onion in skillet until light brown, stirring frequently. Combine with cream cheese, cottage cheese, sour cream, tomato sauce and sugar; mix well. Stir in cooked noodles. Pour into 2-quart baking dish. Bake at 275 degrees for 45 minutes. **Yield: 8 servings.**

Mary Stewart, Kaylor #1396

Roast Turkey à la Bristol

1 12-pound turkey
Salt, pepper and paprika to taste
3/4 cup butter, softened
Flour
1 8-ounce can frozen orange juice concentrate, thawed
1/2 cup boiling water

Rinse turkey and pat dry. Sprinkle inside and outside of turkey with salt, pepper and paprika. Rub with 1/4 cup butter. Dust with flour. Place in roasting pan. Bake at 325 degrees for 30 minutes. Pour orange juice over turkey. Return to oven. Baste with mixture of remaining 1/2 cup butter and boiling water after 20 minutes. Continue basting every 20 minutes with pan drippings until turkey tests done.
Yield: 8 servings.

Zelma K. Pyle, Bernville #1887

Turkey with Chestnut Filling

1 quart chestnuts, blanched, shelled
2 cups soft bread crumbs
2 tablespoons finely chopped celery
1/4 cup melted butter
1 tablespoon finely chopped parsley
1 teaspoon salt
1/2 teaspoon pepper
2 eggs, beaten
1 10 to 12-pound turkey

Boil chestnuts in 2 quarts salted water until tender; drain. Press through coarse strainer. Mix with bread crumbs in bowl; set aside. Sauté celery in butter in skillet until tender. Add to chestnut mixture with parsley, salt, pepper and eggs; mix well. Stuff and truss turkey; place in roasting pan. Roast, loosely covered with foil, at 325 degrees for 4 1/2 hours or to 175 degrees on meat thermometer. **Yield: 8 servings.**

Mildred Wessner, Virginville #1832

Turkey with Corn Bread and Romaine Stuffing

1 onion, chopped
1 cup chopped celery
6 tablespoons margarine
2 teaspoons poultry seasoning
Pepper to taste
4 cups crumbled cornbread
2 cups chopped romaine lettuce
1/2 cup chopped smoked ham
Chicken broth
1 10-pound turkey

Sauté onion and celery in margarine in skillet. Sprinkle with poultry seasoning and pepper. Combine corn bread, lettuce and ham in bowl; mix well. Stir in sautéed mixture. Add enough chicken broth to moisten slightly. Stuff and truss turkey. Roast, covered with foil, at 325 to 350 degrees until 175 to 180 degrees registers on meat thermometer. **Yield: 8 servings.**

Agnes Rabold, Jackson #1506

Easy Stuffed Turkey

12 to 14 slices cooked turkey
1 6-ounce package stuffing mix
1 10-ounce package frozen peas or mixed vegetables
1 10-ounce can cream of celery or mushroom soup
1 soup can milk
1/4 cup shredded Cheddar cheese

Place half the turkey in buttered 9x13-inch baking dish. Prepare stuffing mix using package directions. Spread over turkey. Sprinkle with peas. Layer with remaining turkey. Mix soup and milk in small bowl; pour over turkey. Top with cheese. Bake, covered, at 350 degrees for 30 to 35 minutes or until bubbly. May substitute chicken for turkey. May garnish with French-fried onions. **Yield: 10 servings.**

Barbara Ann Cavalcante, Franklin #1169

Fried River Catfish

1/2 cup cornmeal
6 tablespoons flour
1 teaspoon salt
Pepper to taste
1 egg, slightly beaten
1 tablespoon water
4 catfish
3 tablespoons bacon drippings
1/4 cup oil

Mix cornmeal, flour, salt and pepper in bowl. Beat egg with water in bowl. Dip fish in egg mixture; coat with cornmeal mixture. Fry in hot bacon drippings and oil in large skillet until golden brown on both sides. **Yield: 4 servings.**

Jeannie Chamberlain, Stony Point #1694

Perfect Fish Balls

2 cups chopped potatoes
1 cup flaked codfish
1 tablespoon butter
1 egg
Salt and pepper to taste
Oil for frying

Cook potatoes and fish in a small amount of water in saucepan until tender; drain. Mash potatoes and fish until very smooth. Add butter, egg, salt and pepper; mix well. Drop by spoonfuls into hot oil in skillet, dipping spoon into hot oil to prevent sticking. Cook just until golden brown. **Yield: 4 servings.**

Rose Zorich, Carmichaels #1389

Crispy Baked Fish Filets

1 pound fish filets
1/4 teaspoon salt
Pepper to taste
2 tablespoons oil
1/3 cup cornflake crumbs

Cut fish into serving pieces; sprinkle with salt and pepper. Dip into oil; coat with cornflake crumbs. Arrange in single layer in lightly oiled shallow baking dish. Bake at 500 degrees for 10 minutes; do not turn or baste. Serve immediately.
Yield: 2 servings.

Agnes Blood, Cherry Hill #1214

For best results, thaw frozen seafood in the refrigerator. It will lose moisture and flavor at room temperature or in warm water. Never refreeze thawed seafood.

Baked Fish with Mushroom Sauce

2 packages frozen haddock filets
1 10-ounce can cream of mushroom soup
3/4 cup evaporated milk
1 large onion, sliced
2 tablespoons lemon juice
1 teaspoon paprika
1/4 teaspoon oregano
1/2 teaspoon salt
1/4 teaspoon pepper
1 cup buttered bread crumbs
Additional butter for topping

Place filets in shallow buttered baking dish. Combine soup, evaporated milk, onion, lemon juice, paprika, oregano, salt and pepper in saucepan. Simmer for 10 minutes. Pour over filets. Sprinkle buttered bread crumbs over top; dot with butter. Bake at 375 degrees for 45 minutes. **Yield: 4 to 6 servings.**

Alma Kenny, Westfield #1514

Lively Fish Roll-Ups

1/3 cup margarine
1/3 cup lemon juice
2 teaspoons salt
1/4 teaspoon pepper
1 cup cooked rice
1 10-ounce package frozen chopped broccoli
1 cup shredded cheese
8 4-ounce fish filets
Paprika to taste

Melt margarine in small saucepan over low heat. Stir in lemon juice, salt and pepper. Combine rice, broccoli, cheese and 1/4 cup lemon mixture in bowl; mix well. Spoon mixture onto filets. Roll up to enclose filling. Place seam side down in 8x8-inch baking dish. Pour remaining sauce over top. Bake at 375 degrees for 25 minutes. Sprinkle with paprika. **Yield: 8 servings.**

Marie Traub, Carter Camp #1563

Poor Man's Lobster

1 pound haddock filets
2 cups water
1 tablespoon vinegar
1 teaspoon salt
1 teaspoon seafood seasoning or lemon pepper
Melted butter

Combine haddock, water, vinegar, and seasonings in large saucepan. Bring to boil over medium heat. Reduce heat to low. Simmer for 20 minutes. Drain liquid. Serve with melted butter. **Yield: 2 to 3 servings.**

Goldie I. Durco, Community #1994

Seafood Delight

1 medium onion, finely chopped
2 tablespoons water
1/2 cup chopped tomatoes
1/2 teaspoon basil
1/2 teaspoon garlic powder
2 tablespoons oil
1 1/2 tablespoons lemon juice
1 pound cod filets
1 teaspoon parsley flakes

Combine onion, water and tomatoes in bowl. Stir in basil, garlic powder, oil and lemon juice. Place filets in greased baking dish. Pour onion mixture over top. Sprinkle with parsley. Bake at 350 degrees for 15 minutes. May microwave on High for 7 minutes. **Yield: 4 servings.**

Martha Shannon, Mahoning Valley #1649

Creamed Salmon and Peas

1 16-ounce can salmon
1 16-ounce can peas
1/4 cup butter
1/4 cup flour
1/2 teaspoon salt
1/8 teaspoon pepper
1 cup milk

Drain salmon, reserving liquid. Flake salmon; discard bones. Drain peas; reserving liquid. Melt butter in saucepan over medium-low heat. Stir in flour, salt and pepper. Add milk gradually, stirring constantly. Add reserved liquids. Cook until thickened, stirring constantly. Stir in salmon and peas. Cook until heated through. Serve on toast. **Yield: 5 or 6 servings.**

Helen P. West, Charleston Valley #54

Deviled Salmon

1 16-ounce can salmon
Milk
2 tablespoons butter
2 tablespoons flour
1 teaspoon Worcestershire sauce
8 drops of Tabasco sauce
2 cups bread cubes
1 tablespoon grated onion
2 tablespoons chopped green bell pepper
1/4 teaspoon salt
2 hard-boiled eggs, chopped
1/2 cup dry bread crumbs
2 tablespoons butter, softened

Drain salmon, reserving liquid. Add enough milk to reserved liquid to measure 1 cup. Flake salmon. Melt 2 tablespoons butter in saucepan over medium heat. Stir in flour. Add liquid gradually, stirring constantly. Add salmon, Worcestershire sauce, Tabasco sauce, bread cubes, onion, green pepper, salt and chopped eggs. Cook until thickened, stirring constantly. Spoon into greased baking dish. Mix bread crumbs and 2 tablespoons butter in small bowl. Sprinkle over salmon mixture. Bake at 375 degrees for 20 minutes or until golden brown. **Yield: 6 servings.**

Bonnie Chronister, Mifflin #1725

Salmon Loaf

1 16-ounce can red salmon, drained
6 egg yolks
1 cup cornflake crumbs
1 small onion, grated
1 teaspoon salt
Pepper to taste
6 egg whites, stiffly beaten

Combine salmon, egg yolks, cornflake crumbs, onion, salt and pepper in bowl; mix well. Fold in stiffly beaten egg whites. Spoon into 8-inch baking pan. Bake at 350 degrees for 20 minutes. **Yield: 6 servings.**

Pearle Malone, Mendon #855

Salmon Rolls

1 recipe baking powder biscuits
1½ cups flaked salmon
1 cup chopped green bell pepper
1 onion, chopped
½ teaspoon salt
Salmon liquid

Roll biscuit dough ½ inch thick on floured surface. Combine salmon, green pepper, onion and salt in bowl. Add enough salmon liquid to moisten slightly; mix well. Spread on biscuit dough. Roll as for jelly roll. Cut into 1½-inch slices. Place in greased baking dish. Bake at 400 degrees for 30 minutes. **Yield: 6 servings.**

Dorothy E. Grande, Mahoning Valley #1649

Souper Tuna and Noodles

8 ounces noodles, cooked
1 6-ounce can water-pack tuna, drained
1 cup cooked frozen mixed vegetables
1 can sliced mushrooms, drained
1 10-ounce can cream of mushroom soup
1 soup can water
Grated cheese
Bread crumbs

Place half the noodles in 2-quart baking dish. Layer tuna, vegetables, mushrooms and remaining noodles over top. Mix soup and water in bowl. Pour over layers. Sprinkle with grated cheese and bread crumbs. Bake at 375 degrees for 30 to 35 minutes. **Yield: 6 servings.**

Carole Zimmerman, Ackley #870

Water-pack tuna has about 300 fewer calories per 6½-ounce can than tuna packed in oil.

Stuffed Shells Supreme

12 jumbo macaroni shells
1 10-ounce can cream of celery soup
1/2 teaspoon lemon juice
1/4 teaspoon oregano
1 10-ounce package frozen chopped broccoli, cooked
1/2 cup chopped fresh tomatoes
1 6-ounce can tuna, drained, flaked
1/2 cup shredded Cheddar cheese

Cook shells using package directions; drain. Combine soup, lemon juice, oregano, broccoli, tomatoes and tuna in bowl; mix well. Fill shells with 1/4 cup mixture. Arrange stuffed shells in buttered 1 1/2-quart baking dish. Bake at 400 degrees for 20 minutes. Top with cheese. Bake for 5 minutes. **Yield: 4 to 6 servings.**

Mary Jane Kent, Harveys #1444

Tuna Croquettes

1 10-ounce can cream of mushroom soup
2 6-ounce cans tuna, drained
1/2 cup bread crumbs
2 tablespoons finely chopped onion
1 tablespoon finely chopped green bell pepper
Salt and pepper to taste
Additional bread crumbs
Oil for frying
1/4 cup milk

Combine 1/2 cup soup, tuna, 1/2 cup bread crumbs, onion, green pepper, salt and pepper in bowl; mix well. Shape into patties. Roll in additional bread crumbs. Fry in hot oil in skillet until brown on both sides. Place cooked patties on warm serving plate. Combine remaining soup and milk in saucepan. Cook over medium heat until heated through. Pour over croquettes. **Yield: 4 to 6 servings.**

Alice Beatty, Bell Township #2047

Lemony Tuna Patties

1 12-ounce can chunk light tuna, drained
1/2 cup butter cracker crumbs
1/4 cup chopped onion
2 tablespoons chopped green bell pepper
1 egg, beaten
1/4 cup lemon or lime juice
1/2 teaspoon dillweed
1/2 cup butter cracker crumbs
2 tablespoons margarine or butter

Combine tuna, 1/2 cup cracker crumbs, onion, green pepper, egg, lemon juice and dillweed in bowl; mix well. Shape into 6 patties. Coat with 1/2 cup cracker crumbs. Brown on both sides in margarine in large skillet. Serve with tartar sauce. May microwave on High for 3 to 5 minutes or until heated through, rotating dish once. **Yield: 6 servings.**

Pearle Malone, Mendon #855

Tuna Potpie

1 package all-ready pie pastry
1 12-ounce can chunk light tuna, drained
1 10-ounce package frozen peas and carrots
1/2 onion, chopped
1 10-ounce can cream of potato soup
1/3 cup milk
1/2 teaspoon poultry seasoning
Salt and pepper to taste

Fit half the pastry into pie plate. Combine tuna, vegetables, onion, soup, milk and seasonings in bowl; mix well. Spoon into pastry-lined pie plate. Top with remaining pastry, sealing edge and cutting vents. Bake at 375 degrees for 45 to 50 minutes. **Yield: 6 servings.**

Virginia B. Guthrie, Aleppo #2054

Tuna and Rice Casserole

3 ounces cream cheese
1 10-ounce can cream of mushroom soup
2 cups cooked rice
1 7-ounce can tuna, drained
1 4-ounce can chopped mushrooms, drained
1/4 cup chopped green onions
1 tablespoon chopped parsley
1/8 teaspoon pepper
1/4 cup grated Parmesan cheese
Paprika to taste

Microwave cream cheese in 2-quart glass dish for 20 to 25 seconds or until softened. Blend in soup. Stir in rice, tuna, mushrooms, green onions, parsley and pepper. Microwave on High for 5 minutes; stir to mix. Sprinkle with cheese and paprika. Microwave for 4 to 6 minutes or until heated through. **Yield: 4 to 6 servings.**

Lorraine Keenan, Aleppo #2054

Whitefish with Kiwifruit

1 pound whitefish filets
Flour
Salt and pepper to taste
Butter for frying
1 or 2 kiwifruit, peeled, sliced
Juice of 1 orange

Coat filets with mixture of flour, salt and pepper; shake off excess. Sauté fish in butter in skillet until golden brown on both sides. Remove to warm oven-proof platter. Arrange kiwifruit slices on filets. Pour orange juice over top. Bake in 300 degree oven for 2 minutes or until heated through. **Yield: 4 to 6 servings.**

Lee Faylor Finkenbinder, Mifflin #1725

Deviled Clams

8 large fresh clams in shells
6 potatoes, chopped
1/2 cup chopped onion
1/2 cup chopped celery
1/2 cup butter or margarine
2 eggs
6 slices white bread, cubed
2 tablespoons parsley
Pepper to taste
Milk

Steam clams until shells open; reserve liquid and shells. Chop clams. Cook potatoes and chopped clams in reserved clam liquid in saucepan until potatoes are tender; drain. Mash potato mixture. Sauté onion and celery in butter in skillet. Combine with potato mixture, eggs, bread cubes, parsley and pepper in bowl; mix well. Add a small amount of milk if mixture seems dry. Spoon mixture into reserved clam shells. Arrange in baking dish. Bake at 350 degrees for 20 minutes. **Yield: 6 servings.**

Anna Grace Lorah, Alleghenyville #2065

Steamer-Style Clams

12 fresh littleneck clams in shells, scrubbed
1/4 cup water
Melted butter or cocktail sauce

Combine clams and water in shallow glass baking dish. Microwave, covered, on High for 1 minute. Microwave on Medium for 5 to 6 minutes or until clams open. Serve with melted butter or cocktail sauce. **Yield: 1 or 2 servings.**

Marie E. Schaeffer, Virginville #1832

Deviled Crab

2 cups crab meat
1/2 cup scalded milk
1/3 cup melted butter
2 eggs, well beaten
1 teaspoon salt
2 teaspoons Worcestershire sauce
1 tablespoon minced green bell pepper
1 tablespoon chopped parsley
1/2 teaspoon dry mustard
1/2 teaspoon paprika
1 cup soft bread crumbs
2 tablespoons melted butter

Combine crab meat, milk, 1/3 cup butter, eggs, salt, Worcestershire sauce, green pepper, parsley, dry mustard and paprika in bowl; mix well. Spoon into greased baking dish. Top with mixture of bread crumbs and 2 tablespoons butter. Bake at 375 degrees for 20 minutes or until golden brown. **Yield: 4 to 6 servings.**

Velma Snyder, Virginville #1832

Maryland Lump Crab Cakes

1/4 cup mayonnaise
1 teaspoon Old Bay seasoning
1 teaspoon mustard
1/2 teaspoon Worcestershire sauce
1 egg
3 slices white bread, chopped
1 pound backfin crab meat

Mix mayonnaise, Old Bay seasoning, mustard, Worcestershire sauce, egg and bread in bowl. Fold in crab meat. Shape into 4 patties. Place in buttered baking pan. Bake at 500 degrees for 12 minutes. **Yield: 4 servings.**

Virginia Wade, Vernon #936

Oyster Stew

12 oysters packed in liquid
1/2 cup butter
1 6-ounce can clams
1/2 teaspoon Worcestershire sauce
1/2 teaspoon salt
1/4 teaspoon pepper
1/2 gallon milk

Drain oysters, reserving liquid. Melt butter in saucepan over medium heat. Add oysters. Cook for 3 to 5 minutes or just until edges begin to curl. Add reserved oyster liquid, undrained clams, Worcestershire sauce, salt and pepper. Cook just until heated through. Do not boil. Heat milk in large saucepan over medium heat. Do not boil. Stir in oyster mixture gradually. Serve with oyster crackers. **Yield: 8 servings.**

Doris Koenig, Central #1650

Scalloped Oysters

2 to 3 packages saltine crackers, broken into pieces
1 pint oysters
Salt and pepper to taste
Butter
Milk

Cover bottom of greased 2-quart baking dish with cracker pieces. Place several oysters on top. Season with salt and pepper; dot with butter. Repeat layers until all oysters are used or until mixture reaches to within 3 inches of top of dish. Add enough milk to cover. Bake at 350 degrees for 45 minutes. **Yield: 8 servings.**

Mabel Krieder, Fulton #66

The flavor of allspice is a delicious addition to baked fish or oyster stew.

Shrimp Parmesan

1/2 cup butter
1 cup flour
1/4 teaspoon paprika
1 teaspoon salt
1/4 teaspoon pepper
5 cups milk
16 ounces American cheese, shredded
1 1/2 pounds (or less) shrimp, peeled
8 ounces mushrooms
3 tablespoons minced onion
1 16-ounce package spaghetti, cooked
Parmesan cheese

Combine butter, flour, paprika, salt, pepper and milk in saucepan. Cook over medium heat until thickened, stirring constantly. Add cheese, stirring until cheese melts. Add shrimp, mushrooms and onion. Fold in cooked spaghetti. Spoon into deep 9x13-inch casserole dish. Sprinkle with Parmesan cheese. Bake at 350 degrees for 30 to 45 minutes or until bubbly. **Yield: 6 to 8 servings.**

Ruth Vonada, Logan #109

Shrimp Scampi

1/2 cup chopped onion
4 cloves of garlic, finely chopped
1/4 cup butter or margarine
1/2 cup white cooking wine
2 tablespoons chopped parsley
1 pound large shrimp, peeled
1 teaspoon salt
1/4 teaspoon pepper

Sauté onion and garlic in butter in skillet until golden brown. Add wine. Bring to a boil. Stir in parsley, shrimp, salt and pepper. Cook for 3 to 4 minutes or until shrimp turn pink. Serve over rice. **Yield: 4 servings.**

Hannelore Carle, Sebring #1047

Seafood and Rice

1 pound fresh shrimp, peeled
1 pound scallops
1 or 2 green bell peppers, chopped
1 onion, chopped
Butter
Garlic powder to taste
Lemon juice to taste
1 or 2 tomatoes, cut into wedges
Cooked rice

Combine shrimp, scallops, green pepper and onion in broiler pan. Dot with butter; sprinkle with garlic powder. Add lemon juice. Broil 5 inches from heat source until green pepper and onion are tender, stirring every 5 minutes and basting with pan juices. Add tomato wedges during last 10 minutes of cooking time. Serve over rice. **Yield: 4 to 5 servings.**

Joan Chiea, Beaver Run #2049

Vegetable and Side Dishes

Asparagus Casserole

1 15-ounce can asparagus, drained, chopped
1 2-ounce jar pimento, drained, chopped
1 cup shredded Cheddar cheese
1 cup Ritz cracker crumbs
2 eggs, beaten
1/4 cup melted butter
1 cup milk
1/2 teaspoon salt
1 teaspoon pepper

Combine asparagus, pimento, cheese, cracker crumbs, eggs, butter, milk, salt and pepper in bowl; mix well. Spoon into greased baking dish. Bake at 400 degrees for 30 minutes. **Yield: 4 to 6 servings.**

Jane Darmofal, Kutztown #1836

Grandma's Asparagus Casserole

5 potatoes, sliced
2 onions, chopped
2 cups asparagus
1/2 cup butter
Salt and pepper to taste
4 slices cheese

Layer potatoes, onions and asparagus in baking dish. Dot with butter; season with salt and pepper. Bake, covered, at 325 degrees for 45 minutes. Cover top with cheese. Let stand until cheese melts. **Yield: 6 to 8 servings.**

Eda Hornick, West Pike Run #1928

Stove-Top Baked Beans

1/4 to 1/2 pound bacon
1 40-ounce can Great Northern beans
1 1/2 cups catsup
1 1/2 cups packed brown sugar
2 tablespoons molasses

Brown bacon slightly in heavy 3-quart saucepan. Add beans, catsup, brown sugar and molasses; mix well. Bring mixture to a boil. Reduce heat to low. Simmer for 2 1/2 to 3 hours. May bake at 350 degrees for 3 to 4 hours. **Yield: 8 servings.**

Mrs. Howard Barkley, Community #1767

A few drops of liquid smoke give a "cook-out" flavor to bean dishes.

Baked Beans with Maple Syrup

4 cups dry navy beans
1/2 cup maple syrup
1/2 teaspoon dry mustard
2 teaspoons salt
1 onion, sliced
1/2 pound salt pork or bacon

Soak beans in water to cover overnight. Cook beans using package directions; drain. Combine with maple syrup, dry mustard and salt; mix well. Place onion in 2 1/2-quart baking dish. Layer salt pork and bean mixture over top. Bake, covered, at 250 degrees for 6 hours, adding water as needed. **Yield: 8 to 10 servings.**

Helen F. Snyder, Milford #1744

Baked Beans

1 pound dry navy beans
2 cups chili sauce
1/2 cup packed brown sugar
1/2 teaspoon dry mustard
1 teaspoon salt
Pepper to taste
Sliced bacon

Parboil beans in large saucepan; drain. Add fresh water to cover. Bring to a boil. Cook until beans are almost tender. Spoon beans into 2-quart baking dish. Add chili sauce, brown sugar, dry mustard, salt and pepper; mix well. Place bacon slices on top. Bake at 350 degrees for 1 1/2 hours. **Yield: 10 to 12 servings.**

Lois Moore, Scrubgrass #1705

Mixed Baked Beans

2 16-ounce cans butter beans, drained
1 16-ounce can green lima beans, drained
1 16-ounce can kidney beans, drained
1 16-ounce can baked beans
8 slices bacon
1 cup packed brown sugar
1/2 cup vinegar
1 teaspoon dry mustard
1 1/2 teaspoons salt
3/4 teaspoon garlic salt
Pepper to taste
4 onions, sliced into rings

Combine butter beans, lima beans, kidney beans and undrained baked beans in large baking dish; mix well. Fry bacon in skillet until crisp. Remove bacon; crumble. Add brown sugar, vinegar, dry mustard, salt, garlic salt, pepper and onions to pan drippings in skillet. Simmer for 20 minutes. Add mixture to beans with half the bacon; mix well. Top with remaining bacon. Bake at 350 degrees for 1 hour.
Yield: 10 to 12 servings.

Betty Carlson, Chandlers Valley #846

Baker Beans

4 slices bacon
1 onion, chopped
1 16-ounce can butter beans, drained
1 16-ounce can kidney beans, drained
1 16-ounce can baked beans
4 ounces American cheese, chopped
1/2 cup packed brown sugar
1/3 cup catsup
2 teaspoons Worcestershire sauce
Parmesan cheese

Fry bacon in skillet until crisp. Remove bacon; crumble. Sauté onion in pan drippings. Combine drained beans, undrained baked beans, bacon, onion, American cheese, brown sugar, catsup and Worcestershire sauce in bowl; mix well. Spoon into baking dish. Top with Parmesan cheese. Bake at 375 degrees for 30 to 45 minutes. **Yield: 6 servings.**

Josephine Shutts, South Buffalo #1908

Ma's Beans

2 tablespoons bacon drippings
1 40-ounce can Great Northern beans, partially drained
1 15-ounce can Great Northern beans, partially drained
1 cup sugar
1 cup catsup

Melt bacon drippings in small skillet. Combine with beans, sugar and catsup in bowl; mix well. Spoon into 3-quart baking dish. Bake at 375 degrees for 30 minutes. Reduce oven temperature to 325 degrees. Bake for 1 hour or until most of the liquid is evaporated and top is lightly browned. **Yield: 6 to 8 servings.**

Jean Gensamer, Port Matilda #1284

Sweet Baked Beans

1/2 pound sliced bacon
1 large can marrow beans
1/2 cup packed brown sugar
1/2 cup sugar
1/2 teaspoon pepper

Reserve 4 or 5 slices bacon for topping. Chop remaining bacon. Fry chopped bacon in skillet until crisp; drain. Combine cooked bacon with beans, brown sugar, sugar and pepper in bowl; mix well. Spoon into baking dish. Top with reserved bacon slices. Bake at 350 degrees for 45 minutes. **Yield: 4 servings.**

Karmel Schlieder, Roaring Creek Valley #2041

Welsh Settlement Baked Beans

1 large can Great Northern beans
1 cup packed brown sugar
1 cup sugar
1 small bottle of catsup

Combine beans, brown sugar, sugar and catsup in bowl; mix well. Spoon into baking dish. Bake at 350 degrees for 1 hour. **Yield: 4 to 6 servings.**

Glenora Rogers, Charleston Valley #54

Barbecued Beans

1 pound bacon, crisp-fried, crumbled
1 onion, chopped
1 16-ounce can kidney beans, drained
1 16-ounce can green beans, drained
1 16-ounce can lima beans, drained
1 16-ounce can pork and beans
1/4 cup packed brown sugar
1 cup catsup
2 tablespoons Worcestershire sauce
2 tablespoons mustard

Combine crumbled bacon, onion, drained beans, undrained pork and beans, brown sugar, catsup, Worcestershire sauce and mustard in saucepan; mix well. Simmer for 2 hours. **Yield: 10 to 12 servings.**

Juanita Martin, North Sewickley #1566

Block Party Beans

2 pounds ground beef
2 cups chopped onions
1 cup chopped celery
1 16-ounce can hot chili beans, drained
1 16-ounce can kidney beans, drained
1 16-ounce can pork and beans, drained
1 16-ounce can yellow wax beans, drained
1 16-ounce can green beans, drained
1 16-ounce can lima beans, drained
1 6-ounce can tomato paste
1/2 bottle of catsup
1 10-ounce can tomato soup
1/2 cup packed brown sugar
3 tablespoons prepared mustard

Brown ground beef in large Dutch oven, stirring until crumbly; drain. Add onions and celery. Simmer for 10 minutes. Add beans; stir gently. Add tomato paste, catsup, soup, brown sugar and mustard; mix well. Bake at 300 to 325 degrees for 2 hours or until done to taste. **Yield: 24 servings.**

LaVerne Burkhart, Gouglersville #1743

Four-Bean Bake

1 16-ounce can green beans, drained
1 16-ounce can butter beans, drained
1 16-ounce can kidney beans, drained
1 16-ounce can baked beans
1 small onion, chopped
1/4 cup catsup
2 teaspoons prepared mustard
1 cup packed brown sugar
Kielbasa sausage to taste

Combine drained beans, undrained baked beans, onion, catsup, mustard, brown sugar and kielbasa sausage in baking dish; mix well. Bake at 350 degrees for 1 hour. **Yield: 8 to 10 servings.**

Delores London, Elder #503

Italian Four-Bean Bake

1 large onion, chopped
2 green bell peppers, cut into 1/2-inch pieces
2 cloves of garlic, minced
2 tablespoons oil
1 16-ounce can kidney beans, drained
1 16-ounce can pinto beans, drained
1 16-ounce can garbanzo beans, drained
1 16-ounce can chili beans in sauce
1 16-ounce can stewed tomatoes
3/4 teaspoon ground cumin
1 teaspoon Italian seasoning
Salt and pepper to taste

Combine onion, green pepper pieces, garlic and oil in 3-quart glass dish. Microwave on High for 4 minutes. Add drained beans, undrained chili beans, undrained tomatoes, cumin, and Italian seasoning; mix well. Microwave, covered, for 9 to 11 minutes, stirring once. Add salt and pepper. **Yield: 6 to 8 servings.**

Carrie C. Frederick, Sinking Valley #484

Five-Bean Casserole

1 pound hot or sweet sausage
1 cup chopped onions
1 cup catsup
3/4 cup packed brown sugar
1 16-ounce can green beans, drained
1 16-ounce can pinto beans, drained
1 16-ounce can lima beans, drained
1 16-ounce can kidney beans, drained
1 16-ounce can pork and beans

Fry sausage in skillet until brown and crumbly; drain. Combine with onions, catsup, brown sugar, drained beans and undrained pork and beans in large bowl; mix well. Spoon into baking dish. Bake at 350 degrees for 1 hour. **Yield: 12 to 14 servings.**

Alda L. Tromby, Mt. Joy #537

Old Settler's Baked Beans

1/2 pound ground beef
1/2 pound bacon, chopped
1 small onion, chopped
1 16-ounce can pork and beans
1 16-ounce can butter beans, drained
1 16-ounce can kidney beans, partially drained
1/2 cup packed brown sugar
1/2 cup sugar
1/2 cup catsup
1/4 cup mustard
2 tablespoons molasses

Brown ground beef and bacon with onion in skillet, stirring until ground beef is crumbly; drain. Stir in undrained pork and beans and remaining beans. Mix brown sugar, sugar, catsup, mustard and molasses in bowl. Stir into bean mixture. Spoon into baking dish. Bake at 350 degrees for 1 hour and 15 minutes.
Yield: 8 to 10 servings.

Miriam Sidle, Valley #1360

Denise's Green Bean Casserole

2 10-ounce packages frozen French-style green beans, thawed
2 10-ounce cans cream of mushroom soup
1/4 cup slivered almonds
3 medium potatoes, chopped
1 6-ounce can mushroom pieces, drained
Pepper to taste
2 cans French-fried onions

Combine green beans, soup, almonds, potatoes, mushrooms, pepper and half the onions in bowl; mix well. Spoon into 2-quart baking dish. Top with remaining onions. Bake, loosely covered, at 350 degrees for 35 minutes. Remove cover. Bake for 10 minutes longer or until onions are golden brown. **Yield: 10 to 12 servings.**

Erla Florelle Haas, Shermanata #1796

Green Lima Bean Casserole

3 tablespoons melted butter
2 tablespoons flour
1 teaspoon salt
1/4 teaspoon pepper
1 cup sour cream
4 cups green lima beans
1/2 medium onion, grated
8 ounces Cheddar cheese, shredded
1 tablespoon butter
1/2 cup cornflakes, crushed

Combine 3 tablespoons butter, flour, salt and pepper in saucepan. Cook over low heat for several minutes, stirring constantly. Remove from heat. Stir in sour cream. Fold in beans and onion gently. Spoon into 2-quart baking dish. Cover top with cheese. Dot with 1 tablespoon butter; sprinkle with cornflake crumbs. Bake at 350 degrees for 30 minutes. **Yield: 6 to 8 servings.**

Helen Straub, Pleasant Ridge #1678

Mustard Beans

1 cup sugar
1/2 cup prepared mustard
1/2 teaspoon dried minced onion
1/4 teaspoon salt
1 16-ounce can yellow wax beans

Combine sugar, mustard, onion and salt in 3-quart saucepan. Bring to a boil, stirring until sugar dissolves. Add beans. Simmer for 5 minutes. Let stand until cool. Spoon into serving dish. Chill, covered, overnight. Serve cold. **Yield: 4 to 6 servings.**

Margery Faul, Vernon #936

Harvard Beets with Cloves

1 tablespoon cornstarch
1/2 cup sugar
1/2 teaspoon salt
1/4 cup vinegar
1/4 cup water
3 whole cloves
3 cups sliced cooked beets
2 tablespoons butter or margarine

Blend cornstarch, sugar and salt in saucepan. Combine vinegar and water in bowl. Stir into cornstarch mixture gradually. Cook over low heat until thickened, stirring constantly. Stir in cloves and beets. Let stand in warm place for 30 minutes. Remove cloves. Add butter. Cook until heated through. **Yield: 6 servings.**

Frances Wise, Amity #1540

Broccoli Bake

1 cup chopped onion
1 cup chopped celery
1 cup chopped green bell pepper
1/4 cup margarine
1 10-ounce package frozen chopped broccoli, thawed
2 cups cooked rice
1 10-ounce can cream of mushroom soup
1 8-ounce jar Cheez Whiz

Sauté onion, celery and green pepper in margarine in skillet. Stir in broccoli and rice. Spoon into 2-quart baking dish. Pour soup over top. Dot with Cheez Whiz. Bake at 350 degrees for 1 hour. **Yield: 8 to 10 servings.**

Anna Mary Brenneman, Scotch Valley #510

Chop unused broccoli stems in food processor. Store them in a plastic bag in the freezer for use in soups.

Easy Broccoli Bake

1 10-ounce can cream of broccoli soup
1/2 cup milk
1 teaspoon soy sauce
Pepper to taste
1 bunch broccoli, chopped
1 3-ounce can French-fried onions

Combine soup, milk, soy sauce and pepper in bowl; mix well. Stir in broccoli and half the onions. Spoon into 1 1/2-quart baking dish. Bake at 350 degrees for 25 minutes. Stir mixture. Top with remaining onions. Bake for 5 minutes longer. **Yield: 6 servings.**

Catherine Schwarzbach, Penn #534

Golden Broccoli Casserole

1 20-ounce package frozen broccoli
1 10-ounce can cream of celery soup
1 cup mayonnaise
2 eggs, well beaten
1 cup shredded sharp Cheddar cheese
2 tablespoons chopped onion
Pepper to taste
2 tablespoons butter
1 cup crushed Ritz crackers

Cook broccoli using package directions just until thawed; drain. Combine soup, mayonnaise, eggs, cheese, onion and pepper in bowl; mix well. Stir in broccoli. Spoon into 2-quart baking dish. Dot with butter; sprinkle with cracker crumbs. Bake at 350 degrees for 30 minutes. **Yield: 8 servings.**

Florence E. Hartley, Fort Granville #1902

Broccoli Casserole

1 1/2 pounds frozen chopped broccoli
1/2 teaspoon salt
1 10-ounce can cream of mushroom soup
1/4 cup milk
1 1/2 cups shredded Cheddar cheese
1/4 cup margarine
1 cup baking mix

Cook broccoli in 1 inch salted water in saucepan just until tender; drain. Place in round baking dish. Beat soup and milk in bowl with hand mixer until smooth. Pour over broccoli. Sprinkle cheese over top. Cut margarine into baking mix in bowl until crumbly. Sprinkle over cheese layer. Bake at 400 degrees for 20 minutes or until brown. **Yield: 8 to 10 servings.**

Barbara Handwork, Wills #1690

Broccoli Deluxe

Flowerets of 1 bunch broccoli
2 egg whites
1/2 teaspoon salt
1/2 cup mayonnaise
Parmesan cheese

Cook broccoli in a small amount of water in saucepan until tender; drain. Arrange stem ends toward center on ovenproof serving plate. Beat egg whites with salt in mixer bowl until stiff peaks form. Fold in mayonnaise. Spread on broccoli. Sprinkle with cheese. Broil until golden brown. **Yield: 4 servings.**

Ann Weber, Henderson #1315

Broccoli-Carrot Stir-Fry

1/3 cup orange juice
1 teaspoon cornstarch
1 tablespoon sherry
1 teaspoon grated gingerroot
1 tablespoon (or more) oil
1 1/2 cups diagonally sliced carrots
1 cup broccoli flowerets
2 tablespoons chopped walnuts

Mix orange juice, cornstarch and sherry in small bowl. Set aside. Stir-fry gingerroot in hot oil in wok for 1 minute. Add carrots. Stir-fry for 1 minute. Add broccoli. Stir-fry for 3 to 4 minutes or until tender-crisp. Push vegetables away from center of wok. Add sauce to center. Cook until thickened, stirring constantly. Cook for 1 minute longer. Stir vegetables and walnuts into sauce until coated. Serve immediately. **Yield: 4 servings.**

Nancy B. Matter, Community #2048

Broccoli and Corn

1 12-ounce package chicken-flavored crackers, crushed
1 20-ounce package frozen broccoli
1 16-ounce can cream-style corn
1 16-ounce can whole kernel corn, drained
1/2 cup melted margarine

Reserve 1 cup cracker crumbs for topping. Combine remaining crumbs with broccoli, cream-style corn and whole kernel corn in bowl; mix well. Spoon into greased 9x13-inch baking dish. Top with reserved cracker crumbs. Drizzle margarine over top. Bake at 350 degrees for 25 minutes. **Yield: 12 servings.**

Doris Prosser, Scrubgrass # 1705

Try something different. Look for spaghetti squash, jicama, radicchio, enoki mushrooms, chayote and other new produce at your market.

Broccoli and Creamed Corn Casserole

1 10-ounce package frozen chopped broccoli
1 20-ounce can cream-style corn
1 egg
2 tablespoons melted margarine
2 tablespoons chopped onion
16 to 20 Ritz crackers, crushed
1/4 cup margarine
Paprika to taste

Cook broccoli using package directions. Combine with corn, egg, 2 tablespoons margarine and onion in bowl; mix well. Spoon into buttered 2-quart baking dish. Top with mixture of cracker crumbs and 1/4 cup margarine. Sprinkle with paprika. Bake at 350 degrees for 25 minutes. **Yield: 4 to 5 servings.**

Lesta Schreiber, Perry Valley #1804

Broccoli-Rice Casserole

1/4 cup chopped onion
1 tablespoon plus 1 teaspoon margarine
3 tablespoons flour
1/2 teaspoon dry mustard
1 1/4 cups skim milk
1/8 teaspoon pepper
3 cups coarsely chopped broccoli
1 3/4 cups unseasoned, cooked long grain rice
1 cup shredded reduced-fat sharp Cheddar cheese
1/4 cup nonfat mayonnaise
1 teaspoon melted margarine
1/3 cup crushed unsalted Melba toast

Sauté onion in 1 tablespoon plus 1 teaspoon margarine in skillet for 3 minutes or until tender. Add flour and mustard. Cook for 1 minute, stirring constantly with a wire whisk. Add milk gradually, stirring constantly. Remove from heat. Stir in pepper. Combine broccoli, milk mixture, rice, cheese and mayonnaise in bowl; mix well. Spoon into shallow 2-quart baking dish coated with nonstick cooking spray. Mix 1 teaspoon margarine and toast crumbs in small bowl. Sprinkle over broccoli mixture. Bake at 350 degrees for 25 minutes or until bubbly in center. **Yield: 8 servings.**

Jane M. Madsen, Port Matilda #1284

Stuffed Broccoli

2 10-ounce packages frozen chopped broccoli
1/2 cup butter
4 chicken bouillon cubes, crushed
1/4 cup flour
2 cups milk
6 tablespoons butter
2/3 cup water
1 package stuffing mix

Cook broccoli using package directions; drain. Place in 3-quart baking dish. Melt 1/2 cup butter in small saucepan. Stir in bouillon, flour and milk. Cook over medium heat until thickened, stirring constantly. Pour over broccoli. Melt 6 tablespoons butter in saucepan. Add water. Pour over stuffing mix in bowl; toss until mixed. Spread over broccoli mixture. Bake at 350 degrees for 30 minutes. **Yield: 8 servings.**

Jane Cathcart, Jackson #1506

Cabbage Casserole

1 medium head cabbage, sliced
1 10-ounce can cream of chicken soup
1/2 cup shredded Cheddar cheese
1/2 teaspoon salt
Pepper to taste
1/4 cup bread crumbs
Butter

Parboil sliced cabbage for 5 minutes in saucepan; drain. Alternate layers of cabbage and soup in 1 1/2-quart baking dish. Sprinkle cheese over top. Add salt and pepper. Sprinkle with bread crumbs; dot with butter. Bake at 350 degrees for 30 minutes. **Yield: 6 servings.**

Margery Terwilliger, Kaylor #1396

Golden Cabbage

1/2 head cabbage, coarsely chopped
Salt to taste
1 egg, beaten

Cook cabbage in a small amount of salted water in saucepan until tender; drain. Toss with beaten egg in bowl. Serve immediately. Heat of cabbage will cook egg. **Yield: 2 to 4 servings.**

Pearl Orient, Community #1994

Creamed Cabbage

4 cups sliced cabbage
Salt to taste
1/2 cup water
1 cup whipping cream or half and half
2 tablespoons butter
2 tablespoons flour
1/4 cup milk
1 teaspoon salt
1/2 teaspoon pepper

Cook cabbage in salted water in saucepan over low heat until tender, adding additional water as needed; drain. Return cabbage to saucepan. Add whipping cream, butter, flour, milk, salt and pepper. Cook until thickened, stirring constantly. Spoon into serving dish. **Yield: 4 to 6 servings.**

Walter R. Long, Unity #1710

Cook vegetables such as cabbage with the least amount of water possible to preserve both nutrients and flavor.

Carrot and Apple Casserole

6 tablespoons sugar
2 tablespoons flour
1 teaspoon salt
5 apples, peeled, thinly sliced
2 cups cooked sliced carrots
3/4 cup orange juice

Mix sugar, flour and salt in small bowl. Alternate layers of apple slices and carrots in baking dish, sprinkling sugar mixture between each layer. Pour orange juice over top. Bake at 350 degrees for 20 to 30 minutes. May substitute sweet potatoes for carrots. **Yield: 8 to 10 servings.**

Louise Snyder, Edinboro #947

Carrots with Cheese Sauce

4 cups 1/2-inch carrot slices
1/2 teaspoon salt
1 cup water
2 tablespoons butter
2 tablespoons flour
1 cup milk
1 cup shredded American cheese
1 3-ounce can French-fried onions

Cook carrots in salted water in saucepan until tender; drain. Melt butter in saucepan over medium heat. Stir in flour. Add milk gradually. Cook until thickened, stirring constantly. Stir in cheese until melted. Reserve 1/3 of the onions for topping. Place 1/3 of the carrots in 1 1/2-quart baking dish. Layer onions and carrots 1/2 at a time over top. Pour cheese sauce over layers. Bake at 350 degrees for 15 minutes. Top with remaining onions. Bake for 5 minutes longer. **Yield: 6 servings.**

Lois McAlevy, Logan Valley #664

Carrots and Pineapple

1 16-ounce can pineapple chunks
1/4 cup packed brown sugar
1 tablespoon butter
2 teaspoons cornstarch
1/2 teaspoon cinnamon
1 20-ounce can whole baby carrots, drained

Drain pineapple, reserving juice. Combine reserved pineapple juice with brown sugar, butter, cornstarch and cinnamon in saucepan. Cook over medium heat until thickened and clear, stirring constantly. Stir in pineapple and carrots. Cook until heated through. **Yield: 4 to 6 servings.**

Avonell Clark, Roseville #1290

Add your favorite dry salad dressing mix to white sauce to give a different flavor to vegetables.

Deviled Carrots with Water Chestnuts

1 pound carrots
1/2 cup butter
2 tablespoons brown sugar
1 tablespoon chopped chives
1 teaspoon dry mustard
3/4 teaspoon salt
1/8 teaspoon pepper
1 can sliced water chestnuts, drained

Cut carrots into halves lengthwise. Sauté in butter in skillet over medium heat for 5 minutes. Stir in brown sugar, chives, dry mustard, salt and pepper. Reduce heat to low. Simmer, covered, until carrots are tender. Stir in water chestnuts. Cook until heated through. **Yield: 8 to 10 servings.**

Miriam M. Forney, Star #993

Gingered Carrots

5 or 6 carrots, peeled, cut into chunks
1/2 teaspoon ground ginger
1 teaspoon sugar
1/4 cup butter or margarine
2 tablespoons chopped fresh parsley

Cook carrots in a small amount of water in saucepan until tender; drain. Return carrots to saucepan with ginger, sugar and butter. Cook over low heat until carrots are reheated, stirring to coat carrots with sauce. Sprinkle with parsley. Serve immediately. **Yield: 4 servings.**

Anna Gould, Bell Twp. #2047

Honey-Buttered Carrots

24 baby carrots, peeled
1/2 teaspoon salt
1 cup water
3 tablespoons butter
3 tablespoons honey
1/4 teaspoon cinnamon
1/4 teaspoon nutmeg

Cook carrots in salted water in heavy 2-quart saucepan over medium heat for 10 to 15 minutes or until tender; drain. Add butter, honey, cinnamon and nutmeg. Bring to a boil over medium heat, stirring occasionally. Serve immediately.
Yield: 4 servings.

Mrs. Merle U. Fox, Gideon #2010

For glazed carrots, cook 2 cups carrot slices in 3 cups club soda until tender-crisp and drain. Add 1/4 cup butter and brown sugar to taste and heat until glazed.

Honey-Coated Carrots

4 medium carrots, sliced
2 tablespoons butter or margarine
2 tablespoons honey
2 tablespoons water
1/4 teaspoon salt

Combine carrots, butter, honey, water and salt in 1-quart glass baking dish. Microwave, covered with plastic wrap, on High for 3 to 4 minutes or until carrots are tender-crisp. Let stand, covered, for 3 minutes. Serve immediately.
Yield: 2 to 3 servings.

Renee Calvert, Central #1650

Corn Balls

1 egg
1 small onion, chopped
1/8 teaspoon salt
Pepper to taste
2 cups frozen corn, thawed
3 slices crisp-fried bacon, crumbled
4 slices bread, torn into small pieces
1/4 cup butter

Beat egg in large bowl. Add onion, salt, pepper, corn, bacon and bread pieces; mix well. Melt butter in 1-quart baking dish. Scoop corn mixture into balls with an ice cream scoop. Place in prepared baking dish. Bake at 325 degrees for 30 minutes. May use fresh corn but it should be cooked for 3 minutes before proceeding with recipe instructions. **Yield: 8 servings.**

Helen J. Brown, Somerset #1697

Corn Fritters

3 egg yolks
2 2/3 cups cooked corn
1/2 teaspoon salt
1/4 teaspoon pepper
1/4 cup flour
3 egg whites, stiffly beaten
Oil for frying

Beat egg yolks in bowl until light and lemon-colored. Stir in corn, salt, pepper and flour. Fold in egg whites gently. Drop by spoonfuls into hot oil in skillet. Cook until golden brown, turning once. **Yield: 6 servings.**

Hazel L. Anspach, North Woodbury #1923

Substitute crushed wheat germ for buttered crumbs for a delicious, nutritious and easy casserole topping.

Corn Soufflé

3 tablespoons butter
1/4 cup flour
1/2 teaspoon salt
1/4 teaspoon pepper
1 cup milk
1 cup home-cooked or canned corn
1 tablespoon lemon juice
2 teaspoons grated onion
4 egg yolks, beaten
4 egg whites
1/4 teaspoon cream of tartar

Melt butter in saucepan over medium heat. Stir in flour, salt and pepper. Add milk gradually, stirring constantly. Cook until thickened, stirring constantly. Stir in corn, lemon juice, onion and beaten egg yolks. Let stand until cool. Beat egg whites until frothy. Add cream of tartar. Beat until soft peaks form. Fold gently into corn mixture. Spoon into greased 1 1/2-quart baking dish. Bake at 325 degrees for 1 hour. **Yield: 6 servings.**

Ruth W. Warmkessel, Macungie #1569

Southern-Style Baked Corn

1 16-ounce can whole kernel corn
1 16-ounce can cream-style corn
2 eggs, beaten
1 8-ounce package corn bread mix
1 cup sour cream
1/2 cup melted butter, cooled
Salt and pepper to taste
Parmesan cheese

Mix undrained whole kernel corn corn, cream-style corn, eggs, corn bread mix and sour cream in bowl. Stir in cooled butter. Add salt and pepper. Spoon into 10x10-inch baking dish. Bake at 350 degrees for 30 minutes. Sprinkle with cheese. Bake for 15 minutes longer. **Yield: 8 to 10 servings.**

Lisa Rodgers, East Brook #1706

Baked Eggplant with Cheese

2 medium eggplant, peeled, cubed
1 cup shredded extra-sharp Cheddar cheese
1 cup cracker crumbs
1 cup milk
1 green bell pepper, finely chopped
4 eggs, beaten
2 tablespoons oil
Salt and pepper to taste

Cook eggplant in boiling water until tender; drain. Mash in bowl; set aside. Combine cheese, cracker crumbs, milk, green pepper, eggs, oil, salt and pepper in large bowl; mix well. Stir in eggplant. Pour into greased 2-quart baking dish. Bake at 375 degrees for 35 to 40 minutes or until browned. **Yield: 6 to 8 servings.**

Mildred Neyhard, California #941

Mushroom Business

2 pounds fresh mushrooms, sliced
2 teaspoons butter
1/4 cup chopped onion
1/4 cup chopped celery
1/4 cup chopped green bell pepper
1/2 cup mayonnaise
Salt and pepper to taste
2 teaspoons butter
6 slices bread
1 10-ounce can cream of mushroom soup
1 to 2 cups shredded Cheddar cheese

Sauté mushrooms in 2 teaspoons butter in skillet until tender. Combine with onion, celery, green pepper, mayonnaise, salt and pepper in bowl; mix well. Butter bread slices; cut into 1-inch squares. Place half the bread in 9x13-inch baking pan sprayed with nonstick cooking spray. Spread with mushroom mixture. Layer with remaining bread. Spread mushroom soup over top layer. Chill for 1 hour. Bake at 325 degrees for 50 minutes. Sprinkle with cheese. Bake at 325 degrees for 10 minutes longer. **Yield: 12 servings.**

Olive Smeltzer, Kaylor #1396

Onions au Gratin

2 to 3 large onions, sliced
1 beef or chicken bouillon cube
3/4 cup boiling water
1/4 teaspoon thyme
1 tablespoon butter
Salt and pepper to taste
1/2 cup bread crumbs
2 tablespoons melted butter
1/4 cup shredded sharp Cheddar cheese

Place onion slices in 9x9-inch baking pan. Dissolve bouillon cube in boiling water; add thyme. Pour over onions. Dot with butter; sprinkle with salt and pepper. Bake, covered, at 400 degrees for 20 minutes. Toss bread crumbs with melted butter in small bowl; add cheese. Sprinkle over baked onions. Bake, uncovered, for 10 minutes or until crisp and golden. **Yield: 5 servings.**

Carol L. Etchberger, Ontelaunee #1617

Scalloped Onions

5 onions, sliced
5 slices bread, toasted, cubed
1/2 cup margarine
1/4 cup flour
2 cups milk
1 cup shredded Velveeta cheese

Parboil onions in saucepan in a small amount of water until tender-crisp; drain. Combine with toasted bread cubes in bowl; set aside. Melt margarine in saucepan; stir in flour. Add milk gradually. Cook over medium heat until thickened, stirring constantly. Add cheese. Cook until cheese is melted, stirring frequently. Pour over onion mixture; mix well. Spoon into 1 1/2-quart baking dish. Bake at 350 degrees for 25 to 30 minutes. **Yield: 6 to 8 servings.**

Anita Peffer, Plain Grove #1431

Pea Casserole

2 10-ounce packages frozen green peas
1 green bell pepper, chopped
2 teaspoons chopped pimento
1 stalk celery, chopped
1 8-ounce can sliced water chestnuts
1 10-ounce can cream of mushroom soup
1 package stuffing mix
Melted butter

Cook peas in boiling water in saucepan for 4 minutes; drain. Sauté green pepper, pimento and celery in a small amount of oil in skillet until brown. Stir into peas with water chestnuts and mushroom soup. Spoon into baking dish. Toss stuffing mix with melted butter; sprinkle over top. Bake at 350 degrees for 35 minutes. **Yield: 6 to 8 servings.**

Alta Gannon, Slippery Rock #1441

Baked Potato Patties

1 2-pound package mashed potato flakes
2 eggs, beaten
1/2 teaspoon salt
1 1/2 tablespoons chopped onion
1 tablespoon parsley
2 tablespoons butter
Bread crumbs
Shredded cheese

Cook mashed potato flakes using package directions. Combine with eggs, salt, onion, parsley and butter in bowl; mix well. Add enough bread crumbs to keep mixture together. Shape into patties. Place in greased baking pan. Sprinkle with shredded cheese. Bake at 350 degrees for 30 minutes. Garnish with sliced tomatoes. **Yield: 8 to 10 servings.**

Mildred Reinert, Pioneer #1777

Cheese-Stuffed Baked Potatoes

12 medium potatoes
1/4 cup butter
1 1/2 teaspoons salt
1/2 teaspoon pepper
1 1/2 cups milk
3 cups shredded American or Cheddar cheese
1/2 teaspoon paprika

Bake unpeeled potatoes at 400 degrees for 1 hour or until potatoes test done; cool. Cut into halves lengthwise. Scoop out pulp, reserving shells. Combine potato pulp with butter, salt, pepper, milk and cheese in mixer bowl, beating until smooth. Spoon into reserved shells. Sprinkle with paprika. Bake at 375 degrees for 10 minutes or until heated through. May freeze before second baking if desired. **Yield: 12 servings.**

Velma Snyder, Virginville #1832

Herbed Potato Bake

1/4 cup melted butter or margarine
1 teaspoon seasoned salt
1/2 teaspoon pepper
1/4 teaspoon dried oregano
1/4 teaspoon dried thyme
1/4 teaspoon dried marjoram
3 to 4 potatoes, thinly sliced
2 medium onions, thinly sliced

Combine butter, seasoned salt, pepper, oregano, thyme and marjoram in large bowl; mix well. Add sliced potatoes and onions, tossing to coat. Spoon into greased 2 1/2-quart baking dish. Bake, covered, at 350 degrees for 1 hour. **Yield: 4 servings.**

Nettie A. Kauffman, Ontelaunee #1617

Ham and Cheese Potatoes

8 to 10 medium potatoes, peeled, cubed
8 ounces ham, cubed
8 ounces Velveeta cheese, shredded or cubed
3/4 cup evaporated milk

Cook potatoes and ham in water to cover in saucepan until tender; drain. Combine cheese and evaporated milk in small saucepan. Heat until cheese is melted, stirring frequently. Pour into potato mixture, tossing to coat. Garnish with sprinkle of chopped parsley. Serve hot. **Yield: 8 to 10 servings.**

Letha Levan, Roaring Creek Valley #2041

Holiday Potatoes

4 pounds potatoes, cooked, peeled, chilled
1 1/2 cups shredded Cheddar cheese
1 cup chopped onion
1/4 cup butter
1 10-ounce can cream of celery soup
2 cups sour cream
1/2 cup crushed cornflakes
1 tablespoon melted butter

Shred chilled potatoes into bowl. Stir in cheese; set aside. Sauté onion in 1/4 cup butter in skillet until tender; remove from heat. Stir in soup and sour cream. Pour over potatoes and cheese mixture; mix well. Spoon into greased 9x13-inch baking dish. Chill, covered, overnight. Sprinkle with cornflakes; drizzle with butter. Bake at 350 degrees for 1 hour. **Yield: 6 to 8 servings.**

Esther Blatt, Ontelaunee #1617

To keep boiled potatoes white, add a small amount of milk to the cooking water. The potatoes will taste better, too.

Plotskies (Potato Pancakes)

3 medium potatoes, peeled, chopped
1 medium onion, chopped
1 egg
1 teaspoon baking powder
1/4 cup flour
1 teaspoon salt
Oil for frying

Combine potatoes and onion in blender container. Process until purêed. Add egg, baking powder, flour and salt; mix well. Drop by tablespoonfuls onto hot greased griddle. Bake on both sides over medium heat until brown; drain on paper towels. Serve with sour cream or applesauce. **Yield: 3 to 4 servings.**

Mary E. Alkons, Virginville #1832

Latkes (Potato Pancakes)

6 potatoes, peeled
1/4 cup potato starch
2 eggs
Garlic, salt and pepper to taste
1/2 onion, chopped

Grate potatoes into bowl. Add potato starch and eggs; mix well. Stir in garlic, salt, pepper and onion. Let stand for 6 minutes or until thickened. Drop by tablespoonfuls onto hot greased griddle or skillet. Bake over high heat for 3 minutes or until brown on both sides. **Yield: 6 servings.**

Barbara Weiss, Bottle Run #1301

Mushroom-Potato Casserole

1 cup shredded Gruyère cheese
1 cup shredded Cheddar cheese
1/2 cup sour cream
1/2 cup dry-curd cottage cheese
1 medium onion, finely chopped
1 teaspoon dried thyme
2 pounds potatoes, peeled, thinly sliced
8 ounces fresh mushrooms, sliced
2 tablespoons flour
Salt and pepper to taste
1/4 cup wheat germ
3 tablespoons butter or margarine

Combine cheeses, sour cream, cottage cheese, onion and thyme in medium bowl; mix well. Place 1/3 of the potatoes in buttered 2-quart baking dish. Spoon in half the cheese mixture. Toss mushrooms with flour; arrange half the mushroom mixture over cheese mixture. Sprinkle with salt and pepper. Repeat layers, ending with potatoes. Sprinkle with wheat germ; dot with butter. Bake at 350 degrees for 1 to 1 1/4 hours or until potatoes are tender. Cool for 10 minutes before serving.
Yield: 4 servings.

Mona Bowmaster, Logan #109

Oven-Fried Potatoes

4 large potatoes
1/4 cup oil
1 to 2 tablespoons grated Parmesan cheese
1/2 teaspoon salt
1/4 teaspoon garlic powder
1/4 teaspoon paprika
1/8 teaspoon pepper

Cut each unpeeled potato lengthwise into 4 wedges. Place wedges peel side down in 9x13-inch baking dish. Combine oil, Parmesan cheese, salt, garlic powder, paprika and pepper in small bowl; mix well. Brush over potatoes. Bake at 375 degrees for 45 minutes, basting every 15 minutes with cheese mixture. Turn potatoes. Bake for 15 minutes longer. **Yield: 4 servings.**

Mildred Dumbauld, Kingwood #1765

Cheesy Seasoned Oven-Fried Potatoes

1/4 cup grated Parmesan cheese
1/2 teaspoon garlic powder or garlic salt
1/2 teaspoon onion powder
1/2 teaspoon paprika
1 pound potatoes

Combine Parmesan cheese, garlic powder, onion powder and paprika in paper bag, shaking to mix. Slice potatoes thinly but do not peel. Add to cheese mixture a few at a time, shaking to coat well. Place in baking dish. Bake at 400 degrees for 15 to 20 minutes or until tender. **Yield: 4 to 5 servings.**

Rita Hirschfeld, Burgettstown #1502

Paprika Potatoes Darlene

8 new potatoes, peeled
1 tablespoon margarine
1/2 teaspoon paprika

Place potatoes in saucepan with enough salted water to cover. Bring to a boil; reduce heat. Simmer for 15 to 20 minutes or until tender; drain. Add margarine and paprika, stirring until potatoes are coated. May substitute 2 large baking potatoes, peeled and quartered, for new potatoes. **Yield: 4 servings.**

Darlene Kurtz, Virginville #1832

Cook small new potatoes in your slow cooker on Low for 8 to 10 hours. Serve with dishes of sour cream, crumbled bacon, butter and chopped chives.

Pittsburgh Potatoes

4 cups chopped peeled potatoes
1 large onion, chopped
1 can pimentos, chopped
8 ounces Cheddar cheese, cubed
3 tablespoons butter
3 tablespoons flour
1½ teaspoons salt
1½ teaspoons pepper
1½ cups milk
Buttered bread crumbs

Place potatoes, onion and pimentos in saucepan. Add enough water to cover. Bring to a boil. Cook for 5 minutes. Drain, reserving ½ cup cooking water. Place vegetables in greased baking dish. Sprinkle with cheese. Melt butter in saucepan. Blend in flour, salt and pepper. Stir in milk and reserved cooking liquid slowly. Simmer until thickened, stirring constantly. Pour over vegetable mixture. Top with desired amount of buttered bread crumbs. Bake at 350 degrees for 30 to 40 minutes or until potatoes are tender. **Yield: 4 to 6 servings.**

Levia (Kitten) Crosby, Odin #1254

Potato Dumplings

1 tablespoon butter
¼ cup chopped onion
2 large baking potatoes
¾ teaspoon salt
⅛ teaspoon white pepper
2 tablespoons flour
2 egg yolks, beaten
⅛ teaspoon nutmeg
2 tablespoons chopped fresh parsley
1 gallon water

Melt butter in small skillet. Sauté onion until light brown; set aside. Steam potatoes until tender; cool. Peel and force through potato ricer. Combine with onion, salt, pepper, flour, egg yolks, nutmeg and parsley in bowl; mix well. Heat water in large saucepan until simmering but not boiling. Shape potato mixture by tablespoonfuls into round dumplings. Drop into simmering water; stir gently. Simmer for 12 to 15 minutes or until dumplings rise to surface. Remove to serving platter with slotted spoon . **Yield: 6 servings.**

Mary Lou Templin, Millers Run #2020

Potato Pizza

1 prepared pizza shell
4 to 5 potatoes, peeled
Butter and salt to taste
1 onion, chopped
1 teaspoon margarine

Line pizza pan or baking sheet with prepared pizza shell; set aside. Cook potatoes in saucepan until tender. Mash with butter and salt in bowl until smooth. Spread over pizza shell. Sauté onion in margarine until tender. Spoon onion over potato layer. Bake at 350 degrees until crust is browned. **Yield: 8 servings.**

Catherine Dodd, Kaylor #1396

Cheesy Potato Puffs

$1\frac{1}{4}$ cups water
$\frac{1}{2}$ cup milk
$1\frac{1}{2}$ cups instant potato flakes
$\frac{1}{4}$ cup shredded Cheddar cheese
2 tablespoons butter
Salt to taste
$\frac{1}{2}$ cup fine bread crumbs
$1\frac{1}{2}$ tablespoons melted butter
1 egg, beaten
1 tablespoon water

Combine $1\frac{1}{4}$ cups water and milk in saucepan. Bring to a boil. Whip in potato flakes, cheese, 2 tablespoons butter and salt. Shape mixture into small balls. Toss bread crumbs with melted butter in small bowl. Beat egg with water in separate bowl. Roll potato balls in bread crumbs; dip in egg mixture. Roll again in bread crumbs. Arrange on buttered baking sheet. Bake at 450 degrees for 5 minutes or until golden brown. **Yield: 5 to 6 servings.**

Bernice McMath, Tuscarora Valley #2042

Classic Potato Puffs

1 cup prepared mashed potatoes
2 eggs, beaten
$\frac{1}{2}$ cup flour
2 teaspoons baking powder
$\frac{1}{2}$ teaspoon salt
Pepper to taste
Oil for deep frying

Beat potatoes with eggs in bowl. Stir in flour, baking powder, salt and pepper. Drop by spoonfuls into hot oil in skillet. Fry until golden; drain. **Yield: 4 to 6 servings.**

Mary Jane Neeley, Frankfort Springs, #1989

Princess Potatoes

3 tablespoons butter
$\frac{1}{4}$ cup flour
$\frac{1}{4}$ teaspoon salt
$\frac{1}{4}$ teaspoon pepper
$\frac{1}{4}$ teaspoon celery salt
2 cups milk
$2\frac{1}{2}$ cups sliced cooked potatoes
4 hard-boiled eggs, sliced
1 small onion, sliced
2 tablespoons chopped green bell pepper
2 tablespoons chopped pimento

Melt butter in saucepan. Blend in flour, salt, pepper and celery salt. Stir in milk gradually. Cook until sauce thickens, stirring constantly. Layer potatoes, eggs, onion, green pepper and pimento in baking dish. Pour sauce over top. Bake at 350 degrees for 25 minutes. **Yield: 4 to 6 servings.**

Florence Rarig, Roaring Creek Valley #2041

Ranch Potato Casserole

6 to 8 medium red potatoes
3/4 cup sour cream
1/2 cup ranch salad dressing
1/4 cup bacon bits
2 tablespoons parsley
1 1/2 cups shredded Cheddar cheese
2 cups crushed cornflakes
1/4 cup melted butter

Cook potatoes in water in saucepan until tender; cool. Cut into quarters. Place in greased 8x12-inch baking dish. Combine sour cream, salad dressing, bacon, parsley and 1 cup cheese in bowl; mix well. Pour over potatoes, tossing gently to coat. Sprinkle remaining 1/2 cup cheese over potato mixture. Toss cornflakes with melted butter. Sprinkle over top. Bake at 350 degrees for 40 to 45 minutes or until light brown. **Yield: 6 to 8 servings.**

Lisa Koenig, Central #1650

Hot Potato Salad

4 cups sliced cooked potatoes
1/2 cup mayonnaise
1 cup shredded cheese
1 cup crumbled crisp-fried bacon

Toss potatoes with mayonnaise in bowl to coat. Spoon into 9x9-inch glass baking dish. Sprinkle with cheese and bacon. Bake at 375 degrees for 45 minutes. **Yield: 6 servings.**

Mrs. Sherwood Lerch, Harmony #1692

Scalloped Potatoes

3 tablespoons butter
2 tablespoons flour
1 teaspoon salt
1/2 teaspoon pepper
3 cups milk
3 1/2 to 4 cups thinly sliced potatoes
2 tablespoons minced onion

Melt butter in glass bowl in microwave. Blend in flour, salt and pepper. Stir in milk gradually. Microwave on High for 8 to 10 minutes, stirring every 3 minutes. Place potatoes and onion in glass 9x13-inch baking dish. Pour sauce over top. Microwave, covered, for 17 to 19 minutes, stirring after 10 minutes. Let stand for 5 minutes before serving. **Yield: 6 to 8 servings.**

Sylvia Smith, Fort Granville #1902

Use meat or vegetable leftovers in a cream sauce or cheese sauce as a topper for baked potatoes.

Lean Scalloped Potatoes

2 tablespoons margarine
1/4 cup flour
2 cups 2% milk
1/2 teaspoon salt
Pepper to taste
5 large potatoes, thinly sliced
3 onions, thinly sliced
3 ounces reduced-fat Cheddar cheese, shredded
1/4 cup bread crumbs

Melt margarine in saucepan. Blend in flour. Stir in milk gradually. Cook over medium low heat until thickened, stirring constantly. Stir in salt and pepper; remove from heat. Spread 1/4 cup sauce in 8x12-inch baking dish sprayed with nonstick cooking spray. Layer with potatoes, onions, remaining sauce and half the cheese. Bake, covered, at 375 degrees for 1 hour or until potatoes are tender. Sprinkle with remaining cheese and bread crumbs; spray with nonstick cooking spray. Bake, uncovered, for 5 minutes longer or until cheese is melted. **Yield: 6 to 8 servings.**

Nan Longenberger, Ringtown Valley #2100

The Best Scalloped Potatoes

6 potatoes, thinly sliced
2 stalks celery, chopped
1 small onion, chopped
1/3 cup shredded Cheddar cheese
1/3 cup shredded Swiss cheese
1/3 cup shredded American cheese
1 tablespoon oregano
1 teaspoon salt
1/2 teaspoon pepper
1 10-ounce can cream of chicken soup
1 teaspoon flour
1 tablespoon butter, softened
2 to 3 cups milk

Combine potatoes, celery, onion, cheeses, oregano, salt, pepper, soup, flour and butter in large bowl; mix well. Pour into 9x12-inch baking dish. Cover with milk. Bake at 350 degrees for 1 1/2 hours. **Yield: 8 servings.**

Roxy Knarr, Port Matilda #1284

Dutch Potato Filling

6 large potatoes, peeled
1 medium onion, chopped
1/2 cup finely chopped celery
2 tablespoons butter
3 slices bread, cubed
1/2 cup milk
2 teaspoons salt
Pepper to taste
1 teaspoon poultry seasoning
Chopped parsley to taste
1 egg, beaten
1 cup milk

Boil potatoes in water in saucepan until tender. Drain and mash. Sauté onion and celery in butter in skillet until browned. Add to mashed potatoes with bread cubes, 1/2 cup milk, salt, pepper, poultry seasoning and parsley; mix well. Beat in egg and remaining 1 cup milk until mixture is smooth. Pour into greased 9x13-inch baking dish. Bake at 350 degrees for 30 minutes or until browned. **Yield: 6 servings.**

Ida Rachel Hubbard, Bloomingdale #536

Cheese and Spinach Casserole

1 pound creamed cottage cheese
3 eggs, beaten
4 ounces American cheese, chopped
1/4 cup butter or margarine, cut into pieces
1/2 to 1 10-ounce package frozen chopped spinach, thawed
3 tablespoons flour
Salt to taste

Combine cottage cheese, eggs, cheese and butter in bowl; mix well. Add spinach to mixture with flour and salt, stirring well. Pour into 1 1/2-quart buttered baking dish. Bake at 350 degrees for 1 hour. **Yield: 6 to 8 servings.**

Jean Christy, Conneaut #955

Spinach Casserole

1 10-ounce package frozen chopped spinach
1 cup cooked rice
1 cup shredded sharp cheese
2 eggs, slightly beaten
2 tablespoons butter, softened
1/2 cup milk
1/4 teaspoon crushed rosemary
2 tablespoons chopped onion
1 teaspoon salt
1/2 teaspoon Worcestershire sauce

Cook spinach using package directions; drain. Combine with rice, cheese, eggs, butter, milk, rosemary, onion, salt and Worcestershire sauce in bowl; mix well. Pour into greased 1-quart baking dish. Bake at 350 degrees for 25 minutes or until knife inserted near center comes out clean. **Yield: 4 to 6 servings.**

Mildred Osborne, Menallen #1091

Spinach-Cheese Pie

6 eggs, beaten
8 ounces cream cheese, softened
1 cup sour cream
1/2 to 1 cup melted margarine
12 ounces cottage cheese
2 10-ounce packages frozen chopped spinach, thawed, drained
16 ounces Monterey Jack cheese, shredded

Beat eggs, cream cheese and sour cream in mixer bowl until light and fluffy. Add melted margarine, cottage cheese and spinach. Beat at low speed until well mixed. Fold in Monterey Jack cheese. May add 1 to 2 tablespoons flour to absorb liquid if necessary. Pour into 9x13-inch baking dish. Bake at 350 degrees for 30 to 40 minutes. **Yield: 6 to 8 servings.**

Irene Sinclair, Deemston #1372

Baked Squash

2 cups sliced yellow squash
6 tablespoons melted butter or margarine
1 cup chopped onion
1 cup shredded Cheddar cheese
1/2 cup milk
1/2 cup cream
2 cups bread cubes

Combine squash, butter, onion, cheese, milk and cream in bowl; mix well. Pour into greased 8x10-inch baking dish. Sprinkle with bread cubes. Bake at 350 degrees for 50 minutes. Reduce temperature to 300 degrees. Bake for 10 minutes longer. **Yield: 6 to 8 servings.**

Emma W. Rhoades, Fulton #66

Spaghetti Squash

1 spaghetti squash
Butter to taste
Grated Parmesan cheese to taste

Cook whole squash in water to cover for 30 to 40 minutes or bake at 350 degrees for 1 hour. Cut into halves lengthwise; remove seeds. Scoop out pulp with fork or spoon. Serve with melted butter and grated cheese. May also serve with spaghetti sauce or in casserole as a substitute for pasta. **Yield: 2 to 4 servings.**

Hazel G. Huling, Shavers Creek #353

Sweet Potato and Apple Casserole

5 to 6 sweet potatoes
3 cups thinly sliced apples
1/4 cup packed brown sugar
6 tablespoons margarine or butter
1/3 cup apple cider
2 tablespoons lemon juice
1 teaspoon cinnamon

Cook sweet potatoes in water to cover for 30 minutes or until tender; drain. Peel and slice thinly. Mix with apples in buttered 2-quart casserole. Combine brown sugar, margarine, apple cider, lemon juice and cinnamon in small saucepan; mix well. Bring to a boil; reduce heat. Simmer for 10 minutes. Pour over sweet potato mixture. Bake, covered, at 325 degrees for 30 minutes or until apples are tender, basting occasionally with sauce. **Yield: 6 to 8 servings.**

Lillian Mengel, Virginville, #1832

Make a hot sour cream sauce for vegetables by heating 1/2 cup sour cream, 2 tablespoons mayonnaise, 2 teaspoons lemon juice and seasonings to taste.

Sweet Potato Casserole

1 18-ounce can sweet potatoes, drained
1 12-ounce can Spam, cut into chunks
1 8-ounce can fruit cocktail
2 tablespoons brown sugar
2 tablespoons cornstarch
Cinnamon to taste
Butter to taste

Cut sweet potatoes into chunks; place in greased baking dish. Stir in Spam. Drain fruit cocktail and set aside, reserving juice. Combine reserved juice and brown sugar in saucepan. Bring to a boil; reduce heat. Add cornstarch. Cook until thickened, stirring constantly. Add fruit cocktail, stirring to coat. Pour over sweet potato mixture. Sprinkle with cinnamon and dot with butter. Bake at 350 degrees for 45 minutes or until bubbly. May substitute ham for Spam. **Yield: 8 servings.**

Mavis Gager, Unity #1710

Sweet Potato Fritters

2 cups mashed cooked sweet potatoes
2 tablespoons butter or margarine
2 egg yolks
1 cup milk
1/2 cup flour
1 teaspoon baking powder
1 tablespoon brown sugar
1/2 teaspoon salt
2 egg whites
6 to 8 tablespoons oil

Combine sweet potatoes, butter, egg yolks and milk in bowl, beating until smooth. Sift together flour, baking powder, brown sugar and salt. Stir into sweet potato mixture. Beat egg whites in mixer bowl until stiff peaks form. Fold into mixture. Drop by tablespoonfuls into hot oil in skillet. Fry for 2 to 4 minutes or until browned, turning once; drain. May serve with syrup or butter. **Yield: 6 to 8 servings.**

J. William Gager, Unity #1710

Sweet Potato Patties

2 cups mashed cooked sweet potatoes
1/2 teaspoon salt
1/4 to 1/2 cup pineapple juice
1/2 cup packed brown sugar
1/4 cup butter, softened
4 to 5 slices pineapple

Whip sweet potatoes with salt, pineapple juice, brown sugar and butter until smooth. Arrange pineapple slices on rack in broiler pan. Spoon sweet potato mixture onto pineapple. Broil 3 inches from heat source for 10 minutes. Serve hot. **Yield: 4 to 5 servings.**

Kay Costa, Gillett #884

Crunchy Yams

6 tablespoons margarine
1½ cups sugar
2 eggs
1 cup evaporated milk
Cinnamon to taste
1 20-ounce can yams, drained, mashed
1 cup crushed cornflakes or crisp rice cereal
½ cup chopped pecans or walnuts
½ cup packed brown sugar
6 tablespoons melted butter

Cream margarine and sugar in mixer bowl until light and fluffy. Add eggs; mix well. Stir in evaporated milk and cinnamon. Add mashed yams, stirring to mix. Spoon into glass baking dish. Bake at 400 degrees for 20 minutes. Combine cornflakes, pecans, brown sugar and melted butter in bowl; mix well. Spoon over yams. Bake for 15 minutes longer. **Yield: 6 to 8 servings.**

Mary E. Pees, Eureka #1558

Tzimmes

3 sweet potatoes, peeled, cut into quarters
3 white potatoes, peeled, cut into quarters
6 carrots, peeled, chopped
½ cup honey
1 tablespoon grated lemon rind
1 tablespoon lemon juice
½ teaspoon salt
¼ teaspoon cinnamon
⅛ teaspoon nutmeg
1 cup large dried prunes

Place sweet potatoes, white potatoes and carrots in saucepan with enough water to cover. Bring to a boil; reduce heat. Simmer, covered, for 10 minutes or until vegetables are tender; drain. Pour into greased 1-quart baking dish. Combine honey, lemon rind, lemon juice, salt, cinnamon and nutmeg in bowl; mix well. Pour over vegetables. Add prunes, stirring gently to mix. Bake at 350 degrees for 30 minutes, basting occasionally with sauce. **Yield: 6 servings.**

Lee Faylor Finkenbinder, Mifflin #1725

Creamed Tomato with Hard-Boiled Eggs

3 tablespoons butter or margarine
3 tablespoons flour
1 cup milk
2 cups mashed tomatoes
3 hard-boiled eggs, coarsely chopped

Melt butter in skillet. Blend in flour. Cook until roux is light brown; remove from heat. Add milk gradually, stirring until smooth. Add tomatoes. Bring mixture to a boil; reduce heat. Simmer for 5 minutes, stirring occasionally. Sprinkle eggs into mixture. Simmer, covered, for 1 to 2 minutes longer. Serve on toast or pasta.
Yield: 2 to 3 servings.

Elizabeth Almgren, Pleasant Hill #1405

Green Tomato Casserole

8 medium green tomatoes, sliced
1½ teaspoons salt
½ teaspoon pepper
3 tablespoons chopped chives or onion
1 cup toasted bread crumbs
Lemon juice to taste
Butter to taste
⅓ cup grated Parmesan cheese

Layer tomatoes in baking dish. Sprinkle each layer with salt, pepper, chives, bread crumbs and lemon juice. Dot with butter. Top casserole with Parmesan cheese. Bake at 350 degrees for 45 minutes or until tomatoes are tender. **Yield: 6 servings.**

Viva Santschi, Pine Run #250

Herbed Tomatoes

¾ cup Italian bread crumbs
4 to 6 large tomatoes
¼ teaspoon oregano
¼ teaspoon basil
½ teaspoon each thyme and garlic
Salt and pepper to taste
½ cup shredded Cheddar or Provolone cheese
½ cup grated Parmesan cheese
⅓ cup finely chopped green bell pepper
½ cup finely chopped onion
⅓ cup finely chopped celery
2 teaspoons oil
¼ cup margarine

Sprinkle half the bread crumbs in 9x13-inch baking dish. Dip tomatoes in boiling water. Peel and cut into in 1-inch slices. Layer over bread crumbs. Combine oregano, basil, thyme, garlic, salt, pepper and cheeses in small bowl; mix well. Sprinkle over tomatoes. Sauté green pepper, onion and celery in oil in skillet until tender. Pour over tomato mixture. Sprinkle remaining bread crumbs on top. Drizzle with melted margarine. Bake at 400 degrees for 15 minutes or until tomatoes are tender. **Yield: 10 servings.**

Althea M. Wertman, California #941

Stuffed Tomatoes

6 medium tomatoes
2 cups chopped mushrooms
2 tablespoons butter
½ cup sour cream
2 eggs, beaten
1 teaspoon salt
Pepper and dried thyme to taste
Bread crumbs

Slice tops off tomatoes. Scoop out pulps, leaving thin shells. Chop enough pulp to measure 1 cup; set aside. Sauté mushrooms in butter in saucepan for 5 minutes or until tender. Combine sour cream and eggs. Add to mushrooms. Stir in reserved tomato pulp, salt, pepper and thyme. Cook until bubbly, stirring frequently. Add enough bread crumbs to thicken mixture. Shape into balls. Spoon into tomato shells. Place in 6x10-inch baking dish. Bake at 375 degrees for 30 minutes. **Yield: 6 servings.**

Ruth E. Vonada, Logan #109

Fresh Tomato Scallop

1 tablespoon margarine
2 tablespoons chopped green onions
1/3 cup fine dry bread crumbs
2 tablespoons grated Parmesan cheese
2 tablespoons chopped toasted pecans
5 tomatoes, sliced 1/2 inch thick
1 tablespoon Worcestershire sauce

Place margarine and green onions in 2-cup glass measure. Microwave on High for 1 minute. Add bread crumbs, Parmesan cheese and pecans. Arrange tomatoes in overlapping circles in glass quiche dish. Sprinkle with Worcestershire sauce. Cover loosely with waxed paper. Microwave for 2 to 3 minutes or until tender. Sprinkle with bread crumb mixture. Microwave for 30 to 60 seconds. **Yield: 4 to 6 servings.**

Betty Hall, Halfmoon #290

Butter-Glazed Vegetables

3 tablespoons butter or margarine
1 1/2 teaspoons ground ginger
1 tablespoon sugar
1/2 teaspoon salt
1 pound turnips, peeled, cut into quarters
1/2 cup chicken broth
1 pound carrots, peeled, diagonally sliced
8 ounces parsnips, peeled, sliced 1/2 inch thick

Melt butter in 12-inch skillet over medium heat. Add ginger, sugar, salt, turnips and chicken broth. Bring to a boil; reduce heat to medium. Cook, covered, for 5 minutes. Add carrots and parsnips. Simmer for 12 minutes or until vegetables are tender and liquid is reduced by half. Stir before serving to coat with sauce.
Yield: 6 to 8 servings.

Janice Bowser, Hartslog Valley #375

Vegetable Chili without Carne

1 large onion, chopped
1 green bell pepper, chopped
1 jalapeño pepper, seeded, chopped
3 cloves of garlic, chopped
1 tablespoon olive oil
1 28-ounce can tomatoes in purée
2 cups kidney beans, drained
2 tablespoons dark brown sugar
2 tablespoons mild chili powder
2 tablespoons cumin
2 teaspoons oregano
1/2 teaspoon ground coriander
1/8 teaspoon ground cloves
1/8 teaspoon ground allspice
1 cup uncooked rice
2 cups boiling water

Sauté onion, green pepper, jalapeño pepper and garlic in olive oil in large saucepan for 3 minutes or until tender. Add tomatoes, kidney beans, brown sugar and spices; mix well. Bring to a boil; reduce heat. Simmer, covered, for 30 minutes, stirring occasionally. Cook rice in boiling water in small saucepan using package directions. Serve chili over hot cooked rice. **Yield: 4 servings.**

Martha W. Snyder, Plainfield #1727

Scalloped Carrots, Potatoes, Onions and Celery

1 cup chopped carrots
1 cup cubed potatoes
1 cup chopped onion
1 cup chopped celery
6 tablespoons butter
6 tablespoons flour
1/2 teaspoon salt
1/4 teaspoon pepper
2 cups milk
1 cup shredded Cheddar cheese
Buttered seasoned bread crumbs

Combine carrots, potatoes, onion and celery in saucepan with enough water to cover. Bring to a boil; reduce heat. Simmer until vegetables are tender-crisp; drain. Place in 2-quart baking dish. Melt butter in saucepan. Blend in flour, salt and pepper. Cook over low heat until smooth and bubbly, stirring constantly; remove from heat. Stir in milk. Bring to a boil. Cook for 1 minute, stirring constantly. Stir in 1 cup cheese. Pour over vegetables. Top with seasoned bread crumbs. Bake at 350 degrees for 45 minutes. **Yield: 4 servings.**

Mrs. Robert F. Pardoe, Turbot #249

Creamed Vegetable Croquettes

2 cups cooked mixed vegetables
2 cups bread crumbs
Salt, pepper, nutmeg and parsley to taste
1 egg, beaten
2 tablespoons melted butter
2 cups mashed potatoes
Cracker crumbs
White sauce

Combine vegetables and bread crumbs in bowl, mashing with fork. Stir in salt, pepper, nutmeg and parsley. Add egg, butter and mashed potatoes; mix well. Shape into patties. Coat with cracker crumbs. Fry in hot oil in skillet until browned on both sides; drain. Serve with white sauce. **Yield: 6 to 8 servings.**

Ruth Boyce

Microwave Veggies

Flowerets of 1 1/2 pounds fresh broccoli
Flowerets of 1/2 head cauliflower
2 medium zucchini, sliced
2 medium tomatoes, cut into wedges
3 tablespoons melted butter
1/2 teaspoon garlic salt
1/4 teaspoon thyme
1/4 cup grated Parmesan cheese

Arrange broccoli and cauliflowerets alternately around edge of 12-inch round glass dish. Pile zucchini slices in center; cover with plastic wrap. Microwave on High for 9 to 11 minutes. Arrange tomato wedges over vegetables. Combine butter, garlic salt and thyme in small bowl. Drizzle over vegetables. Sprinkle with Parmesan cheese. Microwave for 1 1/2 to 2 minutes longer or until tender. **Yield: 6 to 8 servings.**

Joan Chiea, Beaver Run #2049

Zucchini Quiche

2 cups chopped or shredded zucchini
1 onion, chopped
4 eggs, well beaten
1 cup baking mix
1/3 cup oil
2 tablespoons grated cheese
3/4 cup chopped cooked ham
Salt, pepper and parsley to taste

Combine zucchini, onion, eggs, baking mix, oil, cheese, ham and seasonings in large bowl; mix well. Pour into greased 9x12-inch baking dish. Bake at 340 degrees for 30 minutes or until golden brown. **Yield: 8 servings.**

Marjorie Slick, North Woodbury #1923

Zucchini "Crab" Cakes

2 eggs, beaten
2 cups grated zucchini, drained
1 tablespoon grated onion
1 tablespoon mayonnaise
1 teaspoon Old Bay seasoning
1 cup bread crumbs
Flour
Oil for frying

Combine eggs, zucchini, onion, mayonnaise, seasoning and bread crumbs in bowl; mix well. Shape into patties; dip in flour. Fry in small amount of oil in skillet until browned on both sides. **Yield: 4 servings.**

Marie Cyphers, Valley #52

Zucchini Casserole Imperial

4 cups peeled sliced zucchini
2 eggs
1 cup mayonnaise
1 onion, chopped
1/4 cup chopped green bell pepper
1 cup grated Parmesan cheese
Salt and pepper to taste
Fresh bread cubes
Butter, melted

Cook zucchini in a small amount of water in saucepan just until tender; drain. Place in greased baking dish. Beat eggs in large bowl. Stir in mayonnaise, onion, green pepper, Parmesan cheese, salt and pepper. Pour over zucchini. Toss desired amounts of bread cubes with melted butter; sprinkle over casserole. Bake at 350 degrees for 30 minutes or until brown and bubbly. Let stand for several minutes before serving. May be made a day ahead and refrigerated. **Yield: 4 servings.**

Marie Sheffler, Community #1994

Make a delicious ***Lemon Butter*** *for vegetables of 1/2 cup softened butter, 1 tablespoon lemon juice and 1 teaspoon salt.*

Zucchini Patties

2 cups grated zucchini
2 eggs, beaten
1/2 cup grated Parmesan cheese
1 cup flour
1/2 cup chopped onion
1/2 teaspoon salt
1/2 teaspoon pepper
1/2 teaspoon garlic salt
1/2 teaspoon parsley flakes
Oil for frying

Mix zucchini and eggs in bowl. Add Parmesan cheese, flour, onion and seasonings; mix well. Heat oil in deep skillet. Drop zucchini mixture by tablespoonfuls into hot oil. Fry until golden brown; drain on paper towels. **Yield: 4 to 6 servings.**

Datha Burkett, Hyndman #1954

Zucchini Provençale

1 medium onion, sliced
1 clove of garlic, minced
1/4 cup vegetable oil
2 pounds zucchini, sliced
4 tomatoes, chopped
1 green bell pepper, chopped
Salt and pepper to taste
Minced parsley to taste
Grated Parmesan cheese to taste

Sauté onion and garlic in oil in large skillet. Add zucchini, tomatoes, green pepper, salt and pepper. Cook until tender. Sprinkle with minced parsley and Parmesan cheese before serving. This dish freezes well. **Yield: 6 to 8 servings.**

Jean Rothrock, Sebring #1047

Stuffed Zucchini

3 medium zucchini
1 1/2 cups soft bread crumbs
1 cup shredded sharp Cheddar cheese
1/4 cup melted butter or margarine
2 tablespoons minced onion
3 tablespoons finely chopped green bell pepper
1 teaspoon salt
Pepper to taste

Cut zucchini into halves lengthwise; scoop out seed. Place cut side down in skillet. Add a small amount of water. Cook until tender. Remove zucchini from skillet. Let stand until cool. Scoop out pulp, leaving shells about 1/4 inch thick. Mash pulp in bowl. Add bread crumbs, cheese, butter, onion, green pepper, salt and pepper; mix well. Pile lightly into shells; place in baking dish. Bake at 350 degrees for 30 minutes or until lightly browned. **Yield: 6 servings.**

Helen Coughanour, Rostraver #919

Barley Casserole

1 cup finely chopped onion
$1/4$ cup finely chopped red bell pepper
$1/4$ cup finely chopped green bell pepper
6 mushrooms, sliced
1 cup pearl barley
$1/2$ cup beef broth
$3/4$ cup chopped parsley
5 cups beef broth
1 broth can water
$1/2$ cup water chestnuts, drained, chopped

Combine onion, red pepper, green pepper, mushrooms, barley and $1/2$ cup beef broth in skillet. Cook over medium heat until tender-crisp, stirring constantly. Pour into 2-quart casserole. Add parsley, 5 cups beef broth and water. Mix well. Bake, uncovered, at 350 degrees for 1 hour and 20 minutes, stirring once. Stir in water chestnuts. Bake for 10 minutes longer or until liquid is absorbed. **Yield: 12 servings.**

Caroline M. Reilly, Scotch Valley #510

Crêpes Marouis

3 eggs
$2/3$ cup flour
$1/2$ teaspoon salt
1 cup milk
2 tablespoons oil
$1/2$ cup chopped green bell pepper
$1/2$ cup chopped onion
2 tablespoons bacon drippings
1 $2 1/2$-ounce jar mushrooms, drained
8 slices crisp-fried bacon, crumbled
2 cups shredded sharp Cheddar cheese
1 8-ounce can tomato sauce

Beat eggs in small mixer bowl until fluffy. Add flour, salt and milk; beat well. Let stand for 30 minutes. Pour $1/4$ cup batter into lightly oiled hot skillet. Rotate pan to spread batter. Bake until brown on one side; remove from skillet. Repeat with remaining batter. Sauté green pepper and onion in bacon drippings in skillet until tender-crisp. Stir in mushrooms, bacon and $1 1/2$ cups cheese. Spoon $1/4$ cup mixture into center of each crêpe; roll. Place seam side down in rectangular baking dish. Pour tomato sauce over top. Bake at 350 degrees for 15 minutes. Sprinkle with remaining $1/2$ cup cheese. Bake until cheese melts. May add $1/2$ cup grated pepperoni if desired. **Yield: 8 servings.**

Virginia Knapp, Buffalo #1523

Substitute herbs, spices or salt-free seasoning blends for salt to add flavor and reduce sodium intake.

Cheese Dumplings

1 egg
2 cups cottage cheese
2 cups flour
1 teaspoon salt
2 quarts boiling salted water
1 large onion, minced
3 tablespoons butter

Combine egg and cottage cheese in mixer bowl; beat until smooth. Add flour and 1 teaspoon salt; stir until soft dough forms. Knead on lightly floured surface until smooth and elastic. Drop by teaspoonfuls into boiling salted water in large saucepan. Cook for 10 minutes or until tender; drain. Place in serving dish. Sauté onion in butter in small skillet until tender. Spoon over dumplings. Serve warm garnished with dollops of sour cream. **Yield: 4 servings.**

Catherine J. Metrick, Unionville #1971

Egg Dumplings

2/3 cup flour
1/4 teaspoon salt
1 teaspoon baking powder
1 egg
3 tablespoons milk
4 cups gravy or broth

Sift flour, salt and baking powder together into bowl. Beat egg in mixer bowl until foamy. Add milk; mix well. Pour into flour mixture; stir until smooth and forms heavy batter. May add additional milk if necessary. Drop by spoonfuls into hot gravy or broth in large saucepan. Cook, covered, for 15 minutes; do not remove cover. **Yield: 2 servings.**

Anna M. Bohn, North Jackson #1740

Big Egg Breakfast

6 eggs
3 tablespoons milk
1/4 teaspoon baking powder
1 tablespoon margarine

Beat eggs in mixer bowl until foamy. Add milk and baking powder; mix well. Melt margarine in large skillet; add egg mixture. Cook, rotating and tilting skillet constantly to keep liquid moving to bottom of skillet, until liquid is puffy and set. Remove to serving plate. **Yield: 4 servings.**

Edith C. Myers, Mt. Joy #537

For a 30-second blender breakfast, process 1 banana, 1/4 cup pineapple, 1 cup milk and 2 tablespoons frozen orange juice concentrate.

Farmer's Breakfast

1/2 pound bacon, cut into 1/2-inch pieces
1 large onion, chopped
5 large potatoes, peeled, sliced julienne-style
Salt and pepper to taste
3 eggs

Sauté bacon in large skillet just until crisp; add onion. Cook until onion is transparent. Add potatoes, salt and pepper; mix well. Cook, covered, until potatoes are tender, stirring occasionally. Beat eggs in mixer bowl until light and fluffy. Pour over potato mixture. Cook, stirring constantly, until eggs are set. **Yield: 4 servings.**

Hannelere Carle, Sebring #1047

Swiss Cheese Scramble Brunch Casserole

2 cups soft bread cubes, crusts trimmed
1 3/4 cups milk
8 eggs, slightly beaten
3/4 teaspoon salt
1/8 teaspoon pepper
2 tablespoons margarine
1/4 teaspoon seasoned salt
8 ounces Swiss cheese, sliced
1/2 cup fine dry bread crumbs
2 teaspoons melted margarine
8 slices crisp-fried bacon, crumbled

Soak bread cubes in milk in bowl for 5 minutes; drain, reserving liquid. Combine eggs, reserved liquid, salt and pepper in mixer bowl; mix well. Melt 2 tablespoons margarine in large skillet; add egg mixture. Cook just until set, stirring constantly. Stir in bread cube mixture. Pour into 9-inch baking dish; sprinkle with seasoned salt. Arrange cheese over top. Combine bread crumbs and 2 teaspoons melted margarine in small bowl; sprinkle over cheese. Top with bacon. Bake at 400 degrees for 10 to 15 minutes or until cheese bubbles around edges and all cheese is melted. Serve hot. **Yield: 8 servings.**

Helen Kramer, Burgettstown #1502

Ham and Cheese Casserole

8 slices stale bread, crusts trimmed, cubed
6 eggs
1 teaspoon dry mustard
2 cups milk
1/2 pound ham, finely chopped
2 cups shredded Cheddar cheese

Arrange bread cubes in greased rectangular baking dish. Beat eggs in mixer bowl until foamy. Add mustard, milk, ham and cheese; mix well. Pour over bread cubes. Chill for 7 hours to overnight. Bake at 350 degrees for 1 hour or until firm. Let stand for 10 to 15 minutes before serving. **Yield: 8 servings.**

Ruth Farmery, Savan #1786

Ham Rarebit Breakfast

1/4 cup butter
1/4 cup flour
1 1/2 cups milk
1 tablespoon mustard
Dash of Tabasco sauce
1/2 cup shredded Cheddar cheese
1 cup diced ham
1/2 cup crushed potato chips

Melt butter in saucepan. Stir in flour gradually until smooth. Stir in milk gradually. Add mustard, Tabasco sauce, cheese and ham; mix well. Pour into baking dish. Bake at 325 degrees for 30 to 40 minutes or until hot and bubbly. Stir well; sprinkle with potato chips. Spoon over toasted English muffins or biscuits. **Yield: 2 servings.**

Robin Hetherington, Ringtown Valley #2100

Welsh Rarebit

1 egg, slightly beaten
2 cups milk
1 cup cubed Cheddar cheese
1 clove of garlic, finely chopped
1 teaspoon salt

Combine egg, milk, cheese, garlic and salt in top of double boiler; mix well. Cook over boiling water until smooth and heated through, stirring frequently. Serve over crackers or toast. **Yield: 4 servings.**

George Shaffer, Linesville #694

Grits Casserole

3 eggs
1 cup milk
1 cup instant grits
1 cup boiling water
1 teaspoon salt
1/2 cup margarine, softened
8 ounces Cheddar cheese, shredded

Beat eggs in mixer bowl until light. Add milk; mix well. Combine grits, boiling water and salt in large saucepan. Cook over medium heat just until thickened, stirring constantly. Add margarine and cheese; beat well. Stir in egg mixture; pour into 1-quart casserole. Bake at 325 degrees for 45 minutes. **Yield: 6 servings.**

Irene Ohlin, Valley #1420

Easy Baked Lasagna

6 cups spaghetti sauce
32 ounces ricotta cheese
2 cups shredded mozarella cheese
1/2 cup grated Parmesan cheese
4 eggs, beaten
1 teaspoon parsley
1 teaspoon salt
1/4 teaspoon pepper
8 ounces uncooked lasagna noodles

Heat spaghetti sauce in large saucepan until heated through. Combine ricotta cheese, mozarella cheese, 1/4 cup Parmesan cheese, eggs, parsley, salt and pepper in large bowl; mix well. Pour 3/4 cup sauce in 9x13-inch baking pan. Layer with 4 noodles, 3/4 cup sauce, 1/3 of cheese mixture and 1/2 cup sauce. Repeat layers twice ending with noodles and remaining sauce. Press noodles gently into cheese mixture. Sprinkle with remaining 1/4 cup Parmesan cheese. Bake, covered with foil, at 375 degrees for 50 minutes or until hot and bubbly; remove foil. Bake for 10 minutes longer. Let stand for 10 minutes before serving. **Yield: 12 servings.**

Lillian Bailey, Amity #1540

Polish Lasagna

16 ounces uncooked lasagna noodles
7 medium potatoes, peeled, chopped
Salt and pepper to taste
1 onion, grated
8 ounces longhorn cheese, shredded
2 pounds sauerkraut, rinsed, drained
1 cup melted margarine

Cook noodles using package directions; drain. Cook potatoes in boiling water in large saucepan until tender; drain. Add salt and pepper; beat until smooth. Add 1/2 of the onion and cheese; mix well. Combine sauerkraut and remaining onion in large saucepan. Cook until tender, stirring constantly. Line greased 9x13-inch baking pan with noodles. Alternate layers of potatoes, noodles and sauerkraut mixture until all ingredients are used, ending with noodles. Drizzle with melted margarine. Bake, tightly covered with foil, at 350 degrees for 45 minutes or until hot and bubbly. **Yield: 12 servings.**

Jessie D. Zitney and Juanita Stasia, Eureka #1011

Starchy foods such as potatoes, pasta, bread and rice are valuable sources of fiber, complex carbohydrates, protein, vitamins and minerals and should not be excluded from any diet. Dieters should avoid the butter and sauces which frequently go with starchy foods.

Vegetable Lasagna

9 lasagna noodles
1 4-ounce can mushrooms, drained
1/2 cup chopped onion
1/2 teaspoon Italian seasoning
1/2 cup margarine, softened
1/2 cup flour
1 teaspoon salt
1/2 teaspoon pepper
4 cups milk
4 ounces mozzarella cheese, shredded
1 10-ounce package each frozen spinach and frozen broccoli, thawed
2 carrots, chopped, cooked
2 cups ricotta cheese
1 egg, beaten

Cook lasagna noodles according to package directions; drain. Sauté mushrooms and onion in skillet until tender. Add Italian seasoning; mix well. Melt margarine over low heat in large saucepan. Stir in flour, salt and pepper gradually until smooth; stir in milk. Bring to a boil. Boil for 1 minute, stirring constantly; remove from heat. Stir in 1/4 cup mozzarella cheese. Squeeze spinach dry. Chop spinach and broccoli. Combine with carrots in bowl; mix well. Combine ricotta cheese and egg in bowl; mix well. Layer 1 cup white sauce, vegetables, noodles, ricotta cheese mixture, mushroom mixture and remaining white sauce in 9x13-inch baking pan. Sprinkle with remaining mozzarella cheese. Bake at 400 degrees for 20 to 25 minutes or until hot and bubbly. **Yield: 8 servings.**

Ruth Mosier, Venango #910

Confetti Casserole

1 cup macaroni
1 medium onion, chopped
1 16-ounce can tomatoes, drained, chopped
1 small green bell pepper, chopped
Salt and pepper to taste
4 ounces sharp Cheddar cheese, sliced

Cook macaroni according to package directions; drain. Combine with onion, tomatoes, green pepper, salt and pepper in bowl; mix well. Pour into casserole. Arrange cheese over top. Bake at 375 degrees for 1 hour. **Yield: 4 servings.**

Carol Drumheller

Hot Macaroni Salad

8 ounces uncooked elbow macaroni
4 slices bacon
1 10-ounce can cream of celery soup
Vinegar to taste
1/2 teaspoon sugar
Dash of pepper
1/2 cup chopped celery
1/4 cup sliced scallions

Cook macaroni according to package directions; drain. Fry bacon in large skillet until crisp; drain, reserve drippings. Combine soup, vinegar, sugar and pepper with bacon drippings; mix well. Fold in macaroni, celery and scallions. Crumble bacon; sprinkle over top. Serve hot. **Yield: 6 servings.**

Naomi Bupp, Red Lion #1781

Spinach Manicotti

12 ounces uncooked manicotti noodles
1½ pounds ground beef
¾ cup finely chopped onion
3 tablespoons margarine
1 10-ounce package frozen spinach, thawed
½ cup soft bread crumbs
¾ cup grated Parmesan cheese
3 eggs, lightly beaten
¾ teaspoon basil
1½ teaspoons salt
Pepper to taste
5½ cups tomato sauce

Cook noodles according to package directions; drain. Brown ground beef in skillet, stirring until crumbly; drain. Sauté onion in margarine in large skillet. Squeeze spinach dry; add to onion mixture. Cook until moisture is absorbed. Add ground beef, bread crumbs, ½ cup cheese, eggs, basil, salt and pepper; mix well. Pour ½ cup sauce into 11x13-inch baking pan. Stuff noodles with ground beef mixture. Arrange over sauce in baking pan. Pour remaining 5 cups sauce over top; sprinkle with remaining ¼ cup cheese. Bake, uncovered, at 350 degrees for 20 minutes. **Yield: 10 servings.**

Kathy Cree, Community #1767

Nana Siebens Specholas

3 eggs
½ cup milk
1 teaspoon salt
Flour

Beat eggs, milk and salt in large mixer bowl until smooth. Stir in enough flour to form stiff dough. Drop by small teaspoonfuls into boiling salted water in large saucepan. Cook until Specholas rise to top; drain. May substitute whole wheat or rye flour. May add parsley flakes, onion flakes or sesame seed for variation. Suggestion: If spoon is dipped in boiling water, dough will slide from spoon easily. **Yield: 6 servings.**

Doris L. Hough, Fulton #66

Pasta with Spinach and Ricotta

1 small onion, minced
2 tablespoons unsalted butter
1 cup chopped, drained, cooked spinach
1 cup heavy cream
1 pound ricotta cheese
1 pound pasta shells, cooked, drained
½ cup grated Parmesan cheese

Sauté onion in butter in large saucepan. Add spinach, cream and ricotta cheese; mix well. Cook for 3 minutes or until heated through, stirring constantly. Add pasta and Parmesan cheese; toss well. Serve hot. **Yield: 4 servings.**

Jane Darmofal, Kutztown #1836

Spaghetti and Cauliflower

8 ounces uncooked spaghetti
2 cloves of garlic, minced
1/4 cup olive oil
2 cups cooked chopped cauliflower
1 teaspoon salt

Cook spaghetti using package directions; drain. Sauté garlic in olive oil in large skillet until brown; add cauliflower and salt. Sauté for 2 minutes. Pour over spaghetti in large serving bowl; toss well. Garnish with fresh parsley. **Yield: 4 servings.**

Cathy Woods, Pleasant Hill #1505

Spaghetti Carbonara

1 pound uncooked spaghetti
1/3 cup grated Romano cheese
1/2 cup grated Parmesan cheese
3 eggs
2 egg yolks
1/4 cup cream
Salt and pepper to taste
8 ounces bacon, crisp-fried, crumbled
1 tablespoon bacon drippings

Cook spaghetti according to package directions; drain, keep hot. Mix Romano cheese and Parmesan cheese together in bowl. Beat eggs and yolks in mixer bowl until foamy. Add cream, half the cheese mixture, salt and pepper; mix well. Pour over hot spaghetti. Add bacon and drippings; toss well. Sprinkle with remaining cheese mixture. **Yield: 4 servings.**

Mildred K. Duran, Burgettstown #1502

Pierogis

4 eggs
1 cup sour cream
1/2 teaspoon salt
2 cups warm water
8 cups flour
1 bunch green onions, finely chopped
2 teaspoons margarine
3 pounds dry cottage cheese
8 ounces cream cheese, softened
2 eggs, beaten
3 tablespoons sour cream
Salt and pepper to taste

Beat eggs, sour cream and salt in large mixer bowl until smooth. Add water and enough flour to make smooth velvety dough. Roll on lightly floured surface to 1/4-inch thickness. Cut into 3 1/2-inch circles. Sauté green onions in margarine in small skillet. Combine cottage cheese, cream cheese, eggs, sour cream, salt and pepper in large mixer bowl; beat until smooth. Stir in green onions. Fill circles with 1 tablespoon filling; seal edges. Drop into boiling water in large saucepan. Cook until Pierogis rise to top; drain. May also fry with onions in skillet. Serve with butter or cheese sauce. May use a sauerkraut and onion mixture or mashed potatoes, onion and cheese mixture as fillings. **Yield: 9 dozen.**

Jean Stiner, Eldred #1604

Pierogi Casserole

1 pound uncooked lasagna noodles
2 cups mashed potatoes
1 tablespoon finely minced onion
Salt and pepper to taste
1/2 cup butter, softened
2 cups shredded Cheddar cheese
2 cups shredded mozzarella cheese
1 tablespoon parsley

Cook noodles using package directions; drain. Combine potatoes, onion, salt and pepper in bowl; mix well. Arrange 1/3 of the noodles in 9x13-inch baking pan. Spread with 1/2 of the potato mixture, dot with 1/3 of the butter and sprinkle with Cheddar cheese. Continue to layer with 1/3 of the noodles, spread with remaining potato mixture, dot with 1/3 of the butter and sprinkle with mozzarella cheese, ending with remaining noodles. Melt remaining butter in small saucepan. Drizzle over noodles; sprinkle with parsley. Bake at 350 degrees for 30 minutes. **Yield: 10 servings.**

James Hoffman, Perry Valley #1804

Baked Pineapple Rice

1 cup uncooked rice
2 cups crushed pineapple
6 tablespoons butter, softened
3/4 cup packed brown sugar
3/4 cup pineapple juice

Cook rice using package directions. Drain pineapple, reserving juice. Layer 1/4 cup rice, 1/4 cup pineapple, 1 1/2 teaspoons butter and 1 tablespoon brown sugar in buttered baking dish until all ingredients are used, ending with rice. Pour pineapple juice over top. Bake, covered, at 350 degrees for 1 hour or until brown.
Yield: 6 servings.

Fern Sonon, Virginville #1832

Side-Dish Rice

1 cup uncooked long grain rice
2 cups water
1 tablespoon butter
1 teaspoon salt
1/2 cup milk
Cinnamon to taste

Combine rice, water, butter and salt in 1-quart microwave-safe casserole; mix well. Microwave, covered, on High for 5 minutes. Reduce to 50% power. Microwave for 15 minutes or until liquid is absorbed. Stir in milk and cinnamon. **Yield: 6 servings.**

Marie Schaeffer, Virginville #1832

Beefy Rice Casserole

1 10-ounce can French onion soup
1 10-ounce can beef consommé
1 4-ounce can mushroom pieces, drained
1 stick margarine, sliced
1 cup uncooked long grain rice

Combine onion soup, beef consommé, mushrooms, margarine and rice in 2-quart baking dish. Bake, covered, at 350 degrees for 1 hour. **Yield: 8 to 10 servings.**

Janet McClellan, Logan #109

Rice Pilaf

3 large onions, chopped
1 4-ounce can mushrooms, drained
1/2 cup margarine
1 cup uncooked rice
1 10-ounce can beef consommé
1 soup can water
1/8 teaspoon MSG

Sauté onions and mushrooms in margarine in skillet until tender. Add rice, consommé, water and MSG. Simmer, covered, for 1 hour, stirring occasionally. **Yield: 8 servings.**

Frances Sullivan, Morning Star #1271

Spanish Rice

1 medium onion, thinly sliced
1/2 medium green bell pepper, chopped
1 cup uncooked rice
1/4 cup butter, margarine or vegetable oil
2 cups stewed tomatoes
1 cup water
1 teaspoon salt
Pepper to taste

Sauté onion, green pepper and rice in butter in saucepan over high heat until lightly browned. Add undrained tomatoes, water, salt and pepper; mix well. Bring to a boil over medium heat. Cover tightly; reduce heat. Simmer for 30 minutes. May add 1/2 pound browned ground beef. **Yield: 4 to 6 servings.**

Sophie Sally Bocz, Brush Valley #1785

Sunny Jim Casserole

1 cup cooked rice
1 cup finely chopped Cheddar cheese
1 cup chopped celery
1 cup dry bread crumbs
1 medium onion, chopped
Salt and pepper to taste
2 eggs, beaten
1 cup milk
2 tablespoons margarine, softened

Combine rice, cheese, celery, bread crumbs, onion, salt, pepper, eggs and milk in bowl; mix well. Pour into 8-inch casserole; dot with margarine. Bake at 375 degrees for 1 hour. **Yield: 4 servings.**

Joan Barker, DuBois #808

Casserole Stuffing

1 cup chopped celery
1/2 cup chopped onion
1/4 cup butter
1 10-ounce can cream of chicken soup
1/2 teaspoon poultry seasoning
8 cups dry bread crumbs

Sauté celery and onion in butter in large skillet until tender; add soup and poultry seasoning; mix well. Add bread crumbs, stirring until moistened. Spoon into 1 1/2-quart casserole. Bake at 350 degrees for 45 minutes or until lightly browned. **Yield: 8 servings.**

Eunice Buchanan, New Lebanon #1445

Southern Corn Bread Stuffing

2 cups chopped onions
1 1/2 cups chopped celery
1 cup margarine, softened
2 tablespoons chopped parsley
2 teaspoons salt
1/2 teaspoon pepper
2 teaspoons poultry seasoning
1 teaspoon sage
5 cups bread crumbs
4 cups crumbled corn bread
2 cups chicken stock
4 egg yolks
4 egg whites

Combine onions, celery, margarine, parsley, salt, pepper, poultry seasoning, sage, bread crumbs, corn bread, chicken stock and egg yolks in large bowl; mix well. Beat egg whites in mixer bowl until stiff peaks form. Fold into stuffing mixture. Spoon into 1 1/2-quart baking dish. Bake at 350 degrees for 45 minutes. **Yield: 8 servings.**

Betty Rodgers, Plain Grove #1431

Stuffing Balls

1 loaf bread, cubed
$1/2$ cup chopped celery
1 onion, chopped
$1/2$ cup chopped parsley
1 cup margarine
2 chicken bouillon cubes
1 egg, beaten
$1/4$ cup milk
1 10-ounce can cream of chicken soup
1 10-ounce can cream of celery soup
1 soup can milk
Salt and pepper to taste

Place bread cubes in large bowl. Sauté celery, onion and parsley in margarine in skillet until tender. Add bouillon cubes, stirring until dissolved. Pour over bread cubes. Add egg and $1/4$ cup milk; mix well. Shape into balls. Mix chicken soup, celery soup and soup can of milk in bowl until well blended. Pour $1/2$ of soup mixture into 9x13-inch baking pan. Arrange stuffing balls over soup mixture. Spoon remaining soup mixture over top. Bake, covered, at 325 degrees for 1 hour. **Yield: 8 dozen.**

Joan Warrick, Sewickley #1897

Slow-Cooker Stuffing

12 cups bread crumbs
$1\frac{1}{2}$ teaspoons poultry seasoning
$1/2$ teaspoon salt
$1/8$ teaspoon pepper
$1/4$ cup margarine
1 cup finely chopped onion
1 cup finely chopped celery
2 tablespoons parsley flakes
2 eggs, well beaten
$1\frac{1}{2}$ cups chicken bouillon

Place bread crumbs in large bowl. Mix poultry seasoning, salt and pepper in small bowl; sprinkle over crumbs. Melt margarine in large skillet; add onion and celery. Sauté until tender; stir in parsley. Pour over crumb mixture. Add eggs and bouillon; toss well. Spoon into slow cooker. Cook, covered, on High for 1 hour; stir. Reduce heat to Low. Cook for $1\frac{1}{2}$ to 2 hours or until liquid is absorbed. **Yield: 8 cups.**

Mrs. Alta Sadler, Mahoning #1732

Scalloped Pineapple

4 eggs
$1/4$ cup flour
1 cup sugar
4 cups crushed pineapple
Cinnamon to taste

Beat eggs in small mixer bowl until smooth. Add flour and sugar; mix well. Stir in pineapple. Pour into baking dish; sprinkle with cinnamon. Bake at 350 degrees for 30 minutes or until brown. **Yield: 4 servings.**

Bina Zeafle, Sebring #1047

Breads

Autumn Apple Pancakes

1 cup chunky applesauce
2 cups pancake mix
2 eggs, beaten
1 cup milk
1 teaspoon cinnamon
3/4 cup packed brown sugar

Combine applesauce, pancake mix, eggs, milk, cinnamon and brown sugar in bowl; mix until smooth. Spray electric skillet with nonstick cooking spray; heat to 375 degrees. Drop 2 tablespoons batter in skillet for each apple cake. Bake for 2 minutes on each side or until browned. Serve with applesauce or syrup. **Yield: 4 servings.**

Alice E. Gilmore, Somerset #1697

Spiced Apple Pancakes

2 cups baking mix
1 egg
1 2/3 cups milk
3/4 cup grated apples
1 cup sugar
2 tablespoons cornstarch
1/4 teaspoon cinnamon
1/4 teaspoon nutmeg
2 cups apple cider
2 tablespoons lemon juice
1/4 cup margarine or butter, softened

Combine baking mix, egg, milk and grated apples in bowl; mix well. Drop by tablespoonfuls onto hot griddle. Bake until browned on each side. Combine sugar, cornstarch, cinnamon and nutmeg in small saucepan. Stir in cider and lemon juice. Bring to a boil. Cook for 1 minute; remove from heat. Add margarine, stirring until melted. Serve over pancakes. May add dollop of sour cream on each pancake. **Yield: 4 to 6 servings.**

Dorothy B. Riffner, Wills #1690

Buckwheat Cakes

4 cups buttermilk
1 cup packed brown sugar
2 pounds buckwheat flour
1/2 cup yeast
Salt to taste
1 teaspoon baking soda

Combine buttermilk, brown sugar, buckwheat flour, yeast and salt in large crock; mix well. Remove 4 cups batter. Add baking soda and enough water to make of desired consistency. Drop by tablespoonfuls onto hot griddle. Bake for 3 to 4 minutes on each side or until browned. Store remaining batter in crock in cool place for several weeks. **Yield: 30 servings.**

Howard McMillin, Westfield #1514

Cornmeal Griddle Cakes

1/2 cup cornmeal
2 tablespoons shortening
1 cup boiling water
3/4 cup milk
2 eggs, beaten
1 tablespoon molasses
1 cup sifted flour
1 teaspoon salt
1 tablespoon baking powder

Combine cornmeal and shortening in bowl. Pour in boiling water. Cover and let stand for 5 minutes or until cooled. Add milk, eggs and molasses, stirring well. Stir in flour, salt and baking powder. Drop by tablespoonfuls onto hot griddle. Bake for several minutes on each side until browned. **Yield: 3 to 4 servings.**

Zelma McWhirter, Mt. Pleasant #1687

German Pancakes

3 egg yolks
1/2 cup milk
1 cup flour
1 teaspoon baking powder
1 teaspoon salt
1/2 cup milk
3 egg whites

Beat egg yolks with fork in bowl until thick and lemon-colored. Add 1/2 cup milk, stirring well. Add flour, baking powder and salt, mixing thoroughly. Stir in remaining 1/2 cup milk. Beat egg whites in mixer bowl until stiff peaks form. Fold into batter gently. Drop by 1/2 cupfuls onto hot greased griddle. Bake for several minutes on each side until browned. **Yield: 8 (5-inch) pancakes.**

Kathryn Fleeger, Mountain #1307

Favorite Pancakes

1 1/2 cups flour
2 tablespoons sugar
3 teaspoons baking powder
1 teaspoon salt
1 egg, beaten
3 tablespoons oil
1 1/4 cups milk

Combine flour, sugar, baking powder and salt in bowl. Add egg and oil gradually, stirring well. Stir in enough milk to make of desired consistency. Drop by tablespoonfuls onto hot greased griddle. Bake for several minutes on each side until browned. May substitute buttermilk for milk. **Yield: 4 to 5 servings.**

Melva Wright, Mifflin #1725

Yellow Cornmeal-Buttermilk Waffles

2 eggs
1¾ cups buttermilk
1 cup yellow cornmeal
1 cup flour
2 teaspoons baking powder
¼ cup melted margarine

Beat eggs and buttermilk in bowl. Sift together cornmeal, flour and baking powder. Add to egg mixture, mixing well. Stir in melted margarine. Pour batter onto hot greased waffle iron. Bake using manufacturer's directions. May freeze cooked waffles and reheat for 10 minutes in a 400-degree oven. **Yield: 6 waffles.**

Ruth Ravenscroft, Ohiopyle #1933

Waffles

2 cups flour
2 teaspoons baking powder
2 teaspoons sugar
¼ teaspoon salt
3 eggs
1½ cups milk
6 tablespoons melted butter

Combine flour, baking powder, sugar and salt in bowl. Beat eggs and milk in small bowl. Add to dry ingredients, mixing well. Stir in melted butter. Pour batter onto hot greased waffle iron. Bake using manufacturer's directions. **Yield: 6 to 8 servings.**

Mildred Reinert, Pioneer #1777

Biscuits

2 cups flour
3 teaspoons double-acting baking powder
1 teaspoon salt
⅓ cup shortening
¾ cup milk

Combine flour, baking powder and salt in bowl. Cut in shortening until mixture is crumbly. Add milk, stirring until soft dough forms. Knead lightly on floured surface. Roll out to ½-inch thickness; cut with biscuit cutter. Place on ungreased baking sheet. Bake at 425 degrees for 12 to 15 minutes or until golden brown.
Yield: 12 servings.

Esther Peters, Turbett #781

Sift dry baking ingredients onto a paper plate. The plate can be bent for easy pouring.

Breakfast Biscuits with Sausage and Gravy

3 breakfast sausages
2 tablespoons butter or margarine
2 tablespoons flour
2 cups warm milk
Salt and pepper to taste
Hot baking powder biscuits

Remove casings from sausages; cut into small pieces. Brown in small skillet until cooked through; drain. Melt butter in saucepan. Blend in flour. Cook over medium heat for 6 to 10 minutes, stirring constantly, but do not brown. Add warm milk gradually. Cook until sauce is thickened, stirring constantly. Stir in sausage, salt and pepper. Serve over hot biscuits cut into halves. **Yield: 3 cups gravy.**

Mary Lou Templin, Millers Run #2020

Peanut Butter Biscuit Twists

1/2 cup packed brown sugar
3 tablespoons water
1 tablespoon margarine
1/4 teaspoon cinnamon
1/2 teaspoon vanilla extract
1 10-count can buttermilk biscuits
Peanut butter

Combine brown sugar, water, margarine, cinnamon and vanilla in saucepan. Cook over medium heat until margarine is melted and sugar dissolved, stirring occasionally. Pour into ungreased 8x8-inch baking pan. Separate biscuits and flatten into 3-inch oblongs. Spread with peanut butter. Twist each biscuit 3 or 4 times. Place in prepared pan. Bake at 400 degrees for 15 to 20 minutes or until browned. Cool for 3 minutes; remove to serving plate. **Yield: 10 servings.**

Beverly Truscott, Hillcrest #1674

Shortcake Biscuits

3 cups flour
4 1/2 teaspoons baking powder
1 1/2 tablespoons sugar
1 teaspoon salt
3/4 cup shortening
3/4 cup milk
1 egg, beaten

Combine flour, baking powder, sugar and salt in bowl. Cut in shortening until crumbly. Add milk and egg, stirring until soft dough forms. Turn out onto lightly floured surface; roll out to desired thickness. Cut out with biscuit cutter. Place on baking sheet. Bake at 400 degrees for 10 minutes or until light brown.
Yield: 10 servings.

Bettie Osborn, Atlantic #344

Applesauce Muffins

1½ cups Homemade Whole Wheat Baking Mix
1 tablespoon sugar
½ teaspoon cinnamon
1 egg white, slightly beaten
½ cup unsweetened applesauce
¼ cup water

Combine Homemade Whole Wheat Baking Mix, sugar and cinnamon in large bowl. Mix egg white, applesauce and water in small bowl. Stir into dry ingredients until moistened. Fill greased muffin cups ⅔ full. Bake at 400 degrees for 20 minutes or until golden brown. **Yield: 8 muffins.**

Homemade Whole Wheat Baking Mix

3 cups whole wheat flour
3 cups all-purpose flour
3 tablespoons baking powder
1½ teaspoons salt
¾ cup nonfat dry milk powder
¾ cup shortening

Combine flours, baking powder, salt and milk powder in bowl. Cut in shortening with pastry blender until mixture is crumbly. Store in airtight container in refrigerator for up to 3 months. Use for biscuits or muffins. **Yield: 7 cups mix.**

Jane Treichler, Virginville #1832

Welsh Currant Cakes

4 cups flour
1 cup sugar
2 teaspoons baking powder
1 teaspoon salt
1 teaspoon nutmeg
½ cup shortening
½ cup butter or margarine
1 cup currants or dark raisins
2 eggs
⅔ cup milk

Combine flour, sugar, baking powder, salt and nutmeg in bowl. Cut in shortening and butter until mixture is crumbly. Stir in currants. Beat eggs with milk in small bowl. Add to mixture, stirring with fork until soft dough forms. Knead lightly into ball. Roll out to ¼-inch thickness on floured surface; cut with 3-inch biscuit cutter. Heat nonstick electric skillet to 350 degrees. Bake for 5 to 8 minutes on each side or until browned. **Yield: 15 to 20 servings.**

Sara Cooper, Briar Creek #146

Make decorative butter pats to serve with bread by pressing softened butter through a decorating tube fitted with desired tip. Store in freezer until needed.

Blueberry Coffee Cake

1/4 cup shortening
3/4 cup sugar
1 egg, beaten
1 1/2 cups flour
2 teaspoons baking powder
1/2 teaspoon cinnamon
1/2 cup milk
1 cup fresh blueberries
1/2 cup packed brown sugar
1/3 cup flour
1/4 cup butter, softened
1/3 cup chopped walnuts

Cream shortening, sugar and egg in mixer bowl until light and fluffy. Combine 1 1/2 cups flour, baking powder and cinnamon. Add to creamed mixture alternately with milk, beating well after each addition. Fold in blueberries. Pour into greased 9x9-inch baking pan. Mix brown sugar, 1/3 cup flour, butter and walnuts in small bowl until crumbly. Sprinkle over blueberry batter. Bake at 350 degrees for 45 to 50 minutes or until coffee cake tests done. **Yield: 8 to 10 servings.**

Luella Ruhf, South Auburn #1188

Easy Coffee Cake

1 2-layer package yellow cake mix
1 3-ounce package coconut cream instant pudding mix
1 cup sour cream
4 eggs
1/2 cup milk
1/2 cup oil
1 1/2 teaspoons cinnamon
3/4 cup chopped nuts
1/2 cup sugar

Combine cake mix, pudding mix, sour cream, eggs, milk and oil in mixer bowl. Beat at medium speed for 5 minutes or until smooth. Spread half the batter in greased and floured 9x13-inch baking pan. Combine cinnamon, nuts and 1/2 cup sugar in small bowl. Sprinkle half the cinnamon mixture over batter. Pour in remaining batter and top with remaining cinnamon mixture. Bake at 350 degrees for 35 to 40 minutes or until coffee cake tests done. **Yield: 8 to 10 servings.**

Veryle Shaffer, North Woodbury #1923

Cinnamon Flop Coffee Cakes

1 cup sugar
1/2 teaspoon nutmeg
2 cups flour
2 teaspoons baking powder
2 tablespoons shortening
1 egg
Milk
Cinnamon to taste
Brown sugar to taste

Sift sugar, nutmeg, flour and baking powder in bowl. Cut in shortening until crumbly. Place egg in 1 cup measure. Add enough milk to measure 1 cup; mix well. Add to dry ingredients, stirring until moistened. Pour into 2 greased and floured 9-inch round baking pans. Sprinkle generously with cinnamon and brown sugar. Bake at 350 degrees for 30 minutes. **Yield: 10 servings.**

Sarah Ellen Mack, Turbot #249

German Christmas Stollen

6 cakes compressed yeast
6 to 8 cups warm milk
6 pounds flour
1 1/2 pounds butter, softened
2 pounds sugar
1 3/4 tablespoons salt
1 4-ounce bottle of almond extract
1 4-ounce bottle of vanilla extract
1 1/4 pounds dark raisins
1 1/2 pounds mixed candied fruit
4 ounces citron
8 ounces ground almonds
Grated rind of 1 lemon
Nutmeg to taste

All ingredients should be weighed on scale and warmed to about 75 degrees. Crumble yeast cakes into half the warm milk in bowl. Let stand until dissolved. Pour 6 to 8 cups flour into large bowl, making well in center. Pour in yeast mixture, mixing with flour to form dough ball. Let rise, covered, in warm place for 1 hour or until doubled in bulk. Stir in remaining milk and remaining flour to form soft, elastic dough. Cream butter in mixer bowl until light and fluffy. Beat in sugar gradually. Add to flour mixture with salt, almond and vanilla extracts, raisins, candied fruit, citron, ground almonds, grated lemon and nutmeg; mix well. Turn out onto floured surface. Knead for 20 minutes or until dough is smooth and elastic. Let rise, covered, in warm place for 3 to 4 hours. Punch dough down. Divide dough into 8 equal portions. Knead each portion well. Shape into loaves; place in greased loaf pans. Let rise, covered, until doubled in bulk. Bake at 350 degrees for 40 to 50 minutes or until light brown. Remove to wire rack to cool. Brush with melted butter; sprinkle with sugar. Wrap tightly in waxed paper and foil and store in cool place. **Yield: 8 loaves.**

Charlotte Rosser, Keystone #2

Quick Buttermilk Coffee Cakes

1 teaspoon baking soda
1 cup buttermilk
2 cups flour
1 1/2 cups sugar
1 teaspoon cream of tartar
1/2 cup oil
2 eggs, beaten
6 tablespoons sugar
6 tablespoons butter
1/2 cup flour

Dissolve baking soda in buttermilk. Combine 2 cups flour, 1 1/2 cups sugar and cream of tartar in bowl. Add oil, eggs and buttermilk mixture; mix well. Pour into 2 ungreased 9-inch cake pans. Mix 6 tablespoons sugar, 6 tablespoons butter and 1/2 cup flour in small bowl until crumbly. Sprinkle over batter. Bake at 375 degrees for 20 to 25 minutes or until coffee cakes test done. **Yield: 16 servings.**

Maria Nyce, Star #993

Use your slow cooker as a bread warmer. Place a damp cloth inside slow cooker and heat on Low for 30 minutes. Remove cloth. Line slow cooker with large napkins. Place bread inside. Bread will remain hot for up to 2 hours.

Orange-Butter Coffee Cakes

1 package dry yeast
1/4 cup warm water
2 eggs, beaten
1/4 cup sugar
1/2 cup sour cream
6 tablespoons butter, softened
1 teaspoon salt
2 3/4 to 3 1/4 cups flour
2 tablespoons melted butter
6 tablespoons sugar
3/4 cup coconut
2 teaspoons grated orange rind
6 tablespoons sugar
1/2 cup sour cream
1/4 cup orange juice
1/4 cup butter
1/4 cup coconut

Dissolve yeast in warm water in bowl. Beat in eggs, 1/4 cup sugar, 1/2 cup sour cream, 6 tablespoons butter and salt. Add 2 3/4 cups flour, mixing well. Turn onto floured surface. Knead, adding enough remaining flour until dough is smooth and elastic. Place in greased bowl, turning to coat surface. Let rise, covered, in warm place until doubled in bulk. Punch dough down. Divide dough into 2 equal portions. Shape into balls. Let rise, covered, for 10 minutes. Roll each portion into 12-inch circle. Brush with 2 tablespoons melted butter. Combine 6 tablespoons sugar, 3/4 cup coconut and orange rind in small bowl. Sprinkle over dough. Cut each circle into 12 wedges. Roll up from wide end to form crescents. Arrange, pinwheel fashion, in 2 greased 9-inch round baking pans. Let rise, covered, for 30 minutes or until doubled in bulk. Bake at 350 degrees for 25 minutes. Remove to wire racks immediately. Combine 6 tablespoons sugar, 1/2 cup sour cream, orange juice and 1/4 cup butter in saucepan. Cook over medium heat until sugar is dissolved, stirring constantly. Bring to a boil. Cook for 3 minutes, stirring constantly. Spread over coffee cakes; sprinkle with 1/4 cup coconut. **Yield: 20 to 24 servings.**

Vera L. Harper, Union #155

Moravian Sugar Cake

1 small potato, peeled, cubed
1 cup water
2 envelopes yeast
1/2 cup sugar
1/4 cup shortening
1/4 cup melted butter or margarine
1/2 teaspoon salt
2 3/4 cups flour
2 eggs, beaten
1/4 cup melted butter or margarine
1/2 cup packed brown sugar
1 teaspoon cinnamon

Cook potato in 1 cup water in saucepan until tender. Cool to 110 to 115 degrees; reserve 1/2 cup cooking liquid. Mash potato with remaining liquid, adding enough reserved liquid to measure 3/4 cup. Beat potato mixture, yeast, sugar, shortening, 1/4 cup butter and salt in mixer bowl. Stir in 1 cup flour. Let rise, covered, in warm place for 30 to 45 minutes or until spongy. Punch dough down. Add remaining flour and eggs; mix well. Let rise, covered, in warm place for 45 minutes or until doubled in bulk. Punch dough down. Spread dough in greased 10x15-inch baking pan. Let rise, covered, for 45 minutes. Make indentations on surface at 1 1/2-inch intervals. Fill indentations with 1/4 cup butter. Sprinkle mixture of brown sugar and cinnamon into indentations. Bake at 375 degrees for 20 minutes or until brown. Cool in pan on rack. **Yield: 12 servings.**

Dorothea Creitz, Central #1650

Moravian Coffee Cake

1/2 recipe Potato Refrigerator Roll Dough (page 242)
1/2 cup butter, softened
1/4 cup cream
1 cup packed brown sugar
2 teaspoons cinnamon

Press dough into 2 greased 9x9-inch baking pans. Let rise, covered, for 1 1/2 to 2 hours or until doubled in bulk. Make 12 indentations in each portion. Spread with butter gently. Pour cream into indentations. Sprinkle with mixture of brown sugar and cinnamon. Bake at 400 degrees for 25 minutes or until golden brown.
Yield: 18 to 24 servings.

Eileen Parrish, Bell Township #2047

Mom's Poviticia (Croatian Walnut Rolls)

1 1/2 cups lukewarm milk
1/4 cup sugar
2 cakes yeast
1/2 cup butter, softened
4 1/2 cups flour
1 teaspoon salt
2 teaspoons vanilla extract
1 teaspoon lemon juice
3 egg yolks, beaten
1/2 to 1 cup warm milk
2 tablespoons butter
1 tablespoon honey
1 tablespoon lemon juice
1 tablespoon vanilla extract
3 egg whites, well beaten
2 cups confectioners' sugar
1 1/2 pounds ground walnuts
1 egg
1 teaspoon water

Combine 1 1/2 cups lukewarm milk, sugar and crumbled yeast cakes in small bowl; mix well. Let stand until yeast is dissolved. Cut 1/2 cup butter into flour in large bowl until crumbly; make well in center. Add salt, 2 teaspoons vanilla, lemon juice, egg yolks and yeast mixture; mix well. Knead dough until smooth and elastic. Divide into 4 equal portions; shape into balls. Place in buttered bowls, turning to butter surfaces. Let rise, covered, in warm place for 30 minutes to 1 hour or until doubled in bulk. Combine 1/2 to 1 cup warm milk and 2 tablespoons butter in large saucepan. Heat over low heat until butter is melted. Add honey, lemon juice, 1 tablespoon vanilla, egg whites, confectioners' sugar and walnuts; mix well. Roll out dough on lightly floured surface. Spoon filling over each portion. Roll up as for jelly roll. Place in buttered baking pan; brush tops with butter. Let rise, covered, until doubled in bulk. Brush tops of rolls with mixture of egg and water. Prick each roll with fork 8 times. Bake at 350 degrees for 30 minutes or until light brown. Brush tops with butter; remove to wire racks to cool. **Yield: 4 loaves.**

Sandra Rumberger, Perry Valley #1804

Light and Luscious Jelly Doughnuts

1 cup flour
1/3 cup sugar
2 envelopes rapid-rise dry yeast
1 teaspoon salt
1/3 cup butter or margarine
1/2 cup milk
1/2 cup water
3 egg yolks, beaten
2 1/2 cups flour
1 egg white, lightly beaten
Strawberry or raspberry jelly
Oil for deep frying

Combine 1 cup flour, sugar, yeast and salt in large mixer bowl; set aside. Heat butter, milk and water in saucepan to 120 to 130 degrees on candy thermometer. Pour into flour mixture. Beat for 2 minutes at medium speed until smooth. Add egg yolks and 1 cup flour, beating well. Stir in remaining flour to form soft dough. Let rise, covered with plastic wrap, in warm place for 1 to 1 1/2 hours or until doubled in bulk. Punch dough down. Divide into two equal portions. Roll out each portion on floured surface to 1/4-inch thickness. Cut each portion into 12 rounds with 3-inch cutter. Brush half the rounds with egg white. Spoon 1 heaping teaspoonful jelly on each top. Cover with remaining rounds, sealing edges. Place on baking sheet or waxed paper. Let rise, covered, for 30 to 45 minutes or until doubled in bulk. Deep-fry in 375-degree oil until brown on both sides. Drain on paper towels. May substitute cream filling made with instant pudding mix for jelly. **Yield: 24 doughnuts.**

Evelyn Gibson, Kaylor #1396

Old-Time Doughnuts

1 1/2 cakes yeast
1 cup warm water
1 cup warm mashed potatoes
3 egg yolks
1 cup sugar
1 cup flour
3 egg whites
1/2 cup shortening
1/2 cup butter
1 cup warm potato water
1 cup sugar
Salt to taste
9 to 10 cups flour
Oil for deep frying

Dissolve yeast in 1 cup warm water. Combine potatoes, egg yolks, sugar, 1 cup flour and yeast mixture in large bowl; mix well. Beat egg whites in mixer bowl until stiff peaks form. Fold into potato mixture. Let stand for 1 to 3 hours. Cream shortening and butter together until light and fluffy. Add to potato mixture with potato water, sugar, salt and remaining flour, stirring to form soft dough. Knead on floured surface until smooth and elastic. Let rise, covered, in warm place for 6 to 6 1/2 hours. Roll out on floured surface to 1/2-inch thickness. Cut into desired shapes. Make slit in each dough portion with knife. Let rise, covered, until doubled in bulk. Deep-fry in 375-degree oil until brown. Drain on paper towels. **Yield: 36 to 40 doughnuts.**

Katie A. Moll, Virginville #1832

Mashed Potato Doughnuts

3 eggs
3/4 cup sugar
3 tablespoons oil
1 cup mashed potatoes
2 3/4 cups flour
4 teaspoons baking powder
1 teaspoon each salt and nutmeg
Oil for deep frying

Beat eggs in large bowl. Add sugar, 3 tablespoons oil and mashed potatoes; mix well. Sift flour, baking powder, salt and nutmeg together. Add to potato mixture. Mix well, adding additional flour if necessary for soft dough. Turn out onto floured surface. Roll out to 3/8-inch thickness. Cut to desired size with floured cutter. Deep-fry in 375-degree oil for 1 to 1 1/2 minutes on each side. Drain on paper towels. Roll in sugar while hot. **Yield: 24 doughnuts.**

Margaret Verbeke, Reynoldsville #1825

Potato Drop Doughnuts

3 tablespoons melted butter
2 cups hot mashed potatoes
2 cups sugar
2 eggs, beaten
1 cup milk
1 teaspoon vanilla extract
1 teaspoon salt
5 teaspoons baking powder
4 1/2 cups flour
Oil for deep frying
Sugar and cinnamon mixture

Stir butter into mashed potatoes. Add sugar, eggs, milk and vanilla; mix well. Stir in salt, baking powder and flour, a little at a time, until soft dough forms. Heat oil to 400 degrees in deep-fryer. Drop dough by teaspoonfuls into hot oil. Deep-fry for 1 to 2 minutes on each side or until golden brown. Drain on paper towels. Roll in mixture of sugar and cinnamon while hot. **Yield: 4 dozen doughnuts.**

Winnie Knox, Buffalo #1523

Sugar-Free Doughnuts

1/2 cup shortening
1/2 cup margarine, softened
1 1/2 cups hot mashed potatoes
1 1/2 cups potato water
1 cup artificial sweetener
2 eggs, beaten
1 package yeast
10 cups unbleached flour
Oil for deep frying

Cream shortening and margarine in mixer bowl. Add mashed potatoes, potato water, artificial sweetener and eggs; mix well. Sprinkle with yeast; stir in gently. Let stand for 1 1/2 to 2 hours in warm place. Stir in flour gradually. Knead on floured surface until smooth. Let rise, covered, in warm place for 5 to 6 hours or until doubled in bulk. Roll out on floured surface to 1/2-inch thickness; cut to desired size. Place on floured towel. Let rise, covered, in warm place for 1 1/2 to 2 hours or until doubled in bulk. Deep-fry in 375-degree oil until light brown. Drain on paper towels.
Yield: 50 doughnuts.

Lester A. Adam, Virginville #1832

Baked French Toast

1 large loaf French bread, cut into 1-inch slices
6 eggs
1½ cups milk
1 cup light cream
1 teaspoon vanilla extract
¼ teaspoon cinnamon
¼ teaspoon nutmeg
¼ cup margarine, softened
½ cup packed light brown sugar
½ cup chopped walnuts
1 tablespoon light corn syrup

Butter 9x9-inch baking pan. Arrange bread slices in overlapping rows to fill pan. Combine next 6 ingredients in large bowl; mix well. Pour over bread slices. Chill, covered, overnight. Combine margarine, brown sugar, walnuts and corn syrup in small bowl. Spread evenly over top of bread. Bake at 350 degrees for 40 minutes or until puffed and golden. Serve with maple syrup. **Yield: 6 to 8 servings.**

Kim Hicks, Pioneer #1777

French Batter Toast

1 cup pancake mix
¼ cup wheat germ
3 eggs, beaten
1½ cups milk
6 thick slices bread
Oil for deep frying
1 cup packed brown sugar
¾ cup water
½ cup sugar

Combine pancake mix, wheat germ, eggs and milk in bowl; mix well. Dip bread slices in mixture. Deep-fry in hot oil until brown. Combine brown sugar, water and sugar in saucepan; mix well. Bring to a boil. Cook for 3 minutes, stirring constantly. Pour over toast. **Yield: 6 servings.**

Nancy B. Matter, Community #2048

Oven French Toast with Nut Topping

1 12-ounce loaf French bread, cut into 1-inch slices
8 eggs
2 cups milk
2 cups half and half
2 teaspoons vanilla extract
½ teaspoon nutmeg
½ teaspoon cinnamon
½ teaspoon mace
¾ cup butter, softened
1⅓ cups packed brown sugar
3 tablespoons dark corn syrup
1⅓ cups coarsely chopped pecans or walnuts

Line buttered 9x13-inch baking pan with bread slices. Process eggs, milk, half and half, vanilla, nutmeg, cinnamon and mace in blender until smooth. Pour over bread. Chill, covered, overnight. Combine butter, brown sugar, corn syrup and pecans in small bowl; mix well. Sprinkle over bread. Bake at 350 degrees for 50 minutes or until puffed and golden. **Yield: 8 to 10 servings.**

Judy Hetzell, Mt. Nebo #1872

Praline Brunch Toast

8 eggs
1 1/2 cups milk
1 tablespoon brown sugar
2 teaspoons vanilla extract
8 3/4-inch thick slices French bread
1/4 cup butter
1/2 cup packed brown sugar
1/4 cup maple syrup
1/2 cup chopped pecans

Beat eggs, milk, 1 tablespoon brown sugar and vanilla in bowl. Pour half the mixture in 9x13-inch dish. Layer bread slices over mixture. Pour remaining egg mixture over top. Chill, covered, for several hours to overnight. Melt butter in 9x13-inch baking dish. Stir in 1/2 cup brown sugar and maple syrup; sprinkle with pecans. Remove bread slices from egg mixture and layer over sugar mixture. Pour any remaining egg mixture over top. Bake at 350 degrees for 30 to 35 minutes or until puffed and golden. **Yield: 4 servings.**

Kay Costa, Gillett #884

Mother's Fried Cakes

6 eggs
3 1/2 cups buttermilk
3 cups sugar
6 tablespoons melted shortening
2 teaspoons salt
2 teaspoons baking soda
4 teaspoons baking powder
2 teaspoons nutmeg
2 teaspoons vanilla extract
Flour
Oil for deep frying

Beat eggs with buttermilk in large bowl. Add sugar, shortening, salt, baking soda, baking powder, nutmeg and vanilla; mix well. Add enough flour to make soft dough, stirring well. Turn out onto floured surface. Roll out to 1/2-inch thickness; cut to desired size. Let stand for 1 hour. Deep-fry in 375-degree oil until brown. Drain on paper towels. **Yield: 50 to 60 fried cakes.**

Cecil Rogers, Charleston Valley #54

Funnel Cakes

2 eggs, beaten
1 1/2 cups milk
2 cups flour
1 teaspoon baking powder
1/2 teaspoon salt
Oil for deep frying
Confectioners' sugar

Combine eggs, milk, flour, baking powder and salt in bowl, stirring until smooth. Pour oil to 3-inch depth in deep-fryer. Heat to 375 degrees. Pour 1/2 cup batter into funnel, blocking bottom opening with finger. Hold funnel over hot oil. Drizzle batter from funnel beginning in center and circling around to outer edge to form a spiral. Deep-fry until golden brown. Drain on paper towels. Sift confectioners' sugar over top. **Yield: 4 to 5 servings.**

Naomi Bupp, Red Lion #1781

Hush Puppies

1 cup coarse cornmeal
1 cup flour
3 eggs, beaten
2 tablespoons sugar
1/2 teaspoon salt
1 tablespoon baking powder
1/3 cup finely chopped green bell pepper
1 to 2 tablespoons finely chopped onion
1 6-ounce can tomato juice
Oil for deep frying

Combine cornmeal, flour, eggs, sugar, salt, baking powder, green pepper, onion and tomato juice in large bowl; mix until moistened. Heat oil to 370 degrees in deep-fryer. Drop batter by tablespoonfuls into hot oil. Deep-fry until brown; drain on paper towels. **Yield: 20 servings.**

Willowa Gates, Corry #55

Johnny Cake

1 1/2 cups flour
1 tablespoon baking powder
1/2 cup cornmeal
1 teaspoon salt
3/4 cup sugar
2 eggs, beaten
1/4 cup oil
2 tablespoons vanilla extract
1 cup milk

Combine flour, baking powder, cornmeal and salt together in large bowl. Combine sugar, eggs, oil, vanilla and milk in medium bowl; mix well. Add to dry ingredients, mixing well. Pour into greased 9x9-inch baking pan. Bake at 350 degrees for 30 to 35 minutes. Cool and cut into squares to serve. **Yield: 9 servings.**

Martha Fenstermaker, Red Brush Community #2085

Apple Butter Bread

2 cups flour
1 cup packed brown sugar
1 1/2 teaspoons baking powder
1/2 teaspoon baking soda
1/2 teaspoon salt
3/4 cup apple butter
1/2 cup apple juice
1/4 cup melted butter or margarine
1 egg, beaten
1 cup raisins
1/2 cup chopped walnuts
3/4 cup apple butter

Combine flour, brown sugar, baking powder, baking soda and salt in large bowl. Add 3/4 cup apple butter, apple juice, butter and egg, stirring until moistened. Fold in raisins and walnuts. Pour half the batter into greased and floured 5x9-inch loaf pan. Spread remaining apple butter over batter. Pour remaining batter over top. Bake at 350 degrees for 1 to 1 1/4 hours or until loaf tests done. Cool in pan on rack for 15 minutes; turn out on wire rack to cool completely. Store in refrigerator wrapped in plastic wrap. **Yield: 1 loaf.**

Mary Harkleroad, Rural Valley #1750

Apple-Pecan Bread

1/2 cup margarine, softened
1 cup sugar
2 eggs, beaten
2 tablespoons milk
1 teaspoon vanilla extract
2 cups flour
1 teaspoon double-acting baking powder
1 teaspoon baking soda
1 cup chopped apples
1/2 cup chopped pecans

Cream margarine and sugar in mixer bowl until light and fluffy. Beat in eggs, milk and vanilla. Add flour, baking powder and baking soda, stirring until moistened. Fold in apples and pecans. Pour into greased 5x9-inch loaf pan. Bake at 350 degrees for 1 hour or until loaf tests done. Remove to wire rack to cool. Wrap in plastic wrap; let stand overnight before slicing. **Yield: 1 loaf.**

Pansy Duke, Bradford #1219

Apricot Bread

1 cup dried apricots
1 cup sugar
2 tablespoons margarine, softened
1 egg, beaten
1/4 cup water
1/2 cup orange juice
2 cups flour
2 teaspoons baking powder
1/4 teaspoon baking soda
Salt to taste

Soak apricots in warm water for 30 minutes; drain. Cut into 1/4-inch pieces; set aside. Cream sugar, margarine and egg in mixer bowl until light and fluffy. Beat in water and orange juice. Sift in flour, baking powder, baking soda and salt, stirring until moistened. Fold in apricots. Pour into greased and floured loaf pan. Bake at 350 degrees for 55 to 60 minutes or until loaf tests done. Cool on wire rack. **Yield: 1 loaf.**

Sandra Null, Eldred #1604

Banana-Nut Bread

1 cup sugar
1 cup packed brown sugar
1/2 cup shortening
2 eggs, beaten
3 large bananas, mashed
1/4 cup sour milk
1 tablespoon vanilla extract
3 cups flour
1 1/2 teaspoons baking soda
1 teaspoon baking powder
Salt to taste
1/2 bottle of maraschino cherries
1/2 bottle of cherry juice
1/2 cup nuts

Cream sugar, brown sugar and shortening in mixer bowl until light and fluffy. Beat in eggs, bananas, sour milk and vanilla. Sift in flour, baking soda, baking powder and salt, stirring until moistened. Stir in cherries and cherry juice. Fold in nuts. Pour into greased and floured loaf pan. Bake at 350 degrees for 1 hour or until loaf tests done. Remove to wire rack to cool. **Yield: 1 loaf.**

Lillian Dentil, Buffalo #1523

Jacy's Honey-Banana Bread

1/4 cup melted margarine
3 bananas, mashed
1/2 teaspoon baking soda
1 1/2 cups whole wheat flour
3/4 cup honey

Combine margarine and bananas in bowl; mix well. Add baking soda, flour and honey, stirring until well mixed. Pour into greased loaf pan. Bake at 350 degrees for 1 hour or until loaf tests done. Remove to wire rack to cool. **Yield: 1 loaf.**

Lois Irwin, Penn #534

Banana-Sour Cream-Walnut Loaf

2/3 cup butter or margarine, softened
1 1/2 cups sugar
2 eggs, beaten
1 1/2 cups mashed bananas
2 3/4 cups flour, sifted
1 teaspoon baking powder
1 teaspoon baking soda
1/2 teaspoon salt
1/2 cup sour cream
1 cup chopped walnuts

Cream butter and sugar in mixer bowl until light and fluffy. Beat in eggs and bananas. Sift together flour, baking powder, baking soda and salt. Add to creamed mixture alternately with sour cream, stirring well after each addition. Fold in walnuts. Pour into greased and floured 5x9-inch loaf pan. Bake at 350 degrees for 1 1/4 hours or until loaf tests done. Cool in pan for 20 minutes; remove to wire rack to cool completely. Store, tightly wrapped, in refrigerator. **Yield: 1 loaf.**

Mary E. Alkons, Virginville #1832

Bishop's Bread

1/2 teaspoon baking soda
3/4 cup sour milk
2 1/2 cups flour
1 1/2 cups packed light brown sugar
1 teaspoon baking powder
1 teaspoon cinnamon
1/2 teaspoon salt
1 egg, beaten

Dissolve baking soda in sour milk; set aside. Combine flour, brown sugar, baking powder, cinnamon and salt in large bowl; mix well. Reserve 1/2 cup crumb mixture for topping. Add egg and sour milk mixture to remaining crumb mixture, stirring to mix. Pour into greased and floured loaf pan. Sprinkle reserved crumb mixture over top. Bake at 350 degrees for 30 minutes or until loaf tests done. Serve hot. **Yield: 1 loaf.**

Faye Knapp, Edinboro #947

Brown Bread

1 cup sugar
1 cup molasses
3 cups buttermilk
2 teaspoons baking soda
2 teaspoons baking powder
2 1/2 cups graham flour
2 cups all-purpose flour
1/2 teaspoon salt

Combine sugar, molasses, buttermilk, baking soda, baking powder, graham flour, all-purpose flour and salt in large bowl. Stir by hand until well mixed. Pour into 2 waxed paper-lined 5x9-inch loaf pans. Let stand for 30 minutes. Bake at 350 degrees for 50 minutes or until loaves test done. Cool on wire rack. May also bake as for muffins. **Yield: 2 loaves.**

Evadna Linder, Valley #876

Healthy Brown Bran Bread

1 cup All-Bran cereal
1/2 cup seedless raisins
2 tablespoons shortening
1/2 cup molasses
3/4 cup boiling water
1 egg, beaten
1 cup sifted flour
1 teaspoon baking soda
1/2 teaspoon salt
1/2 teaspoon cinnamon

Combine All-Bran, raisins, shortening and molasses in large bowl. Add boiling water, stirring until shortening is melted. Add egg; beat well. Sift flour, baking soda, salt and cinnamon together. Add to bran mixture, stirring until moistened. Pour into 2 greased and floured tin cans, filling 2/3 full, or 1 greased and floured medium loaf pan. Bake at 350 degrees for 45 minutes. Remove from cans or loaf pan; wrap in plastic wrap. I have been using this recipe for about 50 years. It's easy and healthy because it contains lots of iron. **Yield: 8 servings.**

Dora Roberts, South Auburn #1188

Carrot and Pineapple Bread

3 eggs, beaten
2 cups sugar
1 cup oil
2 teaspoons vanilla extract
1 cup grated carrots
1 8-ounce can crushed pineapple
1 cup chopped nuts
1 1/2 teaspoons cinnamon
1 teaspoon salt
1 teaspoon baking soda
3 cups flour

Beat eggs with sugar, oil and vanilla in large bowl. Stir in carrots, pineapple and nuts. Add cinnamon, salt, baking soda and flour, stirring to mix. Pour into 2 greased and floured loaf pans. Bake at 325 degrees for 1 hour or until loaves test done. Cool on wire racks. **Yield: 2 loaves.**

Myra Cowan, Harmony #1201

Cheddar-Bacon and Olive Bread

2 1/2 cups flour
2 1/2 teaspoons sugar
2 teaspoons baking powder
1/2 teaspoon baking soda
1 teaspoon salt
1 teaspoon dry mustard
Cayenne pepper to taste
1/4 cup butter, softened
1 cup shredded Cheddar cheese
1 egg, beaten
1 cup buttermilk
1 teaspoon Worcestershire sauce
6 slices crisp-fried bacon, crumbled
1 cup coarsely chopped black olives

Combine flour, sugar, baking powder, baking soda, salt, dry mustard and cayenne pepper in large bowl. Cut in butter with fork until crumbly. Stir in cheese; make well in center of mixture. Beat egg with buttermilk and Worcestershire sauce. Pour into well, stirring until moistened. Stir in bacon and olives. Pour into greased 5x9-inch loaf pan. Bake at 375 degrees for 30 to 40 minutes or until loaf tests done. Remove to wire rack to cool. May also use for muffins, reducing baking time to 20 to 25 minutes. **Yield: 1 loaf.**

Ruth Posten, Deemston #1372

Honey Corn Bread

2 1/2 cups yellow cornmeal
1 cup whole wheat flour
2 1/2 teaspoons baking powder
1 teaspoon salt
3/4 cup (about) buttermilk
2 1/2 cups oil
2 eggs, beaten
2 tablespoons honey

Combine cornmeal, whole wheat flour, baking powder and salt in large bowl; mix well. Mix buttermilk, oil, eggs and honey in small bowl. Add to dry ingredients, stirring until moistened. Pour into greased 9x13-inch baking pan. Bake at 425 degrees for 20 to 25 minutes or until golden brown. Cut into squares to serve. **Yield: 24 servings.**

Sophie Sally Bocz, Brush Valley #1785

Maple Corn Bread

1/2 cup cornmeal
2 cups whole wheat flour
2 tablespoons baking powder
1 teaspoon salt
2 eggs, beaten
1 cup maple syrup
1 1/2 cups milk
6 tablespoons melted shortening

Combine cornmeal, whole wheat flour, baking powder and salt in large bowl. Beat eggs with maple syrup, milk and shortening in mixer bowl. Add to dry ingredients, stirring to moisten. Pour into greased 9x13-inch baking pan. Bake at 400 degrees for 20 minutes. **Yield: 12 to 15 servings.**

Jeanne Tomb, Alert #905

Mexican Corn Bread

1 8-ounce package corn bread mix
1/2 tablespoon finely chopped jalapeño peppers
1 8-ounce can cream-style corn
1 cup sharp Cheddar cheese spread

Prepare corn bread mix using package directions. Stir in jalapeño peppers and corn. Pour half the mixture into greased 8x8-inch baking pan. Drop cheese spread by spoonfuls onto batter. Cover with remaining batter. Bake, covered with foil, at 375 degrees for 25 to 30 minutes or until light brown. **Yield: 8 servings.**

Ellen Marie Wadsworth, Goshen #121

Quick Graham Bread

1/2 cup packed brown sugar
3/4 cup cold water
1/2 cup melted shortening
3/4 cup milk
1 cup all-purpose flour
1 teaspoon salt
1 teaspoon baking soda
2 cups graham flour

Dissolve brown sugar in water in large bowl. Stir in shortening and milk. Sift all-purpose flour with salt and baking soda. Stir into sugar mixture. Add graham flour, mixing well. Pour into greased loaf pan. Bake at 375 degrees for 1 hour. **Yield: 1 loaf.**

Peggy Buchko, Charleston Valley #54

Gingerbread

1 cup sugar
1 egg, beaten
1/2 cup shortening
1/2 cup baking molasses
1 teaspoon ground ginger
2 cups flour
1 teaspoon baking soda
1 cup boiling water

Cream sugar, egg and shortening in large mixer bowl until light and fluffy. Stir in molasses, ginger, flour and baking soda. Add boiling water, mixing well. Pour into nonstick 9x13-inch baking pan. Bake at 350 degrees for 30 minutes. **Yield: 12 to 15 servings.**

Mae Shaffer, Charlesville #698

Add 1 cup chopped dates, dried apricots, raisins or figs to your favorite bread recipe.

Glazed Lemon Bread

1½ cups flour
1 teaspoon baking powder
½ teaspoon salt
⅓ cup melted butter
1 cup sugar
2 eggs, beaten
¼ teaspoon almond extract
½ cup milk
2 teaspoons lemon extract
1½ tablespoons lemon juice
2 tablespoons sugar

Combine flour, baking powder and salt in bowl. Mix butter, 1 cup sugar, eggs and almond extract in large bowl. Add dry ingredients alternately with milk, stirring well after each addition. Stir in lemon extract. Pour into greased and floured 4x8-inch loaf pan. Bake at 350 degrees for 55 to 60 minutes or until loaf tests done. Mix lemon juice and 2 tablespoons sugar in small bowl. Spoon over hot loaf. Cool in pan on wire rack for 10 minutes. Remove to wire rack to cool completely. Let stand overnight, tightly wrapped, before slicing. **Yield: 1 loaf.**

Ruth Ann Fuller, South Auburn #1188

Mincemeat-Bran Bread

2½ cups flour
¼ cup sugar
2½ teaspoons baking powder
½ teaspoon salt
2 eggs, beaten
¾ cup milk
¼ cup oil
1 cup mincemeat
1½ cups bran cereal
½ cup chopped nuts

Combine flour, sugar, baking powder and salt in large bowl. Mix eggs, milk and oil in small bowl. Stir in mincemeat and bran cereal. Let stand for 5 minutes. Stir in nuts. Add to dry ingredients, stirring until moistened. Pour into greased 5x9-inch loaf pan. Bake for 60 to 70 minutes or until loaf tests done. Cool in pan for 15 minutes. Remove to wire rack to cool completely. May sprinkle with confectioners' sugar. Decorate with cherries and green mints for holidays. **Yield: 1 loaf.**

Catherine Halstead

Pineapple-Nut Bread

1 egg, beaten
¼ cup milk
¼ cup melted shortening
1¾ cups flour
½ cup sugar
½ teaspoon salt
1 teaspoon baking powder
½ teaspoon baking soda
1 8-ounce can crushed pineapple
1 cup raisins
½ cup chopped nuts

Beat egg with milk and shortening in large bowl. Sift in flour, sugar, salt, baking powder and baking soda, stirring to mix. Fold in pineapple, raisins and nuts. Pour into 2 greased and floured loaf pans. Bake at 350 degrees for 1 hour. **Yield: 2 loaves.**

Marilyn Teudhope, Harmony #1112

Pumpkin Bread

3 cups flour
1 teaspoon salt
2 cups sugar
4 eggs, beaten
1$^{1}/_{4}$ cups oil
$^{1}/_{2}$ cup chopped nuts
1 teaspoon baking soda
1 tablespoon cinnamon
2 cups cooked pumpkin

Combine flour, salt and sugar in large bowl; make well in center. Add eggs, oil, nuts, baking soda, cinnamon and pumpkin. Stir until moistened. Pour into 2 greased 4x8-inch loaf pans. Bake at 350 degrees for 1 hour. **Yield: 2 loaves.**

A. Elaine Cook, Brandywine #60

Sally Lunn

$^{1}/_{4}$ cup sugar
$^{1}/_{4}$ cup butter, softened
3 eggs, beaten
2 cups flour
4 teaspoons baking powder
$^{1}/_{2}$ teaspoon salt
1 cup milk
1 teaspoon vanilla extract

Cream sugar and butter in mixer bowl until light and fluffy. Beat in eggs. Mix flour, baking powder and salt together. Add to creamed mixture alternately with milk and vanilla, beating well after each addition. Pour into greased 9x9-inch baking pan. Bake at 375 degrees for 30 minutes. Serve warm. **Yield: 9 servings.**

Marian Holloway, Fulton #66

Rhubarb Bread

1$^{1}/_{3}$ cups packed brown sugar
$^{2}/_{3}$ cup oil
1 egg, beaten
1 teaspoon vanilla extract
1 cup sour milk
2$^{1}/_{2}$ cups flour
$^{3}/_{4}$ teaspoon salt
1 teaspoon baking soda
1 teaspoon cinnamon
1$^{1}/_{2}$ to 2 cups chopped rhubarb
$^{1}/_{2}$ cup chopped nuts

Mix brown sugar and oil in bowl. Beat in egg, vanilla and milk. Add flour, salt, baking soda and cinnamon, stirring to moisten. Fold in rhubarb and nuts. Pour into two greased 4x8-inch loaf pans. Bake at 350 degrees for 45 minutes or until loaves test done. Cool on wire rack. **Yield: 2 loaves.**

Sara Cooper, Briar Creek #146

Strawberry Bread

3 cups flour
2 teaspoons baking soda
1 teaspoon salt
2 cups sugar
1¼ cups chopped pecans
3 eggs, well beaten
3 cups mashed strawberries
1¼ cups oil
1 cup butter, softened
3 tablespoons confectioners' sugar
½ cup chopped strawberries

Sift flour, baking soda, salt and sugar into large bowl; make well in center. Combine pecans, eggs, mashed strawberries and oil in small bowl; mix well. Pour into dry ingredients, stirring to moisten. Pour into 2 greased loaf pans. Bake at 350 degrees for 1 hour. Cream butter and confectioners' sugar in small bowl. Stir in chopped strawberries. Serve with hot Strawberry Bread. **Yield: 2 loaves.**

Janet D. Whited, Harmony #1201

Honey-Wheat Loaf

2½ cups whole wheat flour
1½ cups wheat germ
⅓ cup packed brown sugar
½ teaspoon salt
1 cup raisins
2 teaspoons baking soda
1¾ cups buttermilk
⅓ cup honey

Combine flour, wheat germ, brown sugar, salt and raisins in large bowl. Combine baking soda, buttermilk and honey in small bowl; mix well. Let stand until bubbly. Stir into dry ingredients. Spoon into greased 5x9-inch loaf pan. Bake at 350 degrees for 1 hour. Remove to wire rack to cool. **Yield: 1 loaf.**

Anna Angstadt, Pioneer #1777

Spicy Zucchini Bread

3 eggs
1 cup oil
2 cups sugar
2 teaspoons vanilla extract
2 cups shredded zucchini
1 8-ounce can crushed pineapple, drained
3 cups flour
2 teaspoons baking soda
1 teaspoon salt
1 teaspoon cinnamon
½ teaspoon nutmeg
1 cup chopped nuts
1 cup raisins

Beat eggs in large bowl. Add oil, sugar and vanilla, beating until thick and foamy. Stir in zucchini and pineapple. Combine flour, baking soda, salt, cinnamon, nutmeg, nuts and raisins. Add to zucchini mixture gradually, stirring well. Pour into 2 floured loaf pans. Bake at 350 degrees for 1 hour. Remove to wire rack to cool. **Yield: 2 loaves.**

Harry K. Johnson, Wells Valley #1877

Zucchini Bread

3 eggs, beaten
2 cups sugar
1 cup oil
2 cups grated zucchini
2 teaspoons vanilla extract
3 cups flour
1 teaspoon salt
1 teaspoon baking soda
1/4 teaspoon baking powder
3 teaspoons cinnamon
Chopped nuts

Mix eggs, sugar, oil, zucchini and vanilla in large bowl. Sift flour, salt, baking soda, baking powder and cinnamon together. Add to liquid mixture, stirring to moisten. Fold in chopped nuts. Pour batter into 2 greased and floured loaf pans. Bake at 350 degrees for 1 hour or until loaves test done. Cool on wire rack. **Yield: 2 loaves.**

Mitzi Feister, Valley #1360

Easter Bread

2 packages dry yeast
1/3 cup warm water
1/2 cup sugar
1/3 cup margarine, softened
4 eggs, beaten
1 1/2 cups scalded milk
1/4 15-ounce package raisins
2 teaspoons salt
8 to 10 cups flour

Dissolve yeast in warm water. Beat sugar, margarine, eggs and milk in mixer bowl. Stir in raisins and yeast mixture. Sift in salt and enough flour to make smooth dough. Knead on lightly floured surface until smooth and elastic. Place in greased bowl, turning to coat surface. Let rise, covered, in warm place until doubled in bulk. Break off small pieces of dough; shape into small balls. Place in greased round baking pan. Let rise, covered, until doubled in bulk. Bake at 300 degrees for 45 minutes or until golden. **Yield: 36 to 48 servings.**

Violet L. Hicks, East Branch #1262

Never-Fail French Bread

1 cake yeast
1 1/2 cups warm water
1 tablespoon sugar
1 1/2 teaspoons salt
1 tablespoon shortening
4 cups flour
Melted butter

Dissolve yeast in 1/2 cup warm water. Mix sugar and salt with remaining 1 cup water in bowl. Add shortening and yeast mixture, stirring well. Mix in flour. Work dough with spoon at 10-minute intervals for 5 consecutive times. Turn onto lightly floured surface; divide into 2 equal portions. Shape into balls. Let rise for 10 minutes. Shape into 9x12-inch rectangles. Roll up as for jelly rolls beginning with long sides; seal edges. Place on baking sheet. Score each top diagonally 6 times. Let rise, covered with towel, for 1 1/2 hours. Bake at 400 degrees for 30 to 35 minutes. Brush with melted butter. **Yield: 2 loaves.**

Irene Ruffner, Community #1994

Never-Fail Bread

$4^1/_2$ cups warm water
3 packages dry yeast
$^1/_2$ to 1 cup nonfat instant milk powder
$^1/_4$ to 1 cup sugar
$^1/_4$ to 1 cup shortening
4 teaspoons salt
2 to 4 eggs
12 cups flour
Melted shortening

Combine warm water, yeast, milk powder, sugar, shortening, salt, eggs and 6 cups flour in large mixer bowl. Beat at medium speed until smooth. Pour remaining 6 cups flour in large bowl. Pour in liquid mixture, stirring to mix. Turn out onto floured surface. Knead until smooth and elastic. Let rise, covered, for 1 hour or until doubled in bulk. Punch dough down. Let rise for 30 minutes longer or until doubled in bulk. Shape into 4 loaves. Brush all sides with melted shortening. Place in 4 greased loaf pans. Let rise for 30 minutes or until doubled in bulk. Bake at 350 degrees for 30 minutes. Turn out onto wire racks to cool. **Yield: 4 loaves.**

Marian Brennan, Weishample #1898

Rapid-Mix Bread

1 cup flour
2 tablespoons sugar
$^1/_2$ cup nonfat instant milk powder
$1^1/_2$ teaspoons salt
1 package yeast
2 tablespoons oil
$1^1/_4$ cups warm water
$2^1/_2$ cups flour

Combine 1 cup flour, sugar, milk powder, salt and yeast in large mixer bowl. Add oil and warm water. Beat on medium speed for 2 minutes. Add remaining flour, $^1/_2$ cup at a time, beating for 2 minutes after each addition. Turn onto floured surface. Knead for 8 to 10 minutes. Cover with plastic wrap and clean towel; let rest for 20 minutes. Shape into loaf; place in greased loaf pan. Brush with oil. Let rise, covered, for 40 minutes. Bake at 375 degrees for 35 to 40 minutes or until loaf tests done. Remove to wire rack to cool. **Yield: 1 loaf.**

Delores Brooks, Fair View #2080

Peanut Butter Bread

$1^1/_4$ cups warm water
$^1/_4$ cup packed brown sugar
$^1/_2$ cup chunky peanut butter
1 package yeast
$2^3/_4$ cups bread flour

Combine warm water, brown sugar, peanut butter, yeast and bread flour in large bowl, stirring well. Knead until dough is smooth and elastic. Let rise, covered, in warm place until doubled in bulk. Punch dough down. Let rise until doubled in bulk. Shape into loaves; place in 2 greased loaf pans. Let rise, covered, until doubled in bulk. Bake at 360 degrees for 20 minutes. Reduce oven temperature to 250 degrees. Bake for 5 to 10 minutes longer. **Yield: 2 loaves.**

Lois M. Pifer, Henderson #1315

Saffron Bread

1/8 to 1/4 teaspoon saffron
2 tablespoons boiling water
2 packages yeast
1/2 cup warm water
1 cup lukewarm milk
3/4 cup sugar
1 1/2 teaspoons salt
2 eggs, beaten
1/2 cup shortening
1/2 cup currants
1/2 cup raisins
6 1/4 to 7 cups flour

Dissolve saffron in 2 tablespoons boiling water; cool. Dissolve yeast in 1/2 cup warm water; add saffron mixture. Combine with next 7 ingredients in bowl; mix well. Add flour gradually, stirring well. Knead on lightly floured surface until smooth and elastic. Let rise, covered, in warm place for 45 minutes. Shape into 2 loaves; place in greased loaf pans. Let rise, covered, for 30 minutes. Bake at 350 degrees for 20 to 40 minutes or until loaves test done. **Yield: 2 loaves.**

Miriam Warren, Chester Valley #1496

White Bread

1 3/4 to 2 packages dry yeast
1/4 cup warm water
1/2 cup sugar
1/2 cup oil
1 egg, beaten
1 tablespoon salt
2 1/2 cups warm water
10 cups unbleached flour

Dissolve yeast in 1/4 cup water. Let stand for 30 minutes. Combine sugar, oil, egg, salt and yeast mixture in large bowl; mix well. Add 2 1/2 cups water and flour, stirring well. Turn onto floured surface. Knead until smooth and elastic. Place in greased bowl, turning to coat surface. Let rise, covered, for 3 to 4 hours or until doubled in bulk; punch dough down. Let rise for 1 to 1 1/2 hours. Shape into loaves. Place in greased loaf pans. Bake at 350 degrees for 30 to 35 minutes or until loaves test done. Remove to wire rack to cool. **Yield: 5 or 6 loaves.**

Mildred Hawk, Valley #1184

Whole Wheat-Oat Bread

1 1/2 cups whole wheat flour
1 cup quick-cooking oats
2 teaspoons salt
2 packages dry yeast
1 3/4 cups warm water
2 eggs, beaten
1/2 cup margarine, softened
1/2 cup corn syrup
3 to 4 cups all-purpose flour

Combine whole wheat flour, oats, salt, yeast and warm water in bowl; mix well. Let stand for 15 minutes. Add eggs, margarine, corn syrup and enough all-purpose flour to make stiff dough. Turn out on floured board. Knead until smooth and elastic. Let stand for 15 minutes. Punch dough down. Shape into 2 loaves. Place in 2 greased loaf pans. Let rise until doubled in bulk. Bake at 350 degrees for 35 to 40 minutes or until loaves test done. **Yield: 2 loaves.**

Robert W. Terrell, Venango #910

Whole Wheat-Bran Bread

3½ to 4 cups all-purpose flour
2½ cups whole wheat flour
¾ cup raw bran
2 packages dry yeast
1 tablespoon salt
1 cup milk
1 cup water
½ cup honey
3 tablespoons shortening
1 egg, beaten
Melted butter

Combine 1 cup all-purpose flour, 2½ cups wheat flour, bran, yeast and salt in mixer bowl; mix well. Heat milk, water, honey and shortening in saucepan until warm. Stir into flour mixture. Add egg. Beat at medium speed for 3 minutes. Stir in remaining flour until stiff dough forms. Knead for 5 minutes or until smooth and elastic. Place in greased bowl, turning to coat surface. Let rise, covered, in warm place for 1 hour or until doubled in bulk. Shape into 2 loaves. Place in greased loaf pans. Let rise, covered, until doubled in bulk. Bake at 375 degrees for 35 to 40 minutes or until loaves test done. Cool on wire rack. Brush tops with melted butter. **Yield: 2 loaves.**

Deb Elliott, Hookstown #1980

Blueberry Lovers' Muffins

2 cups flour
4 teaspoons baking powder
¼ teaspoon salt
1½ teaspoons cinnamon
⅓ cup sugar
3½ cups bran flakes
1¾ cups skim milk
2 egg whites, beaten
3 tablespoons oil
1½ cups fresh or frozen blueberries

Combine flour, baking powder, salt, cinnamon and sugar in bowl. Mix bran flakes and milk in large bowl. Let stand for 2 minutes. Add egg whites and oil; beat well. Add dry ingredients, stirring until moistened. Fold in blueberries. Spray muffin cups with nonstick cooking spray. Spoon in batter, filling ⅔ full. Bake at 400 degrees for 23 minutes or until light golden brown. Serve warm. **Yield: 12 muffins.**

Marion Greenwood, Schnecksville #1684

Cheesy Muffins

2 cups flour
1 teaspoon salt
1 tablespoon baking powder
3 eggs
1 cup milk
2 teaspoons tarragon
1 tablespoon parsley
2 tablespoons chives
4 cups shredded Cheddar cheese

Combine flour, salt and baking powder in bowl. Beat eggs with milk. Pour into dry ingredients, stirring until mixed. Stir in tarragon, parsley, chives and cheese. Spoon into greased muffin cups. Bake at 425 degrees for 15 minutes. **Yield: 12 muffins.**

Becky Michalka, Burgettstown #1502

Cranberry-Pumpkin Muffins

1½ cups flour
1 teaspoon baking soda
¼ teaspoon baking powder
1 teaspoon cinnamon
1 teaspoon ground cloves
¼ teaspoon salt
¼ cup butter, softened
1¼ cups sugar
2 eggs, beaten
1 cup pumpkin
1 cup finely chopped cranberries
⅓ cup chopped walnuts

Combine flour, baking soda, baking powder, cinnamon, cloves and salt in bowl. Cream butter, sugar and eggs in mixer bowl until light and fluffy. Stir in pumpkin. Add dry ingredients, mixing well. Fold in cranberries and walnuts. Spoon into greased muffin cups, filling to top. May sprinkle with additional walnuts. Bake at 400 degrees for 20 to 25 minutes. **Yield: 12 to 15 muffins.**

Jami Cline, Valley #1420

Stay-Moist Corn Muffins

1¼ cups flour
1 cup cornmeal
½ teaspoon baking powder
½ teaspoon baking soda
2 tablespoons sugar
2 tablespoons honey
2 tablespoons margarine, softened
1 egg, beaten
1 cup sieved cooked squash or pumpkin
¾ cup sour milk

Combine flour, cornmeal, baking powder, baking soda and sugar in bowl. Stir in honey. Beat margarine, egg, squash and milk in small bowl. Pour into dry ingredients, stirring until mixed. Spoon into greased muffin cups. Bake at 375 degrees for 15 to 20 minutes or until golden brown. **Yield: 12 muffins.**

Anna Wellhausen, East New Castle #1536

Low-Fat and High-Fiber Muffins

2 egg whites, beaten
1 cup skim milk
1 tablespoon oil
1 cup miller's bran
1 cup all-purpose or whole wheat flour
½ cup packed brown sugar
1 tablespoon baking powder
½ teaspoon baking soda
1 teaspoon salt
1½ teaspoons cinnamon

Combine egg whites, milk, oil, bran, flour, brown sugar, baking powder, baking soda, salt and cinnamon in large bowl; mix well. Spoon into greased muffin cups. Cook at 400 degrees for 20 to 25 minutes or until golden brown. Cool on wire rack. May add blueberries or raisins. **Yield: 12 muffins.**

Barbara Whritenour, Mineola #1453

Icebox Muffins

4 eggs or egg substitute
2 cups sugar
1 cup margarine, softened
3 cups flour
2 teaspoons baking powder
Salt to taste
1 cup milk
1 teaspoon vanilla extract
1/2 teaspoon lemon extract
1 cup chopped pecans (optional)

Beat eggs in bowl until foamy. Add sugar and margarine, beating well. Sift flour, baking powder and salt together. Add to egg mixture alternately with milk. Stir in vanilla, lemon extract and pecans; mix well. Spoon into greased muffin cups. Bake at 425 degrees for 20 to 30 minutes. May store mixture in airtight container in refrigerator for several weeks. To avoid danger of salmonella, use egg substitute instead of fresh eggs when planning to store batter in refrigerator.
Yield: 2 quarts muffin batter.

Eleanor N. Hunter, Independence #179

Oatmeal Muffins

3/4 cup whole wheat flour
3/4 cup all-purpose flour
1 cup oats
1 tablespoon baking powder
3 tablespoons sugar
1/4 teaspoon salt
1 egg or 2 egg whites, beaten
1 cup skim milk
1/4 cup oil

Combine flours, oats, baking powder, sugar and salt in large bowl; mix well. Beat egg with milk and oil in small bowl. Stir into dry ingredients just until moistened. Spoon into paper-lined or greased muffin cups. Bake at 400 degrees for 15 to 20 minutes or until muffins test done. **Yield: 12 muffins.**

Cathy Woods, Pleasant Hill #1505

Sugar-Free Pineapple Muffins

1/2 cup butter, softened
3 eggs, beaten
1 cup unsweetened pineapple juice
1 teaspoon lemon juice
2 1/2 cups flour
1 teaspoon baking soda
2 teaspoons baking powder
1 cup drained crushed pineapple

Beat butter, eggs, pineapple juice and lemon juice in bowl. Add flour, baking soda and baking powder, stirring until moistened. Stir in pineapple. Spoon into greased and floured muffin cups. Bake at 350 degrees for 20 minutes or until light brown.
Yield: 12 muffins.

Viva Santschi, Pine Run #250

Strawberry Muffins

2 cups flour
1 cup sugar
1 teaspoon baking soda
1 teaspoon cinnamon
1 teaspoon nutmeg
1/2 teaspoon salt
2 eggs, beaten
1/2 cup oil
1/2 cup buttermilk
1/2 cup strawberry jam

Combine flour, sugar, baking soda, cinnamon, nutmeg and salt; make well in center. Beat eggs, oil and buttermilk in small bowl. Pour into dry ingredients, stirring to moisten. Fold in jam. Spoon into paper-lined or greased muffin cups. Bake at 375 degrees for 25 minutes. **Yield: 18 muffins.**

Irene Berry, Penn #534

Strawberry-Oatbran Muffins

1 cup oatbran
1 cup whole wheat flour
1 tablespoon baking powder
1 cup strawberries
1/4 cup honey or maple syrup
2 tablespoons oil
3/4 cup milk
1 teaspoon orange juice (optional)
1/2 cup chopped nuts (optional)

Combine oatbran, flour, and baking powder in large bowl. Process strawberries, honey and oil in blender until puréed. Pour into dry ingredients. Stir in milk, orange juice and nuts. Spoon into greased muffin cups. Bake at 350 degrees for 15 to 20 minutes or until light brown. **Yield: 12 muffins.**

Mamie A. Breininger, Shartlesville #1512

Sweet Potato Muffins

1/2 cup butter, softened
1 1/4 cups sugar
2 eggs
1 1/4 cups mashed sweet potatoes
1/3 cup milk
1 1/2 cups flour
1/4 teaspoon salt
2 teaspoons baking powder
1 teaspoon cinnamon
1/4 teaspoon nutmeg
1/2 cup raisins
1/2 cup chopped pecans
2 tablespoons sugar
1/4 teaspoon cinnamon

Cream butter in mixer bowl until light and fluffy. Add 1 1/4 cups sugar, beating at medium speed. Add eggs 1 at a time, beating well after each addition. Stir in sweet potatoes and milk. Combine flour, salt, baking powder, 1 teaspoon cinnamon and nutmeg. Add to creamed mixture, stirring until moistened. Fold in raisins and pecans. Spoon into greased muffin cups, filling 2/3 full. Combine 2 tablespoons sugar and 1/4 teaspoon cinnamon in small bowl. Sprinkle over batter. Bake at 400 degrees for 20 minutes. **Yield: 12 muffins.**

Colleen R. Shields, Avis #1959

Perfect Pizza Dough

1 package dry yeast
1½ cups warm water
¼ cup sugar
1½ teaspoons oil
1 egg, beaten
5 cups flour

Dissolve yeast in water in bowl. Stir in sugar, oil, egg and flour. Knead until smooth and elastic. Let rise in warm place for 20 minutes. Punch dough down. Spread into 2 nonstick pizza pans. Top with favorite pizza toppings. Bake as desired. **Yield: 1 to 2 pizza crusts.**

Beth Ann Peterson, Rostraver #919

Pizza Crusts

1 tablespoon yeast
1 cup warm water
1 teaspoon sugar
1½ teaspoons salt
¼ cup oil
3 cups flour

Dissolve yeast in warm water in bowl. Add sugar, salt and oil. Stir in flour. Knead for several minutes. Roll into two 13-inch circles; place in greased 12-inch pizza pans. Let rise to desired thickness. Bake at 425 degrees for 10 minutes. Top with favorite pizza toppings. Bake until cheese is browned. **Yield: 2 (12-inch) pizza crusts.**

Jane Treichler, Virginville #1832

Popovers

1 cup flour
⅛ teaspoon salt
3 eggs, beaten
2 tablespoons melted butter
1 cup milk

Combine flour and salt in bowl; make well in center. Add eggs, butter and milk, beating until smooth. Fill greased 5-ounce baking cups or muffin cups half full. Bake at 400 degrees for 35 to 40 minutes or until browned. **Yield: 8 popovers.**

Helena B. Latshaw, Ontelaunee #1617

Soft Pretzels

1 package dry yeast
1½ cups warm water
1 teaspoon salt
1 teaspoon sugar
3½ to 4 cups flour
1 egg, beaten

Dissolve yeast in water in bowl. Add salt, sugar and 2 cups flour; mix well. Stir in remaining flour. Place in greased bowl, turning to coat surface. Let rise, covered, for 45 minutes. Divide into 16 portions. Shape into ropes; twist into pretzel. Place on greased baking sheet. Brush with egg. Bake at 400 degrees for 15 minutes. **Yield: 16 pretzels.**

Dolores Burkett, Elder #503

All-Night Buns

2 packages dry yeast
2 tablespoons sugar
2/3 cup warm water
4 cups warm water
1 1/2 cups sugar
3 teaspoons salt
1 cup oil
14 cups flour

Dissolve yeast and 2 tablespoons sugar in 2/3 cup water. Let stand for 10 minutes. Add remaining ingredients, stirring until soft dough forms. Let rise, covered, in warm place for 2 hours. Knead for several minutes. Let rise, covered, for 2 hours longer. Shape small amounts of dough into balls. Place on greased baking sheets. Let rise, covered, overnight or until doubled in bulk. Bake at 375 degrees for 15 to 20 minutes. **Yield: 5 dozen buns.**

Beatrice Burns, Plum Creek Valley #1702

Breakfast Rolls

1 package dry yeast
1/4 cup warm water
4 cups flour
1 teaspoon salt
1 teaspoon grated lemon rind
1/4 cup sugar
1 cup margarine, softened
2 eggs
1 cup scalded milk, cooled
1 cup sugar
1 tablespoon cinnamon

Dissolve yeast in warm water. Combine flour, salt, lemon rind and sugar in large bowl. Cut in margarine until crumbly. Beat eggs with milk and yeast mixture. Pour into flour mixture; mix well. Chill overnight. Roll on floured surface into two 12x18-inch rectangles. Sprinkle with mixture of 1 cup sugar and cinnamon. Roll from wide ends as for jelly roll. Slice each roll into eighteen 1-inch thick slices. Place on greased baking sheets; flatten slightly. Bake at 400 degrees for 12 minutes. May frost with confectioners' sugar glaze. **Yield: 36 rolls.**

Bernice Kearns, Fort Granville #1902

Cinnamon Twists

1 cake yeast
1 cup lukewarm sour cream
2 eggs, beaten
1 cup melted margarine
1 teaspoon salt
3 1/2 cups sifted flour
1 cup sugar
1 teaspoon cinnamon

Crumble yeast into sour cream in bowl; let stand until softened. Add eggs, margarine and salt; mix well. Stir in flour. Chill for 2 hours. Combine sugar and cinnamon. Sprinkle half the mixture on board. Pat dough on sugared board; sprinkle with remaining sugar mixture. Roll dough; fold over. Roll and fold once more. Roll 1/4 to 1/2 inch thick. Cut into 1x5-inch strips. Twist strips; place on greased baking sheet. Let rise for 30 minutes. Bake at 375 degrees for 12 to 15 minutes. **Yield: 12 to 15 twists.**

Emma Gene Engle, Hillcrest #1674

Danish Pastry

1 package dry yeast
1/4 cup warm water
2 3/4 cups flour
2 tablespoons sugar
1 cup margarine, softened
2 eggs, beaten
1/2 cup margarine, softened
1/2 cup packed brown sugar
1 egg white, beaten
1/2 cup chopped nuts
1/4 cup packed brown sugar

Dissolve yeast in warm water. Combine flour and sugar in large bowl; cut in 1 cup margarine until crumbly. Add yeast mixture and eggs, kneading until smooth. Divide into 4 equal portions. Roll out 2 portions into 9-inch squares. Place in 2 nonstick 8x8-inch baking pans. Cream 1/2 cup margarine with brown sugar in small bowl. Spread over prepared dough in pans. Roll out remaining dough. Cut into 1/2-inch strips. Arrange in criss-cross pattern over filling and edges of pans. Let rise, covered, for 1 to 2 hours or until puffy. Brush with beaten egg white. Sprinkle with nuts and 1/4 cup brown sugar. Bake at 375 degrees for 30 minutes.
Yield: 15 to 20 servings.

Helen Kinder, Buffalo #1523

Onion Rolls

2 packages dry yeast
1/2 cup warm water
1/4 cup sugar
1/4 cup shortening
1 teaspoon salt
3/4 cup scalded milk, cooled
2 eggs, beaten
5 to 5 1/2 cups flour
2 cups chopped onions
1/4 cup butter
1 egg
2 tablespoons cream
1/4 teaspoon salt
Poppy seed or sesame seed

Dissolve yeast in warm water. Combine sugar, shortening, 1 teaspoon salt and lukewarm milk in large bowl. Beat in 2 eggs and yeast. Add flour, stirring to form stiff dough. Knead on floured surface for 3 to 5 minutes or until smooth and elastic. Place in greased bowl, turning to coat surface. Let rise, covered, in warm place for 1 hour or until doubled in bulk. Sauté onions in butter in saucepan until golden brown. Beat egg with cream. Add 2 tablespoons of egg mixture and 1/4 teaspoon salt to onions, reserving remaining egg mixture; cool. Shape dough into 2-inch balls. Place on greased baking sheets. Flatten slightly, making indentations in centers. Place 1 tablespoon onion filling in center of each roll. Brush with reserved egg mixture; sprinkle with poppy or sesame seed. Let rise for 45 minutes or until doubled in bulk. Bake at 400 degrees for 12 to 16 minutes or until golden brown.
Yield: 24 rolls.

Edith Riker, Mt. Nebo #1872

Orange Bowknots

1 package dry yeast
1/4 cup warm water
1 1/4 cups scalded milk
1/2 cup shortening
1/3 cup sugar
1 teaspoon salt
2 eggs, beaten
1/4 cup orange juice
2 tablespoons grated orange rind
5 cups flour
1 cup confectioners' sugar
2 tablespoons orange juice
1 teaspoon grated orange rind

Dissolve yeast in water. Combine milk, shortening, sugar and salt in bowl; cool to lukewarm. Add yeast, eggs, 1/4 cup orange juice and 2 tablespoons orange rind; mix well. Add enough flour to make soft dough. Let rise, covered, in greased bowl for 1 to 2 hours or until doubled in bulk. Punch dough down. Roll on floured surface to 1/2-inch thickness. Cut into strips; tie into knots. Place on greased baking sheet. Let rise until puffy. Bake at 375 degrees for 12 to 15 minutes or until light brown. Brush with mixture of remaining ingredients. **Yield: 7 dozen.**

Luella Schlosser, Hayfield #800

Potato Refrigerator Roll Dough

1 package dry yeast
1 1/2 cups warm water
2/3 cup sugar
1 1/2 teaspoons salt
2/3 cup shortening
2 eggs, beaten
1 cup lukewarm mashed potatoes
7 to 7 1/2 cups flour

Dissolve yeast in warm water in large bowl. Stir in sugar, salt, shortening, eggs and potatoes. Sift in flour; mix well. Knead on lightly floured surface until smooth and elastic. Place in greased bowl, turning to coat surface. Cover with damp cloth. Chill in refrigerator. Shape into rolls 2 hours before baking; place on baking sheet. Let rise, covered, for 1 1/2 to 2 hours or until doubled in bulk. Bake at 400 degrees for 12 to 15 minutes. **Yield: 4 dozen.**

Eileen Parrish, Bell Township #2047

Turnovers

2 packages dry yeast
1 cup warm milk
6 cups flour
3 tablespoons sugar
1 teaspoon salt
2 cups margarine, softened
3 eggs
Filling of choice

Dissolve yeast in warm milk. Combine flour, sugar and salt in bowl. Cut in margarine until crumbly. Beat eggs with yeast mixture. Add to flour mixture; mix well. Let rise in warm place for 2 hours. Roll on floured surface. Cut into squares. Spoon desired filling onto centers of squares. Fold over to enclose filling, sealing edges. Place on baking sheet. Bake at 350 degrees for 10 to 12 minutes. **Yield: 20 to 24 servings.**

Sarah Gault, Mt. Pleasant #1687

Desserts

Apple Cobbler

1/2 cup oats
8 cups sliced peeled apples
3/4 cup unsweetened pineapple juice
1/2 cup raisins
1 teaspoon nutmeg
2 tablespoons honey
1 cup Grape Nuts

Sprinkle oats into nonstick 8-inch baking pan. Combine apples, pineapple juice, raisins, nutmeg and honey in large bowl; mix well. Spoon over oats layer. Cover tightly with foil. Bake at 350 degrees for 1 hour. Remove foil; sprinkle with Grape Nuts. Bake for 15 minutes longer. Serve warm or cold. **Yield: 8 servings.**

Shirley Merkel, Virginville #1832

Apple Crisp

4 cups sliced peeled apples
2/3 cup packed brown sugar
1/2 cup flour
1/2 cup quick-cooking oats
3/4 teaspoon cinnamon
3/4 teaspoon nutmeg
1/3 cup margarine, softened

Arrange apples in 8-inch baking pan. Combine brown sugar, flour, oats, cinnamon and nutmeg in bowl; mix well. Cut in margarine until mixture is crumbly. Sprinkle over apples. Bake at 375 degrees for 30 minutes or until apples are tender. **Yield: 6 servings.**

Juanita Kurten, Brady #1218

Creamy Apple Crisp

3 ounces cream cheese, softened
3/4 cup sour cream
3/4 cup sugar
2 tablespoons flour
1 egg
1/2 teaspoon vanilla extract
3 cups sliced peeled tart apples
1/4 cup quick-cooking oats
1/4 cup flour
1/4 cup packed brown sugar
1/4 cup sugar
1 teaspoon cinnamon
1/4 cup butter, softened

Beat cream cheese, sour cream, 3/4 cup sugar, 2 tablespoons flour, egg and vanilla in mixer bowl until light. Stir in apples. Spoon into 2-quart casserole. Combine oats, 1/4 cup flour, brown sugar, 1/4 cup sugar and cinnamon in bowl; mix well. Cut in butter until mixture is crumbly. Sprinkle over apple mixture. Bake at 350 degrees for 35 to 40 minutes or until golden brown. **Yield: 6 servings.**

Betty Hall, Halfmoon #290

Dietetic Apple Crisp

4 cups sliced peeled apples
1 tablespoon lemon juice
1/3 cup sifted flour
1 cup cornflakes
1/2 teaspoon salt
Granulated brown sugar substitute to equal 1/2 cup sugar
1 teaspoon cinnamon
1/3 cup melted margarine

Arrange apples in greased 8-inch baking dish. Drizzle with lemon juice. Combine flour, cornflakes, salt, brown sugar substitute and cinnamon in bowl; mix well. Stir in margarine. Sprinkle over apples. Bake at 350 degrees for 30 minutes. **Yield: 6 servings.**

Martha A. Milks, Bolivar Run #2060

Apple Dumplings

2 cups flour
5 teaspoons baking powder
1 teaspoon salt
2 tablespoons shortening
3/4 cup milk
6 apples, peeled, chopped
2 cups water
2 cups sugar
1/4 cup margarine
Maple flavoring to taste

Combine flour, baking powder and salt in bowl; mix well. Cut in shortening until crumbly. Stir in enough milk to form soft dough. Roll 1/2 inch thick on lightly floured surface. Cut into 8-inch squares. Spoon apples into centers of squares. Fold over edges to enclose filling; press edges to seal. Arrange seam side down in baking pan. Combine water, sugar, margarine and maple flavoring in saucepan. Bring to a boil, stirring constantly. Pour over dumplings. Bake at 375 degrees for 30 to 40 minutes or until apples are tender. **Yield: 12 servings.**

Kathleen Coleman, Dayton #1819

Apple Fritters

1 cup flour
1 1/2 teaspoons salt
2 tablespoons sugar
1 egg, beaten
1/2 cup milk
3 apples, peeled, thinly sliced
Oil for frying
1/2 cup confectioners' sugar

Combine flour, salt and sugar in bowl; mix well. Stir in egg and milk until smooth. Add apples; mix well. Drop by spoonfuls into 1/2 inch hot oil in skillet. Fry until light brown, turning carefully with spatula once. Drain on paper towels. Sprinkle with confectioners' sugar. Serve hot. **Yield: 15 servings.**

Pauline Sitler, Briar Creek #146

Baked Apples

1/4 cup red-hot cinnamon candies
1 cup hot water
12 apples, cut into quarters
1 cup flour
1 cup sugar
1/2 cup margarine, softened

Dissolve candies in hot water in small bowl. Pour over apples in 2-quart casserole. Mix flour and sugar in small bowl. Cut in margarine until mixture is crumbly. Sprinkle over apple mixture. Bake at 350 degrees for 45 minutes or until apples are tender. **Yield: 8 servings.**

Mrs. Joseph O. Hill, South Buffalo #1908

Danish Pastry Apple Bars

2 1/2 cups flour
1 teaspoon salt
1 cup shortening
2/3 cup (about) milk
1 egg yolk
1 cup crushed cornflakes
8 apples, peeled, sliced
1 cup sugar
1 teaspoon cinnamon
1 egg white
1 tablespoon water
1 cup confectioners' sugar
1/2 teaspoon vanilla extract

Sift flour and salt into bowl. Cut in shortening until crumbly. Add milk and egg yolk; mix to form soft dough. Divide dough into 2 portions. Roll 1 portion at a time on lightly floured surface to fit 10x15-inch baking pan. Place 1 pastry in pan; sprinkle with cornflakes. Arrange apples over cornflakes. Sprinkle with mixture of sugar and cinnamon. Cover with remaining pastry portion; pinch edges to seal. Brush with egg white. Bake at 400 degrees for 50 to 60 minutes or until apples are tender. Combine water, confectioners' sugar and vanilla extract in small bowl; mix well. Drizzle over top while warm. Cut into bars. **Yield: 20 servings.**

Brenda McCauley, Virginville #1832

Saucy Spicy Applesauce Dessert

2 cups applesauce
1/4 cup orange juice
1/2 teaspoon cinnamon
1/4 teaspoon nutmeg

Combine applesauce, orange juice, cinnamon and nutmeg in bowl; mix well. Chill until serving time. This is easy enough for children to prepare. **Yield: 6 servings.**

Melinda Tercha, Pioneer #1777

Zapped Apples

$1/2$ cup sugar
1 teaspoon cinnamon
$1/8$ teaspoon cloves
4 teaspoons cornstarch
8 apples, peeled, sliced
$1/4$ cup raisins

Combine sugar, cinnamon, cloves and cornstarch in large bowl; mix well. Add apples and raisins; toss well. Spoon into glass casserole. Microwave on High for 4 minutes. Mix well. Microwave for 4 minutes longer or until apples are tender. Mix well. Serve hot with ice cream or for breakfast with milk or cream. **Yield: 8 servings.**

Irene Ruffner, Community #1949

Apricots à la Neige

1 cup uncooked rice
6 apricots, cut into halves, pitted
1 cup apricot juice
$1/2$ cup sugar
1 teaspoon cornstarch

Cook rice using package directions or steam until tender. Wring small pudding cloths out of hot water and lay one at a time over a small half-pint bowl. Spread rice $1/3$ inch thick over the cloth. Place one half apricot in center, filling the cavity with rice. Draw cloth around apricot half until entire apricot half is smoothly covered with rice layer. Tie cloth tightly at top. Steam over hot water in steamer for 10 minutes. Remove cloth carefully; arrange on serving platter. Combine apricot juice, $1/2$ cup sugar and 1 teaspoon cornstarch in small saucepan; mix well. Bring to a boil, stirring constantly; strain. Pour over hot apricot balls. May substitute apples and any fruit juice or syrup. This recipe is from *The Boston Cookbook*, Mary J. Lincoln, copyright 1883, 1900 & 1904. **Yield: 6 servings.**

Lorraine Sayward

Alabama Banana Dessert

1 6-ounce package vanilla instant pudding mix
8 ounces cream cheese, softened
1 14-ounce can sweetened condensed milk
16 ounces whipped topping
1 16-ounce package vanilla wafers
8 large bananas, sliced

Prepare pudding mix using package directions. Chill for 5 minutes. Beat cream cheese and condensed milk in mixer bowl. Combine with pudding; mix well. Fold in $1/2$ cup whipped topping. Layer vanilla wafers, banana slices and pudding mixture $1/2$ at a time in 9x13-inch dish. Spread with remaining whipped topping. **Yield: 15 servings.**

Velma Smith, Vernon #936

Banana Split Dessert

2 cups crushed graham crackers
1/2 cup margarine
2 cups confectioners' sugar
1/2 cup margarine, softened
1 egg
1 teaspoon vanilla extract
3 or 4 bananas, sliced
2 16-ounce cans crushed pineapple, drained
12 ounces whipped topping
1 cup chopped pecans
1 cup maraschino cherry halves

Mix graham cracker crumbs and 1/2 cup margarine in bowl. Press into 10x14-inch dish. Combine confectioners' sugar, 1/2 cup margarine, egg and vanilla in mixer bowl; beat well. Spread over graham cracker layer with knife dipped in hot water. Top with banana slices and pineapple. Spread with whipped topping. Sprinkle with pecans and cherries. Chill for 2 hours. **Yield: 15 servings.**

Eileen Wensel, Harmony #1112 and Tiffany Paden, Westfield Jr. #1514

Blueberry Gelatin Dessert

1 6-ounce package blackberry gelatin
2 cups boiling water or pineapple juice
1 21-ounce can blueberry pie filling
1 20-ounce can crushed pineapple, drained
8 ounces cream cheese, softened
1 cup sour cream
1/2 cup sugar
1/2 teaspoon vanilla extract
1/2 cup chopped walnuts

Dissolve gelatin in boiling water in bowl. Stir in pie filling and pineapple. Spoon into 9x13-inch dish. Chill until set. Mix cream cheese, sour cream, sugar and vanilla in bowl until smooth. Spread over congealed layer. Sprinkle with walnuts.
Yield: 15 to 20 servings.

Marilyn Davidson, Bald Eagle #1390

Blueberry Torte

16 graham crackers, crushed
1/4 cup melted margarine
1/4 cup sugar
8 ounces cream cheese, softened
1/2 cup sugar
2 eggs, beaten
1 teaspoon vanilla extract
1 21-ounce can blueberry pie filling
Whipped cream

Mix graham cracker crumbs, margarine and 1/4 cup sugar in bowl. Press into 9x13-inch baking dish. Beat cream cheese, 1/2 cup sugar, eggs and vanilla in mixer bowl until smooth. Spread over graham cracker layer. Bake at 325 degrees for 20 minutes. Let stand until cool. Layer pie filling and whipped cream over baked layer.
Yield: 12 servings.

Marlyn Freu, Liberty #1182

Buster Bar Dessert

1 package Oreo cookies, crushed
1/2 cup melted margarine
1/2 gallon vanilla ice cream, softened
1 jar fudge ice cream sauce
1 cup chopped Spanish peanuts
16 ounces whipped topping

Mix cookie crumbs and melted margarine in bowl. Press half the crumbs into 9x13-inch dish. Layer ice cream, fudge sauce, peanuts and whipped topping over crumb mixture. Sprinkle with remaining crumb mixture. **Yield: 15 servings.**

Charlene F. Lindner, Mt. Joy, #537

Basic Cheesecake

1/4 cup butter or margarine
1 1/2 tablespoons sugar
1 cup graham cracker or vanilla wafer crumbs
1/4 teaspoon ground nutmeg
16 ounces cream cheese, softened
3/4 cup sugar
3 eggs
1 tablespoon lemon juice
1/2 teaspoon vanilla extract
Melba Sauce

Place butter in 8-inch glass cake pan. Microwave on High for 1 minute or until melted. Stir in 1 1/2 tablespoons sugar, graham cracker crumbs and nutmeg. Press into bottom and up side of dish. Microwave for 2 minutes. Let stand until cool. Chill completely. Beat cream cheese in mixer bowl until light and fluffy. Add 3/4 cup sugar, eggs, lemon juice and vanilla; mix well. Spoon into chilled shell. Microwave on Medium for 20 to 25 minutes, turning every 5 minutes. Chill until firm. Top with Melba Sauce just before serving. May also serve with any prepared pie filling. **Yield: 8 servings.**

Melba Sauce

1 10-ounce package frozen raspberries
1/2 cup sugar
2 tablespoons cornstarch
1/2 cup currant jelly
1 teaspoon lemon juice

Place raspberries in 4-cup glass bowl. Microwave on Low for 2 to 3 minutes. Blend sugar and cornstarch together. Stir into raspberries. Add jelly and lemon juice; mix well. Microwave on High for 3 to 5 minutes, stirring after 3 minutes. Let stand until cool. Chill until serving time. May serve over cheesecake, ice cream or fruit.

Mary Lou Templin, Millers Run #2020

Create a quick dessert with fresh fruit slices, a dollop of sour cream or yogurt and a sprinkle of brown sugar or coconut.

Cherry Cheesecake

1 12-ounce package graham cracker crumbs
1/4 cup melted margarine
1/4 cup sugar
16 ounces cream cheese, softened
1/4 cup milk
1/4 cup sugar
1 cup chopped pecans
1 21-ounce can cherry pie filling
8 ounces whipped topping
1 cup chopped pecans

Mix crumbs, melted margarine and 1/4 cup sugar in bowl. Pat into 9x13-inch dish. Combine cream cheese, milk and 1/4 cup sugar in bowl; mix well. Spread over crumb mixture. Layer 1 cup pecans, pie filling and whipped topping over cream cheese mixture. Sprinkle with 1 cup pecans. Chill overnight. **Yield: 15 servings.**

Nancy J. Mihalo, Eldred #1604

Creamy Baked Cheesecake

1 1/4 cups graham cracker crumbs
1/4 cup sugar
1/3 cup melted margarine
16 ounces cream cheese, softened
1 14-ounce can sweetened condensed milk
3 eggs
1/4 cup lemon juice
1 cup sour cream
1 21-ounce can cherry pie filling, chilled

Mix graham cracker crumbs, sugar and melted margarine in bowl. Press onto bottom of 9-inch springform pan. Beat cream cheese in mixer bowl until light and fluffy. Beat in condensed milk gradually. Add eggs and lemon juice; mix well. Pour into prepared pan. Bake at 300 degrees for 50 to 55 minutes or until set. Spread with sour cream. Bake for 5 minutes longer. Cool in pan. Chill thoroughly. Spread with pie filling. **Yield: 12 servings.**

Jean Bagnick, Hope #898

Mary Ferry's Cheesecake

24 ounces cream cheese, softened
1 cup sugar
4 eggs
2 tablespoons vanilla extract
1 9-inch graham cracker pie shell
2 cups sour cream
1/2 cup sugar
2 tablespoons vanilla extract

Mix cream cheese and 1 cup sugar in bowl. Add eggs 1 at a time, beating well after each addition. Stir in 2 tablespoons vanilla. Spoon into pie shell. Bake at 375 degrees for 40 minutes. Chill for 10 minutes. Mix sour cream, 1/2 cup sugar and 2 tablespoons vanilla in bowl. Pour gradually over cheesecake. Bake at 475 degrees for 5 minutes. Refrigerate immediately; chill until serving time. **Yield: 8 servings.**

Karen B. Billig, Central #1650

German Chocolate Cheesecake Squares

$1^1/_2$ cups graham cracker crumbs
$^1/_2$ cup chopped pecans
$^1/_2$ cup sugar
$^1/_3$ cup melted margarine
24 ounces cream cheese
1 14-ounce can sweetened condensed milk
8 ounces melted German's sweet chocolate
3 eggs
1 tablespoon vanilla extract
1 14-ounce can sweetened condensed milk
3 egg yolks, beaten
$^1/_2$ cup margarine
$1^1/_3$ cups flaked coconut
1 cup chopped pecans
1 teaspoon vanilla extract

Mix first 4 ingredients in bowl. Press into 9x13-inch baking pan. Beat cream cheese in mixer bowl until light and fluffy. Beat in 1 can condensed milk gradually. Add melted chocolate, eggs and 1 tablespoon vanilla; beat well. Pour into prepared pan. Bake at 350 degrees for 40 minutes or until set. Cool in pan. Blend 1 can condensed milk, egg yolks and $^1/_2$ cup margarine in heavy saucepan. Cook over medium heat for 8 to 10 minutes or until thickened, stirring constantly. Remove from heat. Stir in remaining ingredients. Cool for 10 minutes. Spread over cheesecake.
Yield: 15 servings.

Hazel Taylor, Odin #1254

No-Bake Cheesecake

8 ounces cream cheese, softened
1 cup sour cream
9 ounces milk
1 4-ounce package French vanilla instant pudding mix
1 9-inch graham cracker pie shell

Beat cream cheese in bowl until light and fluffy. Add sour cream, milk and pudding mix; beat until thickened. Spoon into pie shell. Chill for 2 hours. **Yield: 8 servings.**

Vera G. Ratchford, Hartslog Valley #375

Pineapple Cheesecake

$1^1/_3$ cups graham cracker crumbs
$^1/_4$ cup sugar
$^1/_4$ cup butter
1 8-ounce can crushed pineapple
1 3-ounce package orange gelatin
$1^1/_4$ cups boiling water
3 ounces cream cheese, softened
3 tablespoons sugar
$^1/_2$ teaspoon vanilla extract
1 cup sour cream

Combine graham cracker crumbs, $^1/_4$ cup sugar and butter in bowl; mix well. Press into 8x8-inch dish. Drain pineapple, reserving syrup. Dissolve gelatin in boiling water in medium bowl. Stir in reserved syrup. Cool slightly. Mix $^1/_2$ cup gelatin and pineapple in small bowl. Mix cream cheese, 3 tablespoons sugar and vanilla in large bowl. Stir in remaining gelatin. Fold in sour cream. Spoon into prepared dish. Chill until partially set. Spoon pineapple mixture carefully over top. Chill until set. **Yield: 8 servings.**

Dorothy Aughey, Milford #773

Strawberry Cheesecake

1 cup graham cracker crumbs
2 tablespoons melted butter
4 egg yolks
16 ounces cream cheese, softened
1 cup sugar
2 tablespoons flour
1 cup evaporated milk
4 egg whites, stiffly beaten
1 21-ounce can strawberry pie filling

Mix graham cracker crumbs and melted butter in bowl. Press 2/3 of the crumb mixture onto bottom of 9-inch springform pan. Combine egg yolks, cream cheese, sugar, flour and evaporated milk in bowl; mix well. Fold in egg whites. Pour into prepared pan. Sprinkle with remaining crumb mixture. Bake at 325 degrees for 1 hour. Cool for 1 hour. Spread with pie filling. **Yield: 12 servings.**

Marilyn vonWolffradt, Diahoga #1951

Cherry Dessert

14 graham crackers
1 6-ounce package vanilla instant pudding mix
2 cups cold milk
1 cup whipped topping
1 21-ounce can cherry pie filling

Line 9x9-inch serving dish with half the graham crackers. Combine pudding mix and milk in bowl; mix well. Let stand for 5 minutes. Fold in whipped topping. Layer half the pudding mixture, remaining graham crackers and remaining pudding mixture in prepared dish. Cover with pie filling. Chill for 3 hours. Cut into squares. **Yield: 8 servings.**

Geraldine Steninger, Tuscarora Valley #2042

Cherry Surprise

1 8-count can crescent rolls
16 ounces cream cheese, softened
2/3 cup sugar
1 teaspoon vanilla extract
1 egg white, stiffly beaten
1 21-ounce can cherry pie filling
1 8-count can crescent rolls
1 egg yolk, beaten
1/4 cup sugar

Spread 1 can roll dough in 9x13-inch baking pan. Mix cream cheese, 2/3 cup sugar and vanilla in bowl. Fold in egg white. Layer cream cheese mixture, pie filling and remaining crescent roll dough in prepared pan. Spread egg yolk over top. Sprinkle with 1/4 cup sugar. Bake at 350 degrees for 30 minutes. **Yield: 15 servings.**

Icie Redden, Kerrmoor #1146

Easy Cherry Delight

1/2 cup butter
1 cup flour
1 cup coarsely chopped pecans or walnuts
8 ounces cream cheese, softened
1 cup whipped topping
1 cup sifted confectioners' sugar
1/2 cup rice
1 1/3 cups water
1/2 teaspoon salt
1 1/2 teaspoons butter
4 cups milk
2 4-ounce packages vanilla instant pudding mix
1 21-ounce can cherry pie filling

Cut 1/2 cup butter into flour in bowl until crumbly. Stir in pecans. Press into buttered 9x13-inch baking pan. Bake at 350 degrees for 20 minutes or until lightly browned. Cool in pan. Beat cream cheese and whipped topping in mixer bowl until light and fluffy. Add confectioners' sugar; beat until smooth. Spread in prepared pan. Combine rice, water, salt and 1 1/2 teaspoons butter in saucepan. Cook until rice is tender. Combine milk and pudding mix in bowl; beat until thickened. Stir in rice. Spread over cream cheese layer. Chill until firm. Spread with pie filling. Chill until serving time. Serve with whipped cream. **Yield: 12 servings.**

Shirley Moury, South Auburn #1188

Cherry S'Mores

1 7-ounce chocolate bar, broken into 8 pieces
8 graham crackers
8 large marshmallows
1 cup cherry pie filling

Place 1 piece candy on each cracker. Arrange 4 crackers at a time on microwave-safe dish. Microwave on High for 45 seconds or until chocolate begins to melt. Top each with marshmallow. Microwave for 15 to 30 seconds longer or until soft. Top each with heaping spoonful pie filling. **Yield: 8 servings.**

Ruth Posten, Deemston #1372

Easy Choco-Cherry Dessert

1 2-layer package chocolate cake mix
1 21-ounce can cherry pie filling
2 eggs

Mix cake mix, pie filling and eggs in bowl; do not add additional liquid. Spread in greased 9x13-inch baking pan. Bake at 350 degrees for 25 to 30 minutes or until wooden pick comes out clean. Serve with whipped topping or ice cream.
Yield: 15 servings.

Richard L. Osborne, Morning Star #1271

Chocolate Éclair Dessert

20 (about) graham crackers
2 4-ounce packages vanilla instant pudding mix
$3^1/_2$ cups milk
8 ounces whipped topping
2 packages Choco-Bake
2 teaspoons light corn syrup
2 teaspoons vanilla extract
3 tablespoons margarine, softened
$1^1/_2$ cups confectioners' sugar
3 tablespoons milk

Line buttered 9x13-inch serving dish with half the graham crackers. Beat pudding mix and $3^1/_2$ cups milk in mixer bowl for 2 minutes. Fold in whipped topping. Layer half the pudding mixture, remaining graham crackers and remaining pudding mixture in prepared dish. Chill for 2 hours. Combine Choco-Bake, corn syrup, vanilla and margarine in bowl; beat well. Add confectioners' sugar and 3 tablespoons milk alternately, beating well after each addition. Spread over dessert. **Yield: 15 servings.**

Roberta Windhorst, Pleasant Hill #1505

Chocolate Éclair Dessert

2 4-ounce packages vanilla instant pudding mix
3 cups milk
8 to 12 ounces whipped topping
1 12-ounce package graham crackers
1 16-ounce can chocolate ready-spread frosting

Combine pudding mix and milk in bowl; mix well. Fold in whipped topping. Break graham crackers into squares. Arrange 15 graham cracker squares in buttered 9x13-inch dish. Layer pudding mixture and remaining graham cracker squares $^1/_2$ at a time in prepared dish. Spread frosting over top. Chill, covered, in refrigerator overnight. **Yield: 12 to 14 servings.**

Audrey M. Miller, North Washington #1826

Chocolate Punch Bowl Cake Dessert

1 2-layer package chocolate cake mix
2 4-ounce packages chocolate instant pudding mix
4 cups milk
5 or 6 Reese's cups or Heath Bars, chopped
16 ounces whipped topping

Prepare and bake cake mix using package directions for 9x13-inch baking pan. Cool cake; cut into bite-sized pieces. Prepare pudding mix with milk using package directions. Layer cake pieces, pudding, candy pieces and whipped topping into punch bowl $^1/_2$ at a time. Garnish with chocolate syrup, glaze, chocolate chips or additional candy. **Yield: 12 to 16 servings.**

Barbara L. Minor, Buckhorn #1119

Cinnamon Flop

$2^1/_2$ cups flour
1 cup sugar
2 teaspoons baking powder
$^1/_8$ teaspoon salt
2 tablespoons melted margarine
1 cup milk
$^1/_2$ cup packed brown sugar
2 tablespoons melted margarine
$1^3/_4$ teaspoons cinnamon

Combine flour, sugar, baking powder and salt in mixer bowl; mix well. Add 2 tablespoons margarine and milk; beat well. Pour into greased 9x9-inch baking dish. Combine brown sugar, 2 tablespoons margarine and cinnamon in bowl; mix well. Sprinkle over top of batter. Bake at 350 degrees for 30 minutes or until brown. **Yield: 12 servings.**

Irene Baer, Friendship #2093

Healthy Cream Puffs

1 cup flour
2 envelopes artificial sweetener
$^1/_4$ teaspoon salt
1 cup water
$^1/_4$ cup no-cholesterol margarine
Egg substitute equal to 4 eggs
1 teaspoon vanilla extract
Sugar-free instant pudding

Mix flour, artificial sweetener and salt together. Combine water and margarine in medium saucepan. Heat over medium heat until margarine melts, stirring constantly. Remove from heat. Stir in flour mixture all at once, beating with wooden spoon until well blended. Cook over medium heat for 2 minutes or until mixture forms a ball, stirring constantly. Remove from heat. Cool for 10 minutes. Spray baking pan with nonstick cooking spray. Add egg substitute gradually to mixture, beating until smooth. Stir in vanilla. Drop batter into 12 mounds 3 inches apart on prepared baking pan. Bake at 400 degrees for 30 minutes or until golden brown. Cool slightly. Cut puffs into halves horizontally, removing soft dough. Cool on wire rack. Fill with sugar-free instant pudding. **Yield: 12 servings.**

Anita Peffer, Plain Grove #1431

To reduce calories in your favorite trifle recipe, use sliced angel food cake sprinkled with unsweetened fruit juice instead of pound cake and sherry.

Cream Puff Dessert

1/2 cup margarine
1 cup water
1 cup flour
4 eggs
1 6-ounce package vanilla instant pudding mix
8 ounces cream cheese, softened
Whipped topping
1/4 cup chocolate syrup

Combine margarine and water in saucepan. Bring to a boil. Reduce heat. Add flour all at once, stirring until well mixed. Cook until mixture forms a ball, stirring constantly. Remove from heat. Beat in eggs 1 at a time. Spread in greased 9x13-inch baking dish. Bake at 400 degrees for 30 minutes or until brown. Cool slightly. Prepare pudding using package directions. Add cream cheese; mix well. Spread in prepared dish. Top with whipped topping; drizzle with chocolate syrup. Chill until serving time. **Yield: 12 to 15 servings.**

Ruthanne Litvin, Morning Star #1271

Strawberry Cream Puffs

1 cup water
1/2 cup butter or margarine
1 teaspoon sugar
1/4 teaspoon salt
1 cup flour
4 eggs
Strawberry Cream Filling
Confectioners' sugar

Combine water, butter, sugar and salt in saucepan. Bring to a boil, stirring constantly. Add flour all at once, stirring until smooth. Cook until mixture forms a ball, stirring constantly. Remove from heat. Beat in eggs 1 at a time. Beat until mixture is smooth and shiny. Drop by tablespoonfuls 2 inches apart onto ungreased baking sheet. Bake at 400 degrees for 35 minutes or until golden brown. Cool slightly. Cut off tops, removing soft centers. Cool on wire rack. Fill with Strawberry Cream Filling; replace tops. Sprinkle with confectioners' sugar. Garnish with additional sliced strawberries and mint leaves. **Yield: 10 servings.**

Strawberry Cream Filling

2 pints fresh strawberries, sliced
1/4 cup sugar
2 cups whipping cream
1/4 cup sugar

Combine strawberry slices and 1/4 cup sugar in bowl; mix gently. Chill for 30 minutes. Beat whipping cream in mixer bowl until thickened. Add 1/4 cup sugar gradually, beating until soft peaks form. Fold in strawberries.

Virginia Hay, Hillcrest #1674

Cherry Cream Puff Ring

1 cup water
$1/2$ cup butter
1 cup flour
4 eggs
1 cup milk
$3/4$ cup sour cream
1 4-ounce package vanilla instant pudding mix
$1/4$ teaspoon almond extract
1 21-ounce can cherry pie filling

Combine water and butter in saucepan. Bring to a boil. Stir in flour all at once. Cook until mixture forms a ball, stirring constantly. Remove from heat. Beat in eggs 1 at a time. Line baking sheet with waxed paper. Draw an 8-inch circle on waxed paper. Drop dough by tablespoonfuls around edge inside circle, smoothing top. Bake at 400 degrees for 50 to 60 minutes or until brown. Cool slightly. Cut off top, removing soft dough. Remove to serving plate. Combine milk, sour cream, pudding mix and flavoring in bowl; beat until smooth. Fill cream puff ring with pudding mixture; top with $1/2$ cup pie filling. Replace top; drizzle remaining pie filling over top. Chill until serving time. **Yield: 10 to 12 servings.**

Janet Kelso, Vernon #936

Graham Cracker-Date Roll

24 graham crackers, crushed
$1/4$ teaspoon salt
4 ounces miniature marshmallows
1 8-ounce package dates, chopped
1 cup whipped cream or whipped topping

Reserve 2 tablespoons graham cracker crumbs. Combine remaining crumbs, salt, marshmallows, dates and whipped cream in bowl; mix well. Shape into roll, adding additional whipped cream if too dry to hold together. Roll in reserved graham cracker crumbs. Chill in refrigerator until firm. **Yield: 4 servings.**

M. Leone Remsburg, Warfordsburg #1889

Dirt Dessert

$1/4$ cup margarine, softened
8 ounces cream cheese, softened
1 cup confectioners' sugar
2 4-ounce packages vanilla or chocolate instant pudding mix
$3 1/2$ cups milk
12 ounces whipped topping
2 20-ounce packages Oreo cookies, crushed

Combine margarine, cream cheese and confectioners' sugar in bowl; mix well. Combine instant pudding mix, milk and whipped topping in bowl; mix well. Add cream cheese mixture to pudding mixture; mix well. Spoon $1/3$ of cookie crumbs into foil-lined clay flowerpot. Layer pudding mixture and remaining cookie crumbs $1/2$ at a time in prepared flowerpot. Chill until serving time. May add plastic greenery and flowers and serve with garden spade. **Yield: 10 to 12 servings.**

Phyliss M. Case, Conneaut #955

Dump Cake Dessert

1 16-ounce can crushed pineapple
1 21-ounce can cherry pie filling
1 2-layer package yellow cake mix
1 cup chopped nuts
3/4 cup margarine

Layer pineapple and pie filling in buttered 9x13-inch baking dish. Sprinkle with cake mix and nuts. Dot with margarine. Bake at 350 degrees for 1 hour. **Yield: 15 servings.**

Nina Clawson, Bell Township #1756

Easy Dessert

8 ounces cream cheese, softened
1 cup confectioners' sugar
8 ounces whipped topping
1 angel food cake
1 21-ounce can cherry pie filling

Combine cream cheese and confectioners' sugar in mixer bowl; mix well. Add whipped topping; mix well. Cut cake into bite-sized pieces. Fold into cream cheese mixture. Spread in buttered 9x13-inch dish. Top with pie filling. Chill until serving time. May substitute blueberry or strawberry pie filling for cherry.
Yield: 15 servings.

Ann Yearich, Progress #96

Fruit Salad with Tapioca

2 20-ounce cans pineapple chunks
2 11-ounce cans mandarin oranges
1 10-ounce jar maraschino cherries
2 4-ounce packages vanilla tapioca pudding mix
1 or 2 bananas, sliced

Drain fruits, reserving 3 cups juice. Combine reserved juice and tapioca pudding mix in saucepan; mix well. Cook over medium heat for 3 to 4 minutes or until mixture comes to a boil, stirring constantly. Cool slightly. Combine pudding mixture, pineapple, mandarin oranges and cherries in bowl; mix well. Chill until serving time. Stir in banana slices just before serving. **Yield: 12 to 15 servings.**

Joyce A. Heath, Fort Granville #1902

For an easy but elegant dessert, spoon maple syrup or blueberry syrup over a chilled grapefruit or vanilla ice cream and top with nuts or granola.

Glazed Fruit

2 20-ounce cans pineapple chunks
2 11-ounce cans mandarin oranges
2 4-ounce packages vanilla pudding and pie filling mix
1 10-ounce jar maraschino cherries, drained
2 or 3 bananas, sliced

Drain pineapple and mandarin oranges, reserving 3 cups juice. Combine reserved juice and pudding mix in saucepan; mix well. Cook until thickened, stirring constantly. Cool. Combine pudding, pineapple, mandarin oranges, maraschino cherries and banana slices in bowl; mix lightly. Chill before serving. May be made 1 day ahead. **Yield: 12 servings.**

Deb Elliott, Hookstown #1980

Hot Fruit Compote

1 16-ounce can sliced peaches, drained
1 16-ounce can pear halves, drained, chopped
1 16-ounce can whole purple plums, pitted
1 20-ounce can pineapple chunks, drained
1 6-ounce jar maraschino cherries, drained
2 bananas, sliced
3/4 cup packed brown sugar
1/3 cup butter
1 16-ounce can applesauce
1/2 cup chopped pecans
3 to 6 tablespoons brown sugar

Combine peaches, pears, plums, pineapple, maraschino cherries and bananas in bowl; mix lightly. Pour into buttered 9x13-inch baking dish. Combine 3/4 cup brown sugar, butter and applesauce in saucepan. Cook until butter is melted, stirring occasionally. Spoon over fruit mixture. Sprinkle with pecans and 3 to 6 tablespoons brown sugar. Bake at 300 degrees for 1 hour. Serve hot. **Yield: 10 to 12 servings.**

Melba Emert, Somerset #1697

Marinated Fruit Bowl

2 cups sliced strawberries
1 1/2 cups seedless green grapes
1 cup honeydew balls
2 peeled kiwifruit, sliced
2 peeled oranges, sliced
1 apple, sliced
1/4 cup Triple Sec
2 tablespoons honey
1 tablespoon lime juice
2 bananas, sliced
Mint leaves

Combine strawberries, grapes, honeydew, kiwifruit, oranges and apple slices in large bowl. Mix Triple Sec, honey and lime juice in small bowl. Pour over fruit; toss gently. Chill for 2 hours or longer. Add bananas just before serving. Top with mint leaves. May use any combination of fresh seasonal fruits and may substitute Amaretto for Triple Sec. **Yield: 8 to 10 servings.**

Sandra Null, Eldred #1604

Cranberry Ice

3 pints cranberries
3 pints water
3 cups sugar
3 tablespoons lemon juice
1 cup whipping cream, whipped

Combine cranberries and water in saucepan. Bring to a boil. Cook until berries are soft, stirring occasionally; drain. Force cranberries through food grinder. Combine ground cranberries and sugar in saucepan. Bring to a boil, stirring occasionally. Remove from heat. Cool. Stir in lemon juice. Pour into freezer-proof bowl. Place in freezer until partially frozen, stirring occasionally. Stir in whipped cream. Freeze until ice forms. Spoon into sherbet glasses. **Yield: 8 to 10 servings.**

Phillip Carpenter, Unity #1710

Golden Fruit Freeze

1 11-ounce can mandarin oranges, drained
1 8-ounce can crushed pineapple, drained
1/4 cup sugar
1 cup small curd cream-style cottage cheese
1 2-ounce envelope dessert topping mix
1/2 cup milk
1 teaspoon vanilla extract
1/3 cup mayonnaise or salad dressing

Cut mandarin orange sections into halves. Combine mandarin oranges, pineapple and sugar in bowl; mix well. Combine cottage cheese, dessert topping mix, milk and vanilla in mixer bowl; beat until smooth. Fold in fruit mixture and mayonnaise. Spoon into 8x8-inch pan. Freeze. Let stand at room temperature for 15 minutes before serving. Cut into squares. **Yield: 16 servings.**

Myrtle Lamoreaux, Bloomingdale #536

Ice Cream Birthday Cake

32 chocolate chip cookies, finely crushed
1/4 cup melted margarine
1 cup fudge topping
2 quarts any 2 flavors ice cream, softened
Whipped topping

Combine cookie crumbs and margarine in bowl; mix well. Press into 9-inch deep-dish pie plate. Add fudge topping. Spread 1 quart ice cream over chocolate layer. Freeze for 30 minutes. Add remaining 1 quart different flavor ice cream. Freeze for 30 minutes. Add layer of whipped topping. Garnish with strawberries or cherries. Freeze for 4 hours to overnight. May freeze in oval-shaped roasting pan and decorate to look like football. **Yield: 12 servings.**

Marie Sinclair, Sanborn #2016

Ice Cream Sandwiches Dessert

1 egg
1/2 cup vegetable shortening
1/4 cup margarine, softened
1 teaspoon vanilla extract
1 2-layer package devil's food cake mix
Powdered chocolate drink mix
1/2 gallon brick ice cream

Combine egg, shortening, margarine, vanilla and half the cake mix in mixer bowl; beat well. Add remaining cake mix; mix well. Divide mixture into 4 portions. Roll each portion into 6x10-inch rectangle on surface sprinkled with dry powdered chocolate drink mix. Cut each rectangle into eight 3x2 1/2-inch rectangles; place on greased baking sheet. Bake at 375 degrees for 8 to 10 minutes or until cookies test done. Cool in pan for several minutes. Remove to wire rack to cool completely. Cut ice cream into slightly smaller rectangles than cookies. Place ice cream rectangles on half the cookies; top with remaining cookies. Wrap in waxed paper. Freeze until firm. **Yield: 16 servings.**

Diane Boroi, Valley #1420

Raspberry Ice Cream

1 cup sweetened condensed milk
1/4 cup water
2 cups fresh raspberries, crushed
2 tablespoons lemon juice
1/4 cup whipping cream, whipped

Combine condensed milk and water in bowl; mix well. Add raspberries and lemon juice; mix well. Chill in refrigerator. Fold whipped cream into chilled mixture. Pour into freezer container. Freeze until half frozen. Scrape from sides and bottom of container; beat until smooth but not thawed. Freeze until firm. Spoon into serving dishes. **Yield: 6 servings.**

Jean V. Johnn, Hemlock #2051

Pineapple Sherbet Dessert

Pineapple sherbet
1 cup crushed pineapple
1 cup confectioners' sugar
1 cup fresh buttermilk

Combine pineapple sherbet, pineapple, confectioners' sugar and buttermilk in bowl; stir well. Pour into freezer container. Freeze for 4 hours, stirring 3 or 4 times. **Yield: 4 servings.**

Rebecca Olcus, Kaylor #1396

Homemade Ice Cream

4 eggs, beaten
1 cup sugar
1/2 cup sour cream
2 12-ounce cans evaporated milk, chilled
2 cups half and half
2 cups milk
1 6-ounce package any flavor instant pudding mix

Combine eggs, sugar, sour cream, evaporated milk, half and half, milk and pudding mix in large bowl; mix well. Pour into ice cream freezer container. Freeze using manufacturer's instructions. **Yield: 6 servings.**

Grace Askey, Oak Hill #717

Ice Cream Sherbet

3 cups sugar
9 cups milk
3 envelopes unsweetened orange or strawberry drink mix

Combine sugar, milk and unsweetened drink powder in large container. Pour into ice cream freezer. Freeze using manufacturer's instructions. **Yield: 8 servings.**

Janet McClellan, Logan #109

Icebox Dessert

1/4 cup butter, softened
1 cup confectioners' sugar
1 egg, beaten
1 16-ounce can apricots, drained
8 ounces vanilla wafers, crushed
1/2 cup chopped nuts
2 cups whipped cream or whipped topping

Cream butter and confectioners' sugar in mixer bowl until light and fluffy. Beat in egg. Cut apricots into slices. Layer 1/2 of the vanilla wafer crumbs, 1/4 cup nuts, apricots, confectioners' sugar mixture, half the remaining crumbs, whipped cream, remaining nuts and remaining crumbs in buttered 8x8-inch glass dish. Chill in refrigerator for 24 hours before serving. **Yield: 16 servings.**

Alice L. Voorhies, Hemlock #2051

For a quick dessert, fill cantaloupe halves with vanilla ice cream and top with fresh berries.

Ice Cream Dessert

1/2 cup margarine, softened
1 cup packed brown sugar
1 cup coconut
8 cups rice Chex cereal, crushed
1/2 gallon any flavor ice cream, softened

Cream margarine and brown sugar in mixer bowl until light and fluffy. Stir in coconut and crushed cereal. Spray 9x13-inch dish with nonstick cooking spray. Layer half the cereal mixture, all the ice cream and remaining cereal mixture into prepared dish, pressing lightly on top. Freeze. **Yield: 12 servings.**

Phyllis Moyer, Pleasant Hill #1505

Ice Cream Pudding Dessert

60 butter crackers, crushed
1/2 cup melted margarine
3 4-ounce packages coconut instant pudding mix
1 cup milk
1/2 gallon vanilla ice cream, softened
Whipped topping
Toasted coconut

Combine cracker crumbs and margarine in bowl; mix well. Press into buttered 9x13-inch dish. Combine pudding mix, milk and ice cream in bowl; mix well. Pour over crumb crust. Top with whipped topping; sprinkle with toasted coconut. Chill in refrigerator until serving time. **Yield: 12 servings.**

Jean Moore, Cross Creek Village #1751

Kinaffeh (Shredded Wheat and Nuts)

2 pounds (about) shredded wheat
1 1/2 pounds walnuts, chopped
1 tablespoon cinnamon
3 tablespoons sugar
2 cups melted unsalted butter
3 cups water
4 cups sugar
1 teaspoon lemon juice

Loosen enough shredded wheat to layer in buttered 9x13-inch baking dish. Combine walnuts, cinnamon and 3 tablespoons sugar in bowl; mix well. Sprinkle over shredded wheat layer; top with layer of remaining shredded wheat. Pour hot melted butter over all. Bake at 350 degrees for 1 hour. Combine water and 4 cups sugar in saucepan. Boil for 15 minutes, stirring frequently. Remove from heat. Stir in lemon juice. Cool slightly. Pour over hot baked layer. Cut into squares. **Yield: 12 servings.**

Patricia Scarpelli, Shavers Creek #353

Lemon Bisque

1 prepared crumb shell, crumbled
1 3-ounce package lemon gelatin
1 cup sugar
1 cup boiling water
1 12-ounce can evaporated milk, chilled
Grated rind and juice of 1 lemon

Pat crumb shell in 9x13-inch baking dish. Bake at 350 degrees for 10 minutes. Cool to room temperature. Dissolve gelatin and sugar in boiling water in bowl. Chill in refrigerator until partially set. Beat chilled evaporated milk in bowl until of consistency of whipped cream. Add lemon rind and juice; mix well. Beat partially set gelatin mixture. Fold in evaporated milk mixture. Pour over baked layer. Chill in refrigerator until serving time. **Yield: 15 to 18 servings.**

Irma Keir, Diahoga #1951

Lemon Crackle

2 eggs, beaten
1 cup sugar
2 tablespoons cornstarch
1 cup water
1/2 teaspoon vanilla extract
1/4 cup butter
Juice of 1 lemon
10 soda crackers, crushed
1 cup flour
1/2 teaspoon baking soda
1 cup packed brown sugar
1 cup coconut
1/2 cup melted butter

Combine eggs, sugar, mixture of cornstarch and water, vanilla, butter and lemon juice in saucepan. Cook for 5 minutes or until thickened, stirring constantly. Combine cracker crumbs, mixture of flour and baking soda and brown sugar in bowl; mix well. Stir in coconut and butter; mix well. Layer cracker crumb mixture and lemon mixture 1/4 at a time in buttered 8x8-inch baking dish. Bake at 350 degrees for 50 to 60 minutes or until brown. **Yield: 16 servings.**

Donna McAninch, Reynoldsville #1825

Lime and Pineapple Chiffon

1 6-ounce package lime gelatin
1 20-ounce can crushed pineapple, drained
16 ounces whipped topping

Combine lime gelatin and pineapple in bowl; mix well. Fold in whipped topping. Spoon into serving bowl. May be served immediately or chilled until serving time. **Yield: 6 servings.**

Patricia A. Gutshall, Sebring #1047

Melon Cooler Salad Dessert

1/2 cup frozen lemonade or limeade concentrate, thawed
8 ounces cream cheese, softened
4 cups assorted melon balls

Process lemonade concentrate and cream cheese in blender until well blended. Spoon melon balls into serving dishes; top with cream cheese mixture.
Yield: 8 servings.

Lois M. Pifer, Henderson #1315

Mystery Salad Dessert

2 cups crushed pretzels
3/4 cup melted butter
2 tablespoons sugar
8 ounces cream cheese, softened
1 cup sugar
8 ounces whipped topping
2 3-ounce packages strawberry gelatin
1 cup boiling water
2 10-ounce packages frozen strawberries
4 ounces cream cheese, softened

Combine crushed pretzels, butter and 2 tablespoons sugar in bowl; mix well. Press into buttered 8x12-inch baking dish. Bake at 400 degrees for 5 to 8 minutes or until light brown. Cool to room temperature. Combine 8 ounces cream cheese and 1 cup sugar in bowl; mix well. Fold in whipped topping. Spread over cooled pretzel layer. Chill in refrigerator. Dissolve gelatin in boiling water in bowl. Stir in strawberries until thawed. Pour over cream cheese layer. Chill in refrigerator for several hours or until set. Spread remaining cream cheese over top. **Yield: 12 servings.**

Debbie Fuhr, Plain Grove #1431

Orange Fool

3 eggs
1/2 cup sugar
2 cups light cream or half and half
1/2 teaspoon cinnamon
Juice of 6 oranges, strained

Beat eggs in mixer bowl until frothy. Add sugar, cream, cinnamon and orange juice; beat well. Pour into double boiler. Cook over hot water until thick enough to coat a spoon, stirring constantly. Pour into dessert dishes. Chill until serving time.
Yield: 8 servings.

Walter W. Long, Unity #1710

Orange Fluff

2 3-ounce packages orange gelatin
2 1/2 cups boiling water
1 6-ounce can frozen orange juice concentrate, thawed
1 13-ounce can crushed pineapple
2 11-ounce cans mandarin oranges, drained
1 4-ounce package lemon instant pudding mix
1 cup cold milk
1 cup whipping cream, whipped

Dissolve orange gelatin in boiling water in bowl. Stir in orange juice concentrate. Add undrained pineapple; mix well. Chill in refrigerator until partially set. Stir in mandarin oranges. Pour into serving bowl. Chill until set. Combine pudding mix and milk in bowl; beat well. Fold in whipped cream. Spread over top of congealed gelatin mixture. Chill until serving time. **Yield: 12 servings.**

Lisa Brown, Hillcrest #1674

Pasta Dessert

1 6-ounce package tubetina pasta
6 tablespoons sugar
1 egg
1 tablespoon flour
1/4 teaspoon salt
1 20-ounce can crushed pineapple
1 11-ounce can mandarin oranges
1 4-ounce jar maraschino cherries, sliced
16 ounces whipped topping

Cook pasta for 12 minutes using package directions; drain. Combine sugar, egg, flour and salt in saucepan. Drain pineapple and mandarin oranges, reserving juice. Stir reserved juice into sugar mixture gradually. Cook over medium heat until thickened, stirring constantly. Pour over drained pasta; mix well. Chill, covered, in refrigerator overnight. Add pineapple, mandarin oranges and maraschino cherries to pasta mixture; mix well. Fold in whipped topping. Spoon into serving dish. Chill until serving time. May substitute other small pasta for tubetina.
Yield: 12 to 15 servings.

Frances Hesselgesser, South Buffalo #1908

Peach-Cream Cheese Dessert

2 cups finely crushed graham crackers
1/2 cup sugar
3/4 cup melted margarine
8 ounces cream cheese, softened
1 cup sugar
2 cups whipped topping
1 21-ounce can peach pie filling

Combine graham cracker crumbs, 1/2 cup sugar and margarine in bowl; mix well. Press into buttered 9x13-inch baking dish. Bake at 400 degrees for 5 minutes. Cool to room temperature. Combine cream cheese and 1 cup sugar in mixer bowl; beat well. Fold in whipped topping. Spread over cooled baked layer. Top with pie filling. Chill in refrigerator until serving time. **Yield: 12 servings.**

Janice L. Fox, Prosperity #1700

Pear-Apricot Jubilee

1 cup dried apricots
1 lemon
3/4 cup water
5 cups finely chopped pears
4 cups sugar

Cut apricots into thin strips. Cut lemon into thin slices. Combine apricots, lemon and water in saucepan. Simmer, covered, for 5 minutes, stirring frequently. Combine pears and sugar in heavy 4-quart saucepan. Cook over low heat until thick and clear. Stir constantly until sugar dissolves and then stir frequently to prevent scorching. Add apricot mixture. Cook for several minutes, stirring constantly. Serve over cake. May be canned or frozen. **Yield: 2 pints.**

Marjorie Kennedy, Winfield #1105

Pistachio Pudding Dessert

1 3-ounce package sugar-free pistachio instant pudding mix
1 20-ounce can juice-pack crushed pineapple
16 ounces plain non-fat yogurt

Combine pudding mix and pineapple in bowl; mix well. Fold in yogurt. Chill in refrigerator for several hours before serving. **Yield: 10 servings.**

Lucille Steckler, New Vernon #608

Rosemary's Fruit Pizza

1 20-ounce package chocolate chip or sugar cookie dough
2 3-ounce packages vanilla instant pudding mix
2 1/4 cups milk
1/4 teaspoon almond extract
Sliced apples, bananas, strawberries, kiwifruit and/or pineapple

Spray pizza pan with nonstick cooking spray. Press cookie dough onto pizza pan. Bake at 350 degrees for 12 to 14 minutes or until brown. Cool to room temperature. Combine pudding mix with milk and almond extract in bowl; beat well. Spread over baked crust. Chill in refrigerator until set. Top with fruit slices.
Yield: 8 to 10 servings.

Erla Haas, Shermanata #1796

Substitute low-fat yogurt for whipped cream as a dessert topping.

German Plum Kuchen

1/2 cup flour
2 eggs
1 cup sugar
Milk
1 unbaked 9-inch deep-dish pie shell
Prune plums, pitted
Cinnamon to taste

Combine flour, eggs and sugar in bowl; mix well. Add enough milk to make mixture a little thicker than custard, mixing well. Stand prune plums on end in pie shell until dish is filled. Sprinkle with cinnamon. Pour custard mixture over all. Bake at 350 degrees for 50 minutes or until wooden pick inserted near center comes out clean. **Yield: 8 servings.**

Ardelle Hutcheson, New London #1151

Amish Pudding

1 cup chopped dates
1 teaspoon baking soda
1 tablespoon butter
1 cup boiling water
1 egg
1 1/2 cups flour
1 cup sugar
1 teaspoon vanilla extract
4 or 5 bananas, sliced
2 cups whipped cream

Combine dates, baking soda, butter and boiling water in bowl; mix well. Let stand until cool. Add egg, flour, sugar and vanilla; mix well. Spoon into 9x13-inch baking dish. Bake at 350 degrees for 30 minutes. Let stand until cool. Cut into small pieces. Toss with banana slices and whipped cream in bowl. **Yield: 10 to 12 servings.**

Mildred Osborne, Menallen #1091

Apple Crumb Pudding

1/3 cup butter or margarine
1 16-ounce can applesauce
2 cups toasted bread crumbs
3 egg yolks, beaten
1/2 teaspoon cinnamon
1/3 cup sugar
3 egg whites
1/8 teaspoon salt
1/8 teaspoon cream of tartar
1/2 teaspoon vanilla extract
1/3 cup sugar

Place butter in 2-quart glass bowl. Microwave on High for 1 minute. Stir in applesauce, bread crumbs, beaten egg yolks, cinnamon and 1/3 cup sugar. Microwave, covered with waxed paper, for 5 minutes. Stir. Microwave for 5 minutes longer. Beat egg whites in mixer bowl until foamy. Add salt, cream of tartar and vanilla. Beat until soft peaks form. Add sugar gradually, beating constantly until stiff peaks form. Spread over pudding. Microwave for 2 minutes and 45 seconds, turning after 1 minute. Serve immediately. **Yield: 6 to 8 servings.**

Mary Lou Templin, Millers Run #2020

Apple-Oat Pudding

1/2 cup shortening
1 cup sugar
1 teaspoon baking soda
1 teaspoon water
3 medium unpeeled apples, finely chopped
3 cups quick-cooking oats
2 cups flour
1/2 cup nuts
1/2 teaspoon salt
1 teaspoon cinnamon
1 teaspoon ground nutmeg
1 teaspoon vanilla extract

Cream shortening and sugar in mixer bowl until light and fluffy. Dissolve baking soda in water. Add to creamed mixture with apples, oats, flour, nuts, salt, cinnamon, nutmeg and vanilla; mix well. Spoon into 8x8-inch baking pan. Bake at 350 degrees for 45 minutes. **Yield: 9 servings.**

Effie Yochum, Steuben #858

Rolled Apple Pudding

2 cups flour
2 teaspoons baking powder
1/2 teaspoon salt
1/4 cup shortening
Milk
5 or 6 apples, sliced
1 cup sugar
1/4 cup butter, softened
3 cups hot water

Combine flour, baking powder, salt and shortening in bowl; mix well. Stir in enough milk to make soft dough. Roll dough into rectangle. Spread with apples. Roll as for jelly roll. Place in 9x13-inch baking pan. Mix sugar, butter and water in bowl. Pour over rolled dough. Bake at 350 degrees for 1 hour, basting 3 times. **Yield: 12 servings.**

Edith Brien, Sebring #1047

Bachelor's Pudding

1 cup packed brown sugar
1 cup water
1 1/4 cups flour
1 teaspoon salt
1 teaspoon baking powder
3/4 cup sugar
1 cup milk
1/2 cup chopped nuts
1/2 cup chopped dates or raisins

Dissolve brown sugar in water in baking dish; do not stir. Sift flour, salt, baking powder and sugar in bowl. Stir in milk, nuts and dates, mixing well. Pour over brown sugar mixture; do not stir. Bake at 350 degrees for 20 minutes; cool. Cut into serving portions, turning each portion upside down on plates.
Yield: 12 to 15 servings.

Henry Gaiser, Kaylor #1396

Chocolate Bread Pudding

2 cups soft bread cubes
1/2 cup semisweet chocolate chips
3 eggs, beaten
1/2 cup sugar
1/4 teaspoon salt
1 1/2 cups milk
1/2 teaspoon vanilla extract

Combine bread cubes and chocolate chips in greased 1 1/2-quart baking dish. Beat eggs, sugar, salt, milk and vanilla in bowl. Pour over bread cube mixture. Bake at 350 degrees for 50 to 60 minutes. **Yield: 6 servings.**

Helena B. Latshaw, Ontelaunee #1617

Easy Bread Pudding

8 slices bread, cubed
4 eggs, beaten
1 cup sugar
4 cups milk
1 teaspoon vanilla extract
1/2 cup raisins
Sugar and nutmeg to taste

Place bread cubes in greased 2-quart baking dish. Beat eggs, 1 cup sugar, milk and vanilla in small bowl. Stir in raisins. Pour over bread cubes. Sprinkle with sugar and nutmeg to taste. Bake at 350 degrees for 30 to 40 minutes or until golden brown. **Yield: 6 servings.**

Kathy Wilcox, Watson #1068

Old-Fashioned Bread Pudding

1/4 cup raisins
3 slices whole wheat bread, cubed
2 eggs
1 1/2 cups skim milk
3/4 teaspoon vanilla extract
1/3 cup sugar
1/2 teaspoon cinnamon or nutmeg

Sprinkle half the raisins in greased 1 1/2-quart baking dish. Arrange bread cubes over top; sprinkle with remaining raisins. Beat eggs, milk, vanilla and sugar in bowl until foamy. Pour over bread cubes. Sprinkle with cinnamon. Let stand for 10 minutes. Place baking dish in pan of warm water in oven. Bake at 350 degrees for 30 to 35 minutes or until custard is set. May also microwave, covered, on High for 14 minutes. **Yield: 4 servings.**

Elizabeth Steele, North Woodbury #1923

Quick Bread Pudding

2 eggs
1/2 cup sugar
1 tablespoon vanilla extract
4 cups prepared nonfat dry milk powder
4 slices buttered toasted bread, cut into pieces

Combine eggs, sugar and vanilla in bowl; beat with whisk. Add milk powder; mix well. Spoon into 2-quart baking dish. Arrange toasted bread pieces on top. Place dish in larger pan filled with 1/2 inch water. Bake at 350 degrees for 45 minutes or until water boils. **Yield: 8 servings.**

Althea Kephart, Sanborn #2016

Mother's Cherry Pudding

1 cup sugar
1/2 cup shortening
2 eggs, beaten
3 cups flour
1 tablespoon baking powder
1 1/2 cups milk
1 pint cherries, pitted

Cream sugar and shortening in mixer bowl until light and fluffy. Beat in eggs. Add mixture of flour and baking powder alternately with milk, stirring until smooth. Fold in cherries with spoon. Pour into greased and floured 9x13-inch baking pan. Bake at 350 degrees for 35 to 40 minutes. May substitute blueberries or raspberries for cherries. **Yield: 12 to 15 servings.**

Ruth V. Walker, Oliver #1069

Cracker Pudding

4 cups milk
3/4 cup coconut
3/4 cup sugar
3/4 cup (about) cracker crumbs
2 egg yolks, beaten
2 egg whites
1 tablespoon sugar

Scald milk in saucepan. Add coconut, sugar and enough cracker crumbs to make of desired consistency. Boil for 5 minutes, stirring occasionally. Stir a small amount of mixture into beaten egg yolks. Add egg yolks to mixture, stirring briskly. Cook for 2 minutes longer. Pour into 1 1/2-quart baking dish. Beat egg whites with 1 tablespoon sugar in mixer bowl until stiff peaks form. Spread over pudding. Place under broiler until lightly browned. Pudding will thicken as it cools. **Yield: 6 to 8 servings.**

Miriam M. Forney, Star #993

Baked Custard

1¾ cups milk
¼ cup sugar
3 eggs, beaten
¼ teaspoon salt
½ teaspoon vanilla extract
Nutmeg to taste

Combine milk, sugar, eggs, salt and vanilla in mixer bowl. Beat at medium speed until smooth. Pour into glass custard cups filling ¾ full. Sprinkle with nutmeg. Microwave on Defrost for 15 to 16 minutes or until knife inserted near center comes out clean. Let stand for 5 minutes before serving. **Yield: 4 servings.**

Mary Lou Templen, Millers Run #2020

Date Pudding

1 teaspoon baking soda
16 ounces dates, chopped
1 cup boiling water
1 cup packed brown sugar
1½ cups flour
1 teaspoon baking powder
1 egg
½ teaspoon vanilla extract
1 cup chopped nuts
2 cups packed brown sugar
1½ tablespoons flour
1½ cups milk
1 cup water
2½ tablespoons butter
½ teaspoon salt
½ teaspoon vanilla extract

Sprinkle baking soda over dates in bowl. Pour boiling water over top. Set aside. Combine 1 cup brown sugar, 1½ cups flour, baking powder, egg, ½ teaspoon vanilla and nuts in medium bowl; mix well. Stir in date mixture. Spoon into 2-quart baking dish. Bake at 350 degrees for 45 minutes. Combine 2 cups brown sugar, 1½ tablespoons flour, milk, 1 cup water, butter, salt and ½ teaspoon vanilla in saucepan; mix well. Bring to a boil over medium heat, stirring constantly. Cook until thickened. Serve over date pudding. **Yield: 8 servings.**

Emma L. Hammond, Fairview #1351

Harvest Pudding

6 apples, sliced
1 cup sugar
1 teaspoon cinnamon
1⅓ cups flour
½ cup sugar
2 teaspoons baking powder
¼ teaspoon salt
1 egg, beaten
½ cup milk
¼ cup melted shortening

Arrange apples in buttered 9x13-inch baking dish. Sprinkle with mixture of 1 cup sugar and cinnamon. Sift flour, ½ cup sugar, baking powder and salt together into large bowl. Beat egg with milk. Pour into dry ingredients. Stir in melted shortening. Pour over apple mixture. Bake at 350 degrees for 35 to 45 minutes or until browned. **Yield: 6 to 8 servings.**

Anna Rhine Shirey, Decatur #1920

Indian Pudding

2 cups skim milk
1/4 cup cornmeal
1/4 cup sugar
1/8 teaspoon baking soda
1/2 teaspoon ground ginger
1/2 teaspoon cinnamon
1/4 cup molasses
1 cup skim milk, chilled
Nutmeg to taste

Heat 2 cups skim milk in saucepan over low heat. Add cornmeal gradually, stirring constantly. Cook for 15 minutes or until thickened, stirring constantly; remove from heat. Combine sugar, baking soda, ginger and cinnamon in bowl; mix well. Add to cornmeal mixture. Stir in molasses and 1 cup skim milk, mixing well. Pour into 1-quart baking dish. Bake at 275 degrees for 2 hours. Sprinkle with nutmeg. Serve warm. **Yield: 8 servings.**

Ethel Friede, Stony Point #1694

Philippine Flan Leche

1 cup packed light brown sugar
1/2 cup hot water
2 cups evaporated milk
8 egg yolks, beaten
1 cup sugar
1 teaspoon grated lemon rind or vanilla extract

Caramelize brown sugar in heavy saucepan over low heat. Add 1/2 cup hot water to dissolve caramelized sugar, stirring until syrupy. Pour into 1-quart mold, turning to coat side and bottom. Scald evaporated milk in double boiler for 15 minutes. Beat egg yolks in bowl until frothy. Stir in sugar, lemon rind and scalded milk. Pour into prepared mold. Place mold in large pan half filled with water. Bake at 300 degrees for 1 hour or until firm; cool. Invert onto serving plate gently. **Yield: 6 to 8 servings.**

Alice Campman, Chandlers Valley #846

Molasses Pudding

1 egg
2 tablespoons sugar
2 tablespoons butter or margarine
1/2 cup boiling water
1 teaspoon baking soda
1/2 cup molasses
1 1/2 cups flour

Combine egg, sugar, butter, boiling water, baking soda, molasses and flour in top of double boiler; mix well. Cook over hot water for 1 hour. Serve with milk and sugar, whipped topping or ice cream. **Yield: 4 servings.**

Marie Sinclair, Sanborn #2016

Orange Pudding

Juice and grated rind of 1 orange
1 cup sugar
1 tablespoon butter
2 cups boiling water
1/2 cup milk
1 1/2 tablespoons sugar
1 1/2 tablespoons shortening
1 teaspoon baking powder
1 teaspoon vanilla extract
Flour

Combine orange juice and grated rind, 1 cup sugar, butter and boiling water in deep 6x10-inch baking pan; mix well. Combine milk, 1 1/2 tablespoons sugar, shortening, baking powder and vanilla in bowl; mix well. Add enough flour to make stiff dough. Drop by spoonfuls into orange juice mixture. Bake at 375 degrees until pudding tests done. **Yield: 6 to 8 servings.**

Marlene Yarger, Sanborn #2016

Plum Pudding

1 cup ground suet
1 cup packed brown sugar
2 cups flour
1 teaspoon salt
1 teaspoon baking soda
1 teaspoon baking powder
1 cup chopped nuts
1 cup chopped dates
2 cups chopped apples
1/2 cup currants
1/2 cup raisins
1 teaspoon each cinnamon and nutmeg
1/2 teaspoon ground cloves
1 cup milk

Combine suet, brown sugar, flour, salt, baking soda and baking powder in large bowl. Stir in nuts, dates, apples, currants and raisins. Add cinnamon, nutmeg and cloves. Stir in milk; mix well. Pour into two 6x9-inch pans. Steam in pressure cooker with valve open for 1 hour. Garnish with cherries and nuts. Serve warm with lemon sauce. **Yield: 10 to 12 servings.**

Hazel M. Sipe, Milford #1744

Mock Plum Pudding

1 1/2 cups packed brown sugar
3 tablespoons butter
2 cups boiling water
1/2 cup packed brown sugar
2 tablespoons butter, softened
1/2 teaspoon cinnamon
1/2 teaspoon ground nutmeg
1 tablespoon baking powder
1 1/2 cups flour
1/2 cup milk
1/2 cup chopped nuts
1/2 cup raisins

Combine 1 1/2 cups brown sugar, 3 tablespoons butter and boiling water in 2-quart baking dish; mix well. Combine 1/2 cup brown sugar, 2 tablespoons butter, cinnamon, nutmeg, baking powder, flour, milk, nuts and raisins in large bowl; mix well. Drop by spoonfuls into hot brown sugar mixture. Bake at 350 degrees for 35 to 40 minutes. **Yield: 12 servings.**

Zelda Kozar, Dunkard Township #2045

Vanilla Pudding

1¼ cups Pudding Mix
2½ cups warm water
1 egg, beaten
1 tablespoon butter
¾ teaspoon vanilla extract

Combine Pudding Mix and warm water in saucepan. Bring to a boil over medium heat, stirring constantly. Stir a small amount of hot mixture into beaten egg; stir egg into hot mixture. Add butter and vanilla. Cook until thickened, stirring constantly. For **Chocolate Pudding**, add ¾ cup baking cocoa to Pudding Mix. For **Butterscotch Pudding**, substitute 1½ cups packed brown sugar for sugar in Pudding Mix. For **Lemon Pudding**, substitute ½ teaspoon lemon juice and 1½ teaspoons grated lemon rind for vanilla in Vanilla Pudding. **Yield: 6 servings.**

Pudding Mix

1½ cups sugar
2½ cups instant coffee creamer
1¼ cups flour
1 teaspoon salt

Sift sugar, coffee creamer powder, flour and salt together several times. Spoon into airtight container; mix well. May store in refrigerator for 6 months.

Marie Traub, Carter Camp #1563

Sugar-Free Pumpkin Custard

1½ cups skim milk
2 eggs, beaten
2 teaspoons artificial sweetener
½ teaspoon vanilla extract
1 teaspoon cinnamon
¼ teaspoon salt
1½ cups cooked pumpkin

Combine milk, eggs, artificial sweetener, vanilla, cinnamon and salt in bowl; mix well. Stir in pumpkin. Pour into custard cups. Bake at 350 degrees for 50 to 60 minutes. **Yield: 6 to 8 servings.**

Mildred E. Horting, Perry Valley #1804

Prevent a "skin" from forming on custards and puddings by placing a piece of plastic wrap directly on the surface after removing from heat.

Pumpkin Pudding

1/2 cup mashed pumpkin
1 cup low-fat vanilla yogurt
1/2 teaspoon vanilla extract

Combine pumpkin, yogurt and vanilla in bowl; mix well. Garnish with cinnamon. Serve chilled. **Yield: 2 servings.**

Lynnette White, Willard #1440

Raisin Pudding

1/2 cup raisins
Flour
1/2 cup packed brown sugar
1 tablespoon butter, softened
1/2 teaspoon salt
1 1/4 cups flour
1/2 teaspoon cinnamon
2 teaspoons baking powder
1/2 cup milk
1 cup packed brown sugar
2 cups boiling water

Toss raisins with a small amount of flour to coat; set aside. Mix 1/2 cup brown sugar with butter in large bowl. Add raisins, salt, 1 1/4 cups flour, cinnamon and baking powder; mix well. Stir in milk. Pour into greased 9x13-inch baking dish. Dissolve 1 cup brown sugar in boiling water in bowl. Pour over batter. Bake at 350 degrees for 30 minutes. Syrup will sink to bottom of pan when pudding is done. This is an old recipe belonging to my mother. **Yield: 4 to 6 servings.**

Esther Young, Buffalo #1523

Raisin-Rice Custard Pudding

1/3 cup uncooked rice
1/2 teaspoon salt
3 cups milk
3 eggs, beaten
1/2 cup sugar
1 teaspoon vanilla extract
1/2 cup raisins
Nutmeg to taste

Cook rice in boiling water with 1/2 teaspoon salt until tender; drain. Spoon into shallow 1 1/2-quart baking dish. Scald milk in saucepan; cool. Beat eggs and sugar in bowl. Add scalded milk; mix well. Stir in vanilla and raisins. Pour over rice; sprinkle with nutmeg. Place baking dish in pan filled with 1/2 inch water. Bake at 325 degrees for 1 1/2 hours or until set. Serve warm or cool, with cream. **Yield: 6 servings.**

Helen Stevens, South Auburn #1188

Rice Custard Pudding

4 eggs, slightly beaten
1/2 cup sugar
1/8 teaspoon salt
3 cups scalded milk
1 1/2 cups cooked rice
1 teaspoon vanilla extract
Nutmeg to taste

Combine eggs, sugar, salt, milk, rice and vanilla in bowl; mix well. Pour into buttered baking dish. Sprinkle with nutmeg. Place in pan of hot water. Bake at 325 degrees for 1 to 1 1/2 hours or until knife inserted near center comes out clean. **Yield: 8 servings.**

Elva M. Frick, Bottle Run #1301

Baked Rice Pudding

2 cups uncooked rice
8 cups milk
4 eggs
2/3 cup butter, softened
2 cups sugar

Combine rice and milk in large baking dish. Bake at 350 degrees for 1 hour. Beat eggs in mixer bowl until light and lemon-colored. Add butter and sugar; mix well. Stir into hot rice mixture. Bake for 1 hour longer. May need to add additional milk when adding egg mixture. **Yield: 10 to 12 servings.**

Jean V. John, Hemlock #2051

Easy Hawaiian Rice Pudding

1 16-ounce package rice
1 8-ounce can crushed pineapple
2 4-ounce packages vanilla instant pudding mix
3 cups milk
Whipped topping

Prepare rice using package directions. Rinse; drain well. Combine with pineapple, pudding mix and milk in bowl; mix well. Stir in desired amount of whipped topping. Spoon into serving dish. May add raisins, nuts or coconut. **Yield: 8 to 12 servings.**

Esther Young, Buffalo #1523

Old-Fashioned Rice Pudding

6 cups milk
3/4 cup uncooked long grain rice
1 cup whipping cream
3/4 cup sugar
3 egg yolks, beaten
2 teaspoons vanilla extract
Cinnamon to taste

Rinse saucepan with cold water; do not dry. Pour in milk. Bring to a boil over medium heat. Stir in rice. Bring to a boil once again. Reduce heat to low. Simmer, uncovered, for 55 minutes or until rice is tender, stirring occasionally. Combine whipping cream, sugar, egg yolks and vanilla in small bowl; mix well. Stir into rice. Bring to a boil over medium heat. Spoon into 2-quart serving dish. Sprinkle with cinnamon. Chill for 4 hours or longer. **Yield: 6 servings.**

Nettie A. Kauffman, Ontelaunee #1617

Nutty Rice Pudding

2 cups cooked rice
2 eggs, beaten
3 tablespoons sugar
1/4 teaspoon salt
1 tablespoon butter
2 cups milk
1 teaspoon vanilla extract
1/4 cup raisins
1/4 cup chopped dates
1/4 cup chopped pecans
1/8 teaspoon nutmeg

Combine rice, eggs, sugar, salt, butter, milk, vanilla, raisins, dates and pecans in large bowl; mix well. Pour into buttered baking dish; sprinkle with nutmeg. Place in pan of hot water. Bake at 350 degrees for 1 hour. **Yield: 6 to 8 servings.**

Clara Eaker, Murphy #735

Scandinavian Rice Pudding

2 cups milk
1/2 cup uncooked rice
1/2 cup light cream
1 teaspoon vanilla extract
1/8 teaspoon salt
1/3 cup sugar
1/2 cup raisins
2 tablespoons butter

Heat milk in top of double boiler over hot water. Stir in rice. Cook, covered, for 1 to 1 1/2 hours or until rice is tender, stirring occasionally. Add additional milk if mixture is too thick. Stir in cream, vanilla, salt, sugar, raisins and butter. Remove from heat. Let stand over hot water until serving time. **Yield: 6 to 8 servings.**

Opal Jones, Gretna #1543

Fluffy Fruit and Rice Pudding

1 cup uncooked rice
1 16-ounce can fruit cocktail, drained
8 ounces whipped topping

Cook rice using package directions; drain and rinse. Combine with fruit cocktail in bowl; mix gently. Fold in whipped topping. Chill in refrigerator until serving time. **Yield: 6 to 8 servings.**

Alice Pinnock, South Auburn #1188

Glorified Rice Pudding

2 cups cooked rice
1 cup drained crushed pineapple
2 cups miniature marshmallows
1/2 cup sugar
1/4 cup chopped maraschino cherries
8 ounces whipped topping
1 or 2 drops of red food coloring

Combine rice, pineapple, marshmallows, sugar, and cherries in bowl; mix gently. Whip whipped topping with food coloring. Fold into fruit mixture. Chill until serving time. Garnish with maraschino cherries. **Yield: 6 to 8 servings.**

Ruth Ewig, Harmony #1112

Sponge Pudding

2 cups milk
1/4 cup sugar
1/2 cup flour
Cold milk
1/4 cup butter
5 egg yolks, beaten
5 egg whites, stiffly beaten

Bring 2 cups milk to a boil in saucepan over medium heat. Mix sugar, flour and a small amount of cold milk in bowl. Stir into hot milk. Add butter; mix well. Stir a small amount of hot mixture into beaten egg yolks; stir egg yolks into hot mixture. Fold in stiffly beaten egg whites. Spoon into custard cups. Place cups in shallow baking pan filled with 1/2 inch hot water. Bake at 350 degrees until pudding tests done. May serve with cream sauce. **Yield: 4 to 6 servings.**

Lorraine Sayward, Randolph, Vermont

Suet Pudding

2½ cups flour
1 teaspoon baking soda
½ teaspoon salt
1 teaspoon cinnamon
½ teaspoon nutmeg
1 cup ground suet
1 cup raisins
1 cup milk
1 cup molasses
½ cup sugar
2 tablespoons butter
2 tablespoons cornstarch
2 cups water
1 teaspoon vanilla extract
Nutmeg to taste

Sift flour, baking soda, salt, cinnamon and nutmeg together in bowl. Add suet and raisins. Stir in milk and molasses, mixing well. Pour into buttered 3-quart dish. Set in pan of water. Steam, covered, over low heat for 3 hours. Combine ½ cup sugar, butter, cornstarch, water, vanilla and nutmeg in saucepan; mix well. Cook over medium-low heat until thickened, stirring constantly. Pour over steamed pudding. **Yield: 12 servings.**

Mrs. Warren Pflugh, Kaylor #1396

Tapioca Magic Pudding

2 tablespoons tapioca
⅓ cup sugar
⅛ teaspoon salt
1 egg, beaten
2¾ cups milk
¾ teaspoon vanilla extract

Combine tapioca, sugar, salt, egg and milk in saucepan; mix well. Let stand for 5 minutes. Bring to a boil, stirring constantly; remove from heat. Stir in vanilla. Let stand, covered, for 20 minutes; stir. Serve warm or cold. **Yield: 4 to 6 servings.**

Zelma K. Pyle, Bernville #1887

Pearl Tapioca Pudding

1 cup tapioca
4 cups milk
5 egg yolks, beaten
Grated rind of 1 lemon
Juice of ½ lemon
¾ cup sugar
5 egg whites

Combine tapioca and 1 cup milk in bowl; let stand in refrigerator overnight. Pour into top of double boiler. Add remaining 3 cups milk. Cook over hot water for 3 hours, stirring frequently; cool. Beat egg yolks, lemon rind, lemon juice and sugar in bowl. Stir into cooled tapioca mixture. Beat egg whites until stiff peaks form. Alternate layers of tapioca mixture and egg whites in baking dish, ending with egg whites. Bake at 325 degrees for 15 minutes. **Yield: 10 to 12 servings.**

Delphine Delaney, Kaylor #1396

Frozen Pumpkin Squares

1½ cups graham cracker crumbs
¼ cup sugar
¼ cup melted butter
1 16-ounce can pumpkin
½ cup packed brown sugar
¼ teaspoon ground ginger
½ teaspoon salt
1 teaspoon cinnamon
⅛ teaspoon ground cloves
1 quart vanilla ice cream, softened

Combine graham cracker crumbs, sugar and butter in small bowl. Press into 9x9-inch baking pan. Combine pumpkin, brown sugar, ginger, salt, cinnamon and cloves in bowl; mix well. Fold in ice cream. Spoon into prepared pan. Freeze, covered, until firm. Remove from freezer 30 minutes before serving. Cut into squares. May substitute yogurt for ice cream. **Yield: 16 servings.**

Luella Haynes, Waterford #423

Quick Dessert

1 20-ounce can crushed pineapple, drained
1 21-ounce can cherry pie filling
1 14-ounce can sweetened condensed milk
8 ounces whipped topping
1 cup chopped nuts

Combine pineapple, pie filling, condensed milk, whipped topping and nuts in bowl; mix well. Spoon into serving bowl. Chill until serving time. **Yield: 6 to 8 servings.**

Viola Gudehunst, Jackson #1468

Refreshing Dessert

1 20-ounce can chunk pineapple
2 pears, peeled, sliced
1 cup seedless grapes
2 large apples, sliced
2 oranges, sectioned
2 to 3 bananas, sliced

Combine pineapple, pears, grapes, apples and oranges in large bowl; mix well. Chill until serving time. Stir in banana slices. Spoon into individual serving bowls. Garnish with pineapple sherbet, strawberries, nuts or coconut. **Yield: 6 to 8 servings.**

Donna Nagel, East New Castle #1536

For an easy refreshing dessert, shape scoops of lemon or orange sherbet into balls and roll in flaked coconut; freeze until firm. Serve over sliced strawberries or peaches.

Raspberry Mousse

2 egg whites
3/4 cup sugar
1 10-ounce package frozen raspberries, thawed
1 tablespoon lemon juice
Salt to taste
1 cup whipped cream
1/2 cup chopped walnuts (optional)

Beat egg whites with sugar and raspberries in mixer bowl for 15 minutes. Add lemon juice and salt; mix well. Fold in 3/4 cup whipped cream. Spoon into 3-quart dish. Top with remaining whipped cream and walnuts. May freeze mousse for up to 2 weeks, omitting whipped cream until just before serving. **Yield: 8 to 10 servings.**

Janet McClellan, Logan #109

Baked Rhubarb

1 cup flour
3/4 cup oats
1 cup packed brown sugar
1/2 cup melted butter or margarine
1 teaspoon cinnamon
4 cups chopped rhubarb
1 cup sugar
2 tablespoons cornstarch
1 cup water
1 teaspoon vanilla extract

Combine flour, oats, brown sugar, butter and cinnamon in bowl, stirring until crumbly. Press half the crumb mixture into greased 9x9-inch baking pan. Cover with rhubarb. Combine sugar, cornstarch, water and vanilla in saucepan; mix well. Cook over low heat until thick and clear, stirring frequently. Pour over rhubarb; sprinkle with remaining crumb mixture. Bake at 350 degrees for 1 hour. **Yield: 6 servings.**

Mary Mood, Briar Creek #146

Rhubarb Tart

2 cups flour
2 teaspoons baking powder
6 tablespoons shortening
2 eggs, slightly beaten
1/4 cup milk
4 cups chopped rhubarb
2 3-ounce packages strawberry gelatin
2 cups sugar
1/2 cup butter, softened
1 cup flour

Combine 2 cups flour and baking powder in bowl. Cut in shortening until crumbly. Add eggs and milk, mixing well. Press into 9x13-inch baking pan. Cover with rhubarb. Sprinkle with gelatin. Combine sugar, butter and 1 cup flour in small bowl, stirring until crumbly. Sprinkle over top. Bake at 350 degrees for 40 minutes. **Yield: 12 servings.**

Irene Moore, Scrubgrass #1705

Rhubarb Cake Dessert

1 cup margarine, softened
2 cups flour
2 tablespoons sugar
5 cups finely chopped rhubarb
6 egg yolks, beaten
2 cups sugar
1/4 cup flour
1/4 teaspoon salt
1 cup cream
6 egg whites
3/4 cup sugar
2 teaspoons vanilla extract
Salt to taste

Combine margarine, 2 cups flour and 2 tablespoons sugar in small bowl, stirring until crumbly. Press into greased 9x13-inch baking pan. Bake at 350 degrees for 10 minutes; cool. Combine rhubarb, egg yolks, 2 cups sugar, 1/4 cup flour, 1/4 teaspoon salt and cream in bowl; mix well. Pour into prepared pan. Bake for 40 to 45 minutes or until firm. Beat egg whites in mixer bowl until soft peaks form. Add 3/4 cup sugar, 2 tablespoons at a time, beating constantly until stiff peaks form. Beat in vanilla and salt. Spread over baked layer. Bake for 10 to 15 minutes or until browned.
Yield: 12 servings.

Margaret Coulter, Penn #534

Rhubarb Crunch

1 cup flour
1 cup oats
1 cup packed brown sugar
1/2 cup melted butter
1 teaspoon cinnamon
4 cups chopped rhubarb
1 1/2 cups sugar
2 tablespoons (rounded) cornstarch
1 cup water
1 teaspoon vanilla extract

Combine flour, oats, brown sugar, butter and cinnamon in bowl, stirring until crumbly. Press half the crumb mixture into 9x9-inch baking pan. Cover with rhubarb. Combine sugar, cornstarch and water in saucepan. Cook over medium heat until thick and clear, stirring constantly. Stir in vanilla; cool. Pour over rhubarb. Sprinkle with remaining crumb mixture. Bake at 350 degrees for 1 hour.
Yield: 9 servings.

Dawn M. Dietrich, Virginville #1832

Rhubarb-Strawberry Dessert

4 cups chopped rhubarb
1 3-ounce package strawberry gelatin
4 cups fresh or frozen strawberries

Cook rhubarb in boiling water in saucepan until tender; drain. Mix with gelatin, stirring until gelatin is dissolved; cool. Stir in strawberries. Serve in individual serving dishes with dollop of whipped cream. **Yield: 4 to 8 servings.**

Mae Shaffer, Mt. Pleasant #1687

Snowball Cake

1 prepared angel food cake
1 3-ounce package sugar-free lemon gelatin
1 cup boiling water
1 20-ounce can unsweetened crushed pineapple
16 ounces whipped topping
Coconut or chopped nuts

Slice cake into thin slices; place half the cake slices in 9x13-inch dish. Dissolve gelatin in boiling water in bowl; cool slightly. Stir in pineapple and whipped topping. Alternate layers of pineapple mixture and remaining cake in prepared dish. Top with coconut or nuts. Chill in refrigerator overnight. **Yield: 10 to 15 servings.**

Ellen Walton, East New Castle #1536

Speedy Salad Dessert

1 3-ounce package vanilla instant pudding mix
1 cup whipped cream
1 16-ounce can fruit cocktail, drained
1 11-ounce can mandarin oranges, drained
1 4-ounce jar maraschino cherries, drained
1 cup miniature marshmallows

Prepare pudding mix using package directions. Combine with whipped cream, fruit cocktail, mandarin oranges, cherries and marshmallows in large bowl; mix gently. Chill before serving. **Yield: 6 to 8 servings.**

Marlene E. Sattazahn, Marion #1853

Just a Trifle

1 prepared 10-ounce pound cake
1/2 cup orange juice
3 cups prepared vanilla pudding
1 21-ounce can cherry pie filling
4 ounces whipped topping

Cut cake into 1/2-inch cubes. Layer in glass serving bowl. Sprinkle with orange juice. Alternate layers of pudding, pie filling and cake cubes until all ingredients are used. Top with whipped topping. Chill for 2 hours before serving. **Yield: 8 to 10 servings.**

Peggy Roberts, White Deer #122

Make an easy frozen dessert of torn angel food cake and softened coffee ice cream. Freeze in loaf pan lined with waxed paper and serve sliced with chocolate sauce.

Creamy Yogurt Cups

1 3-ounce package sugar-free gelatin (any flavor)
3/4 cup boiling water
1/2 cup cold water
Ice cubes
1 cup low-fat yogurt
1/2 teaspoon vanilla extract

Dissolve gelatin in boiling water in bowl. Combine cold water with enough ice cubes to measure 1 cup. Add to gelatin, stirring until partially set; remove unmelted ice. Fold in yogurt and vanilla, mixing well. Pour into 5 individual serving dishes. Chill until firm. **Yield: 5 (1/2-cup) servings.**

Carol A. Rhoades, Perry Valley #1804

Zucchini Squares

3 1/2 cups flour
1 cup sugar
1/2 teaspoon salt
1 1/2 cups margarine, softened
8 cups sliced peeled zucchini
2/3 cup lemon juice
1 1/2 cups sugar
1/2 cup flour
1/4 teaspoon nutmeg
1/2 teaspoon cinnamon

Combine 3 1/2 cups flour, 1 cup sugar, salt and margarine in bowl, stirring until crumbly. Press half the mixture into 9x13-inch baking pan, reserving remaining crumbs for topping. Bake at 375 degrees for 10 minutes; cool. Combine zucchini and lemon juice in saucepan. Cook over low heat until zucchini is tender. Stir in 1 1/2 cups sugar, flour, nutmeg and cinnamon a little at a time. Cook for 1 minute longer, stirring frequently; cool. Pour over prepared crust; sprinkle with reserved crumb mixture. May dust with additional cinnamon. Bake for 30 minutes. Cut into squares. **Yield: 15 servings.**

Stella Kollar, Bloomingdale #536

Whole Wheat-Strawberry Shortcakes

1 1/2 cups whole wheat flour
1 1/2 cups all-purpose flour
1 tablespoon baking powder
6 tablespoons margarine, softened
1 cup skim milk
1 cup plain yogurt
2 packets artificial sweetener
2 cups sliced strawberries

Combine flours, baking powder, margarine and milk in large bowl; mix well. Spoon into greased and floured muffin cups. Bake at 400 degrees for 10 minutes or until golden brown. Combine yogurt and artificial sweetener in ice cream freezer container. Freeze using manufacturer's directions. Slice shortcakes into halves. Place layer of frozen yogurt and strawberries on bottom halves; top with remaining halves. **Yield: 12 servings.**

Lorena A. Reilly, Scotch Valley #510

Heavenly Chocolate Fudge Sauce

1/2 cup butter
3 squares unsweetened chocolate
3 cups sugar
1/2 teaspoon salt
1 12-ounce can evaporated milk

Combine butter and chocolate in top of double boiler. Cook over hot water until melted, stirring frequently. Stir in sugar a little at a time. Add salt and evaporated milk gradually. Cook to 234 to 240 degrees on candy thermometer, soft-ball stage, stirring constantly. Serve hot or cold over ice cream. **Yield: 2 cups.**

June Harriger, Roseville #1290

Fruity Pudding Sauce

1 20-ounce can pineapple tidbits
1 20-ounce can fruit cocktail
1 11-ounce can mandarin oranges
1 3-ounce package tapioca pudding mix
1 3-ounce package vanilla pudding and pie filling mix
1 banana, sliced

Drain pineapple, fruit cocktail and mandarin oranges, reserving juices. Add enough water to reserved juices to measure 4 cups liquid. Combine liquid, tapioca pudding mix and vanilla pudding mix in saucepan. Cook using package directions. Pour into bowl. Chill until set. Stir in canned fruits and banana slices. Serve over pound or angel food cake. **Yield: 10 servings.**

Bettie Osborn, Atlantic #344

Peanut Butter Sundae Sauce

1 1/4 cups packed brown sugar
3/4 cup light corn syrup
1/4 cup butter
1 1/4 cups peanut butter
1 1/2 cups (about) light cream

Combine brown sugar and corn syrup in saucepan. Bring to boil over medium heat, stirring until brown sugar dissolves. Stir in butter and peanut butter. Let stand until cool. Stir in enough cream to make of desired sauce consistency.
Yield: 4 to 6 servings.

Robin Hetherington, Ringtown Valley #2100

Make a quick sauce for ice cream or baked pears by melting chocolate-covered mint patties in the microwave.

Vanilla Sauce

3 cups milk
1/2 cup sugar
1/8 teaspoon yellow food coloring
3 tablespoons cornstarch
1/4 cup water
1 1/2 teaspoons vanilla extract

Combine milk, sugar and food coloring in saucepan. Bring to a boil over medium heat, stirring frequently. Dissolve cornstarch in water. Stir into hot liquid. Cook until thickened, stirring constantly. Let stand until cool. Stir in vanilla. Serve with fruit, cake or pudding. May substitute any flavor extract and corresponding food coloring for vanilla and yellow food coloring. **Yield: 4 to 6 servings.**

Mary Lou Templin, Millers Run #2020

Sugar-Free Toppings

Carob Fluff Frosting

2 cups heavy cream
1 teaspoon vanilla extract
6 tablespoons carob powder

Combine heavy cream, vanilla and carob powder in mixer bowl. Beat at high speed until soft peaks form. **Yield: 3 cups.**

Vanilla Topping

1 cup heavy cream
1/2 teaspoon vanilla extract

Combine heavy cream and vanilla in mixer bowl. Beat at high speed until soft peaks form. **Yield: 1 3/4 cups.**

Creamy Orange Topping

1 cup heavy cream
1/2 teaspoon orange extract

Combine heavy cream and orange flavoring in mixer bowl. Beat at high speed until soft peaks form. **Yield: 1 3/4 cups.**

Yogurt Sauce

1 cup yogurt
1 1/2 tablespoons unsweetened fruit juice
1 1/2 tablespoons cornstarch

Combine yogurt, fruit juice and cornstarch in saucepan. Cook over medium heat until thickened, stirring constantly. **Yield: 1 cup.**

Arlene R. Adam, Virginville #1832

Multi-Purpose Fruit Toppings

Apple Spice Topping

2 large apples, peeled, sliced
1 tablespoon lemon juice
Cinnamon to taste

Combine apple slices, lemon juice and cinnamon in bowl; toss. **Yield: 1½ cups.**

Crunchy Topping

½ cup roasted soybeans
1 tablespoon peanut butter
2 tablespoons ground sesame seed

Combine soybeans, peanut butter and sesame seed in bowl; toss. **Yield: ¾ cup.**

Granola Topping

1 cup oats
1 cup chopped sunflower seed
1 cup flaked coconut
1 cup chopped nuts
1 tablespoon oil
Cinnamon to taste

Mix oats, sunflower seed, coconut, nuts, oil and cinnamon in bowl. **Yield: 4 cups.**

Pineapple-Nut Topping

1 cup juice-pack crushed pineapple, well drained
½ cup chopped nuts
Nutmeg to taste

Combine pineapple, nuts and nutmeg in bowl; toss. **Yield: 1½ cups.**

Date-Nut Topping

¾ cup chopped dates
¾ cup chopped nuts
¾ cup flaked coconut
1 tablespoon frozen unsweetened fruit juice concentrate, thawed

Mix dates, nuts, coconut and fruit juice concentrate in bowl. **Yield: 2¼ cups.**

Nutty Pear Topping

1 teaspoon lemon juice
1½ cups chopped pear
1 cup chopped nuts
1 teaspoon nutmeg

Combine lemon juice, pear, nuts and nutmeg in bowl; toss. **Yield: 2½ cups.**

Pineapple Crunch Topping

1 cup unbleached flour
2 teaspoons nutmeg
2 cups chopped nuts
4 to 5 tablespoons oil
1 cup drained juice-pack crushed pineapple

Combine flour, nutmeg, nuts, oil and pineapple in bowl; toss. **Yield: 3 cups.**

Arlene R. Adam, Virginville #1832

Cakes and Frostings

Angel Food Cake

1 cup cake flour
1/2 cup sugar
12 egg whites
1 1/4 teaspoons cream of tartar
1/2 teaspoon salt
1 teaspoon vanilla extract
1 cup sugar

Sift flour and 1/2 cup sugar together. Beat egg whites in mixer bowl at low speed until frothy. Add cream of tartar, salt and vanilla. Beat at medium speed until soft peaks form. Add remaining 1 cup sugar 1 tablespoon at a time, beating constantly at high speed until stiff peaks form; do not underbeat. Fold in flour mixture gently. Spoon into ungreased tube pan. Cut through batter 1 inch from center of pan with knife. Bake at 375 degrees for 30 minutes or until top is brown and dry.
Yield: 12 to 16 servings.

Jean Christy, Conneaut #955

Strawberry Angel Cake

2 cups strawberries
1 package angel food cake mix
1 3-ounce package strawberry gelatin
1 cup boiling water
1/2 cup cold water
8 ounces whipped topping

Reserve several whole strawberries for topping. Slice remaining strawberries. Prepare cake mix using package directions. Slice cake into thirds horizontally. Dissolve gelatin in boiling water in bowl. Add cold water. Chill until partially set. Fold in half the whipped topping gently. Chill until firm. Place bottom third of cake on cake plate. Spread 1/3 of the gelatin mixture over top. Arrange 1/3 of the sliced strawberries on mixture. Repeat layers. Spread remaining whipped topping over top. Garnish with whole strawberries. **Yield: 12 servings.**

Olive Smeltzer, Kaylor #1396

Apple Cake

1/4 cup melted butter or margarine
Sliced apples
1/2 to 2/3 cup packed brown sugar
Cinnamon to taste
1 tablespoon shortening
3/4 cup sugar
1 egg
2 cups flour
2 teaspoons baking powder
1 cup milk

Spread melted butter in 9x13-inch cake pan. Cover bottom with sliced apples. Sprinkle brown sugar and cinnamon over top. Combine shortening, sugar, egg, flour, baking powder and milk in bowl; mix well. Pour into prepared pan, spreading evenly. Bake at 350 degrees for 40 to 45 minutes. **Yield: 15 servings.**

Shirley Alvino, Brokenstraw #407

Apple Sunshine Cake

5 egg whites
Pinch of salt
1/4 teaspoon cream of tartar
1/2 teaspoon vanilla or almond extract
1/2 cup sugar
1/2 cup cake flour
5 egg yolks
3 tablespoons cold water
1/2 cup sugar
1/2 cup cake flour
1 tablespoon cornstarch
1 teaspoon baking powder
1/2 teaspoon vanilla or orange extract

Beat egg whites with salt in mixer bowl at low speed until frothy. Add cream of tartar and 1/2 teaspoon vanilla. Beat at medium speed until stiff peaks form; do not underbeat. Fold in 1/2 cup sugar and 1/2 cup cake flour gently. Set aside. Beat egg yolks in mixer bowl until light and lemon-colored. Add water and 1/2 cup sugar; beat well. Sift in mixture of 1/2 cup cake flour, cornstarch and baking powder; beat well. Stir in 1/2 teaspoon vanilla. Spoon yellow batter into tube pan. Spoon egg white batter over top. Bake at 325 degrees for 50 minutes. Invert onto funnel to cool completely. Loosen cake from side of pan. Invert onto cake plate.
Yield: 12 to 16 servings.

Arlene Waltz, Lycova #2006

Apple Dapple Cake

1 1/2 cups oil
2 cups sugar
3 eggs
3 cups flour
1 teaspoon baking soda
1/2 teaspoon salt
2 teaspoons vanilla extract
3 cups chopped peeled yellow Delicious apples
1 cup flaked coconut
1 cup chopped walnuts
1 cup packed brown sugar
1/2 cup butter
1/2 cup milk

Combine oil, sugar, eggs, flour, baking soda, salt and vanilla in bowl in order listed, mixing well after each addition. Stir in apples, coconut and walnuts. Spoon into greased 10-inch tube pan. Bake at 325 degrees for 1 1/2 hours. Combine brown sugar, butter and milk in saucepan. Bring to a boil. Cook for 2 minutes. Pour over hot cake. Let cake stand until cooled completely. **Yield: 16 servings.**

Matilda Trumbull, Valley #1420

The most convenient way to measure 1/2 cup shortening is to place small dollops of shortening in 1/2 cup water. When water level reaches 1 cup, the shortening measurement below the water level is 1/2 cup.

Apple-Date-Nut Cake

1 1/2 cups flour
2 teaspoons baking cocoa
1 teaspoon baking soda
1 teaspoon cinnamon
1/2 teaspoon ground cloves
3 cups chopped peeled tart apples
1/2 cup chopped walnuts or pecans
1/2 cup chopped pitted dates
1/4 cup flour
1/2 cup butter, softened
1 cup sugar
2 eggs
1/2 cup cold coffee
1/4 cup butter
1/2 cup packed brown sugar
2 tablespoons milk
1 1/2 cups confectioners' sugar
1 teaspoon vanilla extract

Combine 1 1/2 cups flour, baking cocoa, baking soda, cinnamon and cloves in small bowl; mix well. Combine apples, walnuts, dates and 1/4 cup flour in bowl; toss. Cream 1/2 cup butter and sugar in mixer bowl until light and fluffy. Add eggs; mix well. Add flour mixture alternately with coffee, mixing well after each addition. Stir in apple mixture. Spoon into greased and floured 6 1/2-cup tube pan. Bake at 350 degrees for 55 to 60 minutes. Cool in pan for 15 minutes. Loosen cake from side of pan. Invert onto wire rack to cool completely. Melt 1/4 cup butter in small saucepan over medium heat. Add brown sugar. Cook for 2 minutes, stirring constantly. Stir in milk. Bring to a boil, stirring constantly. Remove from heat. Cool slightly. Beat in confectioners' sugar and vanilla until smooth. Spread frosting on cooled cake. May need to add additional milk to make frosting of desired spreading consistency.
Yield: 16 servings.

Marjorie Kennedy, Winfield #1105

Apple-Taffy Cake

1 2-layer package yellow cake mix
1 cup water
1/3 cup margarine, softened
4 eggs
3/4 cup graham cracker crumbs
1 1/2 teaspoons cinnamon
2 1/2 cups chopped peeled apples
3/4 cup packed brown sugar

Combine cake mix, water, margarine, eggs, graham cracker crumbs and cinnamon in large mixer bowl. Beat at low speed for 30 seconds. Beat at medium speed for 2 minutes. Fold in apples. Spoon into lightly greased 9x13-inch cake pan. Sprinkle with brown sugar. Bake at 350 degrees for 38 to 43 minutes on until cake tests done.
Yield: 15 servings.

Marie Elliott, Hookstown #1980

When baking cakes, place pans in center of oven, making sure they do not touch each other or sides of oven. Also, be sure they are not placed directly under each other as this will cut down heat circulation.

Butterscotch-Apple Cake

1 cup oil
2 eggs
2 cups sugar
2½ cups flour
1 teaspoon cinnamon
½ teaspoon salt
1 teaspoon baking soda
3 cups chopped apples
1 cup butterscotch chips

Combine oil, eggs and sugar in bowl. Mix with fork until smooth; do not use electric mixer. Add flour, cinnamon, salt and baking soda; mix well. Stir in apples. Spoon into ungreased 9x13-inch cake pan. Sprinkle butterscotch chips over batter. Bake at 350 degrees for 40 minutes. **Yield: 15 servings.**

Peggy Gordon, Fulton #66

Fresh Apple Cake

1¾ cups coarsely chopped peeled apples
1 cup sugar
1 egg
½ cup oil
1⅓ cups flour
1 teaspoon baking soda
1 teaspoon cinnamon
½ teaspoon nutmeg
½ teaspoon salt
½ cup raisins
½ cup chopped nuts

Combine apples and sugar in bowl; mix well. Let stand for 10 minutes. Add egg, oil, flour, baking soda, cinnamon, nutmeg and salt; mix well. Stir in raisins and nuts. Spoon into greased and floured 8x8-inch cake pan. Bake at 350 degrees for 50 to 55 minutes or until cake tests done. May double recipe to make 9x13-inch cake. **Yield: 9 servings.**

Lori Sindlinger and Shirley Schroer, New Vernon #608

Jewish Apple Cake

4 medium apples, sliced
1 tablespoon cinnamon
3 tablespoons sugar
3 cups flour
1 tablespoon baking powder
2 cups sugar
1 cup oil
¼ cup orange juice
4 eggs
2½ teaspoons vanilla extract

Combine apples, cinnamon and 3 tablespoons sugar in bowl; mix well. Sift flour, baking powder and 2 cups sugar into large bowl. Combine oil, orange juice, eggs and vanilla in medium bowl; mix well. Add to dry ingredients; mix well. Spoon half the batter into greased tube pan. Top with apple mixture. Spoon in remaining batter. Bake at 350 degrees for 1 hour and 25 minutes. **Yield: 16 servings.**

Helen M. Lawson, Shavers Creek #353

Applesauce Cake

2 cups flour
2 teaspoons baking soda
1 teaspoon ground cloves
1 teaspoon cinnamon
1/3 cup butter-flavored shortening
1 cup sugar
1 egg
1 cup applesauce
1 cup raisins, cooked

Sift flour, baking soda, cloves and cinnamon together. Cream shortening and sugar in mixer bowl until light and fluffy. Add egg; mix well. Add sifted ingredients and applesauce; mix well. Stir in raisins. Spoon into greased cake pan. Bake at 375 degrees for 45 minutes. **Yield: 12 servings.**

Charlotte Douthit, Hemlock #1341

Applesauce-Nut Cake

1 2-layer package yellow cake mix
1 4-ounce package vanilla instant pudding mix
1 1/2 cups applesauce
3 eggs or egg substitute
1/4 cup oil
3 tablespoons soy flour
1 teaspoon cinnamon
1/2 to 1 cup chopped nuts
1/2 to 1 cup raisins, cooked

Combine cake mix, pudding mix, applesauce, eggs, oil, soy flour, cinnamon, nuts and raisins in large bowl. Stir with a fork until moistened. Stir vigorously for 1 minute. Spoon batter into ungreased 9x13-inch cake pan, spreading evenly. Bake at 350 degrees for 35 to 40 minutes or until cake tests done. Cool in pan. **Yield: 12 servings.**

Beatrice Latimer, Warfordsburg #1889

Applesauce Fruitcakes

3 cups applesauce
2 cups sugar
1 cup margarine
1 16-ounce package candied red cherries, chopped
1 8-ounce package dates, chopped
1 8-ounce package candied yellow pineapple, chopped
4 cups coarsely chopped pecans
4 1/2 cups flour
1 tablespoon plus 1 teaspoon baking soda
1 teaspoon salt
2 1/2 teaspoons cinnamon
1 teaspoon ground nutmeg
1/2 teaspoon ground cloves

Combine applesauce, sugar and margarine in saucepan. Bring to a boil. Reduce heat to low. Simmer for 5 minutes, stirring constantly. Let stand until cool. Combine chopped fruit and pecans in bowl; mix well. Combine flour, baking soda, salt and spices in large bowl. Add applesauce mixture and fruit mixture; mix well. Fill small loaf cake pans 2/3 full. Bake at 350 degrees for 25 minutes or until loaves test done. Cool in pans for 10 minutes. Remove to wire rack to cool completely. Garnish with red and green cherries. **Yield: 4 to 6 miniature fruitcake loaves.**

Pauline Mains, Mifflin #1725

Banana Cake

1½ cups sugar
1 cup oil
2 eggs
2 cups mashed bananas
1 teaspoon vanilla extract
¾ cup sour milk
1 teaspoon baking soda
1 teaspoon baking powder
2 cups flour
Pinch of salt

Cream sugar and oil in bowl until light and fluffy. Add eggs; mix well. Add bananas, vanilla, milk, baking soda, baking powder, flour and salt; mix well. Spoon into tube pan. Bake at 375 degrees for 1 hour. **Yield: 12 to 16 servings.**

Josephine Smith, Reynoldsville #1825

Banana-Walnut Cake

⅔ cup mashed bananas
½ cup butter, softened
3 eggs
¾ cup water
2 cups unbleached flour
2 teaspoons baking powder
1 teaspoon baking soda
1 teaspoon cinnamon
1 cup chopped walnuts

Beat bananas and butter in mixer bowl until smooth. Add eggs and water; mix well. Add flour, baking powder, baking soda and cinnamon; mix well. Stir in walnuts. Spoon into oiled and floured 9x13-inch cake pan. Bake at 350 degrees for 20 minutes or until knife inserted near center comes out clean. Cool in pan. May substitute mixture of ½ cup walnuts and ½ cup raisins for 1 cup walnuts. **Yield: 8 to 10 servings.**

Arlene Adam, Virginville #1832

Banana-Raisin Cake

1 cup raisins
½ cup water
½ cup butter, softened
3 small bananas, mashed
2 eggs
½ teaspoon vanilla extract
2 cups flour
¼ cup dry milk powder
2 teaspoons baking powder
1 teaspoon baking soda
¼ teaspoon salt
2 teaspoons cinnamon
¼ teaspoon allspice
¼ teaspoon cloves
¼ cup finely chopped nuts

Cook raisins in water in saucepan until plump. Drain, reserving ¼ cup liquid. Combine raisins, reserved liquid, butter, bananas, eggs and vanilla in bowl; mix well. Add mixture of flour, dry milk powder, baking powder, baking soda, salt and spices; mix well. Stir in nuts. Pour into greased and floured 9x13-inch cake pan. Bake at 350 degrees for 30 to 40 minutes or until light brown. **Yield: 12 servings.**

Betty Beck, Reynoldsville #1825

Red Beet Cake

2 ounces unsweetened chocolate, melted
$1^{1}/_{2}$ cups puréed cooked beets
$1^{1}/_{2}$ cups sugar
1 cup oil
3 eggs
1 teaspoon vanilla extract
$1^{3}/_{4}$ cups flour
$^{1}/_{2}$ teaspoon salt
$1^{1}/_{2}$ teaspoon baking soda

Mix melted chocolate and beets in small bowl. Cream sugar, oil, eggs and vanilla in mixer bowl until light and fluffy. Add beet mixture; mix well. Add mixture of flour, salt and baking soda; mix well. Spoon into greased and floured 9x13-inch cake pan. Bake at 350 degrees for 20 to 25 minutes or until cake tests done. **Yield: 12 servings.**

May LeFavor, Virginville #1832

Better-than-Sex Cake

1 2-layer package German chocolate cake mix
7 ounces sweetened condensed milk
$^{3}/_{4}$ cup caramel ice cream sauce
8 ounces whipped topping
3 or 4 Heath bars, crushed

Prepare and bake cake mix using package directions for 9x13-inch cake pan. Pierce cooled cake with wooden spoon handle. Drizzle condensed milk and sauce over cake. Let stand for 1 hour. Cover with whipped topping. Sprinkle with candy. Chill until serving time. **Yield: 15 servings.**

Betty J. Pontius, Harmony #1112

Blueberry Tea Cake

3 cups fresh blueberries
$^{1}/_{4}$ cup sugar
1 cup flour
1 teaspoon baking powder
$^{1}/_{4}$ teaspoon salt
$^{1}/_{4}$ cup shortening
$^{1}/_{2}$ cup sugar
$^{1}/_{4}$ cup milk
2 teaspoons vanilla extract
2 egg whites, stiffly beaten

Mix blueberries and $^{1}/_{4}$ cup sugar in bowl. Spoon into greased cake pan. Sift flour, baking powder and salt together. Cream shortening in mixer bowl. Beat in $^{1}/_{2}$ cup sugar gradually. Add flour mixture and milk alternately to creamed mixture, beating well after each addition. Stir in vanilla. Fold in egg whites. Bake at 350 degrees for 1 hour and 15 minutes. Cool in pan for several minutes. Invert onto serving plate to cool completely. **Yield: 8 servings.**

Martha Fenstermaker, Red Brush Community #2085

Boston Cream Pie

1¹/4 cups cake flour
1 teaspoon baking powder
¹/2 teaspoon salt
3 egg yolks
¹/3 cup water
1 teaspoon grated lemon rind
¹/2 teaspoon vanilla extract
1 cup sugar
2 tablespoons lemon juice
3 egg whites, stiffly beaten
1 cup milk
2 tablespoons butter
¹/3 cup flour
¹/4 teaspoon salt
¹/3 cup sugar
¹/2 cup cold milk
2 egg yolks, slightly beaten
1 teaspoon vanilla extract
¹/2 ounce baking chocolate
¹/4 cup milk
1 tablespoon flour
¹/4 cup sugar
¹/8 teaspoon salt
1 teaspoon butter
¹/2 teaspoon vanilla extract

Sift cake flour, baking powder and ¹/2 teaspoon salt together. Combine 3 egg yolks, water, lemon rind and ¹/2 teaspoon vanilla in bowl; mix well. Stir in 1 cup sugar and lemon juice. Add flour mixture; mix well. Fold in egg whites. Pour into 2 greased and waxed paper-lined 8-inch round cake pans. Bake at 350 degrees for 25 to 30 minutes or until layers test done. Combine milk and 2 tablespoons butter in saucepan. Cook until heated through. Add ¹/3 cup flour, ¹/4 teaspoon salt and ¹/3 cup sugar; mix well. Stir in ¹/2 cup milk. Cook until thickened, stirring constantly. Stir a small amount of hot mixture into beaten egg yolks; stir egg yolks into hot mixture. Cook for 2 minutes, stirring constantly. Cool completely. Stir in 1 teaspoon vanilla. Spread between layers. Combine baking chocolate and ¹/4 cup milk in saucepan. Cook over low heat until chocolate is melted. Stir in mixture of 1 tablespoon flour, ¹/4 cup sugar and ¹/8 teaspoon salt. Cook until thickened and smooth, stirring constantly. Remove from heat. Beat in 1 teaspoon butter and ¹/2 teaspoon vanilla. Spread over top. **Yield: 12 servings.**

Jenny Nicklin, Hemlock #2051

Cold-Oven Butternut Cake

1 cup margarine, softened
¹/2 cup shortening
3 cups sugar
¹/4 teaspoon salt
1 tablespoon plus 2 teaspoons butternut extract
5 eggs
3 cups flour
1 cup milk
¹/2 to 1 cup broken nuts
¹/2 cup maraschino cherries, drained, floured

Cream margarine, shortening, sugar, salt and flavoring in mixer bowl until light and fluffy. Add eggs 1 at a time, beating well after each addition. Add flour alternately with milk, beginning and ending with flour. Beat well after each addition. Fold in nuts and maraschino cherries. Spoon into greased and floured tube pan. Place in cold oven. Turn oven to 325 degrees. Bake for 1 hour and 45 minutes. Invert immediately onto wire rack to cool completely. **Yield: 16 servings.**

Marie Bush, DuBois #808

Coconut-Carrot Cake

2 cups flour
$2\frac{1}{2}$ teaspoons baking soda
2 teaspoons cinnamon
1 teaspoon salt
1 cup oil
2 cups sugar
3 eggs
1 8-ounce can crushed juice-pack pineapple
2 cups grated carrots
$1\frac{1}{2}$ cups flaked coconut
$\frac{1}{2}$ cup chopped nuts

Mix flour, baking soda, cinnamon and salt in bowl. Beat oil, sugar and eggs in bowl. Add flour mixture; beat until smooth. Add pineapple, carrots, coconut and nuts; mix well. Pour into greased 9x13-inch cake pan. Bake at 350 degrees for 50 to 60 minutes or until cake tests done. Frost with cream cheese frosting. **Yield: 15 servings.**

James Hoffman, Perry Valley #1804

Peanutty Carrot Cake

$1\frac{1}{2}$ cups flour
$\frac{3}{4}$ cup sugar
$\frac{1}{2}$ cup packed light brown sugar
$1\frac{1}{4}$ teaspoons baking soda
2 teaspoons cinnamon
$\frac{1}{2}$ teaspoon salt
3 eggs
$\frac{3}{4}$ cup oil
$1\frac{1}{2}$ teaspoons vanilla extract
2 cups shredded carrots
2 cups peanut butter chips
$\frac{1}{2}$ cup chopped walnuts
Nutty Coconut Frosting

Mix flour, sugar, brown sugar, baking soda, cinnamon and salt in bowl. Combine eggs, oil and vanilla in large mixer bowl. Beat until smooth. Add flour mixture; mix well. Fold in carrots, peanut butter chips and walnuts. Spoon into 2 greased and floured 8-inch cake pans. Bake at 350 degrees for 30 to 35 minutes or until layers test done. Cool in pans for 10 minutes. Remove to wire rack to cool completely. Spread Nutty Coconut Frosting between layers and over top and side of cake.
Yield: 16 servings.

Nutty Coconut Frosting

1 5-ounce can evaporated milk
$\frac{2}{3}$ cup sugar
$\frac{1}{4}$ cup butter or margarine
1 egg, beaten
1 cup flaked coconut
$\frac{3}{4}$ cup chopped walnuts
$\frac{1}{2}$ teaspoon vanilla extract

Combine evaporated milk, sugar, butter and egg in saucepan. Bring to a boil over medium heat, stirring constantly. Boil for 2 minutes. Cool slightly. Stir in coconut, walnuts and vanilla. Let stand until cool, stirring occasionally.

Louise Price, Howard #297

Carrot Cake

2 cups sugar
4 eggs
1 cup oil
2 cups flour
1½ teaspoons baking soda
1 teaspoon cinnamon
3 cups shredded carrots

Beat sugar, eggs and oil in bowl until smooth. Add flour, baking soda and cinnamon; mix well. Stir in carrots. Spoon into greased 8x10-inch cake pan. Bake at 350 degrees for 1½ hours. **Yield: 8 to 10 servings.**

Almeda Cape, Gideon #2010

14-Karat Cake

2 cups flour
2 teaspoons baking powder
2 teaspoons cinnamon
1½ teaspoons baking soda
2 cups sugar
1 to 1½ cups oil
4 eggs
1 8-ounce can crushed pineapple, drained
2 cups shredded carrots
1 3-ounce can flaked coconut
1 cup chopped English walnuts
½ cup margarine, softened
8 ounces cream cheese
1 1-pound package confectioners' sugar
1 teaspoon vanilla extract
Milk

Sift flour, baking powder, cinnamon and baking soda into bowl. Add sugar, oil and eggs; mix well. Stir in next 4 ingredients. Spoon into greased 9x13-inch cake pan. Bake at 350 degrees for 35 minutes or until cake tests done. Cool in pan. Cream margarine with next 3 ingredients in bowl until light and fluffy. Add a small amount of milk if needed to make of spreading consistency. Spread over cooled cake. **Yield: 12 servings**

Betty Wilson, Shermanata #1796

Cherry Chiffon Cake

7 to 8 egg whites
½ teaspoon cream of tartar
2 cups flour
1½ cups sugar
1 tablespoon baking powder
1 teaspoon salt
½ cup oil
7 egg yolks
¼ cup maraschino cherry juice
½ cup cold water
1 teaspoon vanilla extract
½ cup maraschino cherries, patted dry
½ cup finely chopped nuts

Beat egg whites in mixer bowl at low speed until frothy. Add cream of tartar. Beat until stiff peaks form; do not underbeat. Add next 9 ingredients in order listed in bowl, mixing at medium speed after each addition. Fold into beaten egg whites. Fold in cherries and nuts. Spoon into lightly greased 10-inch tube pan. Bake at 350 degrees for 45 minutes. Cool on wire rack. **Yield: 16 servings.**

Trudy Wigton, Pleasant Hill #1505

Custard-Chiffon Cake

3/4 cup scalded milk
7 egg yolks, slightly beaten
2 cups sifted flour
1 1/2 cups sugar
1 tablespoon baking powder
1 teaspoon salt
1/2 cup oil
2 teaspoons vanilla
1 cup flaked coconut
1 cup egg whites
1/2 teaspoon cream of tartar

Stir a small amount of scalded milk into beaten egg yolks. Stir egg yolks into scalded milk. Let stand until cool. Sift flour, sugar, baking powder and salt into large mixer bowl. Make well in center. Add oil, vanilla and egg yolk mixture. Beat at medium speed until smooth. Stir in coconut. Set aside. Beat egg whites with cream of tartar at medium speed in mixer bowl until stiff; do not underbeat. Fold in egg yolk mixture. Spoon into ungreased tube pan. Bake at 325 degrees for 55 minutes. Increase temperature to 350 degrees. Bake for 10 minutes or until cake tests done. Invert onto funnel to cool. Loosen cake from side of pan. Invert onto cake plate. **Yield: 12 to 16 servings.**

Marlene Sattazahn, Marion #1853

Chocolate-Chocolate-Chocolate Cake

3 to 4 teaspoons cocoa mix
1/2 cup butter, softened
4 ounces cream cheese, softened
1 1/4 cups sugar
2 eggs
1 teaspoon vanilla extract
3 cups flour
2 teaspoons baking soda
1 teaspoon salt
2 cups milk
4 ounces unsweetened chocolate, melted
1 cup chocolate chips
Creamy Chocolate Frosting

Grease three 8-inch round cake pans; dust with cocoa mix. Cream butter, cream cheese and sugar in mixer bowl for 5 minutes or until light and fluffy. Beat in eggs 1 at a time. Add vanilla. Add mixture of flour, baking soda and salt alternately with milk, mixing well after each addition. Add melted chocolate; mix well. Layer half the batter, chocolate chips and remaining batter in prepared pans. Bake at 350 degrees for 20 to 25 minutes or until layers test done. Cool in pans for 10 minutes. Remove to wire rack to cool completely. Frost with Creamy Chocolate Frosting. **Yield: 12 to 15 servings.**

Creamy Chocolate Frosting

1 cup chocolate chips
1 tablespoon oil
4 ounces cream cheese, softened
1/3 cup butter, softened
4 cups sifted confectioners' sugar
1 teaspoon vanilla extract
1 egg
1 tablespoon milk

Melt chocolate chips with oil in saucepan over low heat. Beat cream cheese and butter in mixer bowl until light and fluffy. Beat in confectioners' sugar and vanilla gradually. Blend in chocolate and egg. Add milk 1 teaspoon at a time until of spreading consistency.

Mary Kaye Shutt, Hookstown #1980

Chocolate-Cherry Cake

1 2-layer package fudge cake mix
1 21-ounce can cherry pie filling
2 eggs, well beaten
1 teaspoon almond extract
1 cup sugar
1/3 cup milk
5 tablespoons butter or margarine
1 cup semisweet chocolate chips

Combine cake mix, pie filling, eggs and flavoring in bowl; mix well. Spoon into greased 9x13-inch cake pan. Bake at 350 degrees for 30 minutes or until cake tests done. Combine sugar, milk and butter in saucepan. Bring to a boil over medium heat, stirring constantly. Boil for 2 minutes. Remove from heat. Stir in chocolate chips until melted. Pour over hot cake. **Yield: 15 to 20 servings.**

Joyce Ross, Harmony #1112

Chocolate-Macaroon Cake

1/2 cup baking cocoa
3/4 cup hot coffee
1 1/4 cups sugar
1/2 cup margarine, softened
3 egg yolks
1 teaspoon salt
1 teaspoon vanilla extract
2 cups sifted flour
1 teaspoon baking soda
1/2 cup sour milk
3 egg whites
1/2 cup sugar
1 egg white
1 teaspoon vanilla extract
1/2 cup sugar
2 cups flaked coconut
1 tablespoon flour

Dissolve baking cocoa in coffee in small bowl. Cream 1 1/4 cups sugar, 1/2 cup margarine, egg yolks, salt, 1 teaspoon vanilla and half the coffee mixture in medium mixer bowl until light and fluffy. Add 2 cups sifted flour, mixture of baking soda and sour milk and remaining coffee mixture to chocolate mixture, stirring well. Beat 3 egg whites in mixer bowl until soft peaks form. Add 1/2 cup sugar gradually, beating until stiff peaks form. Fold into chocolate mixture. Spoon 1/3 of chocolate mixture into greased 10-inch tube pan. Beat 1 egg white with 1 teaspoon vanilla in mixer bowl until soft peaks form. Add 1/2 cup sugar gradually, beating until stiff peaks form. Fold in 2 cups coconut and 1 tablespoon flour. Layer coconut mixture and remaining chocolate mixture in tube pan, 1/2 at a time, ending with chocolate mixture. Bake at 350 degrees for 55 to 65 minutes or until top is brown and dry. Invert onto funnel to cool completely. Loosen cake from side of pan. Invert onto cake plate. **Yield: 16 servings.**

Marilyn Davidson, Bald Eagle #1390

Add 1/2 cup mayonnaise to any 2-layer cake mix for moistness.

Low-Cholesterol Chocolate Cake

5 tablespoons baking cocoa
2 tablespoons margarine
1 cup sugar
3/4 cup packed brown sugar
1/2 cup margarine, softened
5 egg whites
1 teaspoon vanilla extract
1 teaspoon baking soda
1 cup buttermilk
2 cups plus 1 teaspoon cake flour

Heat baking cocoa and 2 tablespoons margarine in saucepan over medium heat until margarine melts, stirring constantly. Cream sugars and 1/2 cup margarine in mixer bowl until light and fluffy. Add chocolate mixture, egg whites and vanilla, beating constantly. Dissolve baking soda in buttermilk in small bowl. Add to creamed mixture alternately with flour, beating well after each addition. Pour into greased 9x13-inch cake pan. Bake at 350 degrees for 35 minutes or until cake tests done. Cool in pan for 5 minutes. Remove to wire rack to cool completely. **Yield: 12 to 15 servings.**

Dorothy Lyon, Cameron County #2081

Deep-Dark Chocolate Cakes

1 3/4 cups flour
2 cups sugar
1 1/2 teaspoons baking soda
1 1/2 teaspoons baking powder
3/4 cup baking cocoa
1 teaspoon salt
2 eggs, beaten
1 cup milk
1/2 cup oil
2 teaspoons vanilla extract
1 cup boiling water

Combine first 6 ingredients in large mixer bowl. Add eggs, milk, oil and vanilla. Beat at medium speed for 2 minutes. Add boiling water stirring until smooth. Pour into 2 greased and floured 9-inch round cake pans or three 8-inch round cake pans. Bake at 350 degrees for 30 to 35 minutes or until cakes test done. Cool in pans for 10 minutes. Remove to wire rack to cool completely. **Yield: 12 servings.**

Sandra Dunn, Pleasant Valley #1074

Eggless Chocolate Cake

1/2 cup shortening
1 1/2 cups sugar
2 teaspoons baking soda
1/2 cup hot water
3 tablespoons (heaping) baking cocoa
Salt to taste
3 cups flour
1 1/2 cups sour milk
1 teaspoon vanilla extract

Cream shortening and sugar in mixer bowl until light and fluffy. Dissolve baking soda in hot water. Add to creamed mixture. Sift baking cocoa, salt and flour together. Add to creamed mixture alternately with milk and vanilla, beating well after each addition. Pour into greased and floured 9x13-inch cake pan. Bake at 350 degrees for 30 minutes or until cake tests done. Cool in pan for 5 minutes. Remove to wire rack to cool completely. **Yield: 20 servings.**

Wandamae Lehner, Bald Eagle #1390

Ho-Ho Cake

1 2-layer package chocolate cake mix
5 tablespoons flour
1 1/4 cups milk
1/2 cup shortening
1/2 cup margarine, softened
1 cup sugar
1 teaspoon vanilla extract
3 1-ounce packets liquid chocolate
2 1/2 tablespoons hot water
1 egg, beaten
1/2 cup margarine, softened
1 teaspoon vanilla extract
3 cups confectioners' sugar

Prepare cake mix using package directions. Pour into 10x15-inch cake pan. Bake at 350 degrees for 20 minutes; cool. Combine flour and milk in saucepan. Cook over medium heat until thickened, stirring constantly; cool. Cream shortening, 1/2 cup margarine, sugar and 1 teaspoon vanilla in mixer bowl until light and fluffy. Add flour mixture, beating until creamy. Spread over cooled cake. Beat liquid chocolate, hot water, egg, 1/2 cup margarine, 1 teaspoon vanilla and confectioners' sugar in mixer bowl until smooth. Spread over top layer. Chill in refrigerator; cut into squares to serve. **Yield: 15 servings.**

Margaret Schwoegl, Mt. Nebo #1872

Wet Chocolate Cake with Buttercream Frosting

2 cups flour
2 cups sugar
3/4 cup baking cocoa
1 teaspoon baking powder
2 teaspoons baking soda
1 cup milk
1 cup boiling water
1 teaspoon vanilla extract
2 eggs, beaten
1/2 cup melted shortening
1/2 cup shortening
1/2 cup butter or margarine, softened
4 cups sifted confectioners' sugar
2 tablespoons milk or water
1 teaspoon vanilla extract

Combine flour, sugar, baking cocoa, baking powder and baking soda in large mixer bowl. Add milk, boiling water, 1 teaspoon vanilla, eggs and melted shortening. Beat at medium speed until smooth. Pour into greased and floured cake pans. Bake at 325 degrees for 25 to 30 minutes or until layers test done. Cool in pans for 5 minutes; remove to wire rack to cool completely. Cream 1/2 cup shortening and butter in mixer bowl until light and fluffy. Add confectioners' sugar, milk and 1 teaspoon vanilla. Beat until creamy. May add additional milk for desired consistency. Spread frosting between layers and over top and side of cooled cake. **Yield: 12 servings.**

Tara Dougherty, Central #1650

The top layer of a layer cake will not slip as you ice it if you hold it in place with a wire cake-tester or thin skewers inserted through all layers. Remove the tester just before completing the job.

Fresh Coconut Sponge Cake

4 egg whites
Dash of salt
1 cup sugar
4 egg yolks
1 cup sugar
2 cups cake flour
2 teaspoons baking powder
1 cup boiling water

Beat egg whites with salt in mixer bowl until soft peaks form. Sift in 1 cup sugar, beating until stiff peaks form. Add egg yolks, beating well. Sift in remaining 1 cup sugar, beating continuously. Sift in flour and baking powder, stirring well. Add hot water gradually, beating well. Pour into 10-inch tube pan. Bake at 325 degrees for 45 to 60 minutes or until top of layer is brown and dry. Invert onto funnel to cool completely. Loosen cake from side of pan. Invert onto cake plate. Spread with white seven-minute frosting; sprinkle with coconut. **Yield: 12 servings.**

Shirley J. Smith, Pine Run #250

Yellow Coconut Cake

1 2-layer package yellow cake mix
3 eggs, beaten
1 1/3 cups water
1/3 cup oil
1 cup flaked coconut
8 ounces whipped topping
1/2 cup flaked coconut
Crushed pecans

Combine cake mix, eggs, water and oil in large mixer bowl. Beat at low speed until moistened. Beat at medium speed for 2 minutes longer. Stir in 1 cup coconut. Pour into greased and floured 9x13-inch cake pan. Bake at 350 degrees for 35 to 38 minutes or until cake tests done; cool. Mix whipped topping with 1/2 cup coconut. Spread over cooled cake; sprinkle with pecans. **Yield: 15 servings.**

Mary Horburger, Roaring Creek Valley #2041

Fruited Coconut Cake

1 2-layer package yellow cake mix
1 4-ounce package lemon instant pudding mix
4 eggs, beaten
1/4 cup oil
1 cup flaked coconut
1 16-ounce can fruit cocktail
1/2 cup packed brown sugar
1/2 cup chopped nuts

Combine cake mix, pudding mix, eggs, oil, coconut and undrained fruit cocktail in mixer bowl. Beat at medium speed for 4 minutes. Pour into greased and floured 9x13-inch cake pan. Sprinkle with brown sugar and nuts. Bake at 325 degrees for 45 minutes or until cake tests done. Cool in pan; cut into serving portions. **Yield: 15 servings.**

Geraldine Steninger, Tuscarora Valley #2042

Cinnamon Crumb Cake

3 cups sugar
4 cups sifted flour
1 cup shortening
2 cups buttermilk
2 eggs, beaten
2 teaspoons cinnamon
1 teaspoon baking soda
1 teaspoon baking powder

Combine sugar and flour in large bowl. Cut in shortening with pastry blender until mixture is crumbly. Reserve 1 cup crumbs for topping. Add 2 cups buttermilk, eggs, cinnamon, baking soda and baking powder to remaining mixture, stirring well. Pour into greased and floured 9x13-inch cake pan. Sprinkle with reserved crumbs. Bake at 350 degrees for 45 minutes or until cake tests done; cool. **Yield: 15 servings.**

Iva Trone, Gideon #2010

Cowboy Crumb Cakes

2 1/2 cups flour
1/2 teaspoon salt
2 cups packed brown sugar
2/3 cup shortening
1/2 teaspoon nutmeg
1/2 teaspoon cinnamon
1/2 teaspoon baking soda
2 teaspoons baking powder
2 eggs, beaten
1 cup sour milk

Combine flour, salt and brown sugar in large bowl. Cut in shortening with pastry blender until mixture is crumbly. Reserve 1/2 cup crumbs for topping. Add nutmeg, cinnamon, baking soda and baking powder; mix well. Beat eggs with sour milk in small bowl. Pour into mixture, stirring until smooth. Pour into 2 greased cake pans. Sprinkle with reserved crumb mixture. Bake at 350 degrees for 20 minutes or until cakes test done; cool. **Yield: 12 to 15 servings.**

Hilda Riedy, Harmony #1692

Molasses Crumb Cake

3 cups flour
1 cup sugar
1/2 cup butter, softened
1 teaspoon baking soda
1 cup baking molasses
1 cup cold water

Combine flour and sugar in bowl. Cut in butter with pastry blender until mixture is crumbly. Reserve 1/2 cup crumbs for topping. Dissolve baking soda in small amount of hot water in bowl. Combine with molasses and 1 cup cold water in small bowl; mix well. Pour into crumb mixture, stirring well. Pour into greased cake pan. Top with reserved crumbs. Bake at 350 degrees for 50 minutes or until cake tests done; cool. **Yield: 15 servings.**

Myrtle M. Schwartz, Harmony #1692

Blue Ribbon Date Brownie Cake

1 cup chopped dates
1 1/4 cups cold water
1 teaspoon baking soda
3/4 cup margarine
2/3 cup fructose sweetener
2 eggs, beaten
1/2 teaspoon salt
1 1/2 cups flour
2 tablespoons baking cocoa
3 tablespoons fructose sweetener
1 cup semisweet chocolate chips
1/2 cup chopped nuts

Combine dates, water and baking soda in saucepan. Bring to a boil; cool. Cream margarine and 2/3 cup fructose in mixer bowl until light and fluffy. Add eggs, salt, flour and baking cocoa, beating well. Stir in date mixture. Pour into greased and floured 9x13-inch cake pan. Sprinkle with 3 tablespoons fructose, chocolate chips and nuts. Bake at 350 degrees for 30 to 35 minutes or until cake tests done. Cool and cut into squares. **Yield: 15 servings.**

Elsie R. Taydus, New London #1151

Fairy Food Cake

4 egg yolks
7 tablespoons cold water
1 1/2 cups sugar
1 1/2 cups sifted flour
1/4 teaspoon salt
1 teaspoon vanilla extract
4 egg whites

Beat egg yolks and cold water in mixer bowl for 5 minutes. Add sugar, beating for 5 minutes longer. Sift flour and salt 3 times. Add to egg mixture with vanilla, beating for 5 minutes longer. Beat egg whites in separate mixer bowl until stiff peaks form. Fold into batter. Spoon into ungreased tube pan. Bake at 375 degrees for 45 to 60 minutes, or until top is brown and dry. Invert onto funnel to cool completely. Loosen cake from side of pan. Invert onto cake plate. **Yield: 16 servings.**

Dorothy A. Rabert, Schnecksville #1684

Fast-Fixing Fruit 'n Cake

1/4 cup oil
1 2-layer package white or yellow cake mix
2 eggs, beaten
1/2 cup water
1 21-ounce can fruit pie filling

Pour oil into 9x13-inch cake pan, turning pan to coat sides and bottom. Add cake mix, eggs and water to pan, stirring for 2 minutes with fork to mix. Spoon pie filling onto batter, swirling with fork for marbleized effect. Bake at 350 degrees for 35 to 45 minutes or until cake tests done. Cool and cut into serving portions.
Yield: 12 servings.

Tiffany Paden, Westfield Junior #1514

Fruitcake

1 cup margarine
2 cups packed brown sugar
4 eggs, beaten
1 cup dark corn syrup
1 cup coffee
3 cups flour
1 teaspoon baking soda
2 teaspoons cinnamon
1 teaspoon nutmeg
$1^1/_2$ pounds mixed candied fruit
1 pound raisins
1 pound chopped nuts
1 cup flour

Cream margarine and brown sugar in mixer bowl until light and fluffy. Add eggs, corn syrup and coffee, beating well. Sift 3 cups flour, baking soda, cinnamon and nutmeg together. Stir into creamed mixture. Toss candied fruit, raisins and nuts with 1 cup flour to coat. Stir into batter. Grease large bundt pan; line with greased brown paper. Pour in batter. Bake at 250 degrees for 4 hours. Remove to wire racks to cool completely. Wrap cooled cake in clean cloth soaked in wine. Store in covered container for 1 week. Remove cloth; decorate as desired. Wrap with plastic wrap and store in cool place or freezer. May also bake in 6 small cake pans for $2^1/_2$ hours each. **Yield: 1 (6-pound) cake or 6 (1-pound) cakes.**

Helen Sipe, Milford #1744

Hickory Nut Cake

$1^1/_2$ cups sugar
$^1/_2$ cup butter, softened
$^3/_4$ cup milk
2 cups flour
2 teaspoons baking powder
4 egg whites
1 cup chopped hickory nuts

Cream sugar and butter in mixer bowl until light and fluffy. Add milk alternately with flour and baking soda, beating well after each addition. Beat egg whites in small mixer bowl until stiff peaks form. Fold into batter with chopped hickory nuts. Pour into greased and floured 8x8-inch cake pan. Bake at 350 degrees for 30 minutes. **Yield: 8 servings.**

Florence D. Houseknecht, Canusarago #27

Holiday fruitcakes can be stored indefinitely. Wrap them in cloths soaked with fruit juice and then in foil. Store in an airtight container in a cool place.

Hummingbird Cake

3 eggs
2 cups sugar
$1\frac{1}{2}$ cups oil
3 cups flour
1 teaspoon salt
1 teaspoon cinnamon
$1\frac{1}{2}$ teaspoons baking soda
1 cup crushed pineapple
2 cups mashed bananas
1 cup crushed nuts

Beat eggs, sugar and oil in mixer bowl until light and fluffy. Add flour, salt, cinnamon and baking soda, beating until smooth. Stir in pineapple with juice, bananas and nuts. Pour into greased tube pan. Bake at 350 degrees for 1 hour. Cool in pan for several minutes; invert onto wire rack to cool completely. **Yield: 16 servings.**

Stella Kollar, Bloomingdale #536

Italian Love Cake

1 2-layer package marble cake mix
2 pounds ricotta cheese
$\frac{3}{4}$ cup sugar
4 eggs
1 teaspoon vanilla extract
1 4-ounce package chocolate instant pudding mix
1 cup milk
8 ounces whipped topping

Prepare cake mix as directed. Pour into greased 11x13-inch glass cake pan. Combine ricotta cheese, sugar, eggs and vanilla in mixer bowl. Beat until smooth. Pour over cake batter. Bake at 350 degrees for 1 hour. Cool in pan. Combine pudding mix and milk in bowl; mix well. Fold in whipped topping. Spread over cooled cake. Chill for 6 hours before serving. **Yield: 20 to 25 servings.**

Babe Hopkins, London Grove #63

Jam Cake

1 cup butter or margarine, softened
2 cups sugar
2 cups jam
$\frac{1}{2}$ cup sour cream
6 egg yolks, beaten
4 cups flour
2 teaspoons baking soda
1 teaspoon cinnamon
$\frac{1}{2}$ teaspoon salt
6 egg whites

Cream butter and sugar in mixer bowl until light and fluffy. Add jam, sour cream and egg yolks, beating well. Sift flour, baking soda, cinnamon and salt together. Stir into creamed mixture until smooth. Beat egg whites in separate mixer bowl until stiff peaks form. Fold into batter. Pour into 2 greased 10-inch round cake pans. Bake at 350 degrees for 30 to 35 minutes or until cake tests done. Cool in pans for several minutes. Remove to wire racks to cool completely. Spread favorite frosting over tops and side of cooled cake. **Yield: 16 servings.**

William E. Gager, Unity #1710

Quick Lunchbox Cake

$2^1/_4$ cups flour
2 teaspoons baking soda
1 teaspoon salt
1 cup packed brown sugar
2 eggs
$^1/_4$ cup butter, softened
1 16-ounce can fruit cocktail
$^1/_2$ cup semisweet chocolate chips
$^1/_2$ cup chopped nuts

Combine flour, baking soda, salt, brown sugar, eggs and butter in mixer bowl. Beat at low speed until blended. Beat at medium speed for 2 minutes. Stir in undrained fruit cocktail. Pour into greased and floured 9x13-inch cake pan. Sprinkle chocolate chips and nuts over top. Bake at 350 degrees for 35 to 40 minutes or until golden brown. Cool; cut into squares to serve. **Yield: 12 servings.**

Edith Patton, Boot Jack #1680

Special Maple Cake

$1^1/_2$ cups sugar
$^1/_2$ cup margarine, softened
3 egg yolks
1 cup warm milk
$2^1/_2$ cups flour
$^3/_4$ cup maple syrup
2 teaspoons baking powder
2 teaspoons vanilla extract
3 egg whites
$^1/_2$ cup maple syrup
3 tablespoons margarine
1 1-pound package confectioners' sugar
4 to 5 tablespoons milk
1 tablespoon vanilla extract

Cream sugar, $^1/_2$ cup margarine and egg yolks in mixer bowl until light and fluffy. Add milk and 2 cups flour alternately, beating well after each addition. Beat for 2 minutes longer. Add remaining $^1/_2$ cup flour, $^3/_4$ cup maple syrup, baking powder and 2 teaspoons vanilla; mix well. Beat egg whites in separate mixer bowl until stiff peaks form. Fold into batter. Pour into 2 greased and floured 9-inch cake pans. Bake at 350 degrees for 25 minutes or until layers test done. Remove to wire rack to cool. Combine $^1/_2$ cup maple syrup and 3 tablespoons margarine in saucepan. Bring to a boil. Cook for 3 minutes, stirring constantly; cool. Add confectioners' sugar, milk and vanilla alternately, beating well after each addition. Continue beating until of desired consistency. Spread frosting between layers and over top and side of cooled cake. May bake in 9x13-inch cake pan for 30 to 35 minutes. **Yield: 15 servings.**

Margaret Ackerman, Friendship #2093

For an easy orange frosting, use vanilla frosting mix, substituting orange juice for water and adding grated orange rind.

Mardi Gras Party Cake

1¼ cups sugar
½ cup shortening
3 eggs
⅔ cup butterscotch chips
¼ cup water
2¼ cups sifted flour
1 teaspoon salt
1 teaspoon baking soda
½ teaspoon baking powder
1 cup buttermilk
Butterscotch Filling
Sea Foam Frosting

Cream sugar and shortening in mixer bowl until light and fluffy. Add eggs 1 at a time, beating well after each addition. Combine butterscotch chips and water in saucepan. Heat until butterscotch is melted, stirring frequently; cool. Stir into creamed mixture. Sift together flour, salt, baking soda and baking powder. Add to creamed mixture alternately with buttermilk, beating well after each addition. Pour into 2 greased and floured 9-inch cake pans. Bake at 375 degrees for 25 to 30 minutes or until layers test done. Remove to wire rack to cool. Spread Butterscotch Filling on top of each layer to within ½ inch of edge. Frost side and top with Sea Foam Frosting. **Yield: 12 servings.**

Butterscotch Filling

⅓ cup sugar
1 tablespoon cornstarch
½ cup evaporated milk
⅓ cup water
⅓ cup butterscotch chips
1 egg yolk, beaten
2 tablespoons butter
1 cup flaked coconut
1 cup chopped pecans or walnuts

Combine sugar and cornstarch in 2-quart saucepan. Add evaporated milk, water, butterscotch chips and egg yolk; mix well. Cook over medium heat until thickened, stirring constantly; remove from heat. Stir in butter, coconut and pecans; cool.

Sea Foam Frosting

⅓ cup sugar
⅓ cup packed brown sugar
⅓ cup water
1 tablespoon corn syrup
1 egg white
¼ teaspoon cream of tartar

Combine sugar, brown sugar, water and corn syrup in saucepan. Cook over medium heat to 236 degrees on candy thermometer, soft-ball stage. Beat egg white in mixer bowl until soft peaks form. Add cream of tartar. Beat until stiff peaks form. Add syrup to egg white slowly, beating until of spreading consistency.

Ivie W. Blayney, Vernon #93

Add chopped dates, candied cherries and almonds to any white frosting to lend a holiday air to ordinary cakes.

Molasses Cake

4 cups flour
2 cups sugar
1 cup margarine, softened
2 cups boiling water
1 cup molasses
1 tablespoon baking soda

Combine flour and sugar in large bowl. Cut in margarine until mixture is crumbly. Set aside, reserving 1 cup crumb mixture for topping. Combine boiling water and molasses in large bowl. Add baking soda. Beat until mixture is foamy. Stir in crumb mixture. Pour into greased 9x13-inch cake pan. Top with reserved crumb mixture. Bake at 350 degrees for 40 minutes or until cake tests done. **Yield: 15 servings.**

Gladys Wohlbach, Harmony #1692

Mounds Cake

1 2-layer package dark chocolate fudge cake mix
1 cup milk
1 cup sugar
24 large marshmallows
1 14-ounce package flaked coconut
1 cup sugar
5 tablespoons butter
1/2 cup milk
2 cups semisweet chocolate chips

Prepare cake mix using package directions, baking in 9x13-inch cake pan. Combine 1 cup milk, 1 cup sugar, marshmallows and coconut in medium saucepan. Cook over medium heat until marshmallows are melted, stirring constantly. Spread hot mixture over warm cake. Combine 1 cup sugar, butter and 1/2 cup milk in small saucepan. Bring to a boil. Boil for 1 minute, stirring constantly. Remove from heat. Add chocolate chips, stirring until melted. Spread over coconut mixture. Cool cake completely before cutting. **Yield: 15 servings.**

Martha Ebersole, Community #1767

Orange Cake

4 egg yolks
1 1/2 cups sugar
1/2 cup orange juice
1 1/2 cups flour
1 teaspoon baking powder
1/4 teaspoon salt
4 egg whites

Beat egg yolks in mixer bowl until thick and lemon-colored. Add sugar and 2 tablespoons orange juice gradually, beating well. Sift together flour, baking powder and salt. Add to egg mixture alternately with remaining orange juice, beating well after each addition. Beat egg whites in small mixer bowl until stiff peaks form. Fold into batter. Pour into greased 12x14-inch cake pan. Bake at 350 degrees for 50 minutes or until cake tests done. **Yield: 12 to 16 servings.**

Pamela Long, Unity #1710

Orange Delight Cake

1 2-layer package yellow cake mix
4 eggs
3/4 cup oil
1 11-ounce can mandarin oranges
8 ounces whipped topping
1 8-ounce can crushed pineapple
1 4-ounce package vanilla instant pudding mix

Combine cake mix, eggs and oil in mixer bowl. Beat for 5 minutes. Fold in oranges and juice; mix well. Pour into greased and floured 9x13-inch cake pan. Bake at 350 degrees for 30 to 35 minutes or until cake tests done; cool. Combine whipped topping, crushed pineapple with juice and pudding mix in bowl; mix well. Spread over cooled cake. Let stand for 2 hours before serving. Store in refrigerator. **Yield: 15 servings.**

Lillie Belle Richards, Bald Eagle #1390

Peanut Butter Cake

1 2-layer package white or yellow cake mix
3 eggs
1 cup peanut butter
1 1/4 cups water

Combine cake mix, eggs, peanut butter and water in mixer bowl. Beat at low speed until moistened. Beat at high speed for 2 minutes longer. Pour into greased and floured 9x13-inch cake pan. Bake at 350 degrees for 30 minutes or until cake tests done; cool. Cut into squares to serve. **Yield: 15 servings.**

Dorothy A. Hammond, Charleston Valley #54

Peanut Butter Melt-Away Cake

1 cup margarine
1/4 cup baking cocoa
1 cup water
2 eggs, well beaten
1/2 cup buttermilk
2 cups sugar
2 cups flour
1 teaspoon vanilla extract
1 teaspoon (heaping) baking soda
1 teaspoon salt
1 1/2 cups peanut butter, melted
1/2 cup margarine
1/4 cup baking cocoa
3 cups confectioners' sugar
6 tablespoons buttermilk
1 teaspoon vanilla extract
1/2 cup peanut butter

Combine 1 cup margarine, 1/4 cup baking cocoa, water, eggs, and 1/2 cup buttermilk in saucepan; mix well. Bring to a slow boil, stirring frequently; remove from heat. Add sugar, flour, 1 teaspoon vanilla, baking soda and salt; beat well. Pour into greased and floured 9x13-inch cake pan. Bake at 350 degrees for 30 minutes; cool. Spread with 1 1/2 cups melted peanut butter. Chill until firm. Combine 1/2 cup margarine and 1/4 cup baking cocoa in saucepan. Bring to a boil. Add confectioners' sugar, 6 tablespoons buttermilk, 1 teaspoon vanilla and 1/2 cup peanut butter. Beat until smooth. Pour over cooled cake. Chill until serving time. **Yield: 18 servings.**

Donna McGary, Penn #534

Pineapple-Zucchini Cakes

2 cups sugar
1 cup oil
3 eggs
2 teaspoons vanilla extract
2 cups grated peeled zucchini
3 cups flour
1 teaspoon each baking powder, baking soda and salt
1 cup crushed pineapple, drained
1/2 cup raisins
1 cup chopped nuts

Cream sugar, oil, eggs and vanilla in mixer bowl until light and fluffy. Stir in zucchini. Sift together flour, baking powder, baking soda and salt. Add to creamed mixture. Stir in pineapple, raisins and nuts. Pour into 2 greased and floured loaf cake pans. Bake at 325 degrees for 1 hour. Cool before slicing. **Yield: 16 servings.**

Dorothy Jane Paul, Hillcrest #1674

Dietetic Pineapple Upside-Down Cake

1/4 cup margarine
2 tablespoons brown or white sugar substitute
1 8-ounce can juice-pack pineapple slices, drained
1 egg, beaten
1/4 cup margarine
2 packets sugar substitute
1/2 cup milk
3 tablespoons baking powder
2 cups sifted flour

Combine margarine and 2 tablespoons sugar substitute in saucepan. Heat until margarine is melted, stirring constantly. Pour mixture into 9-inch round cake pan. Layer with pineapple slices. Combine egg, margarine and 2 packets sugar substitute in bowl; mix well. Add milk, mixing thoroughly. Add baking powder and flour, stirring well. Pour over pineapple slices. Bake at 350 degrees for 30 to 35 minutes or until cake tests done. Invert onto serving plate. **Yield: 6 to 8 servings.**

Martha A. Milks, Bolivar Run #2060

Pineapple Upside-Down Cake

1/4 cup butter
1 cup packed brown sugar
1 8-ounce can pineapple slices
Maraschino cherries
3 egg yolks
1 cup sugar
5 tablespoons pineapple juice
1 cup flour
1 teaspoon baking powder
3 egg whites

Melt butter in 11-inch cast-iron skillet. Sprinkle with brown sugar. Drain pineapple, reserving 5 tablespoons juice. Arrange pineapple slices over brown sugar, placing cherry in center of each slice. Beat egg yolks, sugar, reserved pineapple juice, flour and baking powder in bowl until well mixed. Whip egg whites until stiff peaks form. Fold into batter. Pour over pineapple layer. Bake at 350 degrees for 30 to 35 minutes or until cake tests done. Invert onto serving plate. Serve with whipped cream. **Yield: 6 to 8 servings.**

Florence McElwain, Pleasant Hill #1505

Pink Lozenge Cake

30 Howe's pink lozenges
1 cup boiling water
2 1/2 cups flour
2 teaspoons baking powder
1/4 teaspoon salt
1 cup sugar
1/3 cup butter or margarine, softened
3 egg whites
1 teaspoon vanilla extract

Dissolve lozenges in boiling water in small bowl. Let stand overnight. Sift flour, baking powder and salt together. Cream sugar and butter in mixer bowl until light and fluffy. Add sifted dry ingredients alternately with lozenge syrup, beating well after each addition. Whip egg whites in mixer bowl until stiff peaks form. Fold into batter with vanilla. Pour into 2 greased and floured 9-inch cake pans. Bake at 350 degrees for 30 minutes or until layers test done. Frost with seven-minute or boiled frosting. This recipe is over 100 years old. May substitute 9x13-inch cake pan for two 9-inch cake pans. **Yield: 12 to 15 servings.**

Ethel Matheson, Montmorenci #1704

Buttercup Pound Cake

2 cups sifted cake flour
1/2 teaspoon salt
1 cup sugar
2 1/2 teaspoons baking powder
1/4 cup butter, softened
1/4 cup shortening
3/4 cup milk
5 egg yolks
1 teaspoon vanilla extract
1/4 teaspoon lemon extract

Sift flour, salt, sugar and baking powder together in mixer bowl. Add butter, shortening and milk. Beat at medium speed for 2 minutes or until smooth. Add egg yolks and vanilla and lemon extracts. Beat for 2 minutes. Grease and flour bottom of 9-inch tube pan. Pour in batter. Bake at 350 degrees for 40 to 50 minutes or until cake tests done. Cool on wire rack. Serve plain or with lemon butter frosting. **Yield: 16 servings.**

Mabel L. Kelly, East New Castle #1536

Hot Fudge Pudding Cake

1 cup flour
2 teaspoons baking powder
1/4 teaspoon salt
3/4 cup sugar
2 tablespoons baking cocoa
1/2 cup milk
2 tablespoons oil
1 teaspoon vanilla extract
1 cup chopped nuts
1 cup packed brown sugar
1/4 cup baking cocoa
2 cups hot water

Combine first 5 ingredients in bowl. Stir in milk, oil, vanilla and nuts. Pour into greased and floured 9x9-inch cake pan. Combine brown sugar and 1/4 cup baking cocoa in small bowl; sprinkle over batter. Pour hot water over all. Bake at 350 degrees for 45 minutes. Cool in pan for 5 to 10 minutes before serving. **Yield: 12 servings.**

Arlene Shaffer, Linesville #694

Lemon Pudding Cake

1 2-layer package yellow cake mix
1 4-ounce package lemon instant pudding mix
3/4 cup water
3/4 cup oil
4 eggs, beaten
2 tablespoons melted butter
2 tablespoons water
2 cups confectioners' sugar
1/3 cup orange juice

Combine cake mix, pudding mix, water, oil and eggs in large bowl; beat well. Pour into greased and floured 9x13-inch cake pan. Bake at 350 degrees for 30 to 35 minutes or until cake tests done. Prick top of cake several times with fork. Mix melted butter, water, confectioners' sugar and orange juice in small bowl until smooth. Pour over top of warm cake. **Yield: 12 to 15 servings.**

Dorothy Arnold, Plain Grove #1431

Pumpkin Cake

1 2-layer package yellow cake mix
2 eggs
1/4 cup water
2 teaspoons baking soda
1 15-ounce can pumpkin
2 teaspoons cinnamon
Confectioners' sugar

Combine cake mix, eggs, water, baking soda, pumpkin and cinnamon in mixer bowl. Beat at medium speed for 4 minutes. Pour into greased and floured bundt pan or 9x13-inch cake pan. Bake at 350 degrees for 40 to 45 minutes or until cake tests done. Cool in pan for 10 minutes. Remove to wire rack to cool completely. Sprinkle with confectioners' sugar. **Yield: 12 to 15 servings.**

Sharon Boyer, Hempfield #1958

Butterscotch-Rhubarb Upside-Down Cake

1 cup shortening
1 cup sugar
3 egg yolks
2 cups sifted flour
1 tablespoon baking powder
1/2 teaspoon salt
1/2 teaspoon vanilla extract
2/3 cup milk
3 egg whites
1 1/2 cups packed brown sugar
4 cups sliced rhubarb

Cream shortening and sugar in mixer bowl until light and fluffy. Add egg yolks, beating well. Sift flour, baking powder and salt together. Add sifted dry ingredients alternately with vanilla and milk to creamed mixture, beating well after each addition. Whip egg whites in small mixer bowl until stiff peaks form. Fold into batter. Sprinkle brown sugar evenly into greased 9x13-inch cake pan. Layer with rhubarb. Pour batter over rhubarb. Bake at 350 degrees for 45 minutes or until cake tests done. Cool in pan for 10 minutes. Invert onto serving plate. Serve with whipped cream. **Yield: 15 servings.**

Ada Riel, Chandlers Valley #846

Rhubarb Pudding Cake

1 cup sugar
1 egg
2 tablespoons melted butter or margarine
1 cup buttermilk
1/2 teaspoon salt
1/2 teaspoon baking soda
1 teaspoon baking powder
2 cups flour
1 cup fresh chopped rhubarb
1/2 cup sugar
2 tablespoons melted butter or margarine
1/2 to 1 cup sugar
1/2 cup butter or margarine
1/2 cup evaporated milk
1 teaspoon vanilla extract

Beat sugar, egg and 2 tablespoons melted butter in mixer bowl. Add buttermilk, beating until smooth. Combine salt, baking soda, baking powder and flour. Add to buttermilk mixture, stirring well. Stir in rhubarb. Pour into greased 9x9-inch cake pan. Combine 1/2 cup sugar with 2 tablespoons melted butter in small bowl. Sprinkle over batter. Bake at 350 degrees for 45 minutes or until cake tests done. Cool in pan for 5 minutes; remove to wire rack to cool completely. Combine 1/2 to 1 cup sugar, 1/2 cup butter and 1/2 cup evaporated milk in saucepan; mix well. Bring to a boil. Cook for 1 minute, stirring constantly. Remove from heat. Stir in vanilla. Spoon sauce over cake. **Yield: 12 servings.**

Damaris Irvin, Beech Creek #378

Upside-Down Rhubarb Cake

5 cups finely chopped rhubarb
1 3-ounce package strawberry gelatin
1 cup sugar
3 cups miniature marshmallows
1 2-layer package yellow cake mix

Spread rhubarb in nonstick 9x13-inch cake pan. Sprinkle with gelatin, sugar and marshmallows. Prepare cake mix using package directions. Pour batter over rhubarb mixture. Bake at 350 degrees for 30 minutes or until cake tests done. Cool in pan for 5 minutes. Invert onto serving plate. Serve with whipped cream. **Yield: 15 servings.**

Marian Hollabaugh, Brokenstraw #407

To adapt cake recipes to the microwave: add an extra egg and reduce liquid by about 2 tablespoons; reduce liquid by 1/4 to 1/3 if the recipe contains 3 or more eggs; increase shortening to 1/3 cup for each cup of flour.

Spanish Bar Cakes

4 cups water
2 cups raisins
1 cup shortening
2 cups sugar
2 teaspoons baking soda
4 cups flour
1 teaspoon ground cloves
1 teaspoon cinnamon
1 teaspoon nutmeg
1 teaspoon ground allspice
1/2 teaspoon salt
1 cup chopped walnuts
2 eggs, beaten

Combine water and raisins in saucepan. Bring to a boil. Cook for 10 minutes; remove from heat. Add shortening. Let stand to cool. Sift together sugar, baking soda, flour, cloves, cinnamon, nutmeg, allspice and salt in bowl. Add walnuts. Pour in raisin mixture, stirring well. Stir in eggs. Pour into 2 greased and floured 10x13-inch cake pans. Bake at 350 degrees for 35 minutes. Cool before cutting into squares. May frost with confectioners' sugar icing. **Yield: 15 servings.**

Elcy Blose, Schryock #1359

Roaring Twenties Spice Cake

1 cup sugar
1 cup raisins
1/2 cup shortening
1 teaspoon cinnamon
1 teaspoon nutmeg
1/2 teaspoon ground cloves
Dash of salt
1 1/2 cups water
1 teaspoon baking soda
1 tablespoon water
2 cups flour
1 teaspoon baking powder
1/2 cup sugar
2 tablespoons cornstarch
1 tablespoon butter or margarine
1 tablespoon lemon juice
1/4 teaspoon nutmeg
1 cup water

Combine sugar, raisins, shortening, cinnamon, nutmeg, cloves, salt and 1 1/2 cups water in large saucepan. Bring to a boil. Cook for 5 minutes, stirring frequently; remove from heat. Dissolve baking soda in 1 tablespoon water. Add to raisin mixture with flour and baking powder, stirring well. Pour into greased 8x8-inch cake pan. Bake at 350 degrees for 30 minutes or until cake tests done. Combine 1/2 cup sugar, cornstarch, butter, lemon juice, nutmeg and 1 cup water in saucepan. Cook over medium-low heat until thickened, stirring constantly. Serve over warm cake. **Yield: 9 servings.**

Dorothy E. Boytim, Bald Eagle #1390

Tomato Soup-Spice Cake

4 cups flour
1½ teaspoons baking soda
2 teaspoons cinnamon
1 teaspoon ground cloves
½ teaspoon nutmeg
1 cup butter or margarine
1 1-pound package light brown sugar
2 eggs, beaten
1 10-ounce can tomato soup
1 cup raisins
2 cups chopped walnuts

Combine flour, baking soda, cinnamon, cloves and nutmeg in bowl; set aside. Cream butter and brown sugar in mixer bowl until light and fluffy. Add eggs, beating well. Mix soup with enough water to measure 2 cups. Add to creamed mixture alternately with dry ingredients, beating at low speed after each addition. Fold in raisins and walnuts. Pour into greased and floured cake pans. Bake at 350 degrees for 60 minutes or until layers test done. Cool; frost with cream cheese frosting.
Yield: 12 to 15 servings.

Jean H. Hertzog, Pioneer #1777

Lemon Sponge Cake

1 cup sugar
Dash of salt
2 tablespoons flour
2 egg yolks
1 tablespoon butter, softened
Juice and grated rind of 1 lemon
2 egg whites

Combine sugar, salt, flour, egg yolks, butter, lemon juice and lemon rind in bowl, beating until smooth. Whip egg whites in mixer bowl until stiff peaks form. Fold into batter. Pour into tube pan. Bake at 350 degrees for 45 to 60 minutes or until top is brown and dry. Invert onto funnel to cool completely. Loosen cake from side of pan. Invert onto cake plate. **Yield: 16 servings.**

Blanche Smith, Star #993

Sponge Cake

8 egg whites
¾ teaspoon cream of tartar
1½ cups sugar
6 egg yolks
1 cup flour
2 tablespoons water
2 teaspoons vanilla extract

Beat egg whites in mixer bowl at low speed until frothy. Add cream of tartar. Beat at medium speed until soft peaks form. Add 1 cup sugar, 1 tablespoon at a time, beating constantly at high speed until stiff peaks form. Beat egg yolks in bowl with remaining ½ cup sugar until thick and lemon-colored. Stir in flour, water and vanilla, mixing well. Fold into egg whites. Spoon into 10-inch tube pan. Bake at 325 degrees for 1 hour or until top is brown and dry. Invert onto funnel to cool completely. Loosen cake from side of pan. Invert onto cake plate. **Yield: 16 servings.**

Alice E. Gilmore, Somerset #1697

Strawberry Shortcut Cake

1/2 package miniature marshmallows
1 1/2 cups sugar
1/2 cup butter, softened
1 cup milk
3 eggs
2 1/4 cups flour
1 tablespoon baking powder
1 teaspoon vanilla extract
2 10-ounce packages frozen strawberries, thawed

Spread marshmallows evenly in 9x13-inch nonstick cake pan. Cream sugar and butter in mixer bowl until light. Add milk and eggs, beating until fluffy. Stir in flour, baking powder and vanilla. Pour batter over marshmallows. Spread strawberries over top. Bake at 350 degrees for 45 to 60 minutes or until cake tests done. The strawberries sink and the marshmallows form a glaze on top. Serve with whipped cream or ice cream. **Yield: 12 to 15 servings.**

Ellen Stewart, Plain Grove #1431

Sour Cream Cake

3 ounces semisweet chocolate
1 cup boiling water
1 1/4 teaspoons baking soda
1/2 cup butter, softened
1 teaspoon vanilla extract
1 1/2 cups sugar
3 egg yolks
2 1/2 cups cake flour
1/2 teaspoon salt
1 cup sour cream
1 teaspoon red food coloring
3 egg whites
1/2 cup sugar

Combine chocolate and boiling water in small bowl, stirring until melted; cool. Add baking soda; set aside. Cream butter and vanilla in mixer bowl until light. Stir in 1 1/2 cups sugar, beating until fluffy. Add egg yolks, beating well. Sift flour and salt together. Add to creamed mixture alternately with sour cream, beating well after each addition. Stir in chocolate mixture and food coloring. Whip egg whites in mixer bowl until soft peaks form. Add 1/2 cup sugar gradually, beating constantly until stiff peaks form. Fold into batter. Pour into greased and floured 9x13-inch cake pan. Bake at 350 degrees for 40 to 45 minutes or until cake tests done. **Yield: 15 servings.**

Hazel Winegar, Big Beaver #1578

Swedish Layer Cakes

10 egg whites
1 teaspoon cream of tartar
2 cups sugar
1/2 cup baking cocoa
1 teaspoon vanilla extract
1 cup flour

Beat egg whites in mixer bowl until frothy. Add cream of tartar, sugar and baking cocoa, beating constantly at high speed until stiff peaks form. Add vanilla and fold in flour. Pour into 2 nonstick 9-inch cake pans. Bake at 350 degrees for 30 to 45 minutes or until cakes test done. **Yield: 12 servings.**

Anita Christman, Virginville #1832

Fresh Tomato Cake

1 2-layer package yellow cake mix
1 4-ounce package vanilla instant pudding mix
4 eggs, beaten
1/4 cup oil
1/2 cup golden raisins
1/2 cup chopped nuts
2 cups finely chopped green tomatoes

Combine cake mix and pudding mix in large bowl. Add eggs and oil, beating until smooth. Fold in raisins, nuts and tomatoes. Pour into greased and floured 9x13-inch cake pan. Bake at 350 degrees for 35 to 40 minutes or until cake tests done. Do not underbake. Cool in pan; sprinkle with confectioners' sugar. **Yield: 15 servings.**

Mary Syphrit, Brady #1218

Black Walnut Cakes

4 egg whites
1/4 teaspoon cream of tartar
1/2 cup shortening
1 1/2 cups sugar
1 teaspoon vanilla extract
1/2 teaspoon salt
2 1/4 cups sifted cake flour
3 1/2 teaspoons baking powder
1 cup milk
1 cup chopped black walnuts

Beat egg whites in mixer bowl until frothy. Add cream of tartar, beating until stiff peaks form; set aside. Cream shortening, sugar, vanilla and salt in bowl until light and fluffy. Add flour, baking powder, milk and walnuts; mix well. Fold in egg whites. Pour into greased and floured 9-inch cake pans. Bake at 350 degrees for 30 minutes or until cakes test done. Cool in pans for 5 minutes; remove to wire rack to cool completely. **Yield: 12 servings.**

Mary Reaser, Spring Garden #32

White Wacky Cake

2 cups sugar
3 cups flour
1/2 cup baking mix
2 teaspoons baking soda
1 teaspoon salt
2 cups water
3/4 cup oil
2 tablespoons white vinegar
2 teaspoons vanilla extract

Combine sugar, flour, baking mix, baking soda and salt in mixer bowl. Add water, oil, vinegar and vanilla. Beat at medium speed for 3 minutes. Pour into greased and floured 9x13-inch cake pan. Bake at 350 degrees for 35 to 40 minutes or until cake tests done. Cool in pan; cut into squares to serve. **Yield: 28 servings.**

Clare Richard, Fort Granville #1902

Yum-Yum Cake

2 cups sugar
2 cups crushed pineapple
3 eggs, beaten
2 cups flour
2 teaspoon baking soda
1 cup sugar
1/2 cup margarine
1 5-ounce can evaporated milk
1 cup chopped nuts
1 cup flaked coconut
1 teaspoon vanilla extract

Combine 2 cups sugar, pineapple, eggs, flour and baking soda in large bowl; mix well. Pour into greased and floured 9x13-inch cake pan. Bake at 350 degrees for 40 to 50 minutes or until cake tests done. Boil 1 cup sugar, margarine and evaporated milk in saucepan for 2 minutes, stirring constantly; remove from heat. Add nuts, coconut and vanilla, stirring well. Pour over warm cake. **Yield: 15 servings.**

Tenie Lockhart, Rural Valley #1750

Chocolate-Zucchini Cake

1/2 cup margarine
1/2 cup oil
3/4 cup sugar
2 eggs
1 teaspoon vanilla extract
2 1/2 cups flour, sifted
1 teaspoon baking soda
1/2 teaspoon baking powder
1/4 cup baking cocoa
1/2 teaspoon cinnamon
1/2 teaspoon ground cloves
1/2 cup sour milk
2 cups chopped zucchini
1/2 cup semisweet chocolate chips

Cream margarine, oil, sugar, eggs and vanilla in mixer bowl until light and fluffy. Combine flour, baking soda, baking powder, baking cocoa, cinnamon and cloves. Add to creamed mixture, beating well. Stir in sour milk and zucchini. Pour into greased and floured 9x12-inch cake pan. Sprinkle chocolate chips over top. Bake at 325 degrees for 45 minutes or until cake tests done. Cool in pan on rack. May omit chocolate chips and frost with mixture of 4 ounces cream cheese, 8 ounces confectioners' sugar, 1 teaspoon vanilla and 1/2 cup margarine. **Yield: 15 servings.**

Bertha McClure, Wilmington #1477

Split 2 chocolate cake layers and fill with mixture of 16 ounces whipped topping, 8 ounces softened cream cheese, 4 cups confectioners' sugar, 2 cups miniature chocolate chips and 1/2 cup nuts.

Zucchini Cake

2 cups flour
2 cups sugar
1 tablespoon cinnamon
2 teaspoons baking soda
1 teaspoon baking powder
1 teaspoon salt
1 cup oil
2 teaspoons vanilla extract
3 eggs, beaten
2 cups grated unpeeled zucchini
1 cup raisins
1½ cups chopped nuts

Combine flour, sugar, cinnamon, baking soda, baking powder, salt, oil, vanilla and eggs in large mixer bowl. Beat at medium speed until well mixed. Stir in zucchini, raisins and 1 cup nuts. Pour into greased and floured 9x13-inch cake pan. Sprinkle with remaining ½ cup nuts. Bake at 350 degrees for 50 minutes or until cake tests done. Cool in pan on rack. **Yield: 15 servings.**

Ada M. Peters, Alleghenyville #2065

Ice Cream Roll

3 egg whites
3 egg yolks
1 cup sugar
1 cup flour
Dash of salt
1 teaspoon baking powder
⅓ cup water
1 teaspoon vanilla extract
Confectioners' sugar
Ice cream

Beat egg whites in mixer bowl until stiff peaks form. Add egg yolks, 1 at a time, beating constantly. Add sugar gradually, beating well. Mix flour, salt and baking powder. Add flour mixture alternately with water and vanilla to egg mixture, beating well after each addition. Grease jelly roll pan; line with waxed paper. Pour batter onto pan. Bake at 350 degrees for 15 minutes. Invert onto clean towel sprinkled with confectioners' sugar; remove waxed paper. Roll up towel and cake. Let stand to cool for 1 hour. Unroll; fill with ice cream. Roll up to enclose filling. Dust with additional confectioners' sugar. Store in freezer. **Yield: 8 servings.**

Becky Michalka, Burgettstown #1502

Plump raisins quickly in the microwave. Microwave ½ cup raisins and 1 teaspoon water on High for 15 to 20 seconds and let stand for 1 minute.

Ice Cream Sundae Cake

3 egg whites
$^3/_4$ cup sugar
3 egg yolks
Juice of 1 lemon
$^3/_4$ cup sifted flour
1 teaspoon baking powder
$^1/_8$ teaspoon salt
Grated rind of $^1/_2$ lemon
Ice cream

Beat egg whites in mixer bowl until soft peaks form. Add sugar, beating constantly until stiff peaks form. Beat egg yolks in small bowl until thick and lemon-colored. Mix lemon juice with enough warm water to measure $^1/_4$ cup. Stir into egg yolks. Fold egg yolks into egg whites. Fold in flour, baking powder, salt and lemon rind. Pour into nonstick 7x10-inch cake pan. Bake at 350 degrees for 30 minutes or until cake tests done. Cool in pan. Spread with ice cream; top with fruit or sauce. **Yield: 8 to 10 servings.**

Mona Harmon, Reynoldsville #1825

Pumpkin Roll

3 eggs
1 cup sugar
$^2/_3$ cup cooked pumpkin
1 teaspoon lemon juice
$^3/_4$ cup flour
2 teaspoons cinnamon
1 teaspoon baking powder
1 teaspoon ginger
$^1/_2$ teaspoon nutmeg
$^1/_2$ teaspoon salt
Chopped nuts
$1^1/_2$ cups confectioners' sugar
6 ounces cream cheese, softened
$^1/_4$ cup margarine, softened
$^1/_2$ teaspoon vanilla extract

Beat eggs on high speed in mixer bowl for 5 minutes. Add sugar, pumpkin and lemon juice gradually, beating constantly. Combine flour, cinnamon, baking powder, ginger, nutmeg and salt together. Stir into pumpkin mixture. Spread over 10x15-inch jelly roll pan. Sprinkle with nuts. Bake at 375 degrees for 15 minutes; cool slightly. Turn out onto clean towel sprinkled with $^1/_2$ cup confectioners' sugar; roll up. Let stand until completely cool. Cream confectioners' sugar, cream cheese, margarine and vanilla in mixer bowl until creamy. Unroll cake; spread with cream cheese filling. Roll up; chill in refrigerator. **Yield: 8 servings.**

Beatrice Burns, Plum Creek Valley #1702

To prevent a soggy or heavy cake, be sure that layers, filling and frosting are completely cool before assembling cake.

White Cake Roll

3 eggs
1 cup sugar
5 tablespoons water
1 cup flour
1 teaspoon baking powder
1/4 teaspoon salt
1 teaspoon vanilla
2 tablespoons melted butter
Confectioners' sugar

Beat eggs in mixer bowl until frothy. Add sugar, beating until light. Add water, flour, baking powder, salt, vanilla and butter. Beat at low speed until smooth. Spread over greased jelly roll pan lined with waxed paper. Bake at 350 degrees for 15 minutes; cool slightly. Roll in clean towel sprinkled with confectioners' sugar. Let stand until completely cool. Unroll and fill with ice cream or whipped cream. Roll up; freeze. **Yield: 8 servings.**

Esther E. Adams, Roaring Creek Valley #2041

Chocolate Syrup Cupcakes

1/2 cup margarine, softened
1 cup sugar
1 teaspoon vanilla extract
4 eggs
1 1/4 cups flour
3/4 teaspoon baking soda
1 1/2 cups chocolate syrup

Cream margarine, sugar and vanilla in mixer bowl until light and fluffy. Add eggs 1 at a time, beating well after each addition. Combine flour and baking soda. Add to creamed mixture alternately with chocolate syrup. Pour into paper-lined cupcake cups filling 1/2 full. Bake at 375 degrees for 20 to 25 minutes or until cupcakes test done. **Yield: 30 servings.**

LeWanda Yocum, Morning Star, #1271

Molasses Cupcakes

3 cups flour
1 cup sugar
1/2 cup shortening
1 teaspoon baking soda
1 cup light molasses
1 1/2 cups boiling water
3/4 cup flour
1/2 cup sugar
1/2 cup shortening

Combine 3 cups flour, 1 cup sugar, 1/2 cup shortening, baking soda, molasses and boiling water in bowl; mix until smooth. Pour into paper-lined cupcake cups filling 2/3 full. Mix 3/4 cup flour and 1/2 cup sugar in bowl. Cut in 1/2 cup shortening until mixture is crumbly. Sprinkle over cupcakes. Bake at 350 degrees for 20 to 25 minutes or until cupcakes test done. **Yield: 30 servings.**

Veryle Shaffer, North Woodbury #1923

Dietetic Cupcakes

1 cup raisins
1 cup water
1 cup applesauce
2 eggs, beaten
Sugar substitute to equal 1 cup sugar
3/4 cup oil
1 teaspoon baking soda
2 cups flour
1 1/2 teaspoons cinnamon
1 teaspoon vanilla extract
1/2 teaspoon salt

Simmer raisins in water in small saucepan until soft; drain. Mix applesauce, eggs, sugar substitute and oil in bowl. Add baking soda, flour, cinnamon, vanilla, salt and raisins; mix well. Pour into paper-lined cupcake cups filling 2/3 full. Bake at 350 degrees for 20 to 25 minutes or until cupcakes test done. **Yield: 2 dozen.**

Maude Beatty, Bell Township #2047

Bride's Icing

1 cup shortening
1 teaspoon salt
1 1-pound package confectioners' sugar
2 teaspoons vanilla extract
1/4 cup milk
2 tablespoons butter, softened
2 egg whites
1/4 cup flour

Combine shortening, salt, confectioners' sugar, vanilla, milk, butter, egg whites and flour in large mixer bowl. Beat at high speed for 5 minutes or until smooth. May add 3 tablespoons baking cocoa for chocolate icing. **Yield: 5 3/4 cups.**

Goldie I. Durco, Community #1994

Butter-Marshmallow Party Frosting

2/3 cup milk
32 large marshmallows
3/4 cup butter
1 teaspoon vanilla extract

Combine milk and marshmallows in saucepan. Cook over low heat until marshmallows melt, stirring constantly; cool. Cream butter in mixer bowl at medium speed until light and fluffy. Add marshmallow mixture and vanilla gradually, beating constantly. **Yield: 4 cups.**

Mildred C. Coveleski, Union #152

Cream Cheese Frosting

6 ounces cream cheese, softened
1/4 cup butter or margarine, softened
1 1/2 cups confectioners' sugar
1/2 teaspoon vanilla extract

Beat cream cheese, butter, confectioners' sugar and vanilla in mixer bowl at medium speed until light and fluffy. Spread over cooled cake. **Yield: 2 1/2 cups.**

Catherine Pike, Star #993

Creamy Icing

1 cup milk
1/2 cup shortening
1/2 cup margarine
1 1/4 cups sugar
1 teaspoon vanilla extract

Scald milk in small saucepan; cool. Cream shortening, margarine and sugar in mixer bowl at medium speed for 5 minutes or until light and fluffy. Add milk 1 tablespoon at a time, beating constantly. Add vanilla; beat well. **Yield: 3 1/4 cups.**

Zelma McWhirter, Mt. Pleasant #1687

Fluffy White Icing

1 cup sugar
1/3 cup water
1/4 teaspoon cream of tartar
Dash of salt
2 egg whites
1 teaspoon vanilla extract

Combine sugar, water, cream of tartar and salt in saucepan. Cook over medium heat until bubbly and sugar is dissolved, stirring constantly. Combine egg whites and vanilla in mixer bowl. Add sugar syrup gradually, beating at high speed for 7 minutes or until stiff peaks form. **Yield: 2 to 3 cups.**

Sis Sawhill, Burgettstown #1502

Hickory Nut Frosting

2 3/4 cups sugar
1 cup milk
2 tablespoons light corn syrup
1/4 teaspoon salt
3/4 cup ground hickory nuts
1/2 teaspoon vanilla

Combine sugar, milk, corn syrup and salt in saucepan. Cook over medium heat to 234 to 240 degrees on candy thermometer, soft-ball stage. Cool to lukewarm. Add hickory nuts and vanilla. Beat until of spreading consistency. May add small amount of hot water to thin out. **Yield: 4 cups.**

Mildred E. LaRue, Rush #1167

Creamy Peanut Butter Frosting

1 14-ounce can sweetened condensed milk
2 tablespoons peanut butter

Combine condensed milk and peanut butter in top of double boiler. Cook over boiling water for 5 minutes or until thickened, stirring constantly; cool. **Yield: 2 cups.**

Jean V. Johnn, Hemlock #2051

Candy and Cookies

Apple Candy

8 apples, peeled, cut into quarters
1/2 cup water
4 envelopes unflavored gelatin
4 cups sugar
1 cup chopped nuts
1 teaspoon vanilla extract
1/4 teaspoon orange extract
Confectioners' sugar

Combine apples with water in 2-quart saucepan. Simmer until apples are of consistency of applesauce. Cool to room temperature. Soften gelatin in 1 cup applesauce in small bowl. Add sugar to remaining applesauce in saucepan. Bring to a boil. Stir in gelatin mixture until dissolved. Boil for 20 minutes, stirring frequently; remove from heat. Stir in nuts and flavorings. Spoon into buttered shallow dish. Let stand overnight. Cut into pieces; roll in confectioners' sugar. **Yield: 60 servings.**

Inez Wise, Progress #96

Apricot Half-Dips

1/2 cup semisweet chocolate chips
2 tablespoons margarine or butter
6 ounces dried apricots

Melt chocolate chips with margarine in small saucepan over low heat, stirring to mix well. Place in pan of warm water. Dip 1 end of each apricot into chocolate. Let stand on waxed paper until dry. Store, covered, in refrigerator. May substitute pretzels for apricots. **Yield: 40 to 45 servings.**

Carol A. Rhoades, Perry Valley #1804

Buckeyes

1 pound chunky peanut butter
1 pound creamy peanut butter
1 pound margarine, softened
2 1-pound packages confectioners' sugar
1 13-ounce package graham cracker crumbs
1/2 cup water
1 tablespoon vanilla extract
2 cups chocolate chips
1 cup semisweet chocolate chips
1 block paraffin

Combine peanut butter, margarine, confectioners' sugar, cracker crumbs, water and vanilla in bowl; mix well. Shape into small balls; place on trays. Chill overnight. Melt chocolate chips with paraffin in double boiler, stirring to mix well. Dip peanut butter balls 3/4 of the way into chocolate with wooden pick. Let stand on waxed paper until set. Store in refrigerator. **Yield: 150 servings.**

Betty Master, Scrubgrass, #1705

Butterscotch Marshmallows

1/4 cup light cream
1 1/2 cups packed light brown sugar
3/4 teaspoon vanilla extract
1/3 teaspoon salt
12 ounces marshamllows
1 cup finely chopped nuts or crisp rice cereal

Combine cream, brown sugar, vanilla and salt in 3-quart saucepan; mix well. Cook to 236 degrees on candy thermometer, soft-ball stage, stirring frequently. Place over hot water to keep warm. Drop marshamllows 1 at a time into hot mixture, turning to coat well. Roll in nuts. Place on buttered tray to cool. **Yield: 3 3/4 dozen.**

Joan Milliken, Tuscarora #774

Caramel Bars

14 to 16 ounces caramels
1/4 cup water
1/2 cup peanut butter
4 cups Cheerios
1 cup salted peanuts
1 cup milk chocolate chips
1/4 cup peanut butter
2 tablespoons butter or margarine

Combine caramels, water and peanut butter in large glass bowl. Microwave on High for 3 to 5 minutes or until caramels melt; stir to mix well. Stir in cereal and nuts. Press into buttered 9x13-inch dish. Combine chocolate chips, peanut butter and butter in glass measure. Microwave on Medium for 2 to 4 minutes or until chocolate chips are softened; mix well. Spread over cereal layer. Let stand until cool. Cut into bars. **Yield: 20 to 30 bars.**

Anna M. Bohn, North Jackson #1740

Chocolate-Covered Cherries

1/2 cup candy maker's fondant
4 teaspoons maraschino cherry juice
Chocolate coating
Maraschino cherries

Blend 1/2 cup fondant with 4 teaspoons maraschino cherry juice; cover and set aside. Melt chocolate coating in double boiler over hot water. Coat plastic cordial molds with chocolate, using finger, small spoon or candy coater. Chill just until set. Place 1 cherry in each mold. Spoon fondant mixture over cherry, filling almost full. Cover with chocolate. Chill for 10 minutes. Invert mold and flex gently to unmold. Store at room temperature for 24 to 36 hours; fondant centers will become liquid. May substitute pineapple chunks and juice for cherries. May melt chocolate in oven or microwave if preferred. **Yield: variable.**

Carol A. Crater, Logan #109

Chocolate Fudge

4 cups sugar
1/2 cup butter
1 12-ounce can evaporated milk
2 cups semisweet chocolate chips
1 7-ounce jar marshmallow creme
1 teaspoon vanilla extract

Combine sugar, butter and evaporated milk in saucepan. Bring to a boil. Cook to 234 to 240 degrees on candy thermometer, soft-ball stage, stirring constantly. Add chocolate chips, marshmallow creme and vanilla, stirring until smooth. Pour into buttered 9x13-inch dish. Let stand until firm. **Yield: 3 1/2 pounds.**

Helen Zeh, Big Beaver #1578

Coconut Fudge

1 12-ounce can evaporated milk
4 1/2 cups sugar
2 tablespoons butter
Salt to taste
1 1/2 to 2 pounds white chocolate
2 cups marshmallow creme
1 to 1 1/2 cups coconut

Bring evaporated milk, sugar, butter and salt to a boil in large saucepan over medium heat; reduce heat. Cook for 7 minutes; remove from heat. Stir in white chocolate until melted. Stir in marshmallow creme. Fold in coconut. Spread in large buttered shallow pan. Let stand until firm. Cut into squares. **Yield: 5 pounds.**

Betty J. Pontius, Harmony #1112

Microwave Peanut Butter Fudge

1 1-pound package confectioners' sugar, sifted
1/2 cup margarine
1/4 cup milk
1/2 cup baking cocoa
1/2 cup peanut butter
1 teaspoon vanilla extract

Combine confectioners' sugar, margarine, milk, baking cocoa and peanut butter in glass bowl; do not mix. Microwave on High for 3 minutes. Add vanilla; beat with electric mixer until of desired consistency. Spread in buttered dish. Let stand until firm. Cut into squares. **Yield: 36 servings.**

Althea Woolerton, Odin #1254

Microwave Fudge

3 cups sugar
1/2 cup margarine
1 cup evaporated milk
1 7-ounce jar marshmallow creme
2 cups chocolate chips or peanut butter chips
1/2 teaspoon vanilla extract

Combine sugar, margarine and evaporated milk in deep glass bowl. Microwave on High for 10 minutes, stirring after 4 minutes. Stir in marshmallow creme, chocolate chips and vanilla. Beat until smooth. Spread in buttered 9x9-inch or 9x13-inch dish. Let stand until firm. Cut into squares. **Yield: 36 to 60 squares.**

Ruth Jameson, Brokenstraw #407

Peanut Butter Fudge

1/2 cup milk
2 cups sugar
1 13-ounce jar marshmallow creme
1 18-ounce jar peanut butter

Bring milk and sugar to a boil in saucepan. Boil for 3 minutes; remove from heat. Stir in marshmallow creme and peanut butter. Spread in buttered 9x13-inch dish. Let stand until cool and firm. Cut into 1-inch squares. **Yield: 117 squares.**

Peggy Jamison, Gideon #2010

Old-Fashioned Pumpkin Fudge

2 cups sugar
2 tablespoons light corn syrup
1 tablespoon mashed cooked pumpkin
1/3 cup sweetened condensed milk
1/3 cup milk
1/4 teaspoon pumpkin pie spice
Salt to taste
2 tablespoons butter
1/2 teaspoon vanilla extract
2 drops of orange food coloring (optional)

Combine sugar, corn syrup, pumpkin, condensed milk, milk, pumpkin pie spice and salt in saucepan; mix well. Bring to a boil over medium-high heat; reduce heat. Cook to 238 degrees on candy thermometer, soft-ball stage, stirring occasionally. Cool slightly. Stir in butter until melted. Add vanilla and food coloring. Beat until mixture is creamy and loses its luster. Spread in 5x9-inch dish lined with buttered foil; smooth top. Let stand until cool and firm. Cut into squares. **Yield: 45 squares.**

Kay Costa, Gillett #884

Rocky Road Fudge

3 4-ounce milk chocolate bars, chopped
$1^1/_2$ cups miniature marshmallows
1 cup coarsely chopped walnuts

Melt chocolate in medium saucepan over low heat, stirring constantly until smooth. Stir in marshamllows and walnuts. Drop by teaspoonfuls onto waxed paper. Chill for 15 minutes or until firm. May microwave chocolate on High for $1^1/_2$ to 2 minutes if preferred. **Yield: 28 servings.**

Mary Harkeroad, Rural Valley #1750

White Chocolate Fudge

8 ounces cream cheese, softened
4 cups confectioners' sugar
$1^1/_2$ teaspoons vanilla extract
12 ounces white chocolate
$^3/_4$ cup chopped pecans, walnuts or hickory nuts

Beat cream cheese, confectioners' sugar and vanilla in mixer bowl until smooth. Melt white chocolate in double boiler. Fold in cream cheese mixture and pecans. Spread in buttered 8x8-inch dish. Chill until serving time. Cut into squares.
Yield: 45 squares.

Joyce Ross, Harmony #1112

Homemade Gumdrops

4 envelopes unflavored gelatin
$2^1/_2$ cups cold water
3 cups sugar
$^1/_4$ teaspoon salt
Flavoring
Food coloring

Soften gelatin in 1 cup cold water; set aside. Combine $1^1/_2$ cups water, sugar and salt in large saucepan. Bring to a boil; remove from heat. Stir in gelatin mixture. Bring to a boil. Cook for 15 minutes, stirring occasionally; remove from heat. Sprinkle 2 shallow pans generously with water. Pour in mixture to $^3/_4$-inch thickness. Stir in flavoring of choice and food coloring. Chill for 24 hours. Loosen candy with spatula. Turn onto sugar-coated cutting board. Cut into desired shapes, turning to coat in sugar. Store in loosely covered container to dry for 12 hours.
Yield: 48 (1-ounce) servings.

Mary McMillin, Westfield #1514

Chocolate-Peanut Squares

3/4 cup margarine
2 ounces semisweet chocolate squares
1 1/2 cups graham cracker crumbs
1 cup coconut
1/2 cup chopped unsalted peanuts
16 ounces cream cheese, softened
1 cup sugar
1 teaspoon vanilla extract
1/4 cup margarine
4 ounces semisweet chocolate squares

Combine 3/4 cup margarine and 2 ounces chocolate in microwave-safe bowl. Microwave on High for 1 to 2 minutes or until melted, stirring every 30 seconds. Stir in graham cracker crumbs, coconut and peanuts. Press into 9x13-inch dish. Chill for 30 minutes. Beat cream cheese, sugar and vanilla in mixer bowl until light and fluffy. Spread over graham cracker crust. Chill for 30 minutes. Combine remaining 1/4 cup margarine and 4 ounces chocolate in microwave-safe bowl. Microwave on High for 1 to 2 minutes or until melted, stirring every 30 seconds. Spread over cream cheese layer. Chill until firm; cut into squares. **Yield: 4 dozen.**

Gladys R. Peace, Henderson #1315

Peanut Butter Drops

1 cup sugar
1 cup light corn syrup
1/2 cup peanut butter
4 cups crisp corn cereal
1 cup thin pretzel sticks

Combine sugar and syrup in large saucepan. Bring to a boil. Cook for 30 seconds; remove from heat. Add peanut butter, stirring until smooth. Stir in cereal and pretzels. Drop by spoonfuls onto waxed paper; cool. **Yield: 3 dozen.**

Ardella Cauffman, Perry Valley #1804

No-Cook Easter Eggs

1 14-ounce can sweetened condensed milk
2 pounds shredded coconut
1/4 cup butter, softened
2 teaspoons vanilla extract
1 7-ounce jar marshmallow creme
Almonds
Chocolate coating

Combine sweetened condensed milk, coconut, butter, vanilla and marshmallow creme in bowl; mix well. Shape into egg shapes. Press 2 almonds into each "egg." Chill in refrigerator overnight. Dip in melted chocolate coating.
Yield: 12 to 15 servings.

Mary E. Hiller, Bottle Run #1301

English Toffee

2 cups butter
2 tablespoons corn syrup
1/2 teaspoon salt
6 tablespoons water
2 cups sugar
1 cup slivered almonds
1 teaspoon vanilla extract
1 8-ounce Hershey chocolate bar
1 cup coarsely ground almonds

Combine butter, corn syrup, salt and water in heavy saucepan. Bring to a boil, stirring constantly; remove from heat. Add sugar and slivered almonds. Cook over medium heat to 270 to 290 degrees on candy thermometer, soft-crack stage, stirring frequently. Stir in vanilla. Pour into buttered 10x15-inch pan; cool. Melt chocolate bar in top of double boiler over hot water. Spread half the chocolate over toffee; sprinkle with half the ground almonds. Let stand until cool; turn. Coat with chocolate and sprinkle with remaining almonds. Break into pieces when cool; store in airtight container. **Yield: 3 pounds.**

Irene Ohlin, Valley #1420

Too-Easy Truffles

2 cups semisweet chocolate chips
8 ounces cream cheese, softened
3 cups confectioners' sugar
1 1/2 teaspoons vanilla extract
Ground nuts or toasted flaked coconut

Microwave chocolate in glass bowl on High for 3 to 4 minutes or until melted, stirring every minute. Beat cream cheese in mixer bowl until light and fluffy. Add sugar, beating well. Stir in melted chocolate and vanilla. Chill for 1 hour. Shape into 1-inch balls. Roll in nuts or coconut. Store in refrigerator. **Yield: 5 dozen.**

Ethel Friede, Stony Point #1694

Strawberries

2 3-ounce packages strawberry gelatin
1 14-ounce can sweetened condensed milk
16 ounces chopped coconut
1 teaspoon lemon juice
2 tablespoons sugar
20 drops of red food coloring

Combine 1 1/2 packages gelatin, sweetened condensed milk, coconut, lemon juice, sugar and food coloring in bowl; mix well. Shape into strawberries. Roll in remaining 1/2 package gelatin. Chill until firm. Add plastic leaves or make edible leaves from mixture of confectioners' sugar, green food coloring and small amount of hot water. **Yield: 72 to 75 strawberries.**

Vivian M. Mullin, Mt. Pleasant #975

Turtles

1 14-ounce can sweetened condensed milk
$1\frac{1}{2}$ pounds coating chocolate, melted
Pecan halves

Pour sweetened condensed milk into double boiler; cover. Cook over boiling water for $1\frac{1}{2}$ hours or until thick and light-colored. Beat until smooth; chill. Pour a small amount of melted chocolate into candy papers; top with pecan half. Spoon a small amount of caramel on pecan. Cover with melted chocolate. Let stand until firm. **Yield: 36 to 40 servings.**

Margaret Tau, Hayfield #800

Cinnamon-Walnut Squares

1 cup applesauce
1 tablespoon red-hot cinnamon candies
1 3-ounce package strawberry gelatin
1 cup sugar
3/4 cup coarsely chopped walnuts

Combine applesauce and cinnamon candies in saucepan. Cook over low heat until mixture begins to boil. Stir in gelatin and sugar. Bring to a boil, stirring constantly. Cook for 2 minutes; remove from heat. Stir in walnuts. Pour into buttered 5x9-inch pan. Chill overnight. Cut into squares; coat with sugar. Let stand for 24 hours. Coat with sugar again. **Yield: 3 dozen.**

Helen Paden, Westfield #1514

Jan Hagel Almond Bars

1/2 cup butter, softened
1/2 cup margarine, softened
1 cup sugar
2 egg yolks
1/8 teaspoon almond extract
2 cups flour
2 egg whites
1/4 teaspoon cinnamon
1 tablespoon sugar
1/4 cup sliced almonds

Cream butter, margarine and 1 cup sugar in mixer bowl until light and fluffy. Beat in egg yolks and almond extract. Add flour; mix well. Spread in greased 10x15-inch baking pan. Beat egg whites in mixer bowl until stiff peaks form. Spread on cookie batter. Sprinkle with mixture of cinnamon and 1 tablespoon sugar; top with almonds. Bake at 350 degrees for 25 minutes. Cool for 10 minutes. Cut into 2-inch bars. **Yield: 3 dozen.**

Lee Faylor Finkenbinder, Mifflin #1725

Apricot-Molasses Bars

1 cup flour
1 teaspoon baking powder
1/4 teaspoon baking soda
1/2 teaspoon salt
1/2 cup peanut butter
1/4 cup butter or margarine, softened
1/2 cup packed light brown sugar
1/2 cup molasses
2 eggs
2/3 cup chopped dried apricots

Mix flour, baking powder, baking soda and salt in bowl. Cream peanut butter and butter in mixer bowl until smooth. Add brown sugar and molasses, beating until light and fluffy. Beat in eggs. Add dry ingredients; mix well. Stir in apricots. Spread evenly in 9x9-inch baking pan sprayed with nonstick cooking spray. Bake at 350 degrees for 30 minutes. Cool on wire rack. Cut into squares. **Yield: 1 1/4 dozen.**

Marie E. Ohlinger, Ontelaunee #1617

Caramelitas

50 caramels
1/2 cup evaporated milk
2 cups flour
1 1/2 cups packed brown sugar
2 cups quick-cooking oats
1 cup melted margarine
1 teaspoon baking soda
1/4 teaspoon salt
1 cup chocolate chips
1 cup chopped nuts

Melt caramels with evaporated milk in saucepan over low heat, stirring to mix well. Set aside to cool. Combine flour, brown sugar, oats, margarine, baking soda and salt in bowl; mix well. Press half the crumb mixture in 9x13-inch baking pan. Bake at 350 degrees for 10 minutes. Sprinkle with chocolate chips and nuts. Spread evenly with caramel mixture. Top with remaining crumb mixture. Bake for 15 minutes longer. Cool on wire rack. Cut into 1 1/2-inch squares. **Yield: 4 dozen.**

Lorraine Holt, Port Matilda #1284

Cheese Crunchies

2 cups butterscotch chips
6 tablespoons butter
2 cups graham cracker crumbs
2 cups chopped nuts
16 ounces cream cheese, softened
1/2 cup sugar
4 eggs
1/4 cup flour
2 tablespoons lemon juice

Melt butterscotch chips and butter in microwave or double boiler over hot water. Combine with cracker crumbs and nuts in bowl; mix well. Reserve 2 cups crumb mixture. Press remaining crumbs into ungreased 10x15-inch baking pan. Bake at 350 degrees for 12 minutes. Beat cream cheese and sugar in large mixer bowl until light. Beat in eggs 1 at a time. Add flour and lemon juice; mix well. Spoon evenly over hot baked crust; sprinkle with reserved crumbs. Bake for 25 minutes. Cool completely. Cut into 1x2-inch bars. Store in refrigerator. **Yield: 6 dozen.**

Dot Harris, Iona #272

Chewy Noels

2 tablespoons butter
2 eggs
5 tablespoons flour
1 cup packed brown sugar
1/4 teaspoon baking soda
Chopped nuts to taste
1 teaspoon vanilla extract
Confectioners' sugar

Melt butter in 9x9-inch baking pan over low heat. Beat eggs lightly in bowl. Mix next 4 ingredients in bowl. Stir into eggs. Add vanilla; mix well. Spoon into melted butter in baking pan; do not stir. Bake at 350 degrees for 20 minutes. Invert onto serving plate. Cut into bars. Sprinkle with confectioners' sugar. **Yield: 1 1/2 dozen.**

Virginia Swanson, Ackley #870

Chocolate-Lemon Cream Bars

1 2-layer package devil's food cake mix
1/2 cup butter or margarine, softened
1 egg
1/2 cup chopped nuts
8 ounces cream cheese, softened
1 14-ounce can sweetened condensed milk
1 egg
3 tablespoons lemon juice
1 tablespoon grated lemon rind

Combine cake mix, butter and 1 egg in bowl; mix well. Stir in nuts. Reserve 1 1/2 cups mixture. Press remaining mixture into greased 9x13-inch baking pan. Bake at 350 degrees for 10 minutes. Cool for 5 minutes. Beat cream cheese in mixer bowl until fluffy. Add remaining ingredients; mix well. Spread evenly over baked layer; sprinkle with reserved mixture. Bake for 20 to 25 minutes or until center is set. Cool on wire rack. Cut into bars. Store in refrigerator. **Yield: 3 dozen.**

Fay Hill, South Buffalo #1908

Double Chocolate Crumble Bars

1/2 cup margarine, softened
3/4 cup sugar
1/4 teaspoon salt
2 eggs
1 teaspoon vanilla extract
3/4 cup flour
1/4 teaspoon baking powder
2 tablespoons baking cocoa
1/2 cup chopped nuts
2 cups miniature marshmallows
1 cup chocolate chips
1 cup peanut butter
1 1/2 cups crisp rice cereal

Cream margarine, sugar and salt in mixer bowl until light and fluffy. Beat in eggs and vanilla. Add flour, baking powder and baking cocoa; mix well. Stir in nuts. Spread in greased 9x13-inch baking pan. Bake at 350 degrees for 15 to 20 minutes or until set. Sprinkle with marshmallows. Bake for 3 minutes. Cool slightly. Melt chocolate chips and peanut butter in saucepan over low heat, stirring to mix well. Stir in cereal. Spread evenly over marshmallows. Chill in refrigerator. Cut into bars. **Yield: 2 1/2 to 3 dozen.**

Dorothy Scott, Unionville #1971

Dutch Butter Cookies

1 cup butter, softened
3/4 cup sugar
1 egg yolk
2 cups flour
1 egg white

Cream butter, sugar and egg yolk in mixer bowl until light and fluffy. Add flour; mix well. Press into 10x15-inch baking pan; brush with egg white. Bake at 300 degrees for 1 hour or until golden brown. Cut into squares and remove from pan while hot. **Yield: 2 dozen.**

Scott J. Preston, Steuben #858

Failed Fudge Bars

1 cup peanut butter
6 tablespoons butter, softened
1 1/4 cups sugar
3 eggs
1 teaspoon vanilla extract
1 cup flour
1 pound overcooked chocolate fudge, crumbled

Beat peanut butter and butter in mixer bowl until smooth. Add sugar, eggs and vanilla; mix well. Beat in flour. Add fudge; mix well. Spoon into 9x13-inch baking pan. Bake at 350 degrees for 25 to 30 minutes or until layer tests done. Cool on wire rack. Cut into bars. This recipe was created last Christmas when I overcooked the fudge and used it to make chocolate cookies. **Yield: 3 dozen.**

Barbara Harrison Nauss, Goshen #121

Fred's Bar Cookies

2/3 cup shortening
2 cups packed brown sugar
3 eggs
1 teaspoon vanilla extract
2 cups flour
1 teaspoon baking powder
1/2 teaspoon salt
1 cup chocolate chips
1 cup shredded coconut

Cream shortening and brown sugar in mixer bowl until light and fluffy. Beat in eggs 1 at a time. Add vanilla; mix well. Stir in flour, baking powder and salt. Fold in chocolate chips and coconut. Spread in greased 9x13-inch baking pan. Bake at 350 degrees for 25 minutes. Cool on wire rack. Cut into bars. Our son Fred learned to make these cookies in the fourth grade and we have named them after him. **Yield: 3 1/2 dozen.**

Carolyn Raney, Westfield #1514

French Mint Cream Bars

1/2 cup margarine, softened
1 cup sugar
4 eggs or 1 cup egg substitute
1 16-ounce can chocolate syrup
1 cup flour
1/2 teaspoon baking powder
1/2 cup margarine, softened
2 cups confectioners' sugar
2 tablespoons milk
1 teaspoon peppermint extract
2 or 3 drops of green food coloring
1/2 cup margarine
1 cup semisweet chocolate chips

Cream 1/2 cup margarine and sugar in mixer bowl until light and fluffy. Add eggs, chocolate syrup, flour and baking powder; beat until smooth. Spread in greased 10x15-inch baking pan. Bake at 350 degrees for 20 minutes. Chill in refrigerator. Cream 1/2 cup margarine and confectioners' sugar in mixer bowl until light. Beat in milk, peppermint extract and food coloring. Spread over baked layer. Chill until firm. Melt 1/2 cup margarine with chocolate chips in saucepan over low heat, stirring constantly to mix well. Pour over mint layer; chill slightly. Cut into bars. Chill until firm. **Yield: 6 dozen.**

Betty Oesterling, Eureka #244

Fruit-Filled Cookies

4 ounces dried fruit, chopped
1/2 cup water
4 ounces cream cheese, softened
1/2 cup shortening
1/4 cup sour cream
1 cup flour
1/4 teaspoon salt

Combine dried fruit and water in saucepan. Cook over low heat until thickened. Combine cream cheese, shortening and sour cream in mixer bowl; mix until smooth. Add flour and salt; mix to form dough. Chill for 30 minutes or until firm. Roll half the dough on cookie sheet. Spread with fruit filling. Roll remaining dough on floured surface. Place over filling. Bake at 325 degrees for 20 to 25 minutes or until light brown. Cool on wire rack. Cut into squares. **Yield: 2 dozen.**

Eleanor Hill, Virginville #1832

Cool cookies completely in a single layer on a wire rack before storing. Store soft and chewy cookies in an airtight container and crisp cookies in a jar with a loose-fitting lid.

Tropical Fruit Bars

1 cup boiling water
1 cup finely chopped dried apricots
2 cups flour
1 teaspoon baking powder
1/2 teaspoon baking soda
1/2 cup shortening
1 cup packed brown sugar
2 eggs
2 tablespoons orange juice
1/2 teaspoon grated orange rind
1 cup milk
1 cup chopped walnuts

Pour boiling water over apricots in bowl. Let stand for 10 minutes. Sift flour, baking powder and baking soda together. Cream shortening and brown sugar in mixer bowl until light and fluffy. Beat in eggs. Stir in orange juice and rind. Add dry ingredients alternately with milk, mixing well after each addition. Stir in walnuts and apricots; mix well. Spread in greased 9x13-inch baking pan. Bake at 350 degrees for 25 to 30 minutes or until golden brown. Cool on wire rack. Cut into bars. **Yield: 4 dozen.**

Malissa McFadden, Scrubgrass #1705

Arctic Fudge Bars

1/4 cup butter or margarine, softened
1 cup sugar
4 eggs
6 ounces white chocolate, melted, cooled
1 cup flour
1/2 teaspoon baking powder
1/4 teaspoon salt
8 ounces cream cheese, softened
1/2 cup sugar
1 egg
1 10-ounce packet liquid baking chocolate

Cream butter and 1 cup sugar in medium mixer bowl until light and fluffy. Beat in 4 eggs. Add white chocolate; beat until thick and lemon-colored. Stir in flour, baking powder and salt. Spread in greased 9x13-inch baking pan. Beat cream cheese in small mixer bowl until smooth. Beat in 1/2 cup sugar, 1 egg and baking chocolate. Drop by spoonfuls over white chocolate layer. Swirl lightly with knife to marbleize. Bake at 350 degrees for 40 minutes. Cool on wire rack. Chill in refrigerator. Cut into bars. **Yield: 2 dozen.**

Lorena A. Reilly, Scotch Valley #510

Revive stale cookies by storing them with an apple wedge in an airtight container in the refrigerator for several days.

Hip Huggers

1/2 cup butter or margarine, softened
1 cup packed brown sugar
1 egg
1/4 teaspoon salt
1 1/4 cups flour
1 1/2 cups oats
1/2 teaspoon baking soda
1 teaspoon vanilla extract
Chopped nuts (optional)
1 cup chocolate chips
2 tablespoons butter
1 14-ounce can sweetened condensed milk

Cream 1/2 cup butter and brown sugar in mixer bowl until light and fluffy. Beat in egg and salt. Add flour, oats, baking soda, vanilla and nuts; mix well. Press 2/3 of the mixture into 9x13-inch baking pan. Melt chocolate chips and 2 tablespoons butter with condensed milk in saucepan over low heat, stirring to mix well. Spread over crust. Drop remaining oats mixture by spoonfuls over top. Bake at 350 degrees for 20 minutes. Cool on wire rack. Cut into squares. **Yield: 3 dozen.**

Renee Calvert, Central #1650

Iris' Cookie Bars

2 eggs
1/2 cup shortening
1 cup sugar
2 1/2 cups flour
1 teaspoon baking powder
1 teaspoon baking soda
1/2 teaspoon salt
1/2 cup cold coffee
1 teaspoon vanilla extract
1 cup chocolate chips or floured raisins
3/4 cup packed brown sugar
1 teaspoon cinnamon

Combine eggs, shortening and sugar in mixer bowl; beat until smooth. Add flour, baking powder, baking soda, salt, coffee and vanilla; mix well. Stir in chocolate chips or raisins. Spoon into greased 11x16-inch baking pan. Sprinkle with mixture of brown sugar and cinnamon. Bake at 375 degrees for 15 to 18 minutes or until golden brown; do not overbake. Cool on wire rack. Cut into bars. **Yield: 6 dozen.**

Mildred Harer, Sebring #1047

Crumble stale cookie bars and layer the crumbs with ice cream in parfait glasses for a quick dessert.

Jewish Cookie Bars

3/4 cup margarine, softened
1 1/4 cups sugar
3 eggs
1 teaspoon vanilla extract
1 cup flour
3 tablespoons baking cocoa
Salt to taste
2 cups coconut
1 14-ounce can sweetened condensed milk
3 tablespoons margarine, softened
3 tablespoons baking cocoa
3 cups confectioners' sugar
1 teaspoon vanilla extract
Milk

Cream 3/4 cup margarine and sugar in mixer bowl until light and fluffy. Beat in eggs and 1 teaspoon vanilla. Add flour, 3 tablespoons baking cocoa and salt; mix well. Spread in 9x13-inch baking pan. Bake at 350 degrees for 15 to 20 minutes or until set. Combine coconut and condensed milk in bowl; mix well. Spread over hot baked layer. Bake for 15 minutes longer. Cool on wire rack. Combine 3 tablespoons margarine, 3 tablespoons cocoa, confectioners' sugar and 1 teaspoon vanilla in mixer bowl. Add enough milk to make of spreading consistency, mixing until smooth. Spread over coconut layer. Cut into bars. **Yield: 3 dozen.**

Janice Faust, Jefferson #1373

Best-Loved Lemon Bars

1 cup butter or margarine, softened
1/2 cup confectioners' sugar
2 cups flour
1/4 teaspoon salt
4 eggs, slightly beaten
5 tablespoons lemon juice
1 tablespoon grated lemon rind
2 cups sugar
1/4 cup flour
Confectioners' sugar

Combine butter, 1/2 cup confectioners' sugar, 2 cups flour and salt in bowl; mix to form soft dough. Press evenly into ungreased 9x13-inch baking pan. Bake at 350 degrees for 15 to 20 minutes or until golden brown. Reduce oven temperature to 325 degrees. Combine eggs, lemon juice, lemon rind, sugar and 1/4 cup flour in bowl; mix well. Spread over baked layer. Bake for 25 minutes longer or until set. Cool on wire rack. Sprinkle with additional confectioners' sugar. Cut into bars. **Yield: 3 dozen.**

Orange Bars: Substitute orange juice and rind for lemon and glaze with mixture of 2 ounces melted semisweet chocolate and 1/4 cup melted butter in place of confectioners' sugar topping.

Coconut-Key Lime Bars: Substitute lime juice and rind for lemon and sprinkle top with 1 cup coconut. May tint with green food coloring if desired.

Almond-Amaretto Bars: Substitute Amaretto for lemon juice and rind and sprinkle top with 1 cup sliced almonds.

Cherry Bonbon Bars: Substitute maraschino cherry juice and 24 chopped cherries for lemon juice and rind. Substitute glaze made with mixture of 1 ounce melted semisweet chocolate, 1 ounce melted unsweetened chocolate and 1/4 cup melted butter for confectioners' sugar topping.

Beth Beck, Henderson #1315

Lemon-Coconut Squares

1 1/2 cups sifted flour
1/2 cup packed light brown sugar
1/2 cup butter or margarine, softened
2 eggs
1 cup packed light brown sugar
2 tablespoons flour
1/2 teaspoon baking powder
1/4 teaspoon salt
1/2 teaspoon vanilla extract
1 1/2 cups flaked coconut
1 cup chopped nuts
1 cup confectioners' sugar
1 tablespoon melted butter
2 tablespoons lemon juice

Combine flour, 1/2 cup brown sugar and butter in bowl; mix well. Press into buttered 9x13-inch baking pan. Bake at 275 degrees for 10 minutes. Increase oven temperature to 350 degrees. Combine eggs, 1 cup brown sugar, flour, baking powder, salt and vanilla in bowl; mix well. Stir in coconut and nuts. Spoon over baked layer. Bake for 20 minutes. Blend confectioners' sugar, melted butter and lemon juice in small bowl. Spread over warm layer. Let stand until cool. Cut into squares. **Yield: 4 dozen.**

Marie Swartz, Gibson #798

Magic Cookie Bar

1/2 cup margarine or butter
1 1/2 cups graham cracker crumbs
1 14-ounce can sweetened condensed milk
1 cup semisweet chocolate chips
1 3-ounce can flaked coconut
1 cup chopped nuts

Melt margarine in 9x13-inch baking pan in 350-degree oven. Sprinkle cracker crumbs over margarine. Pour condensed milk evenly over crumbs. Layer chocolate chips, coconut and nuts over top; press down gently. Bake for 25 to 30 minutes or until light brown. Cool on wire rack. Cut into bars. **Yield: 2 to 3 dozen.**

Nancy Horrell, Armstrong #1645

Milk Chocolate-Walnut Bars

1/2 cup packed brown sugar
1/2 cup margarine, softened
1 egg
1 1/2 cups flour
1/2 teaspoon baking powder
1/2 teaspoon vanilla extract
2 cups chocolate chips
1 cup chopped walnuts

Beat brown sugar, margarine and egg in bowl until smooth. Add flour, baking powder and vanilla; mix well. Press into 9x13-inch baking pan. Bake at 350 degrees for 10 minutes. Sprinkle with chocolate chips. Bake for 1 minute longer. Spread chocolate evenly over top; sprinkle with walnuts. Cool on wire rack. Cut into bars. **Yield: 4 dozen.**

Judy Martin, Watson #1068

Mincemeat Bars

3/4 cup flour
1 cup sugar
1/4 teaspoon salt
1/2 18-ounce jar mincemeat
2 eggs, beaten
1 teaspoon vanilla extract
1 cup chopped nuts
Confectioners' sugar

Sift flour, sugar and salt over mincemeat in bowl; mix well. Stir in eggs, vanilla and nuts. Spread in greased and floured 8x8-inch baking pan. Bake at 350 degrees for 50 minutes. Cool on wire rack for 30 minutes. Cut into bars. Sprinkle with confectioners' sugar. Store in airtight container. **Yield: 2 dozen.**

Laura Petergall, Harmony #1112

Pumpkin Bars

4 eggs
1 2/3 cups sugar
1 cup oil
1 16-ounce can pumpkin
2 cups flour
2 teaspoons baking powder
1 teaspoon baking soda
2 teaspoons cinnamon
1 teaspoon salt
1/2 cup butter or margarine, softened
3 ounces cream cheese
1 teaspoon vanilla extract
2 cups confectioners' sugar

Combine eggs, sugar, oil and pumpkin in mixer bowl; beat until smooth. Mix flour, baking powder, baking soda, cinnamon and salt in bowl. Add to pumpkin mixture; mix well. Spread in ungreased 10x15-inch baking pan. Bake at 350 degrees for 25 to 30 minutes or until golden brown. Cool on wire rack. Beat butter and cream cheese in mixer bowl until light. Add vanilla and confectioners' sugar gradually, mixing well after each addition. Spread over baked layer. Cut into bars. **Yield: 6 dozen.**

Mary Whipkey, Aleppo #2054

Snicker Bars

1 14-ounce package caramels
3/4 cup evaporated milk
1 2-layer package German chocolate cake mix
6 tablespoons melted butter
1/2 cup semisweet chocolate chips
1 1/3 cups dry-roasted unsalted peanuts

Combine caramels and 1/3 cup evaporated milk in glass bowl. Microwave on High for 3 minutes or until caramels melt; stir to mix well. Combine cake mix, melted butter and remaining evaporated milk in large bowl; mix to form smooth dough. Roll half the dough between waxed paper. Press evenly into greased and floured 9x13-inch baking pan. Bake at 350 degrees for 8 to 10 minutes or until firm. Sprinkle with chocolate chips. Spread caramel mixture over chips; sprinkle with peanuts. Roll remaining dough between waxed paper. Place over top; press into place. Bake for 15 to 18 minutes longer or until top is firm. Cool on wire rack. Chill until caramel is firm. Cut into bars. **Yield: 3 dozen.**

Jean H. Hertzog, Pioneer #1777

Triple-Good Bars

2 cups raisins
1 14-ounce sweetened condensed milk
1 tablespoon lemon juice
1 tablespoon grated lemon rind
1 cup margarine or butter, softened
1$^{1}/_{3}$ cups packed brown sugar
1$^{1}/_{2}$ teaspoons vanilla extract
2$^{1}/_{2}$ cups oats
1 cup flour
$^{1}/_{2}$ teaspoon baking soda
$^{1}/_{4}$ teaspoon salt
1$^{1}/_{2}$ cups chopped walnuts

Combine raisins, condensed milk, lemon juice and lemon rind in medium saucepan. Cook over medium heat just until mixture begins to bubble, stirring constantly. Cool slightly. Cream margarine, brown sugar and vanilla in mixer bowl until light and fluffy. Add oats, flour, baking soda, salt and walnuts; mix until crumbly. Reserve 2 cups crumb mixture. Press remaining crumb mixture into greased 9x13-inch baking pan Spread raisin mixture over top, leaving $^{1}/_{2}$-inch edge. Sprinkle with reserved crumb mixture; press lightly. Bake at 375 degrees for 25 to 30 minutes or until golden brown. Cool on wire rack. Cut into 1x2-inch bars. **Yield: 4 dozen.**

Helen Coughanour, Rostraver #919

Triple-Layer Bars

16 whole graham crackers
$^{3}/_{4}$ cup sugar
$^{1}/_{2}$ cup packed brown sugar
$^{1}/_{4}$ cup milk
$^{1}/_{2}$ cup margarine
1 cup vanilla wafer crumbs
$^{2}/_{3}$ cup peanut butter
1 cup chocolate chips
$^{1}/_{2}$ cup chopped pecans

Line 9x13-inch dish with graham crackers. Combine sugar, brown sugar, milk and margarine in saucepan. Bring to a boil. Stir in cookie crumbs. Pour over graham crackers. Melt peanut butter and chocolate chips in saucepan. Spread over top; sprinkle with pecans. Cool to room temperature. Cut into bars. **Yield: 3 dozen.**

Mary Fye, Baileyville #1991

Basic Brownies

1 cup butter or margarine, softened
2 cups sugar
4 eggs
2 teaspoons vanilla extract
1 cup baking cocoa
1 cup flour
1 cup chopped nuts

Cream butter and sugar in mixer bowl until light. Beat in eggs and vanilla. Add baking cocoa and flour gradually, mixing well; mixture will be thick. Stir in nuts. Spread in greased and floured 9x13-inch baking pan. Bake at 325 degrees for 35 minutes. Cool on wire rack. Cut into squares. **Yield: 1$^{1}/_{2}$ to 2 dozen.**

Susie K. O'Brien, Bald Eagle #1390

Blond Brownies

1/2 cup shortening
1/2 cup molasses
2 eggs, beaten
3/4 cup packed brown sugar
1 cup flour
1/2 teaspoon baking soda
1/2 teaspoon salt
1 cup chopped walnuts
1 teaspoon vanilla extract
Confectioners' sugar

Melt shortening with molasses in saucepan over low heat. Cool slightly. Beat eggs with brown sugar in mixer bowl. Add molasses mixture. Sift in flour, baking soda and salt; beat until smooth. Stir in walnuts and vanilla. Spread in 9x9-inch baking pan lined with waxed paper. Bake at 350 degrees for 30 to 40 minutes or until brownies test done. Sprinkle with confectioners' sugar. Cool on wire rack. Cut into squares. **Yield: 1 1/2 dozen.**

Eloise Bunnell, Rush #1167

Butterscotch Brownies

3/4 cup butter
1 1-pound package light brown sugar
3 eggs
1 tablespoon vanilla extract
1 1/2 cups flour
1 tablespoon baking powder
Salt to taste
1 1/2 cups chopped English walnuts

Melt butter in saucepan over low heat; remove from heat. Stir in brown sugar. Beat in eggs 1 at a time. Add vanilla, flour, baking powder and salt; mix well. Stir in walnuts. Spoon into greased 9x13-inch baking pan. Bake at 325 degrees for 30 minutes or just until brownies test done; do not overbake. Cool on wire rack. Cut into squares. **Yield: 3 dozen.**

Jane Darmofal, Kutztown #1836

Chocolate Fudge Ribbon Brownies

1 21-ounce package brownie mix
1 12-ounce jar caramel ice cream topping
1/3 cup flour
1 cup coconut

Grease bottom of 9x13-inch baking pan. Prepare brownie mix using package directions. Spread 2 cups of the mixture in prepared pan. Combine ice cream topping and flour in bowl; mix well. Spread evenly over brownie mixture; sprinkle with coconut. Drop remaining brownie mixture by teaspoonfuls over top. Bake at 350 degrees for 35 to 40 minutes or just until brownies test done; do not overbake. Cut into 1 1/2 to 2-inch squares. **Yield: 2 to 4 dozen.**

Barbara Ann Cavalcante, Franklin #1169

Fudge-Topped Brownies

1 cup melted margarine or butter
2 cups sugar
1 cup flour
2/3 cup baking cocoa
1/2 teaspoon baking powder
2 eggs
1/2 cup milk
1 1/2 teaspoons vanilla extract
1 cup chopped walnuts
2 cups chocolate chips
1 14-ounce can sweetened condensed milk
1 1/2 teaspoons vanilla extract

Combine margarine, sugar, flour, baking cocoa, baking powder, eggs, milk and 1 1/2 teaspoons vanilla in large mixer bowl; beat until smooth. Stir in walnuts. Spread in greased 9x13-inch baking pan. Bake at 350 degrees for 40 minutes or until brownies pull from sides of pan. Melt chocolate chips with condensed milk in heavy saucepan, stirring to mix well. Stir in 1 1/2 teaspoons vanilla. Spread over hot brownies. Cool to room temperature. Chill in refrigerator. Cut into bars. **Yield: 3 dozen.**

Jean Bagnick, Hope #898

Hershey Syrup Brownies

1/2 cup margarine, softened
1 cup sugar
4 eggs
1 teaspoon vanilla extract
1 16-ounce can Hershey's chocolate syrup
1 cup plus 1 tablespoon flour
1/2 teaspoon baking powder
1 cup chopped nuts
6 tablespoons margarine
6 tablespoons milk
1 1/2 cups sugar
1/2 cup chocolate chips

Cream 1/2 cup margarine and 1 cup sugar in mixer bowl until light and fluffy. Beat in eggs 1 at a time. Stir in vanilla and chocolate syrup. Add flour, baking powder and nuts; mix well; batter will be thin. Spoon into greased 10x15-inch baking pan. Bake at 350 degrees for 30 minutes. Bring 6 tablespoons margarine, milk and 1 1/2 cups sugar to a boil in saucepan. Boil for 1 minute. Add chocolate chips. Beat until thickened to desired consistency. Spread over warm brownies. Cool on wire rack. Cut into squares. **Yield: 3 dozen.**

Irene Bean, Forest #853

Since glass or dark-colored pans retain more heat than shiny ones, reduce oven temperature by 25 degrees to adjust for this and then bake for the amount of time specified in recipe.

Microwave Brownies

2 eggs
1 cup sugar
1/2 teaspoon salt
1 teaspoon vanilla extract
1/2 cup melted butter
3/4 cup flour
1/2 cup baking cocoa

Combine eggs, sugar, salt and vanilla in medium mixer bowl. Beat at medium speed for 1 minute or until smooth. Beat in butter. Add flour and baking cocoa; mix at low speed. Spread evenly in greased 8x8-inch glass dish. Microwave on High for 6 to 7 minutes or until top appears dry and springs back when lightly touched, rotating dish 1/2 turn after 3 minutes. Cool on wire rack. Cut into squares. **Yield: 1 1/2 dozen.**

Christine Cottrell, Gibson #798

Spice Brownies

1 cup sugar
1 cup water
1 cup raisins
1/2 cup margarine
1 teaspoon cinnamon
1/2 teaspoon nutmeg
1/2 teaspoon cloves
2 cups flour
1 teaspoon baking soda
2 eggs
1/2 cup butter or margarine
1 cup packed brown sugar
1/4 cup milk
2 cups confectioners' sugar
1 teaspoon vanilla extract

Combine first 7 ingredients in saucepan. Bring to a boil. Boil for 6 minutes, stirring constantly. Add flour, baking soda and eggs; mix well. Spoon into baking pan. Bake at 350 degrees until brownies test done. Bring butter and brown sugar to a boil in saucepan. Boil for 2 minutes. Add milk. Bring to a boil; remove from heat. Cool to lukewarm. Beat in confectioners' sugar and vanilla. Spread over brownies. Let stand until cool. Cut into squares. **Yield: 3 dozen.**

Judy Snyder, Penn #534

Zucchini Brownies

1 1/2 cups melted margarine
2 tablespoons water
2 cups packed brown sugar
2 eggs
1 teaspoon vanilla extract
2 cups flour
1 teaspoon baking powder
1 teaspoon baking soda
1 1/2 cups shredded zucchini
1 cup chocolate chips
Chopped nuts

Combine margarine, water, brown sugar, eggs and vanilla in mixer bowl; mix well. Beat in flour, baking powder and baking soda. Fold in zucchini, chocolate chips and nuts. Spoon into greased 9x13-inch baking pan. Bake at 350 degrees for 35 minutes. Cool on wire rack. Cut into squares. **Yield: 3 dozen.**

Louise Hollobaugh, Hickory #1285

Banana and Chocolate Chip Cookies

1 cup sugar or packed brown sugar
1 cup shortening
2 eggs
2 cups flour
2 cups quick-cooking oats
1 teaspoon baking soda
1 teaspoon cloves
1 teaspoon salt
1 teaspoon vanilla extract
3 bananas, mashed
2 cups chocolate chips

Combine sugar, shortening and eggs in mixer bowl; beat until smooth. Mix flour, oats, baking soda, cloves and salt in bowl. Add to egg mixture; mix well. Fold in vanilla, bananas and chocolate chips. Drop by spoonfuls onto cookie sheet. Bake at 350 degrees until light brown. Cool on cookie sheet for 2 minutes. Remove to wire rack to cool completely. **Yield: 4 dozen.**

Doris J. Bacon, Iona #272

Best-Ever Cookies

1 cup shortening
1 cup sugar
1 cup packed brown sugar
2 eggs
1 teaspoon vanilla extract
1½ cups oats
2 cups sifted flour
2 teaspoons baking powder
1 teaspoon baking soda
½ teaspoon salt
1 cup coconut
1 cup chopped nuts

Cream shortening, sugar and brown sugar in mixer bowl until light and fluffy. Beat in eggs and vanilla. Add oats, flour, baking powder, baking soda and salt; mix well. Stir in coconut and nuts. Shape into 1-inch balls; place on cookie sheet. Bake at 325 degrees for 15 to 25 minutes or until firm. Cool on cookie sheet for 2 minutes. Remove to wire rack to cool completely. **Yield: 4 dozen.**

Miriam Sidle, Valley #1360

Butter Dream Cookies

½ cup butter, softened
½ cup shortening
½ cup sugar
2¼ cups flour, sifted
1 teaspoon almond extract
Maraschino cherry halves, drained

Cream butter and shortening in mixer bowl until light. Add sugar, beating until fluffy. Add flour and almond extract; mix well. Shape by tablespoonfuls into balls; place on cookie sheet. Press cherry half onto top of each cookie. Bake at 350 for 8 to 10 minutes or just until golden brown. Cool on cookie sheet for 2 minutes. Remove to wire rack to cool completely. **Yield: 3 dozen.**

Shirley Weibley, Tuscarora #2058

Carrot Cookies

2 cups unbleached flour
1/4 cup wheat germ
1/2 teaspoon baking powder
1/2 teaspoon baking soda
1/4 teaspoon salt
1 cup margarine, softened
3/4 cup packed brown sugar
2 eggs
1 teaspoon vanilla extract
1 teaspoon grated orange rind
2 cups oats
1 cup grated carrots
1 cup chopped nuts
2/3 cup coconut

Mix flour, wheat germ, baking powder, baking soda and salt in bowl. Cream margarine and brown sugar in mixer bowl until light and fluffy. Beat in eggs and vanilla. Add dry ingredients gradually, mixing well after each addition. Stir in orange rind, oats, carrots, nuts and coconut. Drop by teaspoonfuls onto greased cookie sheet. Bake at 350 degrees for 12 minutes or until light brown. Cool on cookie sheet for 2 minutes. Remove to wire rack to cool completely. **Yield: 5 dozen.**

Lillian Mengel, Virginville, #1832

The $250 Chocolate Chip Cookie

2 cups butter, softened
2 cups sugar
2 cups packed brown sugar
4 eggs
2 tablespoons vanilla extract
2 4-ounce chocolate candy bars, chopped
2 cups chocolate chips
3 cups chopped walnuts
5 cups ground oats
4 cups flour
2 teaspoons baking powder
2 teaspoons baking soda
1 teaspoon salt

Cream butter, sugar and brown sugar in mixer bowl until light and fluffy. Beat in eggs and vanilla. Stir in chopped chocolate, chocolate chips, and walnuts. Add oats, flour, baking powder, baking soda and salt; mix well. Drop by teaspoonfuls onto cookie sheet. Bake at 375 degrees for 10 to 15 minutes or until golden brown. Cool on cookie sheet for 2 minutes. Remove to wire rack to cool completely. May add white chocolate if desired. **Yield: 10 dozen.**

Bryson Blair Huling, Shavers Creek #353

Always leave 1 to 2 inches between cookies dropped on cookie sheet to allow room to spread. Thin doughs will spread more than thicker doughs.

Chocolate Chip Cookies

3 eggs
3/4 cup sugar
1 1/2 cups packed brown sugar
1 1/2 cups shortening
1 1/2 tablespoons water
1 1/2 teaspoons vanilla extract
3 3/4 cups flour
1 1/2 teaspoons baking soda
1 1/2 teaspoons salt
3/4 12-ounce package chocolate chips
1 1/2 cups chopped nuts (optional)

Combine first 6 ingredients in large mixer bowl; mix well. Add flour, baking soda and salt gradually, mixing well after each addition. Stir in chocolate chips and nuts. Drop by teaspoonfuls onto cookie sheet. Bake at 350 degrees for 10 minutes or until light brown. Cool on cookie sheet for 2 minutes. Remove to wire rack to cool completely. This recipe placed first in the Junior Grange State competition for 5 to 8 year olds in October of 1991. **Yield: 6 to 8 dozen.**

Rachel Aumiller, East New Castle Junior #224

Chocolate Crinkles

1/2 cup oil
4 squares unsweetened baking chocolate, melted
2 cups sugar
4 eggs
2 teaspoons vanilla extract
2 cups flour
2 teaspoons baking powder
1/2 teaspoon salt
1 cup confectioners' sugar

Mix oil, chocolate and sugar in mixer bowl. Beat in eggs 1 at a time. Add vanilla. Stir in flour, baking powder and salt. Chill for several hours to overnight. Drop by teaspoonfuls into confectioners' sugar; shape into balls. Place on greased cookie sheet. Bake at 350 degrees for 10 to 12 minutes or just until set; do not overbake. Cool on cookie sheet for 2 minutes. Remove to wire rack to cool completely. **Yield: 3 dozen.**

Luella Ruhf, South Auburn, #1188

French Cream Cookies

2 cups flour
1 teaspoon baking soda
1 teaspoon cream of tartar
1/4 teaspoon salt
1/2 cup butter
1/2 cup shortening
1/2 cup peanut butter
1 1/2 cups confectioners' sugar
1 egg, beaten
1 teaspoon vanilla extract

Mix flour, baking soda, cream of tartar and salt in bowl. Cream butter, shortening and peanut butter in mixer bowl until light. Add confectioners' sugar, beating until fluffy. Beat in egg and vanilla. Add dry ingredients; mix well. Chill in refrigerator. Shape into balls. Place on cookie sheet; flatten with fork in crisscross design. Bake at 350 degrees for 12 minutes. Cool on cookie sheet for 2 minutes. Remove to wire rack to cool completely. **Yield: 3 dozen.**

Sarah Preston, DuBois #808

Date and Nut-Filled Cookies

1½ cups chopped dates
⅔ cup sugar
⅔ cup water
1 tablespoon lemon juice
½ cup chopped nuts
1 cup margarine or butter, softened
2 cups packed brown sugar
2 eggs
1 teaspoon vanilla extract
⅓ cup milk
3¼ cups flour
1 teaspoon baking powder
1 teaspoon salt

Combine dates, sugar and water in saucepan. Cook until thickened to desired consistency, stirring frequently. Stir in lemon juice and nuts. Cool to room temperature. Cream margarine and brown sugar in mixer bowl until light and fluffy. Beat in eggs, vanilla and milk. Sift in flour, baking powder and salt; mix well. Drop most of the batter by spoonfuls 2 inches apart onto cookie sheet. Place ½ teaspoon date mixture in center of each cookie. Top each with ½ teaspoon cookie batter. Bake at 375 degrees for 10 minutes or until light brown. Cool on cookie sheet for 2 minutes. Remove to wire rack to cool completely. **Yield: 5 dozen.**

Eleanor Smiley, Waterford #423

Soft Ginger Cookies

1 cup packed brown sugar
1 cup shortening or lard
1 cup molasses
1 egg, beaten
½ cup boiling water
1 tablespoon baking soda
5 cups flour
½ teaspoon salt
1 tablespoon cinnamon
1 tablespoon ginger
1 teaspoon cloves
½ teaspoon nutmeg
½ cup milk
1 teaspoon vanilla extract

Combine brown sugar, shortening, molasses and egg in mixer bowl. Add mixture of boiling water and baking soda; mix until smooth. Mix flour, salt and spices. Add to batter with milk and vanilla; mix well. Drop onto cookie sheet. Bake at 350 degrees for 15 minutes or until brown. Cool on cookie sheet for 2 minutes. Remove to wire rack to cool completely. **Yield: 4 dozen.**

Iva K. Beward, Milford #773

Grandma Rick's Gingersnaps

1½ cups shortening
2 cups molasses
1 1-pound package brown sugar
½ cup water
10 cups flour
1 tablespoon baking soda
1 tablespoon ginger
Sugar (optional)

Combine shortening, molasses, brown sugar and water in mixer bowl; mix until smooth. Add flour, baking soda and ginger; mix well. Shape into balls; roll in sugar if desired. Place on cookie sheet. Bake at 350 degrees for 7 minutes. Cool on cookie sheet for 2 minutes. Remove to wire rack to cool completely. **Yield: 12 dozen.**

Treva Leese, Gideon #2010

Honey and Cheese Oatmeal Cookies

½ cup shortening
1½ cups sugar
1 teaspoon salt
½ cup honey
1 tablespoon lemon juice
1 egg
1 cup flour
½ teaspoon baking soda
1 teaspoon cinnamon
3 cups oats
½ cup cottage cheese
½ cup dried currants or raisins

Cream shortening, sugar and salt in mixer bowl until light. Add honey, lemon juice and egg; mix well. Sift in flour, baking soda and cinnamon; mix well. Add oats alternately with cottage cheese, mixing well after each addition. Stir in currants. Drop by tablespoonfuls 2 inches apart onto greased cookie sheet. Bake at 375 degrees for 10 to 12 minutes or until light brown. Cool on cookie sheet for 2 minutes. Remove to wire rack to cool completely. Store in airtight container. **Yield: 5 dozen.**

Roberta Windhorst, Pleasant Hill #1505

No-Bake Honey-Milk Balls

1 cup honey
1 cup peanut butter
2 cups nonfat dry milk
2 cups oats

Measure honey in 2-cup measure. Add peanut butter to measure 2 cups. Combine with dry milk in mixer bowl. Add oats gradually, mixing well. Shape into small balls. **Yield: 2 dozen.**

Lisa Koenig, Central #1650

Kiffels

1 pound ground poppy seed
2 cups sugar
2 tablespoons melted butter
1/2 teaspoon cinnamon
8 ounces cream cheese, softened
1 cup butter, softened
2 cups flour

Combine poppy seed, sugar, melted butter and cinnamon in bowl; mix well. Combine cream cheese, butter and flour in bowl; mix well. Roll on floured surface. Cut into 2-inch squares. Spoon poppy seed mixture onto squares. Roll up to enclose filling; place on cookie sheet. Bake at 325 degrees on bottom rack of oven for 7 minutes. Bake on top rack for 5 minutes longer or until light brown. Cool on cookie sheet for 2 minutes. Remove to wire rack to cool completely. **Yield: 3 dozen.**

Nut Filling: Combine 1 pound ground nuts, 1 1/2 cups sugar, 1/4 cup melted margarine, 2 beaten egg whites and 2 tablespoons milk.

Rose Buss, Central #1650

Lady Locks

1 egg
1 1/2 cups cold water
1/2 cup margarine
4 cups flour
1 1/2 cups butter, softened
1 tablespoon sugar
7 tablespoons flour
1 cup milk
1 cup sugar
1 cup shortening
1 tablespoon vanilla extract

Beat egg with cold water in small bowl. Cut 1/2 cup margarine into flour in bowl until crumbly. Add egg mixture; mix well. Knead until no longer sticky. Roll on floured surface. Spread with 1/2 cup softened margarine. Fold dough over and wrap with cold wet cloth. Chill for 1 hour. Repeat rolling, spreading and chilling process 2 more times using remaining margarine. Chill overnight. Roll a small portion of the dough at a time; sprinkle with 1 tablespoon sugar. Cut diagonally into 1x4-inch pieces. Roll each piece around round clothespin. Place on ungreased cookie sheet. Bake at 350 degrees for 15 to 20 minutes or until light brown. Let stand for 1 to 2 minutes. Slide cookies off clothespins. Cool on wire rack. Blend flour and milk in saucepan. Cook until thickened, stirring constantly. Cool to room temperature. Cream 1 cup sugar and shortening in mixer bowl until light. Add cooled milk mixture and vanilla; beat until very smooth. Pipe into cookies. **Yield: 6 dozen.**

Margaret S. Bauer, Perry Valley #1804

Old-Fashioned Lemon Cookies

1 cup shortening
1 cup sugar
1 cup packed brown sugar
2 eggs
1 teaspoon lemon extract
1 cup milk
1 tablespoon baking powder
1 teaspoon baking soda
6 to 7 cups flour

Cream shortening, sugar and brown sugar in mixer bowl until light and fluffy. Beat in eggs and lemon extract. Add milk, baking powder, baking soda and enough flour to form dough. Roll on floured surface; cut as desired. Place on cookie sheet. Bake at 400 degrees just until edges begin to brown. Cool on cookie sheet for 2 minutes. Remove to wire rack to cool completely. **Yield: 8 dozen.**

Jewell Brock, East Franklin #1709

Macaroons

1 14-ounce can sweetened condensed milk
1 pound coconut

Combine condensed milk and coconut in bowl; mix well. Drop by teaspoonfuls onto greased cookie sheet. Bake at 300 degrees for 12 minutes or until light brown. Remove to cloth or waxed paper to cool. Reshape cookies that come apart in removing from cookie sheet; cookies will firm as they cool. **Yield: 3 dozen.**

Erla Florelle Haas, Shermanata #1796

Malted Milk Cookies

1 cup margarine, softened
1 cup confectioners' sugar
2 teaspoons vanilla extract
1 tablespoon milk
2 cups flour
1/2 teaspoon baking powder
15 to 20 malted milk balls, crushed
1/2 cup chopped nuts

Cream margarine and confectioners' sugar in mixer bowl until light and fluffy. Beat in vanilla and milk. Add flour and baking powder; mix well. Stir in crushed candy and nuts. Shape by tablespoonfuls into balls. Place on ungreased cookie sheet; press lightly. Bake at 300 degrees for 20 minutes or until very light brown. Cool on cookie sheet for 2 minutes. Remove to wire rack to cool completely. May add maple or black walnut flavoring with vanilla if desired. **Yield: 3 dozen.**

Helen Bishop, Conneaut #955

Soft Molasses Cookies

4 cups flour
$2^1/_4$ teaspoons baking soda
$2^1/_4$ teaspoons ginger
$1^1/_2$ teaspoons ground cloves
$1^1/_2$ teaspoons cinnamon
$^1/_2$ teaspoon salt
$^1/_2$ cup butter, softened
$^1/_2$ cup shortening
$1^1/_2$ cups sugar
$^1/_2$ cup molasses
2 eggs, slightly beaten
Sugar

Mix first 6 ingredients in bowl. Cream butter, shortening and $1^1/_2$ cups sugar in large mixer bowl until light and fluffy. Beat in molasses and eggs. Add dry ingredients, mixing well. Shape into $1^1/_2$-inch balls. Dip tops into additional sugar. Place $2^1/_2$ inches apart on greased cookie sheet. Bake at 350 degrees for 8 to 10 minutes or until light brown; do not overbake. Cool on cookie sheet for 2 minutes. Remove to wire rack to cool completely. Store in airtight container. **Yield: 3 dozen.**

Lola Glass, North Woodbury #1923

Nutmeg Cookies

2 cups butter, softened
1 cup sugar
4 eggs
1 teaspoon vanilla extract
$2^1/_2$ cups flour
3 tablespoons baking powder
$1^1/_2$ teaspoons nutmeg

Cream butter and sugar in bowl until light. Beat in eggs and vanilla. Add mixture of remaining ingredients; mix well. Chill for 4 hours to overnight. Roll on floured surface; cut into squares. Place on cookie sheet. Bake at 375 degrees for 6 to 8 minutes or until light brown. Cool on cookie sheet for 2 minutes. Cool on wire rack. **Yield: 3 dozen.**

Melzena B. Blose, Rural Valley #1750

Filled Oatmeal Cookies

1 cup margarine, softened
$1^1/_2$ cups packed brown sugar
2 eggs
1 teaspoon vanilla extract
$1^1/_2$ cups quick-cooking oats
$3^1/_2$ cups flour
1 teaspoon baking soda
1 teaspoon cream of tartar
1 21-ounce can cherry or other flavor pie filling
Sugar (optional)

Cream margarine and brown sugar in mixer bowl until light and fluffy. Beat in eggs and vanilla. Add oats, flour, baking soda and cream of tartar; mix well. Chill in refrigerator. Shape into 1-inch balls. Place half the balls on ungreased cookie sheet; place remaining balls on waxed paper. Top balls with waxed paper; press with glass to flatten. Peel off waxed paper. Spoon pie filling onto cookies on cookie sheet. Top with remaining cookies. Sprinkle with sugar if desired. Bake at 375 degrees for 20 minutes. Cool on cookie sheet for 2 minutes. Cool on wire rack. **Yield: 3 dozen.**

Ruth Otterman, South Buffalo #1908

Honey-Oatmeal Cookies

1¼ cups sugar
⅓ cup oil
3 egg whites
⅓ cup honey
1 teaspoon baking soda
1 teaspoon salt
2 cups quick-cooking oats
1¾ cups oat flour
1 cup raisins
1 cup chopped pecans

Combine sugar, oil, egg whites, honey, baking soda and salt in bowl; mix until smooth. Add oats, oat flour, raisins and pecans; mix well. Drop by rounded teaspoonfuls 2 inches apart onto ungreased cookie sheet. Press lightly with spoon to flatten. Bake at 375 degrees for 8 to 10 minutes or until light brown. Cool on cookie sheet for 2 minutes. Remove to wire rack to cool completely. **Yield: 4 dozen.**

Edna S. Jones, Shermanata #1796

Powder Puff Cookies

½ cup butter, softened
½ cup packed brown sugar
1 teaspoon vanilla extract
1¼ cups flour
½ teaspoon salt
2 tablespoons milk
2 tablespoons baking cocoa
2 teaspoons butter
2 tablespoons miniature chocolate chips
¾ cup sifted confectioners' sugar
¾ cup miniature chocolate chips
1 tablespoon butter
2 tablespoons light corn syrup
1 tablespoon water
1 teaspoon vanilla extract

Cream ½ cup butter and brown sugar in mixer bowl until light and fluffy. Beat in 1 teaspoon vanilla. Sift in flour and salt; mix well. Add milk, baking cocoa and 2 teaspoons butter; mix well. Stir in 2 tablespoons chocolate chips. Shape into 1-inch balls; place on ungreased cookie sheet. Make small depression in each cookie with thumb. Bake at 350 degrees for 10 to 12 minutes or until cookies test done. Roll in confectioners' sugar, coating well. Cool on wire rack. Combine ¾ cup chocolate chips and 1 tablespoon butter in glass bowl. Microwave on High for 20 seconds at a time until melted, stirring until smooth. Stir in corn syrup, water and 1 teaspoon vanilla. Cool for 5 minutes. Spoon into depressions in cookies. Store cookies in loosely covered container. **Yield: 3 dozen.**

Brandon Treichler, Virginville #1832

Soften 1 stick of butter in the microwave for 1 minute at 20% power. Soften cream cheese for 2 to 2½ minutes at 30% power.

No-Bake Orange and Peanut Butter Drops

3/4 cup sugar
1/4 cup thawed frozen orange juice concentrate
1/4 cup butter
1/4 cup crunchy peanut butter
1 1/2 cups quick-cooking oats
1/2 cup raisins

Combine sugar, orange juice concentrate and butter in medium saucepan. Bring to a boil, stirring constantly; remove from heat. Stir in peanut butter. Add oats and raisins; mix well. Drop by teaspoonfuls onto waxed paper. Chill until firm. **Yield: 2 1/2 dozen.**

Carrie Frederick, Sinking Valley #484

Orange Marmalade Cookies

1 cup orange marmalade
1 egg
1/2 cup shortening
1 teaspoon vanilla extract
2 cups flour
1 teaspoon baking powder
1/2 cup finely chopped nuts (optional)

Combine marmalade, egg and shortening in bowl; mix until smooth. Add vanilla, flour, baking powder and nuts; mix well. Drop by rounded teaspoonfuls onto greased cookie sheet. Bake at 350 degrees for 10 to 12 minutes or until light brown. Cool on cookie sheet for 2 minutes. Remove to wire rack to cool completely. **Yield: 3 to 4 dozen.**

Gertrude Gager, Unity #1710

Magic Peanut Butter Middles

1 1/2 cups flour
1/2 cup baking cocoa
1/2 teaspoon baking soda
1/2 cup margarine, softened
1/4 cup peanut butter
1/2 cup sugar
1/2 cup packed brown sugar
1 teaspoon vanilla extract
1 egg
3/4 cup peanut butter
3/4 cup confectioners' sugar

Mix flour, baking cocoa and baking soda in small bowl. Cream margarine, 1/4 cup peanut butter, sugar and brown sugar in large mixer bowl until light and fluffy. Beat in vanilla and egg. Add dry ingredients; mix well and set aside. Blend 3/4 cup peanut butter and confectioners' sugar in small bowl. Shape into thirty 1-inch balls. Shape reserved dough by tablespoonfuls around balls, enclosing completely. Place 2 inches apart on ungreased cookie sheet. Press with bottom of glass dipped in additional sugar to flatten. Bake at 375 degrees until set with slight cracks. Cool on cookie sheet for 2 minutes. Remove to wire rack to cool completely. **Yield: 2 1/2 dozen.**

Margaret McCoy, Menallen #1091

Quick Peanut Butter Cookies

1 cup peanut butter
1 cup sugar
1 egg

Combine peanut butter, sugar and egg in bowl; mix well. Shape into balls; place on ungreased cookie sheet. Bake at 325 degrees for 10 to 12 minutes or until golden brown. Cool on cookie sheet for 2 minutes. Remove to wire rack to cool completely. **Yield: 1½ dozen.**

Willie Schlemmer Jr., East New Castle Junior #224

Pineapple and Sweet Potato Turnovers

¼ cup drained crushed pineapple
½ cup mashed cooked sweet potato or squash
¼ cup sugar
¼ cup flaked coconut
¼ teaspoon salt
3 ounces cream cheese, softened
½ cup butter or margarine, softened
1 cup sifted flour

Combine pineapple, sweet potato, sugar, coconut and salt in bowl; mix well and set aside. Combine cream cheese, butter and flour in bowl; mix with pastry blender or fingers until mixture forms dough. Chill until dough can be easily handled. Roll ½ at a time to thickness of pie pastry on lightly floured surface. Cut into 3-inch circles. Place 1 heaping teaspoonful of filling on 1 side of each circle. Fold circles over to enclose filling; press edges with fork to seal. Place on cookie sheet. Bake at 375 degrees for 15 minutes or until golden brown. Remove to wire rack to cool. **Yield: 20 turnovers.**

Thelma V. Snyder, Willard #1441

Vanilla Pizzelles

1½ cups sugar
6 eggs, beaten
1 cup melted margarine, cooled
2 tablespoons vanilla extract
3½ cups flour
4 teaspoons baking powder

Beat sugar gradually into eggs in mixer bowl. Add margarine and vanilla; beat until smooth. Sift in flour and baking powder gradually, mixing well after each addition. Drop by spoonfuls onto center of hot oiled pizzelle iron. Bake for 30 seconds or until mixture no longer steams. Remove with fork to wire rack to cool. Store in airtight container. May add ground nuts or substitute other flavoring for vanilla. For **Chocolate Pizzelles**, add ½ cup baking cocoa, ½ cup sugar and ½ teaspoon baking powder. **Yield: 5 dozen.**

Elizabeth Windhorst, Pleasant Hill #1505

Polvorones

1 cup butter or margarine, softened
1/2 cup sifted confectioners' sugar
1 teaspoon vanilla extract
2 cups flour
1/2 cup finely chopped pecans
1/8 teaspoon salt
Confectioners' sugar

Cream butter, 1/2 cup confectioners' sugar and vanilla in medium mixer bowl until light and fluffy. Stir in mixture of flour, pecans and salt. Shape into 1-inch balls; place on ungreased cookie sheet. Bake at 325 degrees for 20 to 25 minutes or until light brown. Roll in additional confectioners' sugar. Cool on wire rack. Roll again in confectioners' sugar. May sprinkle with additional pecans if desired. **Yield: 3 dozen.**

Faye M. Schaeffer, Virginville #1832

Pumpkin Pinwheels

1 16-ounce can solid-pack pumpkin
1 cup sugar
1 teaspoon pumpkin pie spice
1 cup ground nuts
1 cup shortening
2 cups sugar
3 eggs
4 cups flour
1/2 teaspoon cinnamon
1/2 teaspoon salt
2 cups confectioners' sugar
1 tablespoon melted butter
1 teaspoon vanilla extract
2 to 3 tablespoons milk

Combine pumpkin, 1 cup sugar and pumpkin pie spice in saucepan. heat until bubbly; reduce heat. Simmer for 10 minutes. Stir in nuts. Cool to room temperature. Cream shortening and 2 cups sugar in mixer bowl until light and fluffy. Beat in eggs. Add flour, cinnamon and salt; mix well. Divide into 3 portions. Roll 1 portion at a time into 8x12-inch rectangle on floured surface. Spread each with 1/3 of the pumpkin mixture. Roll as for jelly roll to enclose filling. Freeze, wrapped in foil, overnight. Remove 1 roll at a time from freezer and slice 3/8 inch thick. Place on greased cookie sheet. Bake at 400 degrees for 10 to 12 minutes or until golden brown. Cool on cookie sheet for 2 minutes. Remove to wire rack to cool completely. Blend confectioners' sugar, butter, vanilla and enough milk to make of desired consistency in bowl. Drizzle over cookies. **Yield: 8 dozen.**

Dorothy Dengate, Logan Valley #664

You can make an emergency substitute for confectioners' sugar by processing a small amount of granulated sugar at a time in the blender.

Sesame Cookies

1 cup margarine, softened
1/4 cup sugar
1 teaspoon vanilla extract
2 cups flour
1/2 teaspoon salt
Sesame seed
Apricot or strawberry preserves

Cream margarine and sugar in mixer bowl until light and fluffy. Blend in vanilla. Add flour and salt; mix well. Shape into 1-inch balls. Roll in sesame seed; place on cookie sheet. Press each cookie to make indentation. Fill indentations with preserves. Bake at 400 degrees for 10 to 12 minutes or until light brown. Cool on cookie sheet for 2 minutes. Remove to wire rake to cool completely. **Yield: 2 dozen.**

Betty Bittermann, Friendship #1799

Special Sugar Cookies

1 cup shortening
2 cups sugar
2 eggs
1 cup sour cream
1 teaspoon vanilla extract
5 cups flour
1 teaspoon baking soda
1 teaspoon salt

Combine shortening, sugar, eggs, sour cream and vanilla in mixer bowl; beat until smooth. Add flour, baking soda and salt; mix well. Chill for several hours to overnight. Roll on floured surface; cut as desired. Place on ungreased cookie sheet. Bake at 375 degrees for 10 minutes. Cool on cookie sheet for 2 minutes. Remove to wire rack to cool completely. **Yield: 7 dozen.**

Harold Hebets, East Branch #1262

Sugar Cookies

1 cup shortening
1 cup (heaping) sugar
2 eggs, beaten
1/2 cup milk
1 teaspoon vanilla extract
4 cups flour
1 teaspoon baking powder
1 teaspoon baking soda
1/2 teaspoon salt

Combine shortening, sugar and eggs in mixer bowl; beat until smooth. Beat in milk and vanilla. Add mixture of flour, baking powder, baking soda and salt; mix well. Roll 1/4 inch thick on floured surface; cut as desired. Place on cookie sheet. Bake at 375 degrees for 10 minutes. Cool on cookie sheet for 2 minutes. Remove to wire rack to cool completely. **Yield: 5 dozen.**

Mrs. Ralph O'Bryan, Alert #905

Spicy Sugar Cookies

1 cup shortening
1 cup sugar
1 cup packed brown sugar
2 eggs, beaten
1 teaspoon nutmeg
1 teaspoon baking soda
1 cup sour milk
6 cups flour

Cream shortening, 1 cup sugar and brown sugar in mixer bowl until light and fluffy. Beat in eggs and nutmeg. Dissolve baking soda in sour milk in small bowl. Add flour to creamed mixture alternately with sour milk, mixing well after each addition. Roll 1/4 inch thick on floured surface; sprinkle with additional sugar. Cut as desired. Place on cookie sheet. Bake at 400 degrees for 8 minutes or until light brown. Cool on cookie sheet for 2 minutes. Remove to wire rack to cool completely. May substitute butter for half the shortening if desired. **Yield: 3 to 4 dozen.**

Phyllis Robinson, Fassett #1567

Easy Sugar Cookies

3 cups flour
1/2 teaspoon baking powder
1/2 teaspoon baking soda
1 cup butter
2 eggs
1 cup sugar
Colored sugar

Sift flour, baking powder and baking soda into bowl. Cut in butter until crumbly. Beat eggs in mixer bowl. Add 1 cup sugar, beating until thick. Add to crumb mixture; mix well to form dough. Roll 1/2 inch thick on floured pastry cloth. Cut as desired. Sprinkle with colored sugar. Place on cookie sheet. Bake at 375 degrees for 8 to 10 minutes or until golden brown. Cool on cookie sheet for 2 minutes. Remove to wire rack to cool completely. **Yield: 6 dozen.**

Lester Sonon Jr., Virginville #1832

Mother's Sugar Cookies

3 1/2 cups flour
1/2 teaspoon baking powder
1 teaspoon baking soda
1/2 teaspoon nutmeg
2/3 cup shortening
1 cup sugar
1 cup packed brown sugar
2 eggs
1 teaspoon vanilla extract
1 cup light sour cream

Sift flour, baking powder, baking soda and nutmeg together. Cream shortening, sugar and brown sugar in mixer bowl until light and fluffy. Beat in eggs and vanilla. Add dry ingredients alternately with sour cream, mixing well after each addition. Chill dough overnight. Roll on lightly floured surface; cut as desired. Place on cookie sheet. Bake at 325 degrees for 12 minutes. Cool on cookie sheet for 2 minutes. Remove to wire rack to cool completely. May decorate as desired. **Yield: 4 dozen.**

Margaret Townsend, Cross Creek Village #1751

Ellen's Sugar Cookies

1 pound margarine, softened
1 cup shortening
3 1-pound packages light brown sugar
5 pounds (or less) Wondra flour
1½ teaspoons cream of tartar
1 quart buttermilk
2 tablespoons baking soda
2 teaspoons vanilla extract

Cream margarine, shortening and brown sugar in large mixer bowl until light and fluffy. Add flour and cream of tartar; mix well. Add buttermilk, baking soda and vanilla; mix well. Chill overnight. Roll on floured surface; cut as desired. Place on cookie sheet. Bake at 350 degrees until golden brown. Cool on cookie sheet for 2 minutes. Remove to wire rack to cool completely. **Yield: 18 dozen.**

Carol L. Etchberger, Ontelaunee #1617

Sugarless Cookies

1 cup flour
1 cup quick-cooking oats
1 teaspoon baking soda
1½ teaspoons cinnamon
¼ teaspoon nutmeg
1 teaspoon ground cloves
1 teaspoon allspice
½ teaspoon salt (optional)
½ cup oil
2 eggs
1 teaspoon vanilla extract
1 cup unsweetened applesauce
1½ cups raisins
½ cup chopped nuts

Mix flour, oats, baking soda, cinnamon, nutmeg, cloves, allspice and salt in bowl. Add oil, eggs, vanilla and applesauce; mix well. Stir in raisins and nuts. Drop by teaspoonfuls onto greased cookie sheet. Bake at 375 degrees for 12 minutes. Cool on cookie sheet for 2 minutes. Remove to wire rack to cool completely. **Yield: 4 dozen.**

Barbara Dixon, Brady #1218

Swedish Ginger Cookies

¾ cup margarine, softened
1 cup sugar
1 egg
¼ cup molasses
2¼ cups flour
2½ teaspoons baking powder
½ teaspoon baking soda
½ teaspoon ginger
¼ teaspoon ground cloves
1 teaspoon cinnamon
½ teaspoon salt

Cream margarine and sugar in mixer bowl until light and fluffy. Beat in egg and molasses. Add remaining ingredients; mix well. Chill for 2 hours or longer. Shape by scant teaspoonfuls into small balls; place on cookie sheet. Flatten with bottom of glass covered with damp cloth and dipped in additional sugar. Bake at 375 degrees for 10 minutes or until crisp and golden brown. Cool on cookie sheet for 2 minutes. Remove to wire rack to cool completely. **Yield: 5 dozen.**

Ruth S. Carlson, Mountain #1307

Caramel Tassies

6 ounces cream cheese, softened
3/4 cup margarine, softened
2 cups flour
1 package caramels
1/2 cup evaporated milk
1/3 cup sugar
1/4 cup shortening
1/4 cup margarine, softened
1/3 cup evaporated milk
1/2 teaspoon vanilla extract

Beat cream cheese and 3/4 cup margarine in mixer bowl until smooth. Add flour; mix well. Shape into 48 balls. Chill for 2 hours. Press into ungreased tassie cups. Bake at 350 degrees for 15 to 20 minutes or until golden brown. Cool in tassie cups. Remove to serving plate. Melt caramels with 1/2 cup evaporated milk in double boiler, stirring to blend well. Spoon warm mixture into tassie cups. Let stand until cool. Combine sugar, shortening, 1/4 cup margarine, 1/3 cup evaporated milk and vanilla in bowl; beat until smooth. Spread over tassies. **Yield: 4 dozen.**

Della Jones, Jefferson #1373

Peanut Butter Tassies

1/2 cup margarine, softened
1/2 cup peanut butter
1/2 cup sugar
1/2 cup packed brown sugar
1 egg
1/2 teaspoon vanilla extract
1 1/2 cups flour
3/4 teaspoon baking soda
1/2 teaspoon salt
48 1-inch Reese's peanut butter cups

Cream margarine, peanut butter, sugar and brown sugar in mixer bowl until light and fluffy. Beat in egg and vanilla. Add flour, baking soda and salt; mix well. Shape into 1-inch balls. Press into ungreased tassie cups. Bake at 350 degrees for 8 to 10 minutes or until golden brown. Press 1 peanut butter cup into each tassie. Cool in cups for 10 minutes. Remove to wire rack to cool completely. **Yield: 4 dozen.**

Mrs. Joseph O. Hill, South Buffalo #1908

Sugar-Free Tomato Soup Cookies

1 1/2 cups raisins
1/2 cup melted margarine, cooled
2 egg whites, beaten
1 10-ounce can tomato soup
1 1/2 cups flour
2 cups quick-cooking oats
1 teaspoon baking powder
1/2 teaspoon baking soda
2 teaspoons cinnamon
1/2 cup chopped nuts

Soak raisins in hot water to cover in bowl for 5 minutes; drain. Combine margarine, eggs whites and soup in bowl; mix well. Stir in flour, oats, baking powder, baking soda, cinnamon, raisins and nuts. Drop onto lightly greased cookie sheet. Flatten with fork dipped in water. Bake at 350 degrees for 12 to 15 minutes or until golden brown. Cool on cookie sheet for 2 minutes. Remove to wire rack to cool completely. **Yield: 4 dozen.**

Mary Haladay, Berwick #1917

Pies

Christmas Almond Pie

1 6-ounce package vanilla instant pudding mix
$1\frac{1}{2}$ cups cold milk
2 envelopes whipped topping mix
1 cup cold milk
2 cups whipping cream, whipped
2 tablespoons almond extract
1 9-inch graham cracker pie shell
$\frac{1}{4}$ cup slivered almonds
$\frac{1}{4}$ cup chopped maraschino cherries

Mix pudding mix and $1\frac{1}{2}$ cups milk in small bowl. Mix whipped topping mix and 1 cup milk in medium bowl. Combine pudding mixture, whipped topping and whipped cream in large bowl; mix well. Stir in flavoring. Spoon into pie shell. Top with almonds and cherries. Chill for 8 hours or overnight. **Yield: 6 servings.**

Virginia K. Letterman, Port Matilda #1284

Apple Chiffon Pie

3 eggs
$1\frac{1}{2}$ cups sugar
1 cup flour
2 teaspoons baking powder
2 cups finely chopped apples
1 cup chopped pecans
1 10-inch unbaked pie shell

Combine eggs, sugar, flour and baking powder in bowl; mix well by hand. Stir in apples and pecans. Pour into pie shell. Bake at 350 degrees for 40 to 45 minutes or until set. **Yield: 8 servings.**

Edith L. Stoner, Fort Granville #1902

Cheesy Apple Pizza

3 cups flour
1 teaspoon salt
$1\frac{1}{2}$ cups shortening or butter-flavored shortening
1 egg
1 tablespoon vinegar
5 tablespoons ice water
7 tart apples, cored, thinly sliced
$\frac{1}{2}$ cup sugar
1 teaspoon cinnamon
$\frac{1}{4}$ teaspoon nutmeg
1 cup shredded sharp Cheddar cheese
$\frac{3}{4}$ cup flour
$\frac{1}{2}$ cup sugar
$\frac{1}{2}$ cup cold butter, cut into pieces

Combine 3 cups flour and salt in bowl. Cut in shortening until crumbly. Beat egg, vinegar and water in small bowl. Pour over flour mixture; mix well with fork. Use half this mixture for pizza crust; wrap remainder in plastic wrap and store in refrigerator or freezer. Shape dough into large ball. Roll into 15-inch circle. Place on 14-inch pizza pan. Pinch up edge to form smooth rim as for pizza. Cover with overlapping rows of apple slices. Mix $\frac{1}{2}$ cup sugar, cinnamon and nutmeg in bowl. Sprinkle over apples. Spread cheese over all. Mix $\frac{3}{4}$ cup flour and $\frac{1}{2}$ cup sugar in bowl. Cut in butter with pastry blender. Sprinkle over all. Bake at 425 degrees for 30 to 38 minutes or until edge of crust is golden brown. Serve warm. **Yield: 8 servings.**

Beth Beck, Henderson #1315

Creamy Apple Pie

1/2 cup butter, softened
1/4 cup sugar
1/2 teaspoon vanilla extract
1 cup flour
1/4 cup sugar
8 ounces cream cheese, softened
1 egg
1/2 teaspoon vanilla extract
4 cups thinly sliced apples
1/2 teaspoon cinnamon
2/3 cup sugar
1 tablespoon butter
1/2 cup chopped pecans or hickory nuts

Cream 1/2 cup butter, 1/4 cup sugar and 1/2 teaspoon vanilla in mixer bowl until light and fluffy. Add flour gradually until mixture forms soft dough. Press onto bottom and up side of 9-inch deep-dish pie plate. Cream 1/4 cup sugar and cream cheese in mixer bowl until light and fluffy. Add egg and 1/2 teaspoon vanilla; beat until smooth. Spread over crust. Combine apples, cinnamon and 2/3 cup sugar in bowl; mix well. Spoon over cream cheese layer. Dot with 1 tablespoon butter. Sprinkle with pecans. Bake at 400 degrees for 15 minutes. Reduce oven temperature to 350 degrees. Bake for 30 minutes. May cover with foil to prevent excess browning.
Yield: 6 servings.

Catherine Hickernell, Vernon #936

French Apple Pie

1/2 cup margarine
1/3 cup packed brown sugar
1 1/4 cups flour
1/2 cup sugar
1/2 teaspoon vanilla extract
1/4 teaspoon salt
1/4 teaspoon baking soda
7 to 8 cups sliced tart apples
1/2 cup sugar
3 tablespoons flour
1/2 teaspoon cinnamon
1/2 cup flour
1/4 cup packed brown sugar
1/2 teaspoon cinnamon
1/4 cup margarine

Mix 1/2 cup margarine and 1/3 cup brown sugar in bowl. Add 1 1/4 cups flour, 1/2 cup sugar, vanilla, salt and baking soda; stir until crumbly. Press onto bottom and side of 9-inch pie plate. Combine apples, 1/2 cup sugar, 3 tablespoons flour and 1/2 teaspoon cinnamon in bowl; mix well. Spoon onto crust. Mix 1/2 cup flour, 1/4 cup brown sugar and 1/2 teaspoon cinnamon in bowl. Add margarine; stir until crumbly. Sprinkle over apples. Bake at 400 degrees for 15 minutes. Reduce oven temperature to 325 degrees. Bake for 25 to 30 minutes or until apples are tender. Serve warm.
Yield: 6 servings.

Anna L. Craig, Armstrong #1645

To cook a frozen unbaked pie, add 15 to 20 minutes to the time specified in the recipe.

Impossible French Apple Pie

6 cups sliced peeled apples
1 1/4 teaspoons cinnamon
1/4 teaspoon nutmeg
1 cup sugar
3/4 cup milk
1/2 cup baking mix
2 eggs
2 tablespoons margarine, softened
1 cup baking mix
1/2 cup chopped pecans
1/3 cup packed brown sugar
1 tablespoon margarine

Mix apples, cinnamon and nutmeg in bowl. Spoon into greased 10-inch pie plate. Combine sugar, milk, 1/2 cup baking mix, eggs and 2 tablespoons margarine in bowl; beat until smooth. Pour over apples. Mix 1 cup baking mix, pecans, brown sugar and 1 tablespoon margarine in bowl. Sprinkle over all. Bake at 325 degrees for 55 minutes to 1 hour or until knife inserted near center comes out clean. **Yield: 6 servings.**

Claude H. Ohlinger, Ontelaunee #1617

Apple-Cranberry Pie

3/4 cup packed brown sugar
1/4 cup sugar
1/3 cup flour
1 teaspoon cinnamon
4 cups sliced peeled apples
2 cups fresh or frozen cranberries
1 recipe 2-crust pie pastry
2 tablespoons butter

Combine brown sugar, sugar, flour and cinnamon in bowl; mix well. Stir in apples and cranberries. Spoon into pastry-lined pie plate. Dot with butter. Top with remaining pastry, sealing edge and cutting vents. Bake at 425 degrees for 40 minutes or until golden brown. **Yield: 6 servings.**

Janice Bowser, Hartslog Valley #375

Apple Pie Pudding

1 cup sugar
1/2 cup butter, softened
1 egg, slightly beaten
1 cup flour
1 teaspoon baking soda
1/4 teaspoon cinnamon
1/4 teaspoon nutmeg
2 cups chopped apples
1/4 cup chopped pecans
2 tablespoons cornstarch
1 cup sugar
2 tablespoons butter
1 cup boiling water
1 teaspoon vanilla extract

Cream 1 cup sugar and 1/2 cup butter in mixer bowl until light and fluffy. Beat in egg. Sift flour, baking soda, cinnamon and nutmeg together. Stir in apples and pecans. Fold into creamed mixture. Spoon into large pie plate. Bake at 350 degrees for 45 minutes. Combine cornstarch, 1 cup sugar, 2 tablespoons butter, boiling water and vanilla in saucepan. Cook until thickened and clear. Pour over pie. Serve warm. **Yield: 6 servings.**

Bess Yoder, Odin #1254

Banana Split Pie

3 cups graham cracker crumbs
1 cup butter
6 large bananas, sliced
2 eggs
3/4 cup butter, softened
2 cups confectioners' sugar
2 8-ounce cans crushed pineapple, drained
2 cups whipped topping
Chopped pecans
Maraschino cherries

Mix graham cracker crumbs and 1 cup butter in bowl. Press into 10-inch pie plate. Arrange banana slices over shell. Cream eggs, 3/4 cup butter and confectioners' sugar in mixer bowl for 20 minutes. Spread over bananas. Top with pineapple. Cover with whipped topping. Top with pecans and cherries. Chill until serving time. **Yield: 8 servings.**

Esther Knight, Pleasant Hill #1505

Fudge Banana Split Pie

2 or 3 bananas, sliced
Lemon juice
1 pint vanilla ice cream
1 pint chocolate ice cream
1 pint strawberry ice cream
1 11-ounce jar fudge topping

Dip banana slices into lemon juice. Arrange over bottom and side of 9-inch freezer-proof pie plate. Fill with scoops of ice cream. Pour topping over all. Freeze until firm. **Yield: 8 servings.**

Babe Hopkins, London Grove #63

Blackberry Pie

3 cups fresh or frozen blackberries
1/2 cup water
2/3 cup sugar
1/8 teaspoon salt
2 tablespoons cornstarch
2 tablespoons cold water
1 tablespoon butter
1 recipe 2-crust pie pastry

Combine blackberries, water, sugar and salt in saucepan. Bring to a boil. Simmer for 2 to 3 minutes. Add mixture of cornstarch and cold water. Cook until thickened. Stir in butter. Let stand to cool. Spoon into pastry-lined pie plate. Top with remaining pastry, fluting edge and cutting vents. Bake at 350 degrees for 45 minutes. **Yield: 6 servings.**

Ruth Ann Ross, Harmony #1112

Blueberry Icebox Pies

2 to 3 bananas, sliced
2 baked 8-inch pie shells
Lemon juice
8 ounces cream cheese, softened
1 cup sugar
4 cups whipped topping
1 21-ounce can blueberry pie filling

Arrange banana slices in pie shells. Sprinkle with lemon juice. Mix cream cheese and sugar in bowl. Fold in whipped topping. Mound over bananas. Top with pie filling. Chill until serving time. **Yield: 12 servings.**

Eva Southard, Gideon #2010

Buttermilk Meringue Pie

1 cup sugar
1/4 cup flour
1/8 teaspoon salt
1 egg
3 egg yolks
2 cups warm buttermilk
1 tablespoon butter
1 tablespoon lemon extract
1 baked 9-inch pie shell
1 recipe meringue

Combine sugar, flour, salt, egg and egg yolks in double boiler. Stir in buttermilk. Cook until heated through. Cool slightly. Stir in butter and flavoring. Pour into pie shell. Top with meringue, sealing to edge. Bake at 350 degrees until meringue is golden brown. **Yield: 6 servings.**

Althea Kephart, Sanborn #2016

Mom Deal's Butterscotch Pie

1 cup packed light brown sugar
1/4 cup flour
Salt to taste
2 egg yolks, beaten
2 cups milk
1 teaspoon vanilla extract
1 tablespoon butter
1 baked 9-inch pie shell
2 egg whites
1/4 cup sugar

Combine brown sugar, flour, salt, egg yolks and milk in saucepan. Cook until thickened. Add vanilla and butter. Pour into pie shell. Beat egg whites in mixer bowl until soft peaks form. Add sugar gradually, beating until stiff peaks form. Spread over pie. Bake at 350 degrees for 15 minutes. **Yield: 6 servings.**

Thelma I. Deal, Menallen #1091

To prevent ragged edges on a pie meringue when it is cut, dip the knife you use in warm water. Repeat as often as necessary.

Butterscotch Sponge Pie

1 tablespoon butter, softened
1 cup packed brown sugar
2 egg yolks
1 tablespoon flour
1/2 teaspoon salt
1 cup half and half
2 egg whites, stiffly beaten
1 unbaked 9-inch pie shell

Cream butter and brown sugar in mixer bowl until light and fluffy. Add egg yolks, flour and salt; mix well. Stir in half and half. Fold in egg whites. Pour into pie shell. Bake at 350 degrees until set. **Yield: 6 servings.**

Anita Christman, Virginville #1832

Cherry Pie

2 16-ounce cans cherries
1 1/4 cups sugar
1/8 teaspoon salt
1/4 cup tapioca
1 tablespoon flour or cornstarch
1 tablespoon butter
1 1/2 teaspoons lemon juice
1 baked 9-inch pie shell
1/2 cup graham cracker crumbs

Drain cherries, reserving 1/4 cup juice. Combine reserved juice with next 6 ingredients in saucepan. Cook until thickened and clear. Add food coloring if desired. Stir in cherries. Spoon into pie shell. Sprinkle with graham cracker crumbs. Bake at 350 degrees until crumbs are browned. **Yield: 6 servings.**

Mildred Wessner, Virginville #1832

Cherry-Cheese Pie

8 ounces cream cheese, softened
1 1/2 cups sweetened condensed milk
1/3 cup lemon juice
1 teaspoon vanilla extract
1 9-inch graham cracker pie shell
1 21-ounce can cherry pie filling

Combine cream cheese, condensed milk, lemon juice and vanilla in bowl; mix well. Spoon into pie shell. Cover with pie filling. Chill for 4 hours. **Yield: 6 servings.**

Mildred C. Coveleski, Union #152

Chocolate Bar Pie

20 marshmallows
1/2 cup milk
6 small chocolate-almond bars
1/2 cup whipping cream, whipped
1 9-inch graham cracker pie shell

Mix marshmallows and milk in saucepan. Cook until marshmallows are melted. Add candy bars. Cook until candy is melted. Let stand to cool. Fold in whipped cream. Spoon into pie shell. Garnish with whipped topping and slivered almonds. **Yield: 6 servings.**

Alice Campman, Chandlers Valley #846

Chocolate-Peanut Butter Pie

1½ cups cold milk
½ cup peanut butter
2 4-ounce packages chocolate instant pudding mix
2 cups whipped topping
1 9-inch graham cracker pie shell
¼ cup chopped peanuts

Blend milk and peanut butter in bowl. Add pudding mix; mix well. Fold in whipped topping. Spoon into pie shell. Sprinkle with peanuts. Chill until firm.
Yield: 6 servings.

Alice Bish Sylvis, Reynoldsville #1825

German's Sweet Chocolate Pie

4 ounces German's sweet chocolate
⅓ cup milk
2 tablespoons sugar
3 ounces cream cheese, softened
3½ cups whipped topping
1 9-inch graham cracker pie shell

Combine chocolate and 2 tablespoons milk in saucepan. Cook over low heat until chocolate is melted, stirring constantly. Cream sugar and cream cheese in mixer bowl until light and fluffy. Add remaining milk and chocolate mixture to creamed mixture; beat well. Fold in whipped topping. Spoon into pie shell. Freeze for 4 hours or until firm. Let stand in refrigerator for 30 minutes. Garnish with chocolate curls.
Yield: 6 servings.

Thelma Rich, Keystone #2

Coconut Cream Pie

½ cup sugar
½ teaspoon salt
3 tablespoons cornstarch
2½ cups milk
3 egg yolks, beaten
1 tablespoon butter
1 teaspoon vanilla extract
1 baked 9-inch pie shell
3 egg whites
¼ cup sugar
¼ cup shredded coconut

Combine ½ cup sugar, salt, cornstarch and milk in saucepan. Cook over low heat until thickened. Let stand to cool. Stir in egg yolks. Cook over low heat for 5 minutes. Add butter and vanilla. Pour into pie shell. Beat egg whites in mixer bowl until soft peaks form. Add ¼ cup sugar gradually, beating constantly until stiff peaks form. Spread over pie. Sprinkle with coconut. **Yield: 6 servings.**

Mrs. R. Neil Henrie, Lightstreet #31

Toasted Coconut Cream Pie

1 envelope unflavored gelatin
1/2 cup milk
1/2 cup sugar
3/4 cup milk
3 egg yolks
3 egg whites, stiffly beaten
2 cups whipping cream, whipped
1 teaspoon vanilla extract
1 baked 9-inch pie shell
Toasted shredded coconut

Soften gelatin in 1/2 cup milk in small saucepan. Heat until gelatin dissolves, stirring constantly. Cool. Combine sugar, 3/4 cup milk and egg yolks in saucepan; stir with wooden spoon. Cook until blended and smooth, stirring constantly. Let stand to cool. Fold in gelatin mixture, egg whites, whipped cream and vanilla. Pour into pie shell. Sprinkle with coconut. **Yield: 6 servings.**

Nettie A. Kauffman, Ontelaunee #1617

Coconut-Raisin Pie

1/2 cup melted butter
1 1/2 teaspoons vinegar
1 cup sugar
3 eggs, beaten
1/2 cup chopped pecans or walnuts
3/4 cup coconut
3/4 cup golden raisins
1 unbaked 9-inch pie shell

Combine melted butter, vinegar, sugar, eggs, pecans, coconut and raisins in bowl; mix well. Pour into pie shell. Bake at 350 degrees for 30 minutes or until knife inserted near center comes out clean. **Yield: 6 servings.**

Mildred Twentier, Pleasant Hill #1505

Grandmother's Coconut Pie

6 tablespoons melted butter
3 eggs, beaten
1 cup sugar
1/4 cup buttermilk
1 cup flaked coconut
1 9-inch unbaked pie shell

Combine melted butter, eggs, sugar, buttermilk and coconut in bowl; mix well. Pour into pie shell. Bake at 350 degrees for 30 to 40 minutes or until knife inserted near center comes out clean. **Yield: 6 servings.**

Agnes Dillan, Chippewa #1592

To prevent a pie crust from becoming soggy during baking, heat the pie pan or plate before putting the pastry in it.

Cream Pie

1/4 cup flour
3/4 cup sugar
1/8 teaspoon salt
2 cups scalded milk
3 tablespoons margarine
2 egg yolks
1 teaspoon vanilla extract
1 baked 9-inch pie shell
1 recipe meringue

Combine flour, sugar and salt in saucepan. Stir in mixture of scalded milk and margarine. Cook for 15 minutes. Add egg yolks; mix well. Cook until heated through. Let stand to cool. Beat in vanilla. Pour into pie shell. Top with meringue, sealing to edge. Bake until golden brown. May add 2 ounces baking cocoa to flour mixture for chocolate cream pie, substitute brown sugar for white for butterscotch pie or add well drained maraschino cherries for cherry cream pie. **Yield: 6 servings.**

Louise Sutliff, Vernon #936

Impossible Cheesecake Pie

3/4 cup milk
2 teaspoons vanilla extract
2 eggs
1 cup sugar
1/2 cup baking mix
16 ounces cream cheese, softened
1 cup sour cream
2 tablespoons sugar
2 teaspoons vanilla extract

Combine milk, 2 teaspoons vanilla, eggs, 1 cup sugar and baking mix in blender container. Process at high speed for 15 seconds. Add cream cheese. Process for 2 minutes longer. Pour into 9-inch pie plate. Bake at 350 degrees for 40 to 45 minutes or until set. Mix sour cream, 2 tablespoons sugar and 2 teaspoons vanilla in bowl. Spread over cooled pie. **Yield: 6 servings.**

Patty Aumiller, East New Castle #1536

Maple Crumb Pies

1 cup sugar
1 cup maple syrup
1/4 cup flour
1 egg, well beaten
1 teaspoon vanilla extract
2 cups water
2 unbaked 9-inch pie shells
2 cups flour
2 cups packed brown sugar
1 teaspoon cream of tartar
1 teaspoon baking soda
1/2 cup butter
1/4 cup shortening

Combine sugar, maple syrup, 1/4 cup flour, egg, vanilla and water in saucepan. Bring to a full boil. Let stand to cool. Pour into pie shells. Mix 2 cups flour, brown sugar, cream of tartar, baking soda, butter and shortening in bowl. Sprinkle over filling. Bake at 350 degrees for 40 to 45 minutes or until knife inserted near center comes out clean. **Yield: 16 servings.**

Pauline Baumgardner, Somerset #1697

Cheese Custard Pies

1 14-ounce can sweetened condensed milk
3/4 cup (about) water
4 eggs, slightly beaten
1/4 cup flour
1 teaspoon salt
16 ounces small curd cottage cheese
2 unbaked 9-inch pie shells
Cinnamon to taste

Mix condensed milk and enough water to measure 1 quart in large container. Combine eggs, flour and salt in bowl; mix well. Stir in milk mixture. Add cottage cheese; mix well. Pour into pie shells. Sprinkle with cinnamon. Bake at 375 degrees until knife inserted near center comes out clean. **Yield: 16 servings.**

Agnes M. Eckhart, Friendship #1799

No-Sugar Pumpkin Custard Pie

1 12-ounce can evaporated milk
3 eggs
1 can solid-pack pumpkin
Spices to taste
1 tablespoon cornstarch
15 packets artificial sweetener
1 unbaked 10-inch pie shell
1/2 cup crushed cereal flakes of choice
1/4 cup coconut
1/4 cup chopped pecans
1/4 cup butter

Combine evaporated milk, eggs, pumpkin, spices, cornstarch and sweetener in bowl; mix well. Pour into pie shell. Bake at 350 degrees for 30 minutes. Mix crushed cereal, coconut, pecans and butter in bowl. Sprinkle over pie. Bake on top rack of oven for 10 minutes longer. May substitute 2 cups mashed cooked butternut squash for pumpkin or may omit topping. May substitute 2 large grated apples mixed with 1 teaspoon apple pie spices; 2 cups applesauce with spices; 2 cups grated peaches with spices; 2 cups grated pears with spices; 1 1/2 cups flaked coconut with 1 teaspoon vanilla extract or 1 1/2 cups drained canned pineapple with 1 teaspoon vanilla for pumpkin. **Yield: 6 servings.**

Ruth Metzger, Central #1650

Raspberry Custard Pie

2 cups raspberries
1 unbaked 9-inch pie shell
2 eggs
1/2 cup sugar
1 1/2 tablespoons flour
3/4 cup milk

Arrange raspberries in pie shell. Mix eggs, sugar, flour and milk in bowl. Pour over raspberries. Bake at 300 degrees until knife inserted near center comes out clean. May substitute strawberries for raspberries. **Yield: 6 servings.**

Mildred Reinert, Pioneer # 1777

Velvety Custard Pie

4 eggs, slightly beaten
1/2 cup sugar
1/4 teaspoon salt
1 teaspoon vanilla extract
2 1/2 cups scalded milk
1 unbaked 9-inch pie shell
Nutmeg to taste

Combine eggs, sugar, salt and vanilla in bowl; mix well. Stir in hot milk. Pour into pie shell. Sprinkle with nutmeg. Bake at 475 degrees for 5 minutes. Reduce oven temperature to 425 degrees. Bake for 10 minutes or until knife inserted near center comes out clean. **Yield: 6 servings.**

Nellie Miller, Roseville #1290

Fish Pie

3/4 cup shortening
1 egg
1 1/4 cups sugar
1 cup sour milk
1 teaspoon baking soda
1 teaspoon baking powder
Flour
1 1/2 cups molasses
1/2 cup sugar
1/4 cup flour
2 cups water
1 teaspoon vanilla extract

Combine shortening, egg, 1 1/4 cups sugar, sour milk, baking soda and baking powder in bowl; mix well. Add enough flour to make stiff dough. Roll desired amount of dough into two 12-inch circles on lightly floured surface. Store remaining dough in refrigerator. Combine molasses, 1/2 cup sugar, 1/4 cup flour and water in saucepan. Cook until thickened. Stir in vanilla. Pour into pastry-lined pie plate. Top with remaining circle, sealing and fluting edge and cutting vents. Bake at 400 degrees for 10 minutes. Reduce oven temperature to 350 degrees. Bake for 30 to 45 minutes or until golden brown. **Yield: 6 servings.**

Edna Borger, Harmony #1692

Glazed Fruit Pie

1 1/2 cups cold milk or half and half
1 4-ounce package vanilla instant pudding mix
1 baked 9-inch pie shell or graham cracker pie shell
1 3-ounce package peach, orange, strawberry or raspberry gelatin
1 cup boiling water
1/2 cup cold water
2 cups fresh or drained canned fruit

Combine milk and pudding mix in mixer bowl. Beat at low speed for 1 minute. Pour into pie shell. Chill for 1 hour. Dissolve gelatin in boiling water in bowl. Add cold water. Chill until thickened. Spoon 1/2 cup gelatin over pie filling. Top with fruit. Spoon remaining gelatin over fruit. Do not use fresh pineapple, kiwifruit, mango, papaya or figs in this recipe. **Yield: 6 servings.**

Ann Yearick, Progress # 96

Luscious Fresh Grape Pie

4 cups Concord grapes
1 cup sugar
3 tablespoons flour
1 teaspoon lemon juice
1 recipe 2-crust pie pastry
1 tablespoon butter

Remove skins from grapes; reserve. Bring grapes to a boil in saucepan. Press hot grapes through sieve to remove seeds. Combine with reserved skins in bowl. Stir in mixture of sugar and flour. Add lemon juice; mix well. Spoon into pastry-lined pie plate. Dot with butter. Top with remaining pastry, sealing and fluting edge and cutting vents. Bake at 450 degrees for 10 minutes. Reduce oven temperature to 350 degrees. Bake for 30 minutes. **Yield: 6 servings.**

Erma Hebe, Sebring #1047

Lemon Pie

1 14-ounce can sweetened condensed milk
1 6-ounce can frozen lemonade concentrate, thawed
8 to 12 ounces whipped topping
1 9-inch graham cracker pie shell
1/4 cup graham cracker crumbs

Combine condensed milk and lemonade concentrate in bowl; beat well. Fold in whipped topping. Spoon into pie shell. Sprinkle with graham cracker crumbs. Chill for several hours. **Yield: 6 servings.**

Mary Lou McCullough, Big Beaver, #1578

Lemon Custard Sponge Pie

1 1/2 cups sugar
3 egg yolks
1/4 teaspoon salt
1 tablespoon melted butter
2 tablespoons cornstarch
1 cup milk
Juice of 1 lemon
3 egg whites, stiffly beaten
Grated lemon rind to taste
1 unbaked 10-inch pie shell

Combine sugar, egg yolks, salt, melted butter, cornstarch, milk and lemon juice in bowl; mix well. Fold in egg whites and lemon rind. Pour into pie shell. Bake at 450 degrees for 10 minutes. Reduce oven temperature to 400 degrees. Bake for 20 minutes. **Yield: 6 servings.**

Dorothy M. Greis, Pioneer #1777

Pies with cream or custard fillings should be cooled to room temperature and then refrigerated to prevent spoilage.

Lemon Strip Pie

$1\frac{1}{2}$ cups sugar
$\frac{1}{2}$ cup butter
2 cups hot water
$\frac{1}{4}$ cup flour
4 eggs
$\frac{3}{4}$ cup syrup
Grated rind and juice of 1 lemon
1 unbaked 9-inch pie shell
1 cup flour
$\frac{1}{2}$ cup packed light brown sugar
1 teaspoon baking powder
1 tablespoon butter
1 egg, well beaten

Combine sugar, $\frac{1}{2}$ cup butter, hot water, $\frac{1}{4}$ cup flour, 4 eggs, syrup, lemon rind and lemon juice in saucepan. Cook over medium heat until thickened. Let stand to cool. Pour into pie shell. Combine 1 cup flour, brown sugar and baking powder in bowl; mix well. Add butter; mix well. Stir in 1 egg. Roll on lightly floured surface. Cut into strips. Arrange lattice-fashion over pie. Bake at 350 degrees for 30 minutes. **Yield: 6 servings.**

Eva Treichler, Virginville #1832

Cool Lime Pie

1 4-ounce package vanilla pudding and pie filling mix
1 3-ounce package lime gelatin
2 cups water
$\frac{1}{4}$ cup sugar (optional)
$1\frac{1}{2}$ teaspoons grated lime rind
2 tablespoons lime juice
$2\frac{1}{2}$ cups whipped topping
1 9-inch chocolate crumb pie shell
1 cup whipped topping

Combine pudding mix, gelatin, water and sugar in saucepan. Bring to a boil over medium heat, stirring frequently. Stir in lime rind and juice. Pour into bowl. Chill, covered with plastic, until slightly thickened. Fold in $2\frac{1}{2}$ cups whipped topping. Spoon into pie shell. Chill for 3 hours. Spread with 1 cup whipped topping. Garnish with lime slices. **Yield: 6 servings.**

Nellie Chestnut, West Salem, #1607

Old-Fashioned Mincemeat for Pies

1 quart cooked pork
1 quart coarsely ground apples
1 pound raisins
2 cups sugar
$\frac{1}{4}$ cup vinegar
$\frac{3}{4}$ cup water
$\frac{1}{2}$ teaspoon nutmeg
$\frac{1}{2}$ teaspoon allspice
$\frac{1}{2}$ teaspoon cloves
1 teaspoon salt

Combine pork, apples, raisins, sugar, vinegar, water, nutmeg, allspice, cloves and salt in large bowl; mix well. May be used immediately or stored in freezer. **Yield: 12 cups.**

Clarabelle Wells, Deemston #1372

Beef Mincemeat for Pies

2 pounds lean beef, cooked
4 pounds apples, chopped
3/4 cup molasses
1/2 pound packed brown sugar
1 pound raisins
1 pound currants
2 teaspoons cinnamon
2 teaspoons allspice
2 teaspoons cloves
1 1/2 teaspoons pepper
1 1/2 teaspoons salt
Grape juice

Process beef in food grinder. Combine with apples, molasses, brown sugar, raisins, currants, cinnamon, allspice, cloves, pepper and salt in large saucepan; mix well. Add enough grape juice to moisten mixture. Cook until heated through. Pack into hot sterilized jars, leaving 1/4 inch headspace; seal with 2-piece lids. Process in boiling water bath for 10 minutes. Use 1 quart per pie, adding more grape juice if needed. **Yield: 6 quarts.**

Jim Tush, Buffalo #1523

Molasses-Coconut Custard Pie

1 cup molasses
2 eggs
2 tablespoons flour
1/2 teaspoon baking soda
1 cup sugar
1 cup milk
1/2 cup cream
1 cup coconut
1 unbaked 9-inch pie shell

Mix molasses and eggs in bowl. Add mixture of flour, baking soda and sugar; mix well. Add milk, cream and coconut; mix well. Pour into pie shell. Bake at 375 degrees for 50 minutes. **Yield: 6 servings.**

Dorothy M. Miller, Virginville #1832

Montgomery Pies

1 tablespoon flour
1 cup sugar
1 cup molasses
2 cups hot water
1 egg
1 teaspoon vanilla extract
3 unbaked 9-inch pie shells
2 cups sugar
3/4 cup shortening
1 cup milk
3 cups flour
2 eggs
1 tablespoon baking powder
1 teaspoon vanilla extract

Combine 1 tablespoon flour, 1 cup sugar, molasses, hot water and 1 egg in saucepan. Cook until thickened. Stir in 1 teaspoon vanilla. Cool slightly. Pour into pie shells. Cream 2 cups sugar and shortening in mixer bowl until light and fluffy. Add milk, 3 cups flour, 2 eggs, baking powder and 1 teaspoon vanilla; beat well. Pour over fillings. Bake at 350 degrees for 30 to 35 minutes or until golden brown.
Yield: 24 servings.

Margaret E. Crater, Logan #109

Oatmeal Pie

3/4 cup sugar
3/4 cup packed brown sugar
1/4 cup butter
1/4 teaspoon salt
3 eggs, beaten
1 cup milk
3/4 cup oats
3/4 cup shredded coconut
1 teaspoon vanilla extract
1 unbaked 9-inch pie shell

Combine sugar, brown sugar, butter and salt in bowl; mix well. Stir in eggs and milk. Add oats, coconut and vanilla; mix well. Pour into pie shell. Bake at 350 degrees for 35 to 40 minutes or until set. **Yield: 6 servings.**

Helen S. Epting, Virginville #1832

Orange Pie

3/4 cup sugar
Juice of 2 oranges
Grated rind of 1 orange
3 egg yolks
3 tablespoons flour
2 1/4 cups milk
3 egg whites, stiffly beaten
1 unbaked 9-inch pie shell

Combine sugar, orange juice, orange rind, egg yolks, flour and milk in bowl; mix well. Fold in egg whites. Pour into pie shell. Bake at 350 degrees for 45 minutes or until set. **Yield: 6 servings.**

Evelyn Gibson, Kaylor #1396

Orange Meringue Pie

2 tablespoons cornstarch
1 cup water
1 cup sugar
1/8 teaspoon salt
2 egg yolks, beaten
1 cup orange juice
1 tablespoon lemon juice
1 baked 9-inch pie shell
2 egg whites
1/2 teaspoon vanilla extract
1/8 teaspoon cream of tartar
1/4 cup sugar

Dissolve cornstarch in a small amount of water. Bring 1 cup water to a boil in saucepan. Add cornstarch mixture, 1 cup sugar and salt; mix well. Mix egg yolks, orange juice and lemon juice in bowl. Add to saucepan. Cook until heated through. Pour into pie shell. Beat egg whites, vanilla and cream of tartar in mixer bowl until soft peaks form. Add 1/4 cup sugar gradually, beating constantly until stiff peaks form. Spread over pie. Bake at 350 degrees for 10 minutes or until browned.
Yield: 8 servings.

Clare Richard, Fort Granville #1902

Peach-Maraschino Cherry Pie

1/2 cup maraschino cherry juice
1/2 cup sugar
8 peaches, sliced
2 tablespoons cornstarch
1 tablespoon maraschino cherry juice
1 baked 8-inch pie shell

Mix 1/2 cup juice and sugar in small bowl. Pour over peaches in large bowl. Let stand for 1 hour; drain into saucepan. Add mixture of cornstarch and 1 tablespoon juice. Bring to a boil. Simmer until thickened. Let stand to cool. Pour over peaches. Spoon into pie shell. **Yield: 6 servings.**

Elaine Benton, Valley Grange #1420

Peach Pies

1 cup oil
2 tablespoons sugar
1/4 cup milk
1/4 teaspoon salt
3 cups flour
3/4 cup water
3/4 cup sugar
2 tablespoons cornstarch
1 3-ounce package peach or apricot gelatin
8 peaches, peeled, sliced

Mix oil, 2 tablespoons sugar, milk and salt in bowl. Add flour; mix well. Pat into two 9-inch pie plates. Bake at 400 degrees for 15 to 20 minutes or until lightly browned. Combine water, 3/4 cup sugar and cornstarch in saucepan. Bring to a boil. Stir in gelatin. Let stand to cool. Add peaches. Spoon into prepared shells. Top with whipped topping. **Yield: 12 servings.**

Mrs. Robert C. Cook, Hyndman #1954

Peach Pie Alaska

1 3-ounce package apricot gelatin
2/3 cup boiling water
1 cup vanilla ice cream
3 1/2 cups whipped topping
1 cup chopped fresh or canned peaches
1 baked 9-inch deep-dish pie shell

Dissolve gelatin in boiling water in bowl. Add ice cream by spoonfuls, stirring until melted. Stir in whipped topping and peaches. Chill until mixture will mound when dropped from spoon. Spoon into pie shell. Chill for 3 hours. **Yield: 8 servings.**

Jane Reppert, Virginville #1832

Peach-Coconut Pie

1½ tablespoons minute tapioca
⅔ cup sugar
4 cups sliced peaches
1 teaspoon lemon juice
⅛ teaspoon salt
⅓ cup packed brown sugar
¼ cup flour
3 tablespoons butter
¾ cup flaked coconut
1 unbaked 9-inch pie shell

Combine tapioca, sugar, peaches, lemon juice and salt in bowl; mix well. Let stand for 15 minutes. Mix brown sugar, flour, butter and coconut in small bowl. Layer ⅓ of the brown sugar mixture, all the fruit mixture and remaining brown sugar mixture in pie shell. Bake at 425 degrees for 45 minutes or until syrup boils with heavy bubbles that do not burst. **Yield: 6 servings.**

Velma Knorr, Roaring Creek Valley #2041

Peach and Cream Cheese Pie

¾ cup flour
1 teaspoon baking powder
½ teaspoon salt
1 4-ounce package vanilla pudding and pie filling mix
1 egg
½ cup milk
1 quart canned peaches
8 ounces cream cheese, softened
½ cup sugar
3 tablespoons peach juice
1 tablespoon sugar
½ teaspoon cinnamon

Combine flour, baking powder, salt, pudding mix, egg and milk in bowl; mix well. Spoon into greased pie plate. Cover with peaches. Mix cream cheese, ½ cup sugar and peach juice in bowl. Spread over peaches, leaving 1 inch margin around edge. Sprinkle with mixture of 1 tablespoon sugar and cinnamon. Bake at 350 degrees for 30 to 35 minutes or until knife inserted near center comes out clean.
Yield: 8 servings.

Virginia North, Mt. Pleasant #975

Peanut Butter Pie

3 ounces cream cheese, softened
½ cup peanut butter
1 cup confectioners' sugar
½ cup milk
9 ounces whipped topping
1 9-inch graham cracker pie shell

Combine cream cheese, peanut butter, confectioners' sugar, milk and whipped topping in bowl; mix well. Spoon into pie shell. Freeze for 1 to 2 hours or until firm. Store in freezer. **Yield: 10 servings.**

Melissa Null, Eldred #1604

Peanut Butter Chiffon Pie

1 envelope unflavored gelatin
1/4 cup sugar
1/4 teaspoon salt
1 cup milk
2 egg yolks, slightly beaten
1/2 cup creamy peanut butter
2 egg whites
1/4 cup sugar
2 cups whipped topping
1 9-inch graham cracker pie shell

Combine gelatin, 1/4 cup sugar and salt in saucepan. Stir in milk and egg yolks. Bring to a boil over medium heat, stirring constantly. Stir in peanut butter. Chill thoroughly. Beat egg whites in mixer bowl until foamy. Add 1/4 cup sugar gradually, beating constantly until stiff peaks form. Fold into peanut butter mixture. Stir in whipped topping. Spoon into pie shell. Chill for 2 to 3 hours or overnight. **Yield: 8 servings.**

Viola Barrett, Olanta #715

Pear Pie

3/4 cup sugar
1 teaspoon nutmeg or cinnamon
2 tablespoons flour
6 cups sliced peeled pears
1 recipe 2-crust pie pastry
4 teaspoons butter

Mix sugar, nutmeg and flour in small bowl. Stir into pears in large bowl. Spoon into pastry-lined pie plate. Dot with butter. Top with remaining pastry, sealing edge and cutting vents. Bake at 375 degrees for 1 hour. **Yield: 8 servings.**

Kathryn Squiers, Penn #534

Pecan Pie

1/4 cup butter or oil
2 ...
1/8 teaspoon salt
1 teaspoon vanilla extract
1 unbaked 9-inch pie shell
... cup chopped pecans

... and vanilla in bowl; mix well. Pour ... degrees for 15 minutes. Reduce oven ... minutes or until knife inserted near ...

Laura Y. Peake, Charleston Valley #54

Pineapple Pies

2 cups sifted confectioners' sugar
1/2 cup margarine, softened
2 eggs
1/8 teaspoon salt
1 teaspoon vanilla extract
2 baked 9-inch pie shells
1/2 cup confectioners' sugar
1 cup whipped topping
1 cup crushed pineapple, drained
1/2 cup chopped pecans or walnuts

Cream 2 cups confectioners' sugar and margarine in mixer bowl until light and fluffy. Add eggs, salt and vanilla; beat well. Spread in pie shells. Blend 1/2 cup confectioners' sugar into whipped topping in bowl. Stir in pineapple and pecans. Spread over fillings. Chill until serving time. **Yield: 12 servings.**

Gertrude Grindel, Unionville #1971

Mama's Famous Poor Man's Pie

3/4 cup flour
1 unbaked 9-inch pie shell
1 1/2 cups milk
1 1/4 cups sugar
Nutmeg to taste
1 tablespoon (or more) butter

Place flour in pie shell. Add milk; mix well with spoon. Stir in sugar. Sprinkle with nutmeg. Dot with butter. Bake at 450 degrees for 15 minutes. Reduce oven temperature to 350 degrees. Bake for 45 minutes. **Yield: 8 servings.**

Bernie Best, Mt. Joy #537

Colonial Pumpkin Pie

6 eggs
1 cup sugar
1/2 teaspoon ginger
1/2 teaspoon cinnamon
1/2 teaspoon nutmeg
1/2 teaspoon salt
2 cups pumpkin
2 cups cream
1 unbaked 9-inch pie shell

Beat eggs in bowl until light and lemon-colored. Stir in sugar, spices and salt. Add pumpkin and cream; mix well. Spoon into pie shell. Bake at 400 degrees for 10 minutes. Reduce oven temperature to 350 degrees. Bake for 30 minutes or until knife inserted near center comes out clean. **Yield: 6 servings.**

Edna M. Zerbe, Bernville #1887

Prevent a soggy lower pie crust by brushing it with egg white or melted butter before adding the filling.

Double-Layer Pumpkin Pie

3 ounces cream cheese, softened
1 tablespoon sugar
1 tablespoon cold half and half
$1\frac{1}{2}$ cups whipped topping
1 10-inch graham cracker pie shell
1 cup cold half and half
1 4-ounce package vanilla instant pudding mix
1 16-ounce can pumpkin
1 teaspoon cinnamon
$\frac{1}{2}$ teaspoon ginger
$\frac{1}{4}$ teaspoon ground cloves

Mix cream cheese, sugar and 1 tablespoon half and half in bowl. Blend in whipped topping. Spread in pie shell. Combine 1 cup half and half and pudding mix in bowl; beat well. Stir in pumpkin, cinnamon, ginger and cloves. Spread over cream cheese mixture. Chill for 1 hour. May substitute $1\frac{1}{2}$ teaspoons prepared pumpkin pie spice for listed spices. **Yield: 6 servings.**

Helen Anderson, West Pike Run #1928

Pumpkin Pies

1 cup sugar
$\frac{1}{2}$ teaspoon cinnamon
$\frac{3}{4}$ teaspoon salt
1 tablespoon cornstarch
4 eggs
$2\frac{1}{2}$ cups milk
1 teaspoon vanilla extract
2 cups cooked pumpkin
2 unbaked 8-inch pie shells

Combine sugar, cinnamon, salt and cornstarch in bowl; mix well. Stir in mixture of eggs, milk and vanilla. Add pumpkin; mix well. Pour into pie shells. Bake at 425 degrees for 10 minutes. Reduce oven temperature to 350 degrees. Bake for 45 minutes. **Yield: 12 servings.**

Jean Gensamer, Port Matilda #1284

Karen's Pumpkin Chiffon Pie

1 envelope unflavored gelatin
$\frac{1}{4}$ cup water
$1\frac{1}{4}$ cups pumpkin
$\frac{3}{4}$ cup packed brown sugar
$\frac{1}{2}$ teaspoon salt
$\frac{1}{2}$ teaspoon nutmeg
1 teaspoon cinnamon
$\frac{1}{4}$ teaspoon ginger
3 egg yolks, slightly beaten
$\frac{3}{4}$ cup milk
3 egg whites
$\frac{1}{3}$ cup sugar
1 9-inch graham cracker pie shell

Soften gelatin in water in bowl. Add pumpkin, brown sugar, salt, nutmeg, cinnamon, ginger, egg yolks and milk; mix well. Beat egg whites in mixer bowl until soft peaks form. Add sugar gradually, beating constantly until stiff peaks form. Fold into pumpkin mixture. Spoon into pie shell. Chill until serving time. **Yield: 6 servings.**

Marian Holloway, Fulton #66

Pumpkin Custard Pie

1 cup pumpkin
3/4 cup packed brown sugar
2 egg yolks
1 teaspoon butter
1/4 teaspoon salt
2 tablespoons flour
2 cups milk
1/4 teaspoon cloves
1/2 teaspoon cinnamon
1 tablespoon whiskey
2 egg whites, stiffly beaten
1 unbaked 9-inch pie shell

Combine pumpkin, brown sugar, egg yolks, butter, salt, flour, milk, cloves, cinnamon and whiskey in bowl; mix well. Fold in egg whites. Pour into pie shell. Bake at 375 degrees for 45 minutes. **Yield: 6 servings.**

Katie A. Moll, Virginville #1832

Open-Faced Raisin Pies

1 15-ounce package seedless raisins
1 cup sugar
2 unbaked 9-inch pie shells
1 cup margarine
2 cups flour
1 1/2 cups sugar
2 eggs
1 cup milk
2 teaspoons baking soda

Combine raisins, 1 cup sugar and water to cover in saucepan. Bring to a boil. Simmer for 15 minutes. Place in pie shells. Mix margarine, flour and 1 1/2 cups sugar in bowl; reserve 1 cup crumb mixture. Combine remaining crumbs, eggs, milk and baking soda in bowl. Pour over raisins. Sprinkle with reserved crumbs. Bake at 400 degrees for 10 minutes. Reduce oven temperature to 375 degrees. Bake for 30 minutes or until golden brown. **Yield: 16 servings.**

Dorothy Delaney, Progress #96

Raisin Pie

2 cups raisins
1 cup sugar
2 cups water
1/2 teaspoon salt
2 tablespoons butter
3 tablespoons lemon juice
2 tablespoons cornstarch
3 tablespoons cold water
1 teaspoon lemon extract
1 recipe 2-crust pie pastry

Combine raisins, sugar, 2 cups water, salt, butter and lemon juice in saucepan. Cook for 5 minutes. Stir in mixture of cornstarch and 3 tablespoons water. Cook for 5 minutes. Remove from heat. Stir in lemon flavoring. Pour into pastry-lined pie plate. Cut remaining pastry into strips; arrange lattice-fashion on top. Bake at 425 degrees for 25 minutes. **Yield: 6 servings.**

Esther Brest, Westfield #1514

Raisin-Walnut Pie

1/3 cup butter
1 cup sugar
2 eggs
1 cup raisins
1/2 cup chopped walnuts
1/4 cup milk
1 unbaked 8-inch pie shell

Mix butter, sugar and eggs in bowl. Add raisins, walnuts and milk; mix well. Pour into pie shell. Bake at 350 degrees until center is set. **Yield: 8 servings.**

Frances Currie, East New Castle #1536

Sour Cream-Raisin Pie

1 cup raisins
1/4 cup flour
1 cup sour cream
1 cup sugar
2 teaspoons cinnamon
1/2 teaspoon cloves
1 teaspoon vanilla extract
3 egg yolks
1 unbaked 9-inch pie shell
1 recipe meringue

Chop raisins; roll in flour. Combine with sour cream, sugar, cinnamon, cloves, vanilla and egg yolks in bowl; mix well. Pour into pie shell. Spread with meringue. Bake at 400 degrees for 10 minutes. Reduce oven temperature to 350 degrees. Bake for 35 to 45 minutes or until knife inserted near center comes out clean.
Yield: 6 servings.

Elaine Flewellyn, Ulysses #1183

Raspberry Dream Pie

3/4 cup sugar
4 cups raspberries
1/2 cup water
1 teaspoon margarine
1/8 teaspoon salt
1 tablespoon cornstarch
2 to 3 tablespoons water
1 baked 10-inch pie shell
1 envelope unflavored gelatin
1/4 cup water
16 ounces whipped topping

Combine sugar, raspberries and 1/2 cup water in saucepan. Cook for 5 minutes or until softened. Remove 3/4 cup mixture from saucepan; reserve. Add margarine and salt to saucepan. Stir in mixture of cornstarch and water. Pour into pie shell, reserving 1/2 cup. Chill until set. Soften gelatin in 1/4 cup water in bowl. Stir in reserved 3/4 cup sugar mixture. Chill until set. Reserve 1 cup whipped topping; fold remainder into gelatin mixture. Spoon into pie shell. Place reserved 1/2 cup raspberry mixture in center of pie. Spread reserved whipped topping around sauce. Chill until serving time. **Yield: 10 servings.**

Carol A. Witmer, Community #2048

Rhubarb Pie

2 cups rhubarb, cut into 1/2-inch pieces
1 unbaked 9-inch pie shell
2 eggs
1 cup sugar
2 tablespoons (about) flour
1/2 teaspoon salt
2 teaspoons melted butter
1 cup milk

Arrange rhubarb in pie shell. Beat eggs in bowl. Add sugar, desired amount of flour, salt and melted butter; mix well. Stir in milk. Pour over rhubarb. Bake at 400 degrees for 40 minutes or until center is set. **Yield: 6 servings.**

Elvena K. Riegel, Jefferson #1384

Rhubarb-Cream Pie

1 1/2 to 2 cups finely chopped rhubarb
1 cup cream
1 cup sugar
1/2 teaspoon salt
1 teaspoon vanilla extract
3 tablespoons flour
1 recipe 2-crust pie pastry

Combine rhubarb, cream, sugar, salt, vanilla and flour in bowl; mix well. Pour into pastry-lined pie plate. Top with remaining pastry, sealing edge and cutting vents. Bake at 375 degrees until rhubarb is tender. **Yield: 6 servings.**

Mildred Harer, Sebring #1047

Rhubarb Two-Crust Custard Pie

3 tablespoons flour
1 1/4 cups sugar
1 egg, beaten
3 cups chopped rhubarb
1 recipe 2-crust pie pastry
1 tablespoon dark corn syrup
1 tablespoon flour

Sift 3 tablespoons flour and sugar together. Combine with egg in bowl. Add rhubarb; mix well. Pour into pastry-lined pie plate. Drizzle with corn syrup. Sprinkle with 1 tablespoon flour. Top with remaining pastry, sealing edge and cutting vents. Bake at 450 degrees for 10 to 15 minutes or until lightly browned. Reduce oven temperature to 300 degrees. Bake for 35 minutes. **Yield: 6 servings.**

Mary Keck, Briar Creek #146

Patch tears in pastry with a bit of pastry and a touch of ice water rather than rerolling it.

Shoo-Fly Pie

3/4 cup baking molasses
3/4 cup boiling water
1 teaspoon baking soda
1 1/2 cups flour
2/3 cup sugar
1/2 teaspoon cinnamon
1/4 teaspoon ginger
1/8 teaspoon ground cloves
1/4 teaspoon salt
1/3 cup margarine or butter
1 9-inch unbaked pie shell

Combine molasses, boiling water and baking soda in bowl, stirring well; cool. Combine flour, sugar, cinnamon, ginger, cloves and salt in bowl. Cut in margarine until mixture is crumbly. Sprinkle 1/4 of the crumb mixture in pie shell. Pour in molasses mixture. Spread remaining crumb mixture over top. Bake at 350 degrees for 40 minutes. **Yield: 7 servings.**

Florence Williamson, Bottle Run #1301

Lemon Shoo-Fly Pies

1 cup molasses
1 cup sugar
1/4 cup flour
1 egg, beaten
Juice and grated rind of 2 lemons
1 1/2 cups boiling water
2 unbaked 9-inch pie shells
3 cups flour
1 cup sugar
1 teaspoon baking soda
Salt to taste
1 cup shortening

Combine molasses, 1 cup sugar, 1/4 cup flour, egg, lemon juice, lemon rind and boiling water in bowl; mix well. Pour into pie shells. Combine flour, sugar, baking soda and salt in large bowl. Cut in shortening until mixture is crumbly. Sprinkle crumbs over pie filling. Bake at 375 degrees for 30 to 35 minutes or until knife inserted in center comes out clean. **Yield: 12 servings.**

Dorothy Shawver, Progress #96

Strawberry Pie

1 3-ounce package strawberry gelatin
1 cup hot water
1 pint vanilla ice cream
1 10-ounce package frozen strawberries, thawed
1 9-inch baked pie shell

Dissolve gelatin in hot water in mixer bowl. Let stand until partially set. Add ice cream 1 tablespoonful at a time, beating continuously at medium speed. Stir in strawberries. Pour into baked pie shell. Chill for 3 hours before serving.
Yield: 6 servings.

Dorothy E. Grande, Mahoning Valley #1649

Fresh Strawberry Pie

1 cup sugar
1 cup water
3 tablespoons cornstarch
1 3-ounce package strawberry gelatin
1 quart fresh strawberries, hulled
1 9-inch baked pie shell
Whipped topping

Combine sugar, water, cornstarch and gelatin in saucepan; mix well. Cook for 7 minutes, stirring frequently; cool. Place strawberries in baked pie shell. Pour gelatin mixture over strawberries. Top with whipped topping. **Yield: 6 to 8 servings.**

Elizabeth Gardner, Center Road #502

Sweet Potato Pie

1¼ cups sugar
½ teaspoon cinnamon
½ teaspoon nutmeg
2 eggs, beaten
1 12-ounce can evaporated milk
1 teaspoon vanilla extract
1½ cups mashed sweet potatoes
1 unbaked 9-inch pie shell
⅓ cup flour
½ cup packed brown sugar
⅓ cup butter or margarine, softened
½ cup shredded coconut
½ cup chopped pecans or walnuts

Combine sugar, cinnamon and nutmeg in large bowl. Add mixture of eggs, evaporated milk and vanilla, stirring well. Add sweet potatoes, beating until smooth. Pour into pie shell. Bake at 425 degrees for 15 minutes. Reduce temperature to 350 degrees. Bake for 30 minutes longer. Combine flour and brown sugar in bowl. Cut in butter until mixture is crumbly. Stir in coconut and pecans. Sprinkle over pie. Bake for 10 to 15 minutes longer or until topping is golden brown. Cool on wire rack. Serve with whipped topping or vanilla ice cream. Store in refrigerator.
Yield: 6 servings.

Helen Crise, Mendon #855

Green Tomato Pies

6 cups sliced green tomatoes
2 cups sugar
1 cup water
1 teaspoon salt
1 teaspoon cinnamon
1 teaspoon ground cloves
1 teaspoon ground allspice
Flour
2 unbaked 9-inch pie shells

Combine tomatoes, sugar, water, salt, cinnamon, cloves and allspice in saucepan. Cook until tomatoes are tender, adding a small amount of flour if necessary for desired consistency. Pour into pie shells. Bake at 400 degrees for 15 minutes. Reduce temperature to 350 degrees. Bake for 15 to 20 minutes longer or until golden brown.
Yield: 12 servings.

Helen Guss, Milford #773

Vinegar Pie

1 cup sugar
2 eggs, beaten
$2^1/_2$ tablespoons vinegar
2 tablespoons flour
1 cup water
2 tablespoons butter
$^1/_2$ teaspoon lemon juice
1 baked 9-inch pie shell
Chopped nuts

Combine sugar, eggs, vinegar, flour, water, butter and lemon juice in large saucepan. Cook over medium heat until thickened, stirring constantly. Pour into baked pie shell. Sprinkle with chopped nuts. Chill in refrigerator before serving. **Yield: 6 servings.**

Anna P. Moyer, Marion #1853

Zucchini "Apple" Pie

4 cups seeded, sliced zucchini
2 tablespoons lemon juice
Salt to taste
$1^1/_4$ cups sugar
$1^1/_2$ teaspoons cinnamon
$1^1/_2$ teaspoons cream of tartar
Nutmeg to taste
3 tablespoons flour
1 recipe 2-crust pie pastry
Butter to taste

Cook zucchini in boiling water until tender crisp; drain well. Toss with lemon juice and salt. Combine sugar, cinnamon, cream of tartar, nutmeg and flour in large bowl; mix well. Stir in zucchini. Line 9-inch pie plate with pie pastry. Pour in zucchini mixture; dot with butter. Top with remaining pie pastry. Bake at 400 degrees for 40 minutes or until golden brown. **Yield: 6 servings.**

Twila Lyon, Cameron County #2081

Zucchini Pie

1 medium zucchini, peeled, sliced
1 cup sugar
1 cup milk
3 tablespoons flour
1 teaspoon vanilla extract
3 eggs
1 unbaked 9-inch pie shell
Cinnamon to taste

Cook zucchini in a small amount of water in saucepan until tender; drain. Combine 1 cup cooked zucchini with sugar, milk, flour, vanilla and eggs in blender container. Process until well mixed. Pour into pie shell. Sprinkle with cinnamon. Bake at 425 degrees for 10 minutes. Reduce temperature to 350 degrees. Bake for 30 minutes. May substitute uncooked zucchini if desired. **Yield: 6 servings.**

Ruth Ravenscroft, Ohiopyle #1933

Pat-in-the-Pan Pie Shell

1/2 cup margarine, softened
1 cup flour
1/4 cup finely chopped toasted almonds
1/4 cup confectioners' sugar

Cut margarine into flour in bowl until crumbly. Add almonds and confectioners' sugar, stirring to make soft dough. Press firmly on bottom and side of pie plate. Bake at 400 degrees for 12 to 15 minutes. Fill with favorite pudding and pie filling. **Yield: 1 pie shell.**

Margaret Coulter, Penn #534

Low-Cholesterol Pie Pastry

2 cups flour
1/2 teaspoon salt
1/2 cup vegetable oil
6 tablespoons cold water

Sift flour and salt into bowl. Combine oil and water in measuring cup but do not stir. Pour into flour mixture. Stir with fork until mixed. Pat into pie plates or roll out on waxed paper. **Yield: 2 pie shells.**

Leona Krider, Vernon #936

Never-Fail Pie Pastry

3 cups flour
1 teaspoon salt
1 1/2 cups shortening
5 tablespoons water
1 egg
1 teaspoon vinegar

Combine flour and salt in large bowl. Cut in shortening until mixture is crumbly. Mix water, egg and vinegar in small bowl. Pour into flour mixture, stirring well. Roll out on floured surface. Line pastry in pie plates. Bake at 350 degrees for 20 minutes. **Yield: 2 double pastries or 4 single pastries.**

Mildred Thomas, East Branch #1262

Quick Hot Water Pie Pastry

1/4 cup hot water
1/2 cup vegetable oil
2 cups flour
Pinch of salt

Combine hot water and oil in bowl. Add all at once to mixture of flour and salt in bowl. Stir with fork; mix with hands until pastry holds together. Divide dough into 2 portions. Roll between waxed paper into circles 2 inches larger than 9-inch pie plate. May brush top crust with egg beaten with 1 tablespoon water before baking. Bake at 400 degrees for 10 minutes. Reduce temperature to 350 degrees. Bake for 30 to 45 minutes or until brown. **Yield: 2 pastries.**

Twila Lyon, Cameron County #2081

Quantity and
Preserving

Chop Suey

5 to 6 bunches celery
8 to 9 pounds onions
3 1/2 to 4 pounds beef, cubed
2 pounds pork, cubed
Butter
1 large or 2 small cans bean sprouts
2 or 3 small cans mushrooms
Salt and pepper to taste
Cornstarch
Flour

Chop celery and onions into 1/2-inch pieces. Brown beef and pork on all sides in butter in electric roaster set at 350 degrees. Add celery. Cook for 30 minutes. Add onions. Cook until tender. Add bean sprouts, mushrooms, salt and pepper. Cook until heated through. Blend cornstarch and flour with a small amount of water in bowl. Add to roaster. Cook until thickened, stirring occasionally. May cook on top of stove if preferred. **Yield: 24 servings.**

Opal Jones, Gretna #1543

Hamburger Barbecue

60 pounds ground beef
2 gallons chopped onions
2 quarts chopped celery
4 cups packed brown sugar
2 cups vinegar
2 cups lemon juice
12 quarts catsup
1/2 cup dry mustard
1 cup salt

Brown ground beef in large stockpot, stirring until crumbly; drain. Spoon into large roasting pan. Add onions and celery; mix well. Bake at 350 degrees until celery is tender. Add brown sugar, vinegar, lemon juice, catsup, dry mustard and salt; mix well. Bake until bubbly. **Yield: 150 servings.**

Velma Snyder, Virginville #1832

Shirley Chili

7 stalks celery
3 green bell peppers
1 1/2 pounds onions
5 pounds ground beef
1 gallon tomatoes, crushed
3 gallons tomato sauce
3 gallons kidney beans
1 teaspoon cumin
1 teaspoon garlic powder
Onion powder, parsley flakes and celery salt to taste

Chop celery, green peppers and onions in blender. Add to ground beef in 10-gallon stockpot. Cook until ground beef is brown and crumbly, stirring constantly; drain. Add tomatoes, tomato sauce, beans and seasonings; mix well. Cook until of desired consistency, stirring frequently. May cook in electric cooker if preferred.
Yield: 50 servings.

Trudy Wigton, Pleasant Hill #1505

Spaghetti Sauce and Meatballs

25 pounds ground beef
5 pounds ground pork
5 large onions, chopped
2 24-ounce containers Italian-seasoned bread crumbs
12 eggs
4 cans evaporated milk
6 cups (about) milk
3 gallons tomato sauce
3 gallons tomato purée
3 gallons water
2 teaspoons chopped garlic
Sugar to taste
9 ounces Presti's spaghetti seasoning

Combine ground beef, ground pork, onions, bread crumbs, eggs, evaporated milk and enough milk to bind in bowl; mix well. Shape into meatballs. Combine tomato sauce, tomato purée, water, garlic, sugar and spaghetti seasoning in large stockpot; mix well. Add meatballs. Simmer for 8 hours or until thickened. **Yield: 100 servings.**

Rebecca Michalka, Burgettstown #1502

Ham Roll-Ups

25 cups uncooked minute rice
25 10-ounce packages frozen chopped spinach, thawed, drained
48 eggs
12 cups chopped onions
6 cups flour
25 cups sour cream
50 tablespoons Dijon mustard
32 cans cream of celery soup
400 slices boiled ham, sliced on commercial slicer set at #15
Bread crumbs
Paprika

Combine rice, spinach, eggs, onions, flour, sour cream, mustard and 24 cans soup in large bowl; mix well. Place 2 heaping tablespoons mixture on each slice of ham. Roll up ham to enclose filling. Place close together with seam sides down in baking pan. Spoon remaining 8 cans soup over top; sprinkle with bread crumbs and paprika. Bake at 350 degrees for 30 to 35 minutes or until heated through. Let stand for 10 minutes before serving. **Yield: 200 (2-ham roll) servings.**

Pat Rudy, Mt. Nebo #1872

Venison Bologna

1/2 1-pound package brown sugar
15 pounds ground venison
2 teaspoons mustard seed
2 teaspoons mace
1 bottle of liquid smoke
2 teaspoons garlic powder
5 ounces Tender-Quick
2 tablespoons crushed red pepper
2 tablespoons black pepper

Dissolve brown sugar in a small amount of water in large bowl. Add next 8 ingredients; mix for 20 minutes or longer. Stuff into sausage casings. Place in baking pan. Bake at 200 degrees for 4 minutes, turning sausages once. Cool to room temperature. Store, wrapped, in freezer. **Yield: 60 servings.**

Brian and Dwayne Ayers, Shavers Creek #353

Baked Macaroni and Cheese

5 pounds uncooked macaroni
6 tablespoons salt
17 quarts water
10 tablespoons flour
1¼ cups melted butter
15 cups milk
6¾ pounds Velveeta cheese, shredded or sliced

Cook macaroni in salted water in large saucepan until tender; drain. Blend flour into melted butter in large saucepan. Cook until bubbly. Stir in milk gradually. Cook until thickened, stirring constantly. Alternate layers of macaroni, cheese and white sauce in large baking pan until all ingredients are used. Bake at 350 degrees for 1 to 2 hours or until bubbly. **Yield: 60 servings.**

Mary Lehman, Pine Grove Area #2090

Cheese Spread for Sandwiches

4 pounds Velveeta cheese
1 pound sharp Cheddar cheese
16 ounces cream cheese
8 hard-boiled eggs
4 jars pimentos
1 medium onion
8 eggs, beaten
½ cup sugar
½ cup flour
½ cup vinegar
½ cup mustard
2 teaspoons salt

Grind cheeses, hard-boiled eggs, pimentos and onion together. Combine beaten eggs, sugar, flour, vinegar, mustard and salt in saucepan; mix well. Cook until smooth, stirring constantly. Add to ground mixture in large bowl; mix until smooth. Store in refrigerator or freezer. **Yield: 100 servings.**

Mary Lehman, Pine Grove Area #2090

Bean Salad

5 quarts green beans
5 quarts wax beans
1½ quarts white kidney beans
2 quarts red kidney beans
4 quarts chopped carrots
2 quarts chopped onions
5 cups sugar
5 cups vinegar
5 teaspoons salt
5 teaspoons pepper

Cook each vegetable separately in water in saucepan until tender; drain and cool. Combine in large bowl. Combine sugar, vinegar, salt and pepper in bowl. Add to vegetables; mix well. Chill, covered, in refrigerator for 1 or 2 days before serving. **Yield: 150 servings.**

Mary Lehman, Pine Grove Area #2090

Macaroni Salad

10 pounds uncooked macaroni
48 hard-boiled eggs, chopped
$1^1/_2$ gallons chopped celery
4 carrots, grated
1 cup parsley flakes
Celery seed and onion salt to taste
1 gallon (about) coleslaw dressing

Cook macaroni using package directions; rinse and drain. Combine with eggs, celery, carrots, parsley flakes, celery seed, onion salt and salad dressing in large bowl; mix well. Chill until serving time. **Yield: 150 servings.**

Velma Snyder, Virginville #1832

Spinach Salad

12 pounds spinach, torn
12 pounds bacon, crisp-fried, crumbled
6 cups oil
6 cups sugar
$1^1/_2$ cups cider vinegar
$2^1/_4$ cups catsup
$^3/_4$ cup Worcestershire sauce
6 cups chopped red onions
6 dozen eggs, hard-boiled, chopped

Combine spinach and bacon in large salad bowl. Combine oil, sugar, vinegar, catsup, Worcestershire sauce, onions and eggs in bowl; mix well. Add to salad; toss to mix. Serve immediately. May add mushrooms if desired. **Yield: 200 servings.**

Pat Rudy, Mt. Nebo #1872

Coleslaw Dressing

3 jars mayonnaise
2 cups vinegar
2 cups evaporated milk
$^1/_4$ cup prepared mustard
8 cups sugar
1 tablespoon salt

Combine mayonnaise, vinegar, evaporated milk, mustard, sugar and salt in large bowl, stirring until sugar is dissolved. Store in 1-quart containers in refrigerator. **Yield: 5 quarts.**

Peg Byers, Wilmington #1477

For coleslaw to serve 50, use 8 pounds of cabbage, 1 cup chopped pimentos, 3 cups chopped pickles, 1 cup chopped green pepper and $1^1/_2$ quarts salad dressing.

Low-Calorie Salad Dressing

1 envelope unflavored gelatin
1/2 cup cold water
2 eggs, beaten
2 tablespoons dry mustard
2 teaspoons salt
2 tablespoons margarine
1 1/3 cups boiling water
3 to 4 packets artificial sweetener
1/2 cup vinegar

Soften gelatin in 1/2 cup cold water. Combine with eggs, mustard, salt and margarine in top of double boiler; mix well. Add boiling water to bottom of double boiler. Heat until water simmers gently. Cook over simmering water until of desired consistency, stirring constantly. Remove from heat. Stir in artificial sweetener and vinegar; cool. Store in tightly covered 1-quart jar. **Yield: 1 quart.**

Elizabeth Gardner, Center Road #502

Chili Sauce

30 large ripe tomatoes
6 onions
6 peaches, peeled, pitted
6 pears or apples, peeled, pitted
3 green bell peppers, seeded
3 tablespoons salt
4 cups sugar
2 cups vinegar
Spice bag

Force tomatoes, onions, peaches, pears and green peppers through food grinder, finely grinding. Combine in large bowl. Sprinkle with salt. Let stand for 1 hour; drain. Spoon into large saucepan. Stir in sugar, vinegar and spice bag. Cook over medium heat until thickened, stirring frequently. Spoon into hot sterilized jars leaving 1/2 inch headspace; seal with 2-piece lids. May use combination of pears and apples. **Yield: 6 pints.**

Alice L. Voorhies, Hemlock #2051

Spicy Chili Sauce

10 pounds ripe tomatoes
1 hot red pepper, chopped
8 cups finely chopped red bell peppers
1 cup finely chopped onions
4 cups sugar
2 tablespoons salt
5 cups vinegar
1 tablespoon celery seed
1 teaspoon ground cloves
1 tablespoon ground cinnamon

Scald tomatoes; remove peels and cores. Chop finely. Combine with hot pepper, bell peppers and onions in large enamel kettle. Bring mixture to a boil. Cook for 1 1/2 hours, stirring occasionally. Add sugar, salt and vinegar. Cook over low heat for 1 hour longer, stirring frequently. Tie up spices in cheesecloth. Add to mixture. Cook for 30 minutes longer or until thickened, stirring frequently. Discard spices. Pour into hot sterilized jars, leaving 1/2 inch headspace; seal with 2-piece lids.
Yield: 4 pints.

Ada Riel, Chandlers Valley #846

Hot Dog Sauce

3 medium onions, finely chopped
2 tablespoons shortening
2 pounds ground beef
1 tablespoon salt
1 teaspoon pepper
1 2 1/2-ounce can chili powder
1 teaspoon paprika
1 tablespoon ground cloves
1 14-ounce bottle of catsup
8 cups water
1 cup flour

Sauté onions in shortening in large skillet until tender but not browned. Add ground beef, stirring until crumbly. Add salt, pepper, chili powder, paprika, cloves and catsup. Cook over medium heat, stirring frequently. Combine 2 to 3 cups water and flour in bowl, stirring until paste forms. Stir into hot mixture gradually. Add remaining water, stirring well. Cook over low heat for 1 1/2 hours, stirring frequently to prevent burning. Pour into hot sterilized jars leaving 1/2 inch headspace; seal with 2-piece lids. May prepare in slow cooker. **Yield: 8 pints.**

Catherine Dodd, Kaylor #1396

Chicken Corn Soup

12 large bunches celery, chopped
4 boxes dehydrated soup greens
Noodles to taste
120 hard-boiled eggs, chopped
25 chickens, cooked, boned, cut up
Chicken broth
2 boxes MSG
4 boxes bouillon cubes
2 large boxes salt
1 large box pepper
5 pounds butter
500 ears of corn, cut

Divide ingredients into 4 equal portions. Fill four 15-gallon kettles 1/3 full of water. Bring to a boil. Add celery. Bring to a boil. Add soup greens, noodles, eggs, cut up chicken, enough chicken broth for desired consistency, MSG, bouillon cubes, salt, pepper, butter and corn; mix well. Simmer until vegetables are tender, stirring occasionally. **Yield: 60 gallons.**

Velma Snyder, Virginville #1832

Split Pea Soup

3 pounds green or yellow split peas
3 gallons ham stock
4 pounds ham, cubed
2 cups chopped celery
2 cups chopped onions
8 ounces carrots, grated
Garlic, salt, pepper, bay leaf and thyme to taste
1 cup flour
2 cups warm water

Place peas in large stockpot with enough water to cover. Add ham stock, ham, celery, onions, carrots and seasonings. Simmer until thickened, stirring frequently. Mix flour with 2 cups warm water in bowl, stirring until smooth. Stir into soup gradually to thicken. **Yield: 50 servings.**

Mary Lehman, Pine Grove Area #2090

Fresh Tomato Soup

½ bushel tomatoes
2 bunches celery, chopped
14 carrots, chopped
10 onions, chopped
1 cup flour
2 cups sugar
¼ cup salt
2 bay leaves

Cook tomatoes in large kettle until tender; drain. Put through food grinder, reserving 2 cups. Return to kettle. Cook celery, carrots and onions in water to cover until tender. Process in food processor until puréed. Add to tomatoes. Whisk flour, sugar and salt with reserved tomatoes until smooth. Add to tomato mixture. Add bay leaves. Simmer until of desired consistency, stirring occasionally. Discard bay leaves. Pour into hot sterilized jars leaving ½ inch headspace; seal with 2-piece lids. Process in cold pack for 5 minutes. **Yield: 14 to 16 quarts.**

Wayne Kramer, Burgettstown #1502

Old-Fashioned Tomato Soup

1 peck tomatoes
12 small onions
2 teaspoons celery seed
1 teaspoon pepper
¼ cup salt
1 cup sugar
½ cup cornstarch
½ cup cold water

Cook tomatoes with onions in large kettle until tender. Strain through food mill. Return to kettle. Add celery seed, pepper, salt and sugar; mix well. Mix cornstarch with ½ cup water to form paste. Add to tomato mixture gradually. Simmer for 20 minutes longer, stirring frequently. Pour into hot sterilized jars leaving ½ inch headspace; seal with 2-piece lids. **Yield: 6 to 8 quarts.**

Martha H. Anderson, Hartslog Valley #375

Frozen Corn

16 cups whole kernel corn
5 cups water
½ cup margarine
8 teaspoons sugar
1 teaspoon salt

Combine corn, water, margarine, sugar and salt in large saucepan. Bring to a boil. Boil for 10 minutes, stirring occasionally; cool. Spoon into freezer containers or plastic freezer bags and freeze. **Yield: 4 quarts.**

Sandra Kinney, Liberty #1182

Potato Filling

1 bunch parsley, chopped
6 cups chopped celery
3 cups chopped onions
1 pound butter
3 pounds moist bread cubes
2 gallons mashed potatoes
1 quart warm milk
6 eggs, beaten
Salt and pepper to taste

Saute parsley, celery and onions in butter in large saucepan until tender. Add bread cubes, potatoes, milk, eggs, salt and pepper; mix well. Chill mixture for several hours to overnight. Spoon into 2 to 3 large baking pans; cover with foil. Bake at 325 degrees for 45 minutes; remove foil. Bake for 15 to 20 minutes longer or until slightly browned. **Yield: 60 servings.**

Ruth Steeley, Plumsteadville #1738

Regal Chocolate Sauce

2 1/2 cups light corn syrup
5 cups sugar
5 cups water
16 ounces unsweetened chocolate squares
5 teaspoons vanilla extract
1 teaspoon salt
5 cups evaporated milk

Combine corn syrup, sugar and water in large saucepan. Cook to 236 degrees on candy thermometer, soft-ball stage, stirring occasionally; remove from heat. Add chocolate, stirring until melted. Stir in vanilla and salt. Add evaporated milk gradually, stirring well; cool. **Yield: 100 (1-ounce) servings.**

Ruth Walker, Buffalo #1523

Peach Cobbler

6 29-ounce cans sliced peaches
3/4 cup cornstarch
2 cups water
4 1/2 cups sugar
1 tablespoon salt
2 tablespoons cinnamon
3 quarts baking mix
1/2 cup sugar
1 quart milk

Drain peaches, reserving 10 cups juice. Pour reserved juice into two 5-quart saucepans. Mix cornstarch and water in bowl until smooth. Stir equal amounts into peach juices. Stir in 4 1/2 cups sugar and salt into peach juice mixtures. Bring to a boil, stirring constantly. Stir in peach slices. Pour mixtures into 4 greased 9x13-inch baking dishes; sprinkle with cinnamon. Combine baking mix, 1/2 cup sugar and milk in bowl; mix well. Drop by spoonfuls over peach mixtures. Bake at 400 degrees for 25 minutes. **Yield: 50 servings.**

Mary Lehman, Pine Grove Area #2090

Apple Butter

36 cups applesauce
18 cups sugar
2 cups sweet apple cider
2 tablespoons cinnamon

Combine applesauce, sugar, cider and cinnamon in baking pan; mix well. Bake at 325 degrees for 5 to 6 hours or until of desired consistency, stirring frequently. Spoon into hot sterilized jars, leaving 1/2 inch headspace; seal with 2-piece lids. May reduce amounts and cook in slow cooker if preferred. **Yield: 20 pints.**

Shirley J. Smith, Pine Run #250

Slow-Cooker Apple Butter

4 quarts apples
1 quart apple cider
2 cups sugar
2 teaspoons cinnamon
2 teaspoons ground cloves

Cook unpeeled apples with cider in saucepan until very tender. Put through food mill. Combine with sugar, cinnamon and cloves in slow cooker. Cook on High for 10 hours or until thickened to desired consistency, stirring occasionally. Spoon into hot sterilized jars, leaving 1/2 inch headspace; seal with 2-piece lids. **Yield: 3 pints.**

Gladys M. Durlin, California #941

Spicy Apple Butter

6 quarts applesauce
6 pounds sugar
1 cup vinegar
1/4 cup cinnamon
1 1/2 tablespoons allspice

Combine applesauce, sugar, vinegar, cinnamon and allspice in large baking pan; mix well. Bake at 300 degrees for 5 hours, stirring frequently. Spoon into hot sterilized jars, leaving 1/2 inch headspace; seal with 2-piece lids. **Yield: 7 quarts.**

Colleen R. Shields, Avis #1959

Old-Fashioned Apple Butter

35 gallons apple cider
2 1/2 bushels apple schnitz
35 pounds sugar
2 tablespoons cinnamon

Cook cider in large copper kettle for 7 hours or until reduced by half. Cut up apples. Add apple schnitz to cider. Cook for 6 or 7 hours or until apples absorb no more cider, stirring frequently. Add sugar. Cook for 1 hour longer; remove from heat. Stir in cinnamon. Spoon into jars, leaving 1/2 inch headspace. Cover jars with paper and cloth. Let stand overnight. Seal with 2-piece lids. **Yield: 14 gallons.**

Grace Hershberger, Bedford #619

Autumn Pumpkin Butter

8 cups pumpkin purée
4 cups sugar
Juice of 4 lemons
1½ teaspoons cinnamon
1 teaspoon ginger
¼ teaspoon ground cloves
¼ teaspoon nutmeg

Combine pumpkin purée, sugar, lemon juice, cinnamon, ginger, cloves and nutmeg in slow cooker; mix well. Cook on High until thickened to desired consistency. Spoon into hot sterilized jars, leaving ½ inch headspace; seal with 2-piece lids. **Yield: 4 pints.**

Trudy Wigton, Pleasant Hill #1505

Tomato Butter

2 cups white vinegar
2 cups sugar
3 cups packed brown sugar
2 teaspoons cinnamon
1 teaspoon allspice
1 teaspoon ground cloves
1 tablespoon salt
5 quarts ripe tomatoes, peeled, ground
3 medium onions, ground

Combine vinegar, sugar, brown sugar, cinnamon, allspice, cloves and salt in heavy enameled saucepan. Bring to a boil. Add tomatoes and onions. Simmer over low heat or bake at 350 degrees until thickened to desired consistency, stirring frequently. Spoon into hot sterilized jars, leaving ½ inch headspace; seal with 2-piece lids. Serve with biscuits or over cream cheese with crackers. **Yield: 5 pints.**

Betty Hunter, Independence #179

Tomato-Apple Butter

8 tomatoes, chopped
8 apples, chopped
2½ pounds brown sugar
1 cup cider vinegar
1 teaspoon cinnamon
1 teaspoon allspice
1 teaspoon ginger
1 teaspoon ground cloves

Combine tomatoes and apples in large saucepan. Cook until very tender. Put through sieve or food mill. Combine with brown sugar, vinegar, cinnamon, allspice, ginger and cloves in saucepan. Bring to a boil; reduce heat. Simmer for 25 minutes or until thickened to desired consistency, stirring constantly. Spoon into hot sterilized jars, leaving ½ inch headspace; seal with 2-piece lids. May spoon into freezer containers and freeze if preferred. **Yield: 3 pints.**

Evelyn Lauer, Washington #1949

Dark Rich Catsup

3/4 bushel tomatoes
4 onions
2 green bell peppers
1/2 cup cornstarch
2 1/4 cups cider vinegar
2 pounds brown sugar
1 tablespoon each garlic powder, paprika, dry mustard, allspice, ground cloves, cinnamon and pepper
3 tablespoons salt

Purée tomatoes, onions and green peppers in blender; mixture will measure about 30 cups. Cook in large saucepan for several hours or until reduced by half. Dissolve cornstarch in 1/4 cup vinegar. Add to tomato mixture with remaining 2 cups vinegar, brown sugar, garlic powder, paprika, dry mustard, allspice, cloves, cinnamon, pepper and salt; mix well. Cook until thickened, stirring constantly. Spoon into hot sterilized jars, leaving 1/2 inch headspace; seal with 2-piece lids. Process in boiling water bath for 15 minutes. **Yield: 8 pints.**

Betty Lou Kauffman, Pleasant Hill #1505

Catsup

4 quarts strained tomatoes
3 cups vinegar
3 cups sugar
1 tablespoon allspice
2 tablespoons cinnamon
1 teaspoon ground cloves
2 tablespoons salt
1 tablespoon pepper

Combine tomatoes, vinegar, sugar, allspice, cinnamon, cloves, salt and pepper in large saucepan. Cook until reduced by half, stirring frequently. Spoon into hot sterilized jars, leaving 1/2 inch headspace; seal with 2-piece lids. May increase recipe and cook in electric roaster if desired. **Yield: 5 pints.**

Clem Harkleroad, Rural Valley #1750

Golden Pear Jam

4 cups ground pears
1 cup drained crushed pineapple
4 cups sugar

Combine pears, pineapple and sugar in saucepan. Cook for 30 minutes, stirring frequently. Spoon into 5 hot sterilized half-pint jars, leaving 1/2 inch headspace; seal with 2-piece lids. **Yield: 2 1/2 pints.**

LaVerne Burkhart, Gouglersville #1743

Rhubarb Jam

2½ pounds rhubarb, chopped
3 cups sugar
½ cup water
Juice and grated rind of 2 oranges

Combine rhubarb, sugar, water, orange juice and orange rind in saucepan. Cook for 30 minutes, stirring occasionally. Spoon into hot sterilized jars, leaving ½ inch headspace; seal with 2-piece lids. **Yield: 6 (6-ounce) jars.**

Jean V. Johnn, Hemlock #2051

Papaya and Coconut Jelly

1 cup papaya purée
1 cup sugar
½ cup coconut

Combine papaya purée, sugar and coconut in saucepan. Bring to a boil. Cook for 7 to 8 minutes or until of desired consistency, stirring constantly. Cool to room temperature. Store in refrigerator or freezer. **Yield: 1½ cups.**

Katie M. Mengel, Centerport #1600

Raspberry Jelly

6 cups beet juice
½ cup lemon juice
8 cups sugar
2 packages pectin
1 6-ounce package red raspberry gelatin

Combine beet juice, lemon juice, sugar and pectin in saucepan; mix well. Boil for 6 minutes; remove from heat. Stir in gelatin until dissolved. Spoon into hot sterilized jars, leaving ½ inch headspace; seal with 2-piece lids or paraffin. **Yield: 4 or 5 pints.**

Dorothy Martin, Harmony #1112

Violet Jelly

1 quart violets
2½ cups boiling water
2 tablespoons lemon juice
4 cups sugar
1 package pectin

Wash and stem violets and pack tightly into 1-quart container. Pour boiling water over violets. Let stand to steep. Strain infusion into 6-quart saucepan, pressing to remove all moisture; discard violets. Add lemon juice, sugar and pectin to infusion in saucepan; mix well. Bring to a full rolling boil that cannot be stirred down, stirring constantly. Boil for 1 minute. Spoon into hot sterilized jars, leaving ½ inch headspace; seal with 2-piece lids. **Yield: 2 to 3 pints.**

Esther Dietterick, Light Street #31

Tomato Marmalade

2 oranges
2 lemons
12 cups drained chopped tomatoes
10 cups sugar
1 teaspoon cinnamon
2 tablespoons whole cloves

Slice oranges and lemons; cut slices into quarters. Combine with tomatoes, sugar and cinnamon in saucepan. Tie cloves in cheesecloth bag; add to tomato mixture. Bring to a boil over high heat. Cook for 50 minutes or until thickened to desired consistency, stirring frequently. Remove spice bag. Spoon marmalade into hot sterilized jars, leaving 1/2 inch headspace; seal with 2-piece lids. Process in boiling water bath for 10 minutes. **Yield: 4 pints.**

Joan Milliken, Tuscarora #774

Zucchini Marmalade

6 cups shredded zucchini
4 1/2 cups sugar
1 20-ounce can crushed pineapple
1/2 cup lemon juice
2 3-ounce packages apricot or strawberry gelatin

Combine zucchini with a small amount of water in saucepan. Cook for 6 minutes; drain well. Add sugar, pineapple and lemon juice. Cook for 3 minutes, stirring frequently. Stir in gelatin until dissolved. Spoon into hot sterilized jars, leaving 1/2 inch headspace; seal with 2-piece lids. **Yield: 4 pints.**

Betty Rodgers, Plain Grove #1431

Tomato Juice

1 bushel very ripe tomatoes, peeled, cored, puréed
1 1/2 cups sugar
5 tablespoons lemon juice
3 tablespoons Worcestershire sauce
1/3 cup celery salt
3 tablespoons pickling salt

Place tomato purée in large saucepan. Cook for 30 minutes, stirring frequently. Add sugar, lemon juice, Worcestershire sauce and celery salt; mix well. Cook for 15 minutes longer, stirring frequently. Spoon into hot sterilized 1-quart jars, adding 1/2 teaspoon pickling salt to each jar; seal with 2-piece lids. Process in boiling water bath for 10 minutes. Let stand for 1 month before serving. **Yield: 18 quarts.**

Robin Hetherington, Ringtown Valley #2100

Iodized salt used in pickling will cause pickles to darken.

Dilled Green Peppers

12 green bell peppers
5 tiny hot peppers
5 cloves of garlic
5 small sprigs of dill or 1¼ teaspoons dried dillweed
⅝ teaspoon alum
3 cups vinegar
5 cups water
¼ cup salt

Cut bell peppers into 1½-inch pieces. Pack into 5 hot sterilized 1-pint jars, leaving 1 inch headspace. Add 1 hot pepper, 1 clove of garlic, 1 small sprig of dill and ⅛ teaspoon alum to each jar. Bring vinegar, water and salt to a boil in saucepan. Simmer for 5 minutes. Pour into prepared jars; seal with 2-piece lids. Process in boiling water bath for 10 minutes. **Yield: 5 pints.**

Jean Ball, South Auburn #1188

Hot Peppers

4 teaspoons salt
12 cloves of garlic
¾ cup oil
2 teaspoons oregano
8 cups sliced hot peppers
Water
Vinegar

Place 1 teaspoon salt, 3 cloves of garlic, 3 tablespoons oil and ½ teaspoon oregano in each of 4 hot sterilized 1-pint jar. Fill jars with sliced hot peppers. Bring equal parts of water and vinegar to a boil in saucepan. Pour into prepared jars, leaving ½ inch headspace; seal with 2-piece lids. **Yield: 4 pints.**

Karen Harvey, East New Castle #1536

Cinnamon Rings

2 gallons cucumbers, peeled, sliced, seeded
2 cups dehydrated lime
8½ quarts water
1 cup vinegar
1 tablespoon alum
1 1-ounce bottle of red food coloring
2 cups each water and vinegar
10 cups sugar
8 cinnamon sticks
1 9-ounce package red-hot cinnamon candies

Combine cucumbers, lime and 8½ quarts water in large crock. Let stand for 24 hours. Drain and rinse until water is clear. Add fresh water to cover. Let stand for 3 hours; drain. Combine with 1 cup vinegar, alum, food coloring and water to cover in saucepan. Simmer for 10 minutes; drain and place cucumbers in large crock. Combine 2 cups water, 2 cups vinegar, sugar, cinnamon sticks and cinnamon candies in saucepan. Bring to a boil. Pour over cucumbers in crock. Let stand for 3 days; drain, reheat and pour liquid over cucumbers each day. Spoon into hot sterilized jars, leaving ½ inch headspace; seal with 2-piece lids. Process in boiling water bath for 10 minutes. **Yield: 8 to 9 pints.**

Mary Syphrit, Brady #1218

Mom's Ripe Cucumber Recipe

4 quarts cucumbers, peeled, seeded, chopped
1/2 cup chopped green, red or yellow bell pepper
1/2 cup chopped onion
1 cup vinegar
2 cups sugar
1/4 teaspoon turmeric
2 tablespoons salt

Combine cucumbers, bell pepper, onion, vinegar, sugar, turmeric and salt in saucepan. Bring to a rolling boil, stirring frequently. Spoon into hot sterilized jars, leaving 1/2 inch headspace; seal with 2-piece lids. **Yield: 4 quarts.**

Gladys Sheffer, Red Lion #1781

Bread-and-Butter Pickles

25 cucumbers, sliced
1 quart cider vinegar
2 cups sugar
1/2 teaspoon turmeric
1 tablespoon celery seed
1/2 teaspoon ground cloves
1/2 cup pickling salt

Cover cucumbers with salted water in large bowl. Soak for 3 hours to overnight; drain. Pack into hot sterilized jars. Bring vinegar, sugar, turmeric, celery seed, cloves and pickling salt to a boil in saucepan. Pour over cucumbers, leaving 1/2 inch headspace; seal with 2-piece lids. Process in pressure cooker at 10 pounds pressure for 10 minutes. May add hot peppers, green bell pepper strips, sliced onions or garlic if desired. **Yield: 6 pints.**

Hazel Winegar, Big Beaver #1578

Old-Fashioned Bread-and-Butter Pickles

4 quarts thinly sliced cucumbers
3 onions, sliced
2 red bell peppers, chopped
1 cup vinegar
2 cups packed brown sugar
1 tablespoon horseradish (optional)
1/4 cup mixed pickling spices
1 teaspoon celery seed
1/2 teaspoon turmeric (optional)
1 tablespoon salt

Sprinkle cucumbers and onions in large bowl with salt. Let stand for 4 hours to overnight; drain. Combine with bell peppers, vinegar, brown sugar, horseradish, mixed spices, celery seed, turmeric and 1 tablespoon salt in saucepan. Heat just to the boiling point; do not boil. Spoon into hot sterilized jars, leaving 1/2 inch headspace; seal with 2-piece lids. **Yield: 6 to 8 pints.**

Martha Shannon, Mahoning Valley #1649

Sweet Garlic-Dill Pickles

4 cloves of garlic
4 large sprigs of dill
4 quarts cucumbers sliced 1/8 inch thick
2 cups white vinegar
3 cups sugar
2 cups water
2 tablespoons salt

Place 1 clove of garlic and 1 sprig of dill in each of 4 hot sterilized 1-quart jars. Fill jars with cucumbers. Combine vinegar, sugar, water and salt in saucepan. Bring to a boil. Pour over cucumbers, leaving 1/2 inch headspace; seal with 2-piece lids. Process in boiling water bath for 10 minutes. May pickle blanched cauliflower in the same manner. **Yield: 4 quarts.**

Ruth E. Vonada, Logan #109

Polish Dill Pickles

24 cucumbers
1 gallon water
1/2 cup salt
4 sprigs of dill
4 teaspoons turmeric
4 cloves of garlic
Alum
1 cup vinegar
2 cups sugar
2 cups vinegar
1 tablespoon salt

Cut cucumbers into quarters lengthwise. Combine with water and 1/2 cup salt in crock. Let stand overnight; drain. Place 1 sprig of dill, 1 teaspoon turmeric, 1 clove of garlic and a pinch of alum in each of 4 hot sterilized 1-quart jars. Combine cucumbers with 1 cup vinegar and water to cover in large saucepan. Cook just until cucumbers change color; drain. Pack cucumbers into prepared jars. Combine sugar, 2 cups vinegar and 1 tablespoon salt in saucepan; mix well. Bring to a boil. Pour over cucumbers in jars, leaving 1/2 inch headspace; seal with 2-piece lids. Place in 250-degree oven. Turn off heat. Let stand in oven until cool. **Yield: 4 quarts.**

Margaret Bullman, Kaylor #1396

Nellie's Fancy Pickles

1 quart small onions
1 quart carrots, sliced
1 quart cucumbers, sliced
12 red or green bell peppers, coarsely chopped
3 cups vinegar
4 cups sugar
2 tablespoons mustard seed

Combine onions, carrots, cucumbers and bell peppers with salted water to cover in large saucepan. Cook until tender; drain. Bring vinegar, sugar and mustard seed to a simmer in saucepan. Simmer for several minutes. Add vegetables. Simmer for 30 minutes, stirring occasionally. Spoon into hot sterilized jars, leaving 1/2 inch headspace; seal with 2-piece lids. **Yield: 3 quarts.**

Dot Cupper, Sebring #1047

Freezer Pickles

7 cups thinly sliced cucumbers
1 tablespoon salt
1 cup vinegar
2 cups sugar
1/2 teaspoon celery seed
1/2 teaspoon mustard seed
1 medium onion, chopped
1 medium green bell pepper, chopped

Sprinkle cucumbers with salt in large bowl. Let stand for 2 hours; drain. Combine vinegar, sugar, celery seed and mustard seed in large bowl; mix well to dissolve sugar. Add onion, green pepper and cucumbers; mix well. Spoon into freezer containers. Store in freezer for 5 days before using. **Yield: 3 pints.**

Emily Werner, Gouglersville #1743

No-Salt Pickles

3 1/2 pounds medium cucumbers
3 cloves of garlic
3 sprigs of dill or dillseed to taste
2 cups vinegar
3 cups water
1/2 cup sugar

Cut cucumbers into strips lengthwise. Soak in ice water in refrigerator until well chilled. Place 1 clove of garlic and 1 sprig of dill in each of 3 hot sterilized 1-quart jars. Drain cucumbers and pack into prepared jars. Bring vinegar, 3 cups water and sugar to a boil in saucepan. Boil for 1 minute. Pour over cucumbers in jars, leaving 1/2 inch headspace; seal with 2-piece lids. Process in boiling water bath for 10 minutes. **Yield: 3 quarts.**

Barbara H. Aurand, Fort Granville #1902

Shake Pickles

12 cups sliced cucumbers
4 to 8 onions, sliced
3 1/2 cups sugar
3 cups vinegar
1 teaspoon alum
1 teaspoon mustard seed
1 teaspoon turmeric
1 teaspoon celery salt
1/3 cup salt

Place cucumbers and onions in 1-gallon jar. Combine sugar, vinegar, alum, mustard seed, turmeric, celery salt and salt in bowl; mix well. Add to cucumbers. Chill for 6 days before serving, shaking once a day. Store in refrigerator for 3 to 6 months. **Yield: 1 gallon.**

Mary L. Bradnick, Tuscarora Valley #2042

Sweet Pickles

2 quarts dill pickles, drained
3 cups sugar
2 tablespoons vinegar
2 tablespoons mixed spices

Cut pickles into pieces and return to jars. Combine sugar, vinegar and mixed spices in large bowl; mix until sugar dissolves. Pour over pickles in jars; seal. Store for up to 1 year in refrigerator. **Yield: 2 quarts.**

Anna Dumbroski, Hemlock #2051

Easy Sweet Pickles

12 pounds cucumbers, thinly sliced
1 cup pickling salt
2 quarts vinegar
9 tablespoons sugar
3 tablespoons powdered alum
6 tablespoons mustard seed
1 tablespoon celery seed
3 tablespoons mixed spices
18 cups sugar

Sprinkle cucumbers with pickling salt in crock. Add boiling water to cover. Let stand overnight. Drain and rinse with cold water. Combine vinegar, 9 tablespoons sugar, alum, mustard seed, celery seed and mixed spices in saucepan. Bring to a boil. Pour over cucumbers in crock. Let stand for 24 hours. Stir in 3 cups sugar until dissolved; cover crock. Add 3 cups sugar each day for 5 additional days. Store pickles, covered, in crock for up to 6 months. **Yield: 1 crock.**

Annabel Wakefield, Charlesville #698

Barbecue Relish

8 ripe tomatoes
8 apples
6 red bell peppers
6 green bell peppers
6 onions
Salt
1 cup vinegar
3 cups packed brown sugar
1/2 teaspoon cinnamon
1/2 teaspoon ground cloves
2 tablespoons salt

Grind tomatoes, apples, bell peppers and onions together. Sprinkle with salt. Let stand for several minutes; drain well. Combine with vinegar, brown sugar, cinnamon, cloves and 2 tablespoons salt in saucepan. Cook for 20 to 25 minutes, stirring frequently. Spoon into hot sterilized jars, leaving 1/2 inch headspace; seal with 2-piece lids or paraffin. **Yield: 8 pints.**

Margret Barackman, Penn Line #1784

Green Tomato Barbecue Relish

1 gallon green tomatoes
10 green bell peppers
10 red bell peppers
15 onions
1/2 cup salt
1 quart vinegar
4 cups sugar
3 tablespoons cornstarch
1 10-ounce jar mustard
1 tablespoon celery seed

Grind tomatoes with bell peppers and onions. Combine with salt in muslin bag. Drain overnight. Bring vinegar and sugar to a boil in saucepan. Stir in mixture of cornstarch and mustard. Add vegetables. Boil for 20 minutes, stirring occasionally. Stir in celery seed. Spoon into hot sterilized jars, leaving 1/2 inch headspace; seal with 2-piece lids. **Yield: 8 to 9 pints.**

LeWanda Yocum, Morning Star #1271

Corn Relish

Ears of corn
4 cups shredded cabbage
4 cups chopped onions
2 red bell peppers, chopped
4 cups chopped tomatoes
4 cups chopped cucumbers
Chopped celery to taste
7 cups weak vinegar
4 1-pound packages brown sugar
1 teaspoon white mustard seed
1 teaspoon each celery seed, turmeric and cinnamon

Boil corn in water in saucepan until tender. Cut off enough corn kernels to measure 4 cups. Combine cabbage, onions and bell peppers with water to cover in saucepan. Cook until tender; drain. Combine tomatoes, cucumbers and celery in saucepan. Cook until tender. Combine remaining ingredients in large saucepan; mix until brown sugar dissolves. Add vegetables; mix well. Bring to a boil. Boil for 20 minutes. Spoon into hot sterilized jars, leaving 1/2 inch headspace; seal with 2-piece lids. **Yield: 3 quarts.**

Rose M. B. Stephens, Charleston Valley #54

Hot Dog Relish

4 cups ground green tomatoes
4 cups ground red and green bell peppers
4 cups ground onions
4 cups ground cabbage
1/2 cup salt
4 cups vinegar
2 cups water
6 cups sugar
1 1/2 teaspoons turmeric
1 1/2 tablespoons celery seed
1 1/2 tablespoons mustard seed

Combine tomatoes, bell peppers, onions and cabbage with salt in large bowl. Let stand for several hours. Rinse and drain well. Combine vinegar, water, sugar, turmeric, celery seed and mustard seed in large saucepan. Bring to a boil. Boil for 15 minutes. Add vegetables; mix well. Cook until heated through. Spoon into hot sterilized jars, leaving 1/2 inch headspace; seal with 2-piece lids. **Yield: 8 pints.**

Lisa Huling Juliana, Shavers Creek #353

Zucchini Relish

10 cups chopped peeled zucchini
4 cups chopped onions
2 green bell peppers
1 red bell pepper
5 tablespoons salt
2 tablespoons cornstarch
2 1/2 cups vinegar
6 cups sugar
1 teaspoon turmeric
1 teaspoon dry mustard
2 teaspoons celery seed
1/2 teaspoon alum
1/2 teaspoon pepper

Grind zucchini, onions and bell peppers together. Combine with salt in large bowl. Let stand overnight. Rinse and drain well. Dissolve cornstarch in vinegar in saucepan. Add vegetables, sugar, turmeric, dry mustard, celery seed, alum and pepper; mix well. Cook for 30 minutes, stirring occasionally. Spoon into hot sterilized jars, leaving 1/2 inch headspace; seal with 2-piece lids. **Yield: 5 to 6 pints.**

Glenora Rogers, Charleston Valley #54

Homemade Sauerkraut

10 pounds cabbage, shredded
4 ounces salt

Layer cabbage 1/2 at a time in crock, sprinkling layers with salt and pressing down. Let stand until pickled. This recipe is in memory of Mary E. Askey. **Yield: 10 pounds.**

Grace Askey, Oak Hill #717

Freezer Cantaloupe

2 cups cold water
3 cups sugar
6 cups cantaloupe balls

Combine water and sugar in bowl; mix until sugar dissolves. Chill in refrigerator. Add cantaloupe balls. Spoon into freezer containers. Store in freezer. **Yield: 6 cups.**

Lenora Adams, Alleghenyville #2065

Preserved Peaches

18 peaches
3/4 cup to 1 1/2 cups sugar

Blanch, peel and pit peaches. Pack into hot sterilized 1-quart jars. Add 1/4 to 1/2 cup sugar to each jar. Add water to within 1/2 inch of top; seal with 2-piece lids. Process in boiling water bath for 15 minutes. Sugar will dissolve completely in 2 or 3 weeks. **Yield: 3 quarts.**

Ethel Matheson, Montmorenci #1704

Finger Paint

3 cups dry laundry starch
$1\frac{1}{2}$ cups soap flakes
$1\frac{1}{2}$ cups talcum powder
4 cups boiling water
Powdered paint

Combine starch, soap flakes and talcum powder in large bowl. Add boiling water gradually, stirring until smooth. Add powdered paint to make desired colors. Store in airtight containers.

Patricia Lynette Kent, Harveys #1444

Halloween Makeup

1 tablespoon shortening
2 tablespoons cornstarch
Food coloring

Blend shortening and cornstarch in small bowl. Use as basic white makeup. Blend desired food coloring into basic white makeup to achieve desired effect.

Patricia Lynette Kent, Harveys #1444

Kooky Clay

1 cup flour
$\frac{1}{4}$ cup salt
$\frac{1}{3}$ cup water

Combine flour, salt and water in bowl; mix with wooden spoon until smooth. Test consistency by pressing between fingers. Add a small amount of flour if too mushy or several drops of water if too dry. Store in plastic bag in refrigerator. Warm to room temperature before using. Shape as desired, paint with water-based paints and allow to air-dry. Spray with clear acrylic to seal and preserve.

Marie Sinclair, Sanborn # 2016

Clay Christmas Ornaments

2 cups flour
1 cup salt
1 cup water

Mix flour and salt in bowl. Stir in water gradually. Knead for 7 to 10 minutes. Add food coloring as desired. Roll out $\frac{1}{4}$ inch thick; cut into desired shapes. Insert hook for hanging; place on baking sheet. Bake at 325 to 350 degrees for 30 minutes.

Jean Moore, Cross Creek Village #1751

Amy Jo's Kool-Aid Play Dough

1 cup sifted flour
1/2 cup salt
3 tablespoons oil
1 envelope unsweetened drink mix
1 cup boiling water

Combine all ingredients in small bowl. Knead until mixture forms soft dough.

Catherine J. Metrick, Unionville #1971

Cooked Play Dough

1 cup flour
1/2 cup salt
2 tablespoons cream of tartar
1 cup water
1 tablespoon vegetable oil
Food coloring

Mix flour, salt and cream of tartar in saucepan. Combine water, oil and food coloring in small bowl. Stir into flour mixture gradually. Cook over medium heat for 5 minutes or until very thick, stirring constantly. Knead until smooth. Cool and store in airtight container. This clay is safe. The little ones won't get sick even if they eat it.

Susan Delaney, DuBois #808

Cornstarch Play Dough

2 cups baking soda
1 cup cornstarch
1 1/4 cups cold water
Food coloring

Combine baking soda, cornstarch, cold water and desired food coloring in saucepan. Cook over medium heat until thickened, stirring constantly. Invert onto plate; cover with damp cloth. Let stand until cool. Knead on surface dusted with cornstarch until smooth and pliable. Store in airtight container.

Patricia Lynette Kent, Harveys # 1444

Little Angel Peanut Butter Play Dough

1 cup creamy peanut butter
1 tablespoon honey
1 cup dry milk powder

Blend peanut butter and honey in bowl. Add dry milk powder gradually, mixing until dough is stiff enough to mold into shapes. Decorate with raisins, seeds, nuts or candies.

Viva Santschi, Pine Run # 250

Equivalents Chart

	When the recipe calls for	Use
Baking	1/2 cup butter 2 cups butter 4 cups all-purpose flour 4 1/2 to 5 cups sifted cake flour 1 square chocolate 1 cup semisweet chocolate chips 4 cups marshmallows 2 1/4 cups packed brown sugar 4 cups confectioners' sugar 2 cups granulated sugar	4 ounces 1 pound 1 pound 1 pound 1 ounce 6 ounces 1 pound 1 pound 1 pound 1 pound
Cereal - Bread	1 cup fine dry bread crumbs 1 cup soft bread crumbs 1 cup small bread cubes 1 cup fine cracker crumbs 1 cup fine graham cracker crumbs 1 cup vanilla wafer crumbs 1 cup crushed cornflakes 4 cups cooked macaroni 3 1/2 cups cooked rice	4 to 5 slices 2 slices 2 slices 28 saltines 15 crackers 22 wafers 3 cups uncrushed 8 ounces uncooked 1 cup uncooked
Dairy	1 cup shredded cheese 1 cup cottage cheese 1 cup sour cream 1 cup whipped cream 2/3 cup evaporated milk 1 2/3 cups evaporated milk	4 ounces 8 ounces 8 ounces 1/2 cup heavy cream 1 small can 1 13-ounce can
Fruit	4 cups sliced or chopped apples 1 cup mashed bananas 2 cups pitted cherries 2 1/2 cups shredded coconut 4 cups cranberries 1 cup pitted dates 1 cup candied fruit 3 to 4 tablespoons lemon juice plus 1 tablespoon grated lemon rind 1/3 cup orange juice plus 2 teaspoons grated orange rind 4 cups sliced peaches 2 cups pitted prunes 3 cups raisins	4 medium 3 medium 4 cups unpitted 8 ounces 1 pound 1 8-ounce package 1 8-ounce package 1 lemon 1 orange 8 medium 1 12-ounce package 1 15-ounce package

	When the recipe calls for	Use
Meats	4 cups chopped cooked chicken 3 cups chopped cooked meat 2 cups cooked ground meat	1 5-pound chicken 1 pound, cooked 1 pound, cooked
Nuts	1 cup chopped nuts	4 ounces shelled 1 pound unshelled
Vegetables	2 cups cooked green beans	1/2 pound fresh or 1 16-ounce can
	2 1/2 cups lima beans or red beans	1 cup dried, cooked
	4 cups shredded cabbage	1 pound
	1 cup grated carrot	1 large
	8 ounces fresh mushrooms	1 4-ounce can
	1 cup chopped onion	1 large
	4 cups sliced or chopped potatoes	4 medium
	2 cups canned tomatoes	1 16-ounce can

Measurement Equivalents

1 tablespoon = 3 teaspoons	1 6 1/2 to 8-ounce can = 1 cup
2 tablespoons = 1 ounce	1 10 1/2 to 12-ounce can = 1 1/4 cups
4 tablespoons = 1/4 cup	1 14 to 16-ounce can = 1 3/4 cups
5 1/3 tablespoons = 1/3 cup	1 16 to 17-ounce can = 2 cups
8 tablespoons = 1/2 cup	1 18 to 20-ounce can = 2 1/2 cups
12 tablespoons = 3/4 cup	1 29-ounce can = 3 1/2 cups
16 tablespoons = 1 cup	1 46 to 51-ounce can = 5 3/4 cups
1 cup = 8 ounces or 1/2 pint	1 6 1/2 to 7 1/2-pound can or Number 10 = 12 to 13 cups
4 cups = 1 quart	
4 quarts = 1 gallon	

Metric Equivalents

Liquid			Dry		
1 teaspoon	=	5 milliliters	1 quart	=	1 liter
1 tablespoon	=	15 milliliters	1 ounce	=	30 grams
1 fluid ounce	=	30 milliliters	1 pound	=	450 grams
1 cup	=	250 milliliters	2.2 pounds	=	1 kilogram
1 pint	=	500 milliliters			

NOTE: The metric measures are approximate benchmarks for purposes of home food preparation.

Substitution Chart

	Instead of	Use
Baking	1 teaspoon baking powder	1/4 teaspoon soda plus 1/2 teaspoon cream of tartar
	1 tablespoon cornstarch (for thickening)	2 tablespoons flour or 1 tablespoon tapioca
	1 cup sifted all-purpose flour	1 cup plus 2 tablespoons sifted cake flour
	1 cup sifted cake flour	1 cup minus 2 tablespoons sifted all-purpose flour
	1 cup dry bread crumbs	3/4 cup cracker crumbs
Dairy	1 cup buttermilk	1 cup sour milk or 1 cup yogurt
	1 cup heavy cream	3/4 cup skim milk plus 1/3 cup butter
	1 cup light cream	7/8 cup skim milk plus 3 tablespoons butter
	1 cup sour cream	7/8 cup sour milk plus 3 tablespoons butter
	1 cup sour milk	1 cup milk plus 1 tablespoon vinegar or lemon juice or 1 cup buttermilk
Seasoning	1 teaspoon allspice	1/2 teaspoon cinnamon plus 1/8 teaspoon cloves
	1 cup catsup	1 cup tomato sauce plus 1/2 cup sugar plus 2 tablespoons vinegar
	1 clove of garlic	1/8 teaspoon garlic powder or 1/8 teaspoon instant minced garlic or 3/4 teaspoon garlic salt or 5 drops of liquid garlic
	1 teaspoon Italian spice	1/4 teaspoon each oregano, basil, rosemary plus dash of cayenne
	1 teaspoon lemon juice	1/2 teaspoon vinegar
	1 tablespoon mustard	1 teaspoon dry mustard
	1 medium onion	1 tablespoon dried minced onion or 1 teaspoon onion powder
Sweet	1 1-ounce square chocolate	1/4 cup cocoa plus 1 teaspoon shortening
	1 2/3 ounces semisweet chocolate	1 ounce unsweetened chocolate plus 4 teaspoons granulated sugar
	1 cup honey	1 to 1 1/4 cups sugar plus 1/4 cup liquid or 1 cup corn syrup or molasses
	1 cup granulated sugar	1 cup packed brown sugar or 1 cup corn syrup, molasses or honey minus 1/4 cup liquid

Quantities to Serve 100

Baked beans	5 gallons
Beef	40 pounds
Beets	30 pounds
Bread	10 loaves
Butter	3 pounds
Cabbage for slaw	20 pounds
Cakes	8 cakes
Carrots	33 pounds
Cauliflower	18 pounds
Cheese	18 pounds
Chicken for chicken pie	40 pounds
Coffee	3 pounds
Cream	3 quarts
Fruit cocktail	1 gallon
Fruit juice	4 (No. 10) cans
Fruit salad	20 quarts
Ground beef	30 to 36 pounds
Ham	40 pounds
Ice cream	4 gallons
Lettuce	20 heads
Meat loaf	24 pounds
Milk	6 gallons
Nuts	3 pounds
Olives	1¾ pounds
Oysters	18 quarts
Pickles	2 quarts
Pies	17 pies
Potatoes	35 pounds
Roast pork	40 pounds
Rolls	200 rolls
Salad dressing	3 quarts
Scalloped potatoes	5 gallons
Soup	5 gallons
Sugar cubes	3 pounds
Tomato juice	4 (No. 10) cans
Vegetables	4 (No. 20) cans
Vegetable salad	20 quarts
Whipping cream	4 pints
Wieners	25 pounds

Bread Baking Guide

The pleasure of baking homemade bread is matched only by eating it, except when something goes wrong. Most problems can be determined and easily avoided the next time.

Problem...	***Cause...***
Bread or biscuits are dry	Too much flour; too slow baking; over-handling
Bread has too-open texture or uneven texture	Too much liquid; overhandling in kneading
Strong yeast smell from baked bread	Too much yeast; over-rising
Tiny white spots on crust	Too rapid rising; dough not covered properly while rising
Crust has bad color	Too much flour used in shaping
Small flat loaves	Old yeast; not enough rising or rising much too long; oven temperature too high
Heavy compact texture	Too much flour worked into bread when kneading; insufficient rising time; oven temperature too high
Coarse texture	Too little kneading
Crumbly texture	Too much flour; undermixing; oven temperature too low
Yeasty sour flavor	Too little yeast; rising time too long
Fallen center	Rising time too long
Irregular shape	Poor technique in shaping
Surface browns too quickly	Oven temperature too high
Bread rises too long during baking and is porous in center and upper portion of loaf	Oven temperature too low

Cake Baking Guide

Problem...	*Cause...*	
	Butter-Type Cakes	**Sponge-Type Cakes**
Cake falls	Too much sugar, liquid, leavening or shortening; too little flour; temperature too low; insufficient baking	Too much sugar; overbeaten egg whites; egg yolks underbeaten; use of greased pans; insufficient baking
Cake cracks or humps	Too much flour or too little liquid; overmixing; batter not spread evenly in pan; temperature of oven too high	Too much flour or sugar; temperature too high
Cake has one side higher	Batter spread unevenly; uneven pan; pan too close to side of oven; oven rack or range not even; uneven oven heat	Uneven pan; oven rack or range not level
Cake has hard top crust	Temperature too high; overbaking	Temperature too high; overbaking
Cake has sticky top crust	Too much sugar or shortening; insufficient baking	Too much sugar; insufficient baking
Cake has soggy layer at bottom	Too much liquid; eggs underbeaten; undermixing; insufficient baking	Too many eggs or egg yolks; underbeaten egg yolks; undermixing
Cake crumbles or falls apart	Too much sugar, leavening or shortening; batter undermixed; improper pan treatment; improper cooling	
Cake has heavy, compact quality	Too much liquid or shortening; too many eggs; too little leavening or flour; overmixing; oven temperature too high	Overbeaten egg whites; underbeaten egg yolks; overmixing
Cake falls out of pan before completely cooled		Too much sugar; use of greased pans; insufficient baking

No-Salt Seasonings

Salt is an acquired taste and can be significantly reduced in the diet by learning to use herbs and spices instead. When using fresh herbs, use 3 times the amount of dried herbs. Begin with small amounts to determine your favorite tastes. A dash of fresh lemon or lime juice can also wake up your taste buds.

Herb Blends to Replace Salt

Combine all ingredients in small airtight container. Add several grains of rice to prevent caking.

No-Salt Surprise Seasoning — 2 teaspoons garlic powder and 1 teaspoon each of dried basil, oregano and dehydrated lemon juice.

Pungent Salt Substitute — 3 teaspoons dried basil, 2 teaspoons each of summer savory, celery seed, cumin seed, sage and marjoram, and 1 teaspoon lemon thyme; crush with mortar and pestle.

Spicy No-Salt Seasoning — 1 teaspoon each cloves, pepper and coriander, 2 teaspoons paprika and 1 tablespoon dried rosemary; crush with mortar and pestle.

Herb Complements

Beef — bay leaf, chives, cumin, garlic, hot pepper, marjoram, rosemary

Pork — coriander, cumin, garlic, ginger, hot pepper, savory, thyme

Poultry — garlic, oregano, rosemary, savory, sage

Cheese — basil, chives, curry, dill, marjoram, oregano, parsley, sage, thyme

Fish — chives, coriander, dill, garlic, tarragon, thyme

Fruit — cinnamon, coriander, cloves, ginger, mint

Bread — caraway, marjoram, oregano, poppy seed, rosemary, thyme

Salads — basil, chives, tarragon, parsley, sorrel

Vegetables — basil, chives, dill, tarragon, marjoram, mint, parsley, pepper

Basic Herb Butter

Combine 1 stick unsalted butter, 1 to 3 tablespoons dried herbs or twice that amount of minced fresh herbs of choice, 1/2 teaspoon lemon juice and white pepper to taste. Let stand for 1 hour or longer before using.

Basic Herb Vinegar

Heat vinegar of choice in saucepan; do not boil. Pour into bottle; add 1 or more herbs of choice and seal bottle. Let stand for 2 weeks before using.

Index